# The Just Practice Framework in Action

# The Just Practice Framework in Action

*Contemporary Case Studies*

EDITED BY JANET L. FINN
University of Montana

New York   Oxford
OXFORD UNIVERSITY PRESS

Oxford University Press is a department of the University of Oxford.
It furthers the University's objective of excellence in research, scholarship,
and education by publishing worldwide. Oxford is a registered trade mark
of Oxford University Press in the UK and certain other countries.

Published in the United States of America by Oxford University Press
198 Madison Avenue, New York, NY 10016, United States of America.

© Oxford University Press 2022

For titles covered by Section 112 of the US Higher Education
Opportunity Act, please visit www.oup.com/us/he for the latest
information about pricing and alternate formats.

All rights reserved. No part of this publication may be reproduced, stored in
a retrieval system, or transmitted, in any form or by any means, without the
prior permission in writing of Oxford University Press, or as expressly permitted
by law, by license, or under terms agreed with the appropriate reproduction
rights organization. Inquiries concerning reproduction outside the scope of the
above should be sent to the Rights Department, Oxford University Press,
at the address above.

You must not circulate this work in any other form
and you must impose this same condition on any acquirer.

**Library of Congress Cataloging-in-Publication Data**

Names: Finn, Janet L., 1956- editor.
Title: The just practice framework in action : contemporary case studies /
   edited by Janet L. Finn, University of Montana.
Description: New York, NY: Oxford University Press, [2021]
Identifiers: LCCN 2021013412 (print) | LCCN 2021013413 (ebook) | ISBN
   9780197529041 (paperback) | ISBN 9780197529058 (epub) | ISBN
   9780197529065 (pdf)
Subjects: LCSH: Social justice—Case studies. | Social service—Case
   studies.
Classification: LCC HM671 .J877 2021 (print) | LCC HM671 (ebook) | DDC
   303.3/72—dc23
LC record available at https://lccn.loc.gov/2021013412
LC ebook record available at https://lccn.loc.gov/2021013413

*To all those dedicated to the pursuit of social justice.
Together we can realize our visions of a just world.*

# Contents

*Preface, Janet L. Finn, MSW, PhD* xi
*Acknowledgments* xv

1. Introduction to the Just Practice Framework   1

Part One   INTEGRATING SOCIAL JUSTICE IN DIRECT SOCIAL
           WORK PRACTICE

2. "Just as I Am": Moving from Biopsychosocial to Just Practice
   Assessments   10
   ROBYN BROWN-MANNING, LMSW, PHD, AND WILLIE TOLLIVER, DSW

3. Just Practice with Midlife and Older LGBTQ Adults   25
   CHARLES PITRE HOY-ELLIS, LCSW, PHD

4. Just Practice in the Context of a Therapeutic Group Home   37
   SARAH FIELDING, LCSW

5. A Very Good Day: Just Practice and the Therapeutic Alliance   46
   ELIZABETH URSCHEL, MFA, LCSW

Part Two   INTEGRATING SOCIAL JUSTICE IN NEIGHBORHOOD
           AND COMMUNITY CONTEXTS OF PRACTICE

6. Just Process: Determining the Location of a Homeless Shelter   58
   AMIE THURBER, MSW, PHD

7. Just Practice for Housing Equality   69
   KARA BYRNE, MSW, PHD

8. Just Practice for Water as a Human Right  81
   ANN P. RALL, MSW, PHD

9. Just Practice in a Gentrifying Neighborhood  94
   AMIE THURBER, MSW, PHD

10. Practicing Social Justice Work in Refugee Resettlement
    JEN BARILE, MSW, AND JESSE LITTMAN, MSW  104

Part Three   INTEGRATING SOCIAL JUSTICE IN SCHOOL SETTINGS

11. Just Practice and Restorative Justice in Schools  116
    JEN MOLLOY, MSW, PHD

12. Verbatim Theater and Social Work: A Just Practice Approach to Trauma-Informed Education  127
    ERIN BUTTS, MSW, AND SARAH BUTTS, MFA

13. Social Workers in Schools: A Just Practice Perspective  138
    KATIE BAUMLER, MSW

Part Four   INTEGRATING SOCIAL JUSTICE IN THE CRIMINAL JUSTICE SYSTEM

14. Social Justice Work in Jail: Navigating Tensions of Care and Control  150
    DEANNA COOPER, LCSW

15. Diane's Story: From Incarceration to Social Justice Advocacy  162
    VICKII COFFEY, MSA, PHD

Part Five   INTEGRATING SOCIAL JUSTICE IN UNIVERSITY CONTEXTS OF PRACTICE

16. Healthy Market: Addressing Food Insecurity at an Urban College Campus  174
    SONYA CRABTREE-NELSON, LCSW, PHD, MARISSA CIRILO, LCSW, AND ERIC CRABTREE-NELSON, LCSW

17. Using Just Practice to Structure Learning in Field   184
    LAURA DRESSER, MSW, PHD

18. Just Practice for Disability Rights   193
    AMY CAPOLUPO, LCSW

Part Six   INTEGRATING SOCIAL JUSTICE IN ORGANIZATIONAL
            CONTEXTS OF PRACTICE

19. Just Practice: Lessons from the East Side Clinic
    DIANE KEMPSON, MSW, PHD   206

20. Bringing Just Practice Into a Corporate Law Context
    KAO NOU L. MOUA MSW, PHD   216

21. Social Justice and the Triple Bottom Line: Integrating Social, Environmental, and Economic Sustainability
    KATHERINE DEUEL, MS, MSW   226

Part Seven   INTEGRATING SOCIAL JUSTICE IN INDIGENOUS
              AND INTERNATIONAL CONTEXTS OF PRACTICE

22. Just Practice in Indigenous Communities
    ASHLEY TRAUTMAN, MSW, JD, AND MARILYN BRUGUIER ZIMMERMAN, MSW, PHD   238

23. Indigenous Knowledges, Social Justice, and Disaster Risk Reduction
    MARJORIE BALAY-AS, PHD, AND JAY MARLOWE, MSW, PHD   250

24. Social Work and Social Justice on the U.S.–Mexico Border: From Critical Consciousness to Collaborative Action
    JANET L. FINN MSW, PHD   261

*Epilogue*   271
*Contributors*   272
*Index*   276

# Preface

JANET L. FINN, MSW, PHD

*The Just Practice Framework in Action: Contemporary Case Studies* presents a collection of essays illustrating the application of the Just Practice framework in diverse contexts of social work practice. It is designed to serve as a companion reader to *Just Practice: A Social Justice Approach to Social Work* (Finn, 2020) and as a stand-alone text. The Just Practice framework provides a model for the integration of social justice into social work from the most intimate spaces of individual, clinical practice to macro-level policy analysis, advocacy, and community building. The contributors to this volume show how they have brought the Just Practice framework to bear to inform and transform their practice as clinicians, researchers, advocates, organizers, educators, and program directors. Their stories bring the framework to life, illustrating its potential for transformative social work practice. Their accounts offer grounded insights into challenges and possibilities of social justice–oriented social work that both strengthen and inform the Just Practice framework.

The Just Practice framework is organized around five key concepts—*meaning, context, power, history,* and *possibility*. As we consider them in relation to one another, they provide a guide for social justice–oriented thought and practice. How do we give meaning to the experiences and conditions that shape our lives? What are the contexts in which those experiences and conditions occur, and how might context limit or expand courses of action? How do structures and relations of power shape people's lives and their choices for individual and collective action? How might a historical perspective help us grasp the interplay of sociopolitical structures and human agency, the ways in which struggles over meaning and power have played out, and the human consequences of those struggles? How might an appreciation of those struggles help us claim a sense of possibility for critical, creative social work? How might our thinking and practice be transformed by ongoing attention to these independent yet interrelated concepts (Finn, 2020, p. xix)?

The five key concepts of Just Practice are translated into action through *seven core processes* that link theory and practice: *critical reflection, engagement, teaching-learning, action, accompaniment, evaluation,* and *celebration*. The processes are familiar in that they build on dominant social work approaches to planned change, which focus on engagement, assessment, intervention, and evaluation. What is unique here is that they are informed by and enacted within the broader frame of meaning, power, context, history, and possibility. They are explicitly dialogical and collaborative processes. In Chapter 1 I provide readers with an overview of the Just Practice concepts and processes. Taken together, these concepts and processes provide a framework that integrates critical thinking, historical consciousness, political and ethical commitment, and practical skills. It is grounded in a question-posing approach that encourages social workers to challenge internalized ways of thinking, disrupt certainties, engage in critical inquiry, and open themselves to new possibilities. This collection of case studies illuminates these facets of the Just Practice framework in action.

Over the past several years, I have been engaged in critical scholarship using the Just Practice framework (see, for example, Finn, 2005; Finn & Molloy, 2020). I have also been teaching the framework as the foundation of the Master of Social Work (MSW) program at the University of Montana since 2002 and engaging with scholars, educators, and practitioners who are applying the framework in a variety of arenas of pedagogy and practice. Thus, this volume features several case studies grounded in Montana, where practitioners have been utilizing the Just Practice framework for the past 2 decades.

Montana is a predominantly rural state with a few key metropolitan areas. The state is reported to have the nation's fastest growing rate of income inequality as the percentage of non-wage income makes up an increasing proportion of the state's economy (Michels, 2018). The toll of social and economic inequities is manifest in pervasive issues of trauma, economic insecurity, and addiction. Montana had the nation's highest suicide rate in 2019 (Ellison, 2019). Health disparities, poverty, and racism pose ongoing challenges to the resilience of Montana's American Indian communities. The Montana context, while unique in some aspects, offers a microcosm of the social justice issues facing social workers across the United States and beyond.

This collected volume brings together the work of more than 30 social work practitioners and educators who have utilized the framework in rethinking and transforming their social work practice. While some authors reflect on cases from their past practice or the evolution of programs and practices over time, others draw readers into here-and-now practice moments. Contributors make links between theory and practice. They provide concrete examples that show readers how practitioners bring the concepts and processes of *Just Practice* to bear in grappling with real-life challenges. They speak to the nuances of meaning that shape practice; their navigation of complex power relations; the historical, cultural, political, organizational, and community contexts of their work; and the possibilities and constraints they have faced. They critically reflect on both the successes and failures they have experienced in their work. The diversity of the case studies demonstrates the applicability of the Just Practice framework in individual direct practice, community change work, systems change, organizational development, and action research. They illustrate the value of the Just Practice framework in guiding an integrated approach to social work practice that challenges the false dichotomy of "micro" and "macro" social work practice.

The contributors apply the Just Practice framework to address issues of housing rights and homelessness, refugee resettlement, neighborhood gentrification, Indigenous rights, and immigration. They explore campus and community action around food security, mental health care access, disability rights, and students organizing for social justice. They demonstrate the potential for just practice in schools, group homes, jails, law offices, and nonprofit organizations. They consider how the processes of social work assessment can be transformed and how Just Practice provides a new lens through which to consider direct practice with children and youth. Some contributors speak directly to issues of oppression, privilege, difference, and diversity. Some explore the complex ethical terrain of justice-oriented practice. Others show how participatory and community-based research is a critical component of practice. Authors address challenges of engagement, the potential of teaching-learning, the power of accompaniment, possibilities for participatory action and evaluation, the importance of critical reflection, and reasons for celebration. They bring their passion and authenticity to bear in offering "out-of-the box" possibilities for practice.

This volume was coming to fruition as the United States and our world were being profoundly transformed by a global pandemic. The health crisis wrought by Covid-19 has mapped onto and exacerbated deep social, racial, and economic inequalities. The gap between rich and poor, both globally and nationally, had become a chasm prior to the pandemic (Oxfam America, 2020). It became more deeply entrenched during 2020 as millions faced loss of jobs, housing, and healthcare access. The disproportionate death toll for African Americans and other communities of color in the United States as a result of Covid-19 has laid bare the historically deep and systemically broad inequalities in the country wrought by centuries of racist policies and practices steeped in the logic of White supremacy (Abedi et al., 2020; Kendi, 2019).

This volume also took shape in a context of profound social violence and political disruption. One hundred and sixty-four Black persons were killed by police in the United States in the first 8 months of 2020 (CBS News, 2020). Grassroots mobilizations demanding justice and accountability were frequently met with violent suppression. A parallel process was playing out in the political realm through systematic efforts at voter suppression targeting voters of color; threats of violence against elected officials seeking to enforce health regulations in the face of Covid-19; and relentless attacks on the foundations of democracy in the United States by an autocrat and his supporters seeking to retain power. The Just Practice framework and the case studies presented here do not pretend to provide solutions to these deep and disturbing injustices. Rather, they help us see that our social work practice is never outside of these larger realities. Further, they show how justice-oriented action can stem from seemingly intractable situations, whether at the individual, organizational, or community level. They offer a gateway to new thinking, inspire hope and possibility, and create ripple effects beyond what we are able to appreciate in the moment. Taken together, this collection of case studies enriches and enhances understanding of the Just Practice framework and prepares students to embrace the framework as a guide to their social work thought and practice.

## REFERENCES

Abedi, V., Olulana, O., Avula, V., Chaudhary, D., Khan, A., Shahjouei, S., Li, J., & Zand, R. (2020). Racial, economic, and health inequality and COVID-19 infection in the United States. *Journal of Racial and Ethnic Health Disparities.* https://doi.org/10.1007/s40615-020-00833-4

CBS News. (2020). *Police in the U.S. killed 164 Black people in the first 8 months of 2020.* https://www.cbsnews.com/pictures/black-people-killed-by-police-in-the-u-s-in-2020/

Ellison, A. (2019, December 11). *U.S. states ranked by suicide rate.* https://www.beckershospitalreview.com/rankings-and-ratings/us-states-ranked-by-suicide-rate-121119.html

Finn, J. (2005). La Victoria: Claiming memory, history, and justice in a Santiago población. *Journal of Community Practice, 13*(3), 9–31.

Finn, J. (2020). *Just practice: A social justice approach to social work* (4th ed.). Oxford University Press.

Finn, J., & Molloy, J. (2020, December 1). Advanced integrated practice: bridging the micro-macro divide in social work pedagogy and practice. *Social Work Education.*

Kendi, I. (2019). *How to be an anti-racist.* Penguin Random House.

Michels, H. (2018, March 13). *Montana's income inequality is growing faster.* Montana Primary Care Association. https://www.mtpca.org/2018/03/montanas-income-inequality-growing-faster-state/

Oxfam America. (2020). *Inequality and extreme poverty* [Fact sheet]. https://www.oxfamamerica.org/explore/issues/extreme-inequality-and-poverty/

# Acknowledgments

I am grateful to the many students, alumni, and faculty from the University of Montana–Missoula School of Social Work who have shaped and challenged my thinking about *Just Practice* over the past 20 years. Special thanks to the contributors to this volume who have expanded the possibilities for social justice work through their creative and critical practice. Our many conversations over the course of this project have enriched and inspired my thinking and teaching. Thanks to Emma Sobremonte de Mendicuti, social work faculty member of Universidad de Deusto and chair of the Third International Social Work Congress held in Bilbao, Spain, in November 2018, for the invitation to give a keynote talk on Just Practice in action. The presentation provided the impetus for this book project.

Thanks to the wonderful team at Oxford University Press—Alyssa Palazzo, Sarah Butcher, Lisa Ball, Ryan Chavis, Rebecca Olley, Stefano Imbert, Mary Anne Shahidi, and Matthew Dix for their unfailing support through every phase of the publishing process. I am also grateful to reviewers Jacqueline Anderson, Erica Balderrama, Anthony Campbell, Jen Evers, Jillian Graves, Ebony Hall, Jane Hereth, Kelly Martin, Lori McNeel, Natalie Moore-Bembry, Paula Sheridan, and Aloha Van Camp, whose critiques and suggestions were key to bringing this volume to fruition. Finally, thanks to my husband, Dave Ames, for his gentle reminders that social justice is nourished with food, drink, love, laughter, music, and friendship.

# 1

# Introduction to the Just Practice Framework

> Promoting social justice . . . in an unequal world provides the raison d'etre for social work.
> —Lena Dominelli

## Just Practice Key Concepts

In this chapter I provide readers with an overview of the concepts and processes that comprise the Just Practice framework. Let's start with the five key concepts—*meaning, context, power, history,* and *possibility*. As we consider them in relation to one another, they provide a guide for social justice–oriented thought and practice. They call on social workers to continually reflect on how we make sense of experiences and life circumstances; how we understand the complex contexts that shape and constrain human experience; how we name and navigate structures and relations of power; how we bring a sense of history to bear in understanding present concerns and future trajectories; and how we claim a sense of possibility to inspire and transform social work practice.

The concept of meaning starts with recognition of meaning-making as a fundamental human capacity. We continually seek to make sense of our experience and do so from our social locations in the world. Searching for meaning requires reflexivity, which entails both examination of one's own "conceptual baggage" and implicit assumptions (Kirby & McKenna, 1989) and examination of self in relation to others and the broader social context (Gardner, 2012, p. 107). Attention to meaning helps social workers recognize the partiality of our views and open ourselves to hearing and appreciating how service users give meaning to their experiences and how their experiences might be understood by others, such as loved ones, helping professionals, and policymakers (Finn, 2020, p. 23).

The concept of context gets to the heart of social work's legacy of a "person-in-environment" perspective. Context shapes meaning and helps us make sense of people, events, and circumstances. If we ignore context, we may miss or misinterpret intricate connections, patterns, and possibilities for change beyond the individual. A focus on context challenges us to critically consider how organizational, community, societal, and cultural-political arenas shape our practice. Social work plays out within multiple contexts. The agency-based context of practice is further embedded in community and policy contexts and is shaped by broader social, political, and economic logics and forces. Our work is never outside broader contexts of racism, White supremacy, sexism, heterosexism, and cisgenderism. The challenge—and opportunity—here is to help social workers grasp that context is not merely the arena or "container" in which social work takes place. Rather, contexts are productive forces. Contexts *produce* us as particular kinds of social workers and service users (Finn, 2020, p. 25).

The Just Practice framework seeks to make power a talkable theme in all aspects of our social work practice. Some view power from a standpoint of domination and repression. Others see power in connection and collaboration (Homan, 2016). Power may be both possessive and relational; people can both have power and exercise it (Mullaly, 2010). "Power over" others represents only one form of power. Power may also come from within and from joining with others. It is manifest in human agency and resistance. The Just Practice perspective helps social workers gain a critical understanding of power by interrogating relations of power that shape practice. Social workers are often well positioned to evoke power within, power with others, and power to act (Townsend et al., 1999). Part of Just Practice is recognizing how powerful a social work voice of advocacy and resistance can be (Finn, 2020, p. 26).

History and a critical historical consciousness are fundamental to effective social justice work. Humans are historical beings, and it is through consciousness of our histories that we can better appreciate present complexities and future possibilities. History can serve as a warning device by helping us see how flawed assumptions have led to harmful practices in the past. History helps us create linkages and identify threads of connection across time. History permeates the present as we build on and respond to ideas and practices that came before us. History helps us understand how power works. A historical perspective provides us the opportunity to see who has the power to name and frame what counts as a problem and to develop strategies and mobilize resources for action. History inspires us to act; it reminds us that change is possible and that "ordinary" people can be powerful agents of change (Finn, 2020, p. 27).

Finally, a sense of possibility enables us to look at what has been done, what can be done, and what can exist. Possibility challenges us to think differently about practices, people, programs, and policies. It draws attention to human agency, or the capacity to act in the world as intentional, meaning-making beings, whose actions are shaped but never fully determined by life circumstances. A sense of possibility can help us to get unstuck as we look at what has been done and envision what can be done. As we expand our possibilities for thinking, we may change the way a problem is perceived and envision new courses of action (Finn, 2020, p. 28).

## Just Practice Core Processes

The five key concepts of Just Practice are translated into action through seven core processes that link theory and practice: *critical reflection, engagement, teaching-learning, action, accompaniment, evaluation,* and *celebration.* Critical reflection entails *problematizing* social work by continually questioning embedded assumptions about social problems, interventions, and ourselves as social workers. Through critical reflection we become cognizant of our positionalities and how they may shape our approach to practice. We deepen our self-awareness, question our certainties, and reframe our inquiry to open up new possibilities. Critical reflection enables us to examine the dynamics of oppression and privilege and question presumptions of White privilege and power that have infiltrated social work history, theory, and practice.

Engagement is the process through which the social worker enters the world of the participant(s) and begins to develop a working relationship. It recognizes relationship as the "heart" of social work (Perlman, 1979). Engagement is a process of listening, communication, translation, and connection that seriously addresses questions of trust, power, intimacy, and difference. Social workers begin from a place of openness and acknowledge the partiality of their knowledge. Engagement provides the entrée to social justice work in community, organizational, group, and interpersonal contexts. It is a process of coming together with others to create a space of respect and hope in which we can learn from and about one another. Engagement is enhanced by curiosity, humility, compassionate listening, and respect.

Teaching-learning is a process of discovery and critical inquiry. While it entails, at least in part, the processes of data collection, assessment, and interpretation, teaching-learning reframes them as collaborative rather than unilateral activities. Teaching-learning connotes a two-way street and a relationship of interchange among participants. The teaching-learning approach positions the social worker as co-learner in a process where meaning is co-constructed rather than extracted or imposed. It entails mutual question-posing, collaboratively collecting information, identifying resources and supports, discussing root causes of presenting concerns, and discovering personal and collective capacities for action. Teaching-learning is also a process wherein we question top-down, "expert" approaches to assessment and dominant assumptions, examine power relations, and move beyond a problem focus to honor strengths, capabilities, and rights.

Action is the process of carrying out plans and sustaining the momentum. We prefer the concept of "action" to that of "intervention" in that action suggests an opening up of possibilities. Action may take many forms. It includes animating, facilitating, awakening the spirit and sense of possibility, advocating, and taking responsibility to speak for the values of social justice. Action is informed by reflection.

It demands vigilance and a commitment to the ongoing search for one's own competence (Freire, cited in Moch, 2009. Action honors the human agency of all participants in the process and calls for critical and respectful attention to resistance.

Action goes hand in hand with accompaniment. Accompaniment consists of the actual people-to-people partnerships through which action is realized. In its simplest sense, accompaniment means to go with, to support and enhance the process. It reflects a commitment to being part of the journey over the long haul. The process entails ongoing dialogue regarding difference, power, and positionality among participants. It keeps us mindful of the challenges of collaboration and the need for conscious work in building alliances, mediating conflicts, and negotiating power. It calls for an intentional relationship with those with whom we work grounded in love, dignity, and respect (Villarreal Sosa, Diaz, & Hernandez, 2019).

Evaluation is an ongoing process of stepping back, taking stock at different moments, and assessing the effectiveness of our efforts. Evaluation is interwoven with reflection and teaching-learning. In evaluation, we systematically examine the processes and outcomes of our efforts. Evaluation is a collaborative process done *with* rather than *to* others. Through evaluation we honor our responsibilities and accountability to those with whom we work. Evaluation allows time for rethinking and reorganizing change efforts. It enables participants to see gains, growth, and successes and to use these as springboards into subsequent action. Evaluation also calls attention to the challenges of our change efforts and provides a process to address these challenges and build new knowledge to forge subsequent efforts.

Celebration is the act of commemorating the successes, big and small, in the process of change. It consists of the activities that allow us to have fun with and in the work. Celebration is a process of bringing joy to the work and honor to the workers. Celebration is too easily ignored, but it is a fundamental way in which we can give voice to the beauty and power of our work. We see celebration as an essential component of a just world and the struggle to achieve it. Taken together, these concepts and processes provide a framework for an integrated, social justice approach to social work practice.

## Overview of the Case Studies

The case studies show how the Just Practice framework translates into action in the real world. Each chapter concludes with questions for reflection and discussion. Where relevant, contributors include links to additional resources. Table 1.1 provides a summary showing the key themes, core processes, and Council on Social Work Education competencies addressed in each chapter.

Table 1.1: Summary of Chapters

| Chapter | Five Key Themes: Meaning, Power, Context, History, Possibility | Seven Core Processes: Critical Reflection, Engagement, Teaching-Learning, Action, Accompaniment, Evaluation, Celebration | CSWE 2022 Competencies |
|---|---|---|---|
| 1 | Introduction and overview of key themes | Introduces and provides an overview of seven core processes | 3: Advance social justice |
| 2 | Brings key themes to bear to rethink biopsychosocial assessments | Features teaching-learning, critical reflection, and concept of positionality | 3: Advance social justice; 7: Assessment |
| 3 | Addresses key themes in clinical practice with older LGBTQ adults | Illustrates engagement, teaching-learning, action, accompaniment, and celebration using two case examples | 2: Diversity, equity, inclusion; 3: Advance social justice; 6: Engagement; 8: Intervention |
| 4 | Examines key themes in context of adolescent group home | Explores engagement, teaching-learning, accompaniment, and critical reflection through three case examples | 3: Advance social justice; 6: Engagement; 8: Intervention |
| 5 | Draws on key themes to summarize life story of 12-year-old client | Addresses engagement, teaching-learning, action, accompaniment, and celebration | 6: Engagement; 8: Intervention; 9: Evaluation |
| 6 | Uses key themes to describe process of site selection for a homeless shelter | Features engagement, teaching-learning, action, accompaniment, and critical reflection | 3: Advance human rights; 6: Engagement; 7: Assessment; 8: Intervention |
| 7 | Key themes guide process of participatory research for housing equality | Illustrates engagement, teaching-learning, accompaniment, and critical reflection | 3: Advance social justice; 2: Diversity, equity, inclusion; 4: Practice-informed research |
| 8 | Brings key themes to bear in addressing water as a human right in Detroit | Highlights engagement, teaching-learning, and action | 3: Advance human rights; 5: Policy practice; 6: Engagement; 7: Assessment; 8: Intervention |
| 9 | Applies key themes to analyze gentrification in Nashville neighborhoods | Describes engagement and teaching-learning in a participatory research project | 3: Advance social justice; 4: Practice-informed research 5: Policy practice; 6: Engagement; 7: Assessment |

| Chapter | Five Key Themes: Meaning, Power, Context, History, Possibility | Seven Core Processes: Critical Reflection, Engagement, Teaching-Learning, Action, Accompaniment, Evaluation, Celebration | CSWE 2022 Competencies |
|---|---|---|---|
| 10 | Uses key themes to illustrate work in a refugee resettlement program | Highlights engagement, teaching-learning, accompaniment, critical reflection, celebration, and evaluation | 3: Advance human rights; 6: Engagement; 7: Assessment; 8: Intervention; 9: Evaluation |
| 11 | Examines a school-based restorative justice process through lens of key themes | Features discussion of engagement, teaching-learning, critical reflection, and evaluation | 3: Advance social justice; 4: Research-informed practice; 6: Engagement; 7: Assessment; 9: Evaluation |
| 12 | Uses themes to describe a school-based documentary theater project | Addresses engagement, teaching-learning, accompaniment, and action | 2: Diversity, equity, inclusion; 3: Advance social justice; 6: Engagement; 8: Intervention |
| 13 | Considers school-based practice with a young student through lens of key themes | Highlights engagement, teaching-learning, and critical reflection | 3: Advance social justice 6: Engagement; 7: Assessment; 8: Intervention |
| 14 | Brings key themes to bear in describing a jail-based substance-use treatment program | Features engagement, teaching-learning, action, accompaniment, and critical reflection | 1: Professionalism and interprofessional teams; 3: Advance social justice; 6: Engagement; 8: Intervention |
| 15 | Applies key themes to describe one woman's journey from prison to advocacy work | Illustrates engagement, teaching-learning, and critical reflection and use of a social-justice-oriented research methodology | 3: Advance social justice; 4: Research-informed practice; 6: Engagement; 7: Assessment |
| 16 | Uses key themes to describe project to address food insecurity on a college campus | Addresses teaching-learning and critical reflection in establishing a healthy market | 1: Professionalism and inter-professional teams 3. Advance social justice; 6: Engagement; 7: Assessment |
| 17 | Shows how key themes guide a yearlong MSW field education seminar | Explores engagement; teaching-learning, action, accompaniment, and critical reflection | 3: Advance social justice; 6: Engagement; 8: Intervention |

| Chapter | Five Key Themes: Meaning, Power, Context, History, Possibility | Seven Core Processes: Critical Reflection, Engagement, Teaching-Learning, Action, Accompaniment, Evaluation, Celebration | CSWE 2022 Competencies |
|---|---|---|---|
| 18 | Applies keys themes to guide a campus-based effort to improve accessibility | Describes engagement, teaching-learning, action, and accompaniment | 1: Promote socially just use of technology; 2: Diversity, equity, inclusion; 3: Advance human rights; 4: Engage in policy practice |
| 19 | Uses key themes to examine response to closure of a community health center | Considers engagement, teaching-learning, action, accompaniment, and critical reflection | 1: Address ethical dilemmas; 3: Advance social justice; 6: Engagement; 8: Intervention |
| 20 | Shows how key themes guided collective change effort within a law firm | Addresses engagement, teaching-learning, action, and accompaniment | 2: Diversity, equity, inclusion; 3: Advance social justice; 6: Engagement; 7: Assessment; 8: Intervention |
| 21 | Examines key themes in the context of a building materials reuse store | Explores engagement, teaching-learning, action, accompaniment; critical reflection, and celebration | 2: Diversity, equity, inclusion; 3: Advance environmental justice; 6: Engagement; 7: Assessment: 8: Intervention |
| 22 | Shows how key themes guide trauma-informed practice in Indigenous communities | Highlights critical reflection, engagement, and accompaniment with attention to positionality | 2: Diversity, equity, inclusion; 3: Advance social justice; 4: Policy practice; 6: Engagement; 7: Assessment; 8: Intervention; 9: Evaluation |
| 23 | Uses key themes to explore disaster risk reduction in Indigenous communities | Features engagement and teaching-learning with attention to grounded research to inform practice | 3: Advance social and environmental justice; 4: Policy practice; 5: Research-informed practice; 6: Engagement; 7: Assessment |
| 24 | Shows how key themes informed a course on social justice and U.S.-Mexico border | Highlights engagement, teaching-learning, action, and accompaniment | 3: Advance social justice and human rights; 4: Policy practice; 6: Engagement |

## REFERENCES

Finn, J. (2020). *Just practice: A social justice approach to social work* (4th ed.). Oxford University Press.

Gardner, F. (2012). The care, the rain, and meaningful conversation. In S. Witkin (Ed.), *Social construction and social work practice* (pp. 103–126). Columbia University Press.

Homan, M. (2016). *Promoting community change: Making it happen in the real world* (6th ed.). Cengage.

Kirby, S., & McKenna, K. (1989). *Methods from the margins: Experience, research, social change.* Garamond Press.

Moch, M. (2009). A critical understanding of social work by Paulo Freire. *Journal of Progressive Human Services, 20*, 92–97.

Mullaly, B. (2010). *Challenging oppression and confronting privilege: A critical social work approach* (2nd ed.). Oxford University Press.

Perlman, H. H. (1979). *Relationship: The heart of helping people.* University of Chicago Press.

Townsend, J., Zapata, E., Rowlands, J., Alberti, P., & Mercado, M. (1999). *Women and power: Fighting patriarchies and poverty.* Zed Books.

Villarreal Sosa, L., Diaz, S., & Hernandez, R. (2019). Accompaniment in a Mexican immigrant community: Conceptualization and identification of biopsychosocial outcomes. *Journal of Religion & Spirituality in Social Work: Social Thought, 38*(1), 21–42.

Part One

# INTEGRATING SOCIAL JUSTICE IN DIRECT SOCIAL WORK PRACTICE

# 2

# "Just as I Am"

## Moving from Biopsychosocial to Just Practice Assessments

ROBYN BROWN-MANNING, LMSW, PHD,
AND WILLIE TOLLIVER, DSW

**Contributors:** Eden Wall, MSW Student, Silberman School of Social Work; Erica Turett, MSW Student, Silberman School of Social Work

> I cannot assume to know what K needs or wants based on my understanding of her social identity; instead, I defer to her as the expert on her own experience.
> —Eden Wall

### Overview

In Chapter 2 Robyn Brown-Manning and Willie Tolliver reimagine biopsychosocial assessments from a Just Practice perspective. They describe how traditional biopsychosocial assessments often neglect an important voice—that of the service user. As a result, the individual's experiences and situations are often pathologized, as they are void of context, meaning, and history. The chapter highlights how students are guided in developing Just Practice assessments by shifting their positioning from "all-knowing" authorities to humble learners, with service users as teachers and crafters of their own narratives.

## Introduction

The introduction of *Just Practice* as a foundation-year textbook for the MSW program at a large public university in New York City served as a catalyst for changing the approach to biopsychosocial assessment. Biopsychosocial assessments, which have been a part of social work since the 1970s, were embraced by social workers for their comprehensive, multidimensional approach that aligned with social work's commitment to a person-in-environment approach (Engel, 1977). The biopsychosocial assessment is a process and instrument almost solely associated with the social work profession. Biopsychosocial assessments typically capture an overview of a service user's physical and emotional health and vulnerability, family circumstances, education and employment status, and coping skills. However, these assessments also have limitations. First, the social identities of the service users are interpreted through the eyes of the social worker with little opportunity for individuals to construct their own narratives regarding how social markers of identity shape their everyday lives. Second, they focus on the here and now and the recent past of the individual, often with little attention to the broader sociopolitical, cultural, or economic context of their experience. Third, they tend to be problem-focused, emphasizing individual pathology and person-changing interventions rather than focusing on how forces of oppression in the larger society imprint, impact, and disrupt people's lives.

## The Assignment: Just Practice Assessment

At the forefront of our thinking when the Just Practice framework was introduced in the MSW program was the school's commitment to a curriculum that authentically represented its mission to

> promote civic engagement and dedication to public services in the City of New York. Our student body, field agencies, and alumni are the primary social work workforce of the public human service departments and not-for-profit agencies in New York City. (Silberman School of Social Work, n.d.)

All entering students (approximately 600 annually) are required to take a foundational yearlong course titled the Social Work Practice and Learning Lab. The course focuses on the oppressive contexts in which social work is practiced and the differential use of practice methods in contemporary professional social work. Among several assignments given to students throughout the year was a biopsychosocial assessment. With the introduction of the Just Practice framework, it became increasingly clear, however, that there was a disconnect between the traditional biopsychosocial assessment, the economic and social justice mission of the social work profession, and the tenets of the Just Practice framework. As students tested the Just Practice processes in their internships, especially that of teaching-learning, they found that it was challenging to effectively incorporate what they were learning from the service user. Finn (2020 states that "the biopsychosocial assessment process is often structured and formulaic with primary attention given to the traditional assessment categories and less attention paid to the environmental and structural arrangements that shape individual experience" (p. 253). In response, one instructor suggested that we transition from a biopsychosocial to a Just Practice assessment. We changed the title of the assignment and enlisted the support of the director of the writing center to provide clear instructions for it, as illustrated in the following:

## Just Practice Framework Assessment

### Aims

1. To understand the importance of ascertaining the meaning that service users give to the experiences and the conditions in their lives.
2. To ensure that the five themes of the Just Practice Framework—meaning, context, power, history, and possibility—are consistently applied when working with service users.

### Introduction (half a page)
- What is the topic?
- What is the connection to social work?
- What does your paper do?

### Identity and Issues (one page)
- Think of a person you are working with and identify where you are in the process (i.e., engagement, assessment/planning/review). Identify the issues being addressed in the situation presented by the person.

### Meaning (two pages)
- How are you working with the service user to ascertain what their understanding of the situation is? How are you identifying the **MEANING** they give to the experiences and conditions that shape their lives?

### Context (two pages)
- **CONTEXT** is the background and set of circumstances and conditions that surround and influence particular events and situations in life. How are you taking into consideration the **contexts** in which the client's experiences and conditions unfold? What are those contexts? How are contexts adding to the meaning given by the person to their lived experience and conditions? How are contexts impacting your understanding of the situation?

### Similarities in Positionality (one page)
- Consider how your approach is/may be affected by any similarities or dissimilarities between you and the person (e.g., in age, gender, ability, ethnicity, sexual orientation, class status, and/or education).

**Power and History (two pages)**
- As an individual in a "professional position," the social worker has to be aware of how their role might connote **POWER** to the service user.
- Where is the service user experiencing someone having power over them and their life? Where in their life is the service user exercising power over people?
- Where in their personal life are people close to them having power over them? Where is the service user exercising power to act with people close to them?
- Where is it happening in their external environment, as in a child welfare system having power over them? Or do the police and or justice system have power over them? Are the service recipients having issues with the school system? Where is the service user exercising power within relationships that are a part of their external environment?
- How much weight/consideration are you giving to this person's story about the experiences and conditions of their life as well as their wishes and feelings?
- How has **HISTORY** marked the person or their group or community for oppression? How has history shaped their resilience? What might their history tell us about **POSSIBILITY** for the service user?

**Power and Possibility (one page)**
- What other avenues are there for the service user's meaning, wishes, and feelings to be presented—including them doing so for themselves? Are you sure that you have adequately explored their meaning, wishes, and feelings?

**Conclusion (half a page)**
- What is the biggest takeaway from this essay?
- How will this information make you a better social worker?

The change in assignment, which seemed somewhat minor at the time, was transformative for the students. One individual said it best at the end of her Just Practice assessment assignment:

> When I recently completed an ego-oriented assessment of K for my clinical course, I ultimately produced a story that was largely deficit-based, hardly anchored in context or history, and frankly unhelpful; by contrast, the Just Practice framework enabled me to create an understanding that is nuanced, holistic, and strengths-based. Equipped with the Just Practice framework, I will approach my work with more self-awareness and sensitivity, understanding individuals for the resilient, complex, and unique people they are. (E. Wall, personal communication, December 20, 2019)

In the following section, we offer excerpts taken from a traditional biopsychosocial assessment (Mr. O), followed by illustrations that we draw from two Just Practice assessments (K and LG). We draw alternately on the examples of K and LG to demonstrate how they contrast with the assessment of Mr. O. For clarity, we follow the structure of the assignment instructions and offer brief comments and questions after each example.

# Introduction

In the introduction, students declare a topic for the paper, identify the topic's relation to social work, and forecast what will be accomplished in the paper. While this seems to be a straightforward task, we noted differences in how students framed the assessment from the start. They recognized their privileged position in being able to share service users' narratives and recognized the power of the written word. As they began to apply Just Practice tenets and processes, they honored the humanity of service users as the authority and the craftspeople of their own stories.

### BIOPSYCHOSOCIAL EXAMPLE: "MR. O"

*Mr. O is a 30-year-old African-American male with a diagnosis of schizophrenia, chronic, undifferentiated type, polysubstance abuse in remission, and a history of pervasive development disorder. It must be noted that as an African American male, Mr. O has been a victim of systems of oppression (Finn, 2020). This systemic oppression and positionality (Finn, 2020, p.46) experienced by Mr. O will be highlighted in this bio-psycho-social.*

### JUST PRACTICE EXAMPLE #1: "K"

*The Just Practice framework "puts social work's expressed commitment to social justice at center stage" (Finn, 2020, p. xviii). Through the application of the five themes of meaning, context, power, history, and possibility, the framework allows us, as social workers, to engage in deep self-reflection and to develop more holistic understandings of the individuals with whom we work so we can serve them meaningfully and justly. This paper applies the Just Practice framework to one of the students at my field placement; in doing so, I am able to gain deeper and more meaningful insight into her experiences and the ways in which I can best support her.*

### JUST PRACTICE EXAMPLE #2: "LG"

*Understanding the meaning a service user makes of their life is key to social work, but it is often brushed aside in service of the mandates of the sector or agency. This paper applies the Just Practice framework to my work with a service user in my first-year social work internship at a child welfare organization.... It is important to note that in writing her own story, LG may add or subtract from what I have deemed notable. This paper is my attempt to humbly practice a framework that has been transformative for me and that I am still learning to apply.*

## REFLECTION

All three opening statements address the relevance of the Just Practice framework. However, in the two examples where students are intentionally applying the Just Practice framework to guide their assessment, they situate themselves as self-reflective learners open to different interpretations of the lived experiences of service users. They adopt a teaching-learning tone that informs the remainder of the written assignment.

## Identity and Issues

### BIOPSYCHOSOCIAL EXAMPLE: MR. O

*Mr. O has recently been discharged from a psychiatric center to supported housing. He has also been referred to a psychosocial clubhouse that focuses on strength-based practice with the adult mental health population. His goals while attending the clubhouse are to increase socialization, build vocational skills, and obtain employment. He has had an extensive psychiatric history that included multiple hospitalizations for violent and aggressive behavior and non-compliance with medication. He has not displayed this behavior since being institutionalized, and a brief period of incarceration. Mr. O participates in individual therapy and a weekly Narcotics Anonymous group.*

### JUST PRACTICE EXAMPLE #1: K

*At my field placement, I work with first-semester students at a public college. One of my students, K, is a 48-year-old African American woman. K is gregarious, passionate, and funny. She is an artist and plans to study film in college. K draws immense support and joy from her relationship with her three grown children. As a child, she was verbally abused and neglected by her single mother and sisters. As an adult, K experienced extensive domestic abuse from her partner, which culminated in a near-death experience and a home eviction. She shared that she has a diagnosis of anxiety disorder and dysthymia and was looking for help to "not feel so overwhelmed." As such, most of our work this semester has focused on developing skills for managing and coping with overwhelming feelings, which often manifest as either anger or anxiety, as she faces the new challenges of college life. . . .*

### JUST PRACTICE EXAMPLE #2: LG

*LG is a Black, 38-year-old mother of 6 children who are between 4 and 16 years of age. She currently lives with 3 of her 6 children. LG's family was referred to the agency for preventive services as a response to the family's open child protection cases. We have been working together for 2.5 months and are currently in action and accompaniment phase, which involves us working collaboratively to create change; this phase emphasizes the relational nature of action.... Additionally, I am always learning more about how LG makes meaning and offering alternative information or perspective to her context, which means we are also continually teaching-learning together (Finn, 2020, p. 223).*

*I see the presenting problems in LG's situation as twofold. First, there are the issues that the child protection agency deems problematic in LG's home and family: excessive corporal punishment, educational neglect, medical neglect, and improper cleaning of the home, and physical violence and sexual abuse between the children. Child Protection Services (CPS) has responded in many ways to the cases, including removing, at different times, 4 of LG's 6 children from her home. The family has many mandated services and workers that monitor behavior in the home. This leads to the second presenting problem: the fallout from these cases. (CPS) involvement for LG means that almost every day, she has a meeting she is required to go to. She is not currently employed largely because she is required to be available daily for mandatory meetings and managing her children's foster care.*

### REFLECTION

The biopsychosocial example focuses on Mr. O's psychiatric conditions, thus positioning him as a person with a singular identity. There is no discussion of the possible impact of institutionalization or incarceration on his mental health status. In contrast, the Just Practice examples acknowledge institutional barriers that create both context and meaning for the service users. The students using the Just Practice approach also demonstrate their ability to "hold the environment" for the service users to construct their own narratives, while simultaneously acknowledging and naming the systemic practices that are often ignored in traditional biopsychosocial assessments. Are there other points of similarity or difference that you note here?

## Meaning

"Just Practice means grappling with the ways in which we individually and collectively make sense of our worlds" (Finn, 2020, p. 24). In this section, students are asked to consider their practice and what helps them learn about the service users' understanding of their situations. Here we contrast the assessment of Mr. O with that of K.

### BIOPSYCHOSOCIAL EXAMPLE: MR. O

*When analyzing the member's ego function in terms of reality testing, Mr. O struggled at a young age with perception of external environment and internal world. According* to Goldstein (1984), when someone is "unable to experience the internal nature of his struggle, he projects his guilt onto external objects he then views as attacking him" (p. 54). Mr. O reports at the time of the incident when he attacked his grandmother, he was delusional and viewed his grandmother as a demon attacking him. This could be a result of his inability to decipher his own internal struggle from trauma inflicted on him at a young age. . . .

## JUST PRACTICE EXAMPLE: K

*As social workers, we must "attempt to understand how others make sense of their world" (Finn, 2020, p. 23). . . . I have worked to make space for K to lead and tell her story without interruption, practicing skills of observing and both active and radical listening (Finn, 2020, p. 207.) . . . In doing so, my work is discerning the meaning she makes of her experiences and challenges. . . . K was expected to take care of the household and was not allowed to participate in any family events or outings. . . . As K recalls these memories through tears, her pain is palpable, as is her pride in how far she has come. . . . she wants to succeed for her "younger self" who is still in an immense amount of pain from childhood. . . . She tells me, "Every good day I have, I feel like it is taking a bad day away from her."*

## REFLECTION

Words are powerful. In the Just Practice examples, the students present the service users' statements as fact. There is no interpretation offered. There are no such words as "alleges" or "denies," which are so often used in traditional biopsychosocial assessments. The service users truly construct their own narratives, with the workers receiving the information as presented. Conversely, the biopsychosocial example begins with the student "analyzing the member's ego functioning in terms of reality testing." There is a quiet yet profound blaming of Mr. O for his inability to comprehend what is happening internally, resulting in problems with his grandmother. With a narrow focus on the service user's mental health issues as his sole identity, there is no consideration of other lenses through which meaning could be examined. Are there other points of contrast that you see here?

# Context

The Just Practice framework conceptualizes context as "the circumstances and conditions that surround and influence particular events and situations" (Finn, 2020, p. 24). In a departure from traditional biopsychosocial assessments, the Just Practice assessment is intentional in its inclusion of state and federal policies as intimate "players" in the ways services are delivered and in defining what is considered a social problem (Finn, 2020). We present excerpts from Mr. O's biopsychosocial example and LG's Just Practice example here.

## BIOPSYCHOSOCIAL EXAMPLE: MR. O

Mr. O has a strong history of trauma. He reports a history of physical abuse at the hands of his mother and stepfather. He also reported that his stepfather watched pornographic movies with him when he was a young child. He reported he was abused sexually by his older stepbrother. Mr. O's mother has a diagnosis of schizoaffective disorder with bipolar features. Despite the lack of extensive history Mr. O describes his family as all mentally ill. When he was fourteen, four boys that he knew from summer camp beat him, held him at gunpoint, and forced him to take them to his home, which they ransacked and cut the phone line. He and his family were threatened repeatedly following the incident and therefore relocated.

## JUST PRACTICE EXAMPLE: LG

Learning LG's context has helped me understand how her experiences . . . inform the meaning she makes. In terms of the meaning she makes of CPS and the foster care system, important context is that LG spent time in foster care herself as a young person, giving her founded knowledge of how the system works. In foster care, she experienced violence and abusive mismanagement by the system. After being assaulted by a foster parent who hit her on the head with a crystal ashtray, leaving a scar that remains over twenty years later, LG went through the proper channels she was taught for reporting a foster parent for violence. Instead of protecting her, the agency called the foster parent to tell her she had been reported and left LG living in heightened danger in the same home, where she was at risk of retaliation. This informs her efforts to keep her children out of foster care and provides context for her assessment of CPS as incompetent and abusive of power.

## REFLECTION

The biopsychosocial example continues its trajectory of pathology with mental illness that resides within the family context as the primary focus. In contrast, the Just Practice assessment of LG enables us to see how powerful the contexts of foster care and CPS have been in shaping LG's life and her current struggles. Are there other observations regarding contexts that you glean from these excerpts?

# Positionality

Although positionality is not an explicit tenet of the Just Practice framework, it is important for students to consistently appreciate the many ways in which their own social identities interface with those of the service users. Variations in race, ethnicity, gender identities, class, religion, and so on impact how the social work student hears, interprets, and responds to elements of the service user's narrative. One's location in the social hierarchy also shapes the social work student's approach to the work; engaging in reflexive praxis is critical to effective assessments that are grounded in social justice concepts. Here we present the examples of Mr. O and K and show how the social workers addressed their positionalities.

## BIOPSYCHOSOCIAL EXAMPLE: MR. O

*My own practice must involve recognizing the member's strengths and linking him to employment which he can be successful in. This involves setting up employment partnerships and building strong communication between an employer and Mr. O. This involves a strength-based perspective recognizing the capacities and strengths of the service user. As a practitioner it is important to look at my own* **positionality** *as a social worker. I must align my position of privilege and power as a practitioner with the goals of Mr. O.*

## JUST PRACTICE EXAMPLE: K

*It is important to account for both my and K's positionalities, and how the differences and similarities between them might affect our relationship and work (Finn, 2020). K and I are both cisgender women, which is the only obvious similarity in our positionalities. It is worth noting that my gender is my only non-dominant social identity, whereas it is one of many of K's intersecting identities that is often accompanied by marginalization and discrimination. However, I cannot and have not assumed the fact that we are both women means we share similarities in perspective or experience, given our intersectional identities as well as the fact that there is always variation among individuals.*

*K's and my positionalities differ in several ways—some of which are very explicit and some of which are subtler. K is 16 years older than I am with significantly more life experience (including the experience of being a mother, a part of K's identity that she values deeply). I am the worker; she is the service user. She is Black, and I am White. She has spent her entire life living in poverty, while I grew up in a middle-upper-class family. While I have attended mostly private educational institutions and am now pursuing my second master's degree, K attended public high schools, took a range of GED programs, and is now beginning her undergraduate career. I am able-bodied and healthy; K, by contrast, struggles with chronic pain and has several mental health diagnoses. It is worth noting that many of our differences—in class, health, education—result from systemic and structural racism and oppression and result in, for K, unique experiences of discrimination.*

*Given our very different social identities, it is crucial that I assume my role as a learner in our relationship. . . . I cannot assume to know what K needs or wants based on my understanding of her social identity; instead, I defer to her as the expert on her own experience, taking the necessary care and time to understand the meaning she ascribes to her experiences and her identity. I must also examine my own biases and interrogate my own assumptions to ensure that I am not projecting my meaning or imposing my values onto K (Finn, 2020). Finally, it is crucial that I recognize the power I hold as a White middle-upper-class individual and be thoughtful about the ways in which this power comes into our working relationship (Finn, 2020). With*

K centered as the teacher and expert, the "treatment plan should be a collaborative process . . . [and should not] place the therapist in an overly powerful position in relation to the client" (Hook, Davis, Owen, & DeBlaere, 2017, p. 108).

### REFLECTION

While Mr. O's social worker names positionality as an aspect to consider, there is little elaboration regarding how the worker's positionality comes into play in the helping relationship. K's social worker, in contrast, critically considers the interplay of positionality between worker and service user and anticipates how their distinctive social identities could affect the helping relationship. Further, K's social worker also acknowledges how institutional practices might further bestow privilege on her and simultaneously further disadvantage K. What else do you notice in these two approaches to addressing positionality as a part of the assessment process?

## Power and History

In the first semester of the MSW program, students in the Social Work Practice and Learning Lab choose from three books on U.S. history—*A People's History of the United States* by Howard Zinn, *An Indigenous People's History of the United States* by Roxanne Dunbar-Ortiz, and *Harvest of Empire* by Juan Gonzalez. With this foundational history, students have a real feel for how the impact of history manifests in current-day human relations, particularly as it relates to power differentials between people based on gender, race, class, sexual orientation, and immigration status. We compare examples from Mr. O and LG here.

### BIOPSYCHOSOCIAL EXAMPLE: MR. O

*One must also consider the service user's collective trauma he experiences as an African American. African Americans have historically been victims of trauma inflicted by racist institutions that date back to slavery, continued during Jim Crow laws, and persist today. These present-day institutions that reinforce trauma prominently include the criminal justice system. This collective trauma goes beyond the scope of the individual's trauma. However, it must be noticed that in the face of this trauma, resiliency skills are developed and can be seen historically.*

### JUST PRACTICE EXAMPLE: LG

*History marks LG and her family for oppression in housing, education, income, health, and, most notably, the child welfare system. As a Black family living in New York City they have been subjected to redlining, which prohibited people of color from participating in purchasing homes and accessing capital. Education is segregated and unequally provided based on race; White and resourced children receive more education and less criminalization than Black children in New York.*

*The United States has an excessive history of violently and unreasonably removing children of color from their families and homes. Slavery, Black Codes and apprenticeship laws, as well as boarding schools for Indigenous children, all involved mass forcible separation of children of color from their families; the unlawful removal of children of color by the state and into state custody has been woven into government policy since colonialism began on U.S. land (Hunter, 2018). Today, this legacy continues in full force, but takes on different forms, such as immigrant detention, incarceration, and the child welfare system. The child welfare system flags mothers of color and sole parent mothers as lacking in nurturance and ability to raise their children. LG's family is stuck in a system that chooses to believe they are unfit for common courtesy and empathy. History marks LG's family to not be believed or treated humanely because she is Black and poor and is parenting alone. The bias of child welfare does not allow for nuance: It does not see that LG was assaulted in foster care, that she works daily to manage her children's care and CPS cases, and that she and her children care deeply for each other.*

## REFLECTION

While both social workers highlight the importance of collective as well as individual and familial history, LG's social worker links this larger, collective narrative to LG's present-day reality, which Mr. O's social worker does not do. What else do you notice here?

# Power and Possibility

People who are systemically oppressed for years develop capacity to exercise power without disturbing the power hierarchy that pervades the United States. Social work students must be supported to see and recognize service users' use of power—for example, queer, Black youth who refuse to pretend to be someone other than who they are. Service users may also use their power to join together to hold agencies and providers accountable for just, equitable services. We present excerpts from Mr. O and K to illustrate this here.

## BIOPSYCHOSOCIAL EXAMPLE: MR. O

*Mr. O's goal of obtaining and maintaining part-time employment is the focus of the work. He currently receives SSI but would like to supplement this income with part-time employment that he can sustain. He has expressed interest in porter maintenance work and dishwashing. He actively participates in work-based volunteer activities at the clubhouse. When Mr. O was placed in a supported employment dishwashing position, he struggled with a fixed schedule and strict supervision from his boss. He was let go after 3 weeks of employment. This deterred his motivation for a few months. With* staff counseling, he feels compelled to return to the workforce but would like to be placed in the right position where he can succeed.

### JUST PRACTICE EXAMPLE: K

*Through our work together and as we navigate this appeal process, I see the possibility of serving as a bridge between K and the systems she is confronting. I have the opportunity to explicitly acknowledge the broken, punitive systems in which we are working. I can communicate to K that she is not at fault or incapable, instead focusing my work on helping her navigate them so that she can get what she needs and continue to build the life she wants to live. Importantly, I must acknowledge the unearned power I hold as not only a worker but also a White woman that allows me to do this. . . .*

*K is teeming with possibility; she is powerful, passionate, and persevering. While she sometimes doubts herself, K also speaks about, and truly believes in, her potential and possibility. It seems that K may find solace and a sense of liberation through her storytelling. In the short term, K's appeal letter is an opportunity to use her voice and speak her truth, to share her meaning, and to identify her needs. As a social worker and an advocate, I believe it is my role to encourage her to do this through a strengths-based orientation (Holden et al., 2017)—and to use my own power in ways that challenge the voices that say otherwise and work to dismantle the systems that stand in her way.*

### REFLECTION

It seems that Mr. O's social worker is empathetic to his struggles, and yet there may be a missed opportunity here to find possibility in struggles. Might his struggles with structure be a sign of healing and finding voice? K's social worker, however, sees possibilities to name and leverage power with K, to value her story, and to name and support her strengths. Where do you see points of contrast here? Where do you see further opportunities for social justice work with Mr. O and K?

## Conclusion

The final section of the Just Practice assessment assignment invites students to once again engage in reflexive praxis. We want students to think critically about the utility and application of the Just Practice tenets and processes in their work and to see their roles in fulfilling the social work profession's social justice mandate on micro, mezzo, and macro levels. Moreover, we want students to tap into their own power and possibility, knowing that they are quite capable of affecting change with service users, service organizations and with policymakers.

### JUST PRACTICE EXAMPLE #1: K

*The Just Practice assessment framework introduces texture and richness to K and her experience. In providing K with the opportunity to tell her story, and then grounding that story in context and history, I begin to better understand her perspectives, feelings, and goals and can work to better support her. This exercise has demonstrated the drastically different understandings that are produced through using different frameworks and approaches.*

## JUST PRACTICE EXAMPLE # 2: LG

*As a White person with no significant system involvement, seeing the way LG's family is treated in the child welfare system has floored me. Having a framework for understanding the meaning LG makes of her life, the context she comes from, and power dynamics at play allows me to hold a sense of possibility for an otherwise very painful situation. The Just Practice framework also offers social workers a way out of exercising power over services users; while this is often the goal of social work, there are too few methods that understand how to be anti-oppressive and humanizing. . . . The framework allows me to take a step back, suspend judgment, and look at the whole picture of a person. It allows me to see people not through agency goggles, but rather through empathy for their whole experience.*

# Closing Reflection

This chapter has explored a tangible way in which students have implemented the Just Practice framework, which has the potential for being transformative to practice. The biopsychosocial assessment has a central place in social work. In its current form, while capturing significant aspects of a service user's life and presenting issues, it is often missing its most important voice—that of the service user. As a result, the individual's experiences and situations are often pathologized and void of context, meaning, and history. Rarely is possibility even considered, beyond what an agency can offer through its toolkit. The chapter has highlighted how students have been guided in developing Just Practice assessments, in lieu of biopsychosocial assessments, by shifting their positionalities from places of "all-knowing" authorities to humble learners, with service users as the teachers and the crafters of their own narratives. Students are bringing this type of assessment into other core courses, electives, and internships, promising a much-needed culture change in how social work is practiced within the current sociopolitical environment and beyond.

### QUESTIONS FOR REFLECTION AND DISCUSSION

1. Take a moment to think about a biopsychosocial assessment that you have completed. What did you learn from that assessment? What might have been missing? How might a Just Practice assessment offer a different perspective?
2. Consider the case of Mr. O above. How might Mr. O's story look different if approached through a Just Practice lens?
3. How might an intervention informed by a Just Practice assessment differ from that informed by a traditional biopsychosocial assessment?

4. Imagine advocating for a shift from a traditional biopsychosocial assessment to a Just Practice assessment approach in a social work setting such as a mental health center. What barriers might you encounter? How would you address those barriers? Where might you find sources of support?

## REFERENCES

Engel, G. (1977). The need for a new medical model: A challenge for biomedicine. *Science 196*(4286), 129-136.

Finn, J. (2020). *Just practice: A social justice approach to social work* (4th ed.). Oxford University Press.

Goldstein, E. (1984). The ego and its functions. In *Ego psychology and social work practice*. Free Press.

Holden, K., Hernandez, N., Wrenn, G., & Belton, A. (2017). Resilience: Protective factors for depression and post-traumatic stress disorder among African American Women? *Health, Culture and Society, 9,* 12–29.

Hook, J. N., Davis, D. D., Owen, J., & DeBlaere, C. (2017). *Cultural humility: Engaging diverse identities in therapy*. American Psychological Association.

Hunter, T. (2018). The long history of child snatching. *New York Times* June 4, P. A23. Retrieved from https://www.nytimes.com/2018/06/03/opinion/children-border.html

Silberman School of Social Work. (n.d.). *About*. Retrieved November 2019 from https://sssw.hunter.cuny.edu/about/

# 3

# Just Practice with Midlife and Older LGBTQ Adults

CHARLES PITRE HOY-ELLIS, LCSW, PHD

> We're all born naked and the rest is drag.
> —RuPaul

---

**Overview**

In this chapter Charles Pitre Hoy-Ellis brings the Just Practice framework to bear in his practice with midlife and older LGBTQ adults. Hoy-Ellis addresses the diversity, history, and context of LBGTQ individuals and communities. He examines historical constructions of homosexuality as pathology, considers the impact of pathologizing discourses and practices on people's lives, and speaks to the importance of resistance and liberation movements. Hoy-Ellis offers readers vignettes of two clients to show how he incorporates the concepts and processes of Just Practice in clinical social work.

---

## Introduction

In this chapter, I consider questions of context, meaning, power, and history in shaping lived experiences of midlife and older LGBTQ adults. When I started my MSW program in clinical/contextual practice nearly 20 years ago, the most typically used term for people who did not identify as heterosexual or cisgender was *lesbian, gay, bisexual, and transgender* (LGBT). At that time, the term "queer" was, for many people, still highly derogatory based on its socially constructed, historical usage. However, many in the community began arguing that excluding queerness was another example of heterosexist oppression *within* the LGBT community. One powerful challenge to this exclusion was the rallying cry of the early 1990s anti-LGBT-violence political organization Queer Nation, "We're here! We're Queer! Get used to it!" (Queer Nation NY, 2016). Hence, I use the more inclusive acronym LGBTQ in this chapter.

One of the most commonly held and erroneous ideas was that LGBTQ people are a relatively homogenous group. This is reflected in social workers' understandable urge to "know how to work with [fill in the social identity group]." We rarely if ever seek to "know how to work with White folx" or "straight folx." When considering dominant positionalities, we assume heterogeneity. Conversely, learning "how to do therapy with LGBTQ people" implies homogeneity and an implicitly oppressive approach. To engage in just practice with midlife and older LGBTQ adults, we must recognize the diversity, history, and contexts of LGBTQ people and communities.

In the context of my social work professor drag, I teach MSW courses in diversity, social justice, and reflexive social work practice along with advanced practice in aging. In my scholar drag, I focus on the social determinants of health and mental health disparities among sexual and gender minorities (SGM), particularly among midlife and older adults. As a licensed independent clinical social worker (LCSW) with more than 15 years' direct practice with LGBTQ communities, my practice drag depends on whether I am working with individual clients or community agencies and organizations. I draw on these varied contexts in reflecting on socially just practice with midlife and older LGBTQ adults. I share highlights from two clients' stories to illustrate how I bring processes of Just Practice to bear (Finn, 2020). I do not provide a manual on "how to work with midlife and older LGBTQ adults." If you are willing to actually hear their stories and truly enter into their worlds, they will tell you.

## Mental Health and the Context of LGBTQ Experiences

First, let's consider the context of LGBTQ people's experiences. Compared to the general population, LGBTQ people of all ages are at significantly greater risk for mood and anxiety disorders, such as depression, suicidality, and substance use disorders (Hoy-Ellis, 2016). This increased risk is not due to their sexual orientations or gender identities. It is the result of the exhausting work of navigating a social *context* that highly stigmatizes them, day in and day out. LGBTQ people experience external minority stressors, including acute and chronic discriminatory events and conditions such as hate crimes and discriminatory laws and policies. They experience internal minority stressors such as fear of rejection by important others. They may practice camouflage to make themselves less visible as targets. But camouflage itself becomes a stressor over time. Both long-term concealment and internalized heterosexist and cisgender stigma significantly increase the risk for depression (Hoy-Ellis & Fredriksen-Goldsen, 2016). Therefore, it is crucial to understand the social contexts of clients' lives.

## History and LGBTQ Experiences

It is equally important to understand the histories of oppression and resistance that have shaped the experiences of LGBTQ individuals and communities. Today's midlife and older adults came of age in the mid- to late 20th century. I provide a brief historical overview to show the interplay of meaning and power in constructing homosexuality and constraining LBGTQ lives.

## CONSTRUCTING HOMOSEXUALITY AS SICKNESS AND PERVERSION

The historical construction of homosexuality reveals a pathologizing interplay of meaning and power. The first known appearance of the term "homosexuality" in English was in an 1892 translation of *Psychopathia sexualis* (Krafft-Ebing, 1886). It was an umbrella term for "sexual inversion," a pseudoscientific notion that implied an inborn, pathological reversal of gender traits. Sexual activity among two or more persons of the same sex, commonly referred to as sodomy, had been criminalized in the United States since colonial times (Frank et al., 2009). Sodomy was a felony in all 50 states until 1962, when Illinois became the first state to decriminalize it (Carpenter, 2012). It was during the Great Depression, however, that constructions of homosexuality as a deviant identity, versus behavior, began to develop.

New Deal policymakers were concerned with the problem of "unattached persons," single, transient adults with no means of support (Canaday, 2009, p. 91). Welfare support during this era was provided through the family unit, so these people were not eligible for government aid. In an attempt to address this "problem," the Civilian Conservation Corps (CCC) and the Federal Transient Program (FTP) were established in 1933. The CCC engaged unemployed young men in conservation projects (p. 92). The FTP provided direct relief. While the CCC was hailed for its success, the FTP ended rather suddenly in 1935. "Transients" were associated with homosexuality and sexual perversion in the mid-20th-century popular imagination, and the FTP became plagued by discourses of "unworthy" older migrants preying on "worthy" youthful migrants (Canaday, 2009). This casting of a program as inherently one of sexual perversion led to its demise and contributed to a discourse of homosexuality as sickness and perversion.

## FROM WORLD WAR II TO THE LAVENDER SCARE

Constructions of homosexuality as identity were further solidified within the military during World War II. According to Canaday (2009), soldiers identified as having engaged in "homosexual acts" were separated into two categories—one being "just a youthful drunken indiscretion" (i.e., behavior), the other as "innately homosexual" (i.e., identity). Upon separation from military service, the innately homosexual's dishonorable discharge was printed on blue paper. These blue discharges carried the mark of stigma. Individuals given blue discharges were disqualified from benefits offered under the GI Bill. Prospective employers routinely requested an applicant's discharge form—the DD-214. A blue DD-214 meant that it was extremely unlikely one would be offered employment (Canaday, 2009).

The Lavender Scare emerged as a key feature of the McCarthy era of the 1950s. Senator Joseph McCarthy, convinced that the federal government was a hotbed of communist spies, sought to root them out. McCarthy also initiated a witch-hunt to find and expose homosexuals. He claimed that if homosexuals in government weren't already communists, they were uniquely poised to be blackmailed by communists lest their homosexuality be exposed. The McCarthy hearings were televised and broadcast into the homes of millions of Americans. As a result of these attacks, President Eisenhower signed an executive order in 1953 banning homosexuals from employment in the federal government.

At this same time, legal and political institutions were reconstructing homosexuality from the merely "criminal'" into the more horrific "sexual perversion." Police raids of locations where known or suspected homosexuals congregated (e.g., nightclubs, bars) were routine. People dancing with someone of the same sex were arrested on morals charges. Women who wore three or fewer visibly "female" garments could be arrested as sex perverts. Newspapers published sensationalized accounts naming those arrested. As a result, these "sex perverts" would often lose their jobs, be rejected by family, and be forced to relocate. Thus, camouflaging—hiding one's sexual and/or gender identities—became a survival trait.

## THE POWER OF DIAGNOSTIC LABELS

In 1952 the American Psychiatric Association (APA) published the first edition of the *Diagnostic and Statistical Manual of Mental Disorders (DSM-I)*. Homosexuality was officially declared a "sociopathic personality disturbance" (Silverstein, 2009). The medical establishment became empowered to identify and implement treatments to "cure" homosexuality. Individuals were involuntarily institutionalized and subjected to putative cures, including castration, lobotomy, electroshock therapy, intravenous camphor, and induced diabetic comas (Silverstein, 2009). Many people mistakenly believe that the APA removed homosexuality as a mental illness from the *DSM-II* in 1973—it did not. While homosexuality as psychiatric sickness per se was removed, experiencing "ego-dystonic" distress around one's homosexual orientation was still considered a psychiatric disorder (Drescher, 2015).

## PRIDE AND LIBERATION

In the predawn hours of Saturday, June 28, 1969, the New York City police arrived at the Stonewall Inn, a well-known "gay bar" in Greenwich Village, to conduct a routine raid. Instead of allowing themselves to be taken into custody, some patrons began fighting back. Whether it was a thrown shot glass or a drag queen's high heels, the incident sparked three days of rioting against police oppression and brutality against the LGBTQ community. At that time there were only a handful of "homophile" organizations in the nation, such as the Daughters of Bilitis and the Mattachine Society (Canaday, 2014). One year later, there were thousands. The queer community flexed its previously unrecognized agency, countering the dominant discourse of sickness and perversion with new language—that of pride and liberation. Today's Pride month, parades, and festivals commemorate the Stonewall Riots.

## 1980s BACKLASH

A few years later, in response to the passage of civil rights protection for lesbians and gays in Dade County, Florida, Anita Bryant launched her "Save the Children" campaign, claiming that "homosexuals cannot reproduce, so they must recruit [children]" (https://www.pbs.org/outofthepast/past/p5/1977.html). The religious right, under the leadership of Jerry Falwell, then launched an attack on the LGBTQ liberation movement. This coincided with the beginning of the HIV/AIDS pandemic in America. The religious right countered that HIV/AIDS was God's punishment for those who "chose" to lead an LGBTQ lifestyle. They sought to silence LBGTQ rights claims and return to discourses of sickness and perversion. In testament to the indomitability of human agency, "in 1987 with AIDS deaths in the thousands and government policy still criminally indifferent, activists formed ACTUP (AIDS Coalition to Unleash Power) with the sentiment "turn anger, fear, and grief into action" (https://actupny.org/video.1.html).

## PERSISTENCE OF PATHOLOGIZING LABELS

It was not until 1987 that the APA finally removed distress with one's non-heterosexual orientation as a psychiatric disorder from the *DSM-III-R* (Drescher, 2015). Unfortunately, the decades-long arc of injustice persists regarding the pathologizing of gender identity and sexual orientation. The *DSM-V*, published in 2013, reclassified gender identity disorder (i.e., mental disorder per se) as gender dysphoria (mental disorder if one experiences distress between their gender identity and their biological sex; American Psychiatric Association, 2013). Today's midlife and older adults came of age within the sociocultural and historical context of the 1940s through the 1980s. Thus, it is important to situate their experiences within this broader history.

# Expanding the Possibilities: Promoting Health Equity

My colleagues and I recognize that LGBTQ people experience minority stressors that emerge from both current social contexts and a cumulative history of oppressive discourses, policies, and practices. In response, we developed the health equity promotion model. This model specifically brings an intersectional lens to bear in understanding LGBTQ identities, contextualizes LGBTQ experience within a life course perspective, and considers pathways for navigating adversity and achieving positive health outcomes (Fredriksen-Goldsen et al., 2014). Comprehensive discussion of the model is beyond the scope of this chapter. The model aligns with Just Practice principles and guides my approach to practice.

## Working with Midlife and Older LGBTQ Adults

I now turn to two specific clients whom I have worked with to show how the work we did illustrates core processes of Just Practice (Finn, 2020).

### CASE STUDY #1: MICAH

*Engagement*

Engagement begins before the first contact with a potential client. I make clear in registry information that, in addition to being an LCSW, I am also an LGBTQ-affirming therapist, and that I have certification as a sexual and gender minority specialist. This signals to potential clients that I have knowledge and experience to work with self-identified LGBTQ people. During the initial assessment, I gather information specific to being LGBTQ that is not generally collected in a typical mental health assessment. In addition to gathering typical sociodemographic information (e.g., race/ethnicity) I go deeper. I normalize information that is specific to being LGBTQ. When I ask about sexual orientation, I always preface the question by clarifying that this is a routine question I ask everyone. I follow this up by sharing my own sexual orientation as a gay man. Most clients I have worked with identify as LGBTQ, although some do identify as heterosexual. Micah (pseudonym), age 58 at the time (now in their early 70s), identified as heterosexual and White.

I then pose routine questions around gender and gender identity and share my own gender/identity as a cisgender man. This communicates that while I do not identify as transgender/gender-nonconforming myself, I am aware of these ways of beingness. With some hesitancy Micah responded, "Well, as you can tell I'm a man" (referring to visible facial hair stubble and significant hair on forearms, deeper voice), "but I feel like I'm a woman." Micah's apprehension as to how I would respond was clear; their relief was visible when I thanked them for the gift of sharing and further validated them by acknowledging, "It can't be easy to share something like that with someone you just met!" Micah smiled and agreed.

*Teaching-Learning*

Teaching-learning reframes assessment as a collaborative process rather than one where I am the all-knowing professional. While I acknowledge that I do have some "expert knowledge" (and I always use air quotes with this) on why people think, feel, and act as they do in a general sense, I strongly reinforce that the client is the expert on their life and experience. I told Micah, "Between our collective expertise, I bet we can find ways forward to get a better sense of what's going on that hinders you and find ways to shift those dynamics in ways that are more helpful for you." Micah nodded in agreement, smiled ever so slightly, and said that sounded like a plan.

I then asked Micah about their preferred pronouns. Some confusion was evident, so I talked a bit about the function of pronouns and how they are gendered and, importantly, how they are about identity. We had a brief Pronouns 101 course, which goes to the heart of identity. Micah hesitantly suggested that in public they used masculine pronouns (i.e., he/him/his) and added that it might be cool to experiment with feminine pronouns (i.e., she/her/hers) in more private spaces. Since the therapeutic setting is a private space, I asked if Micah would be okay with me using feminine pronouns in exploring their experiences. Micah's face lit up. [I now shift to using feminine pronouns in describing the therapeutic process with Micah.] I also introduced the idea of *sex as biology* as the template upon which social constructions of gender are overlaid. I asked Micah how old she was when she first thought of herself as a woman. Not atypically, she responded that as long as she could remember she knew there was something different about her; she just didn't have the language or concept to pin down what that difference was.

Micah was born in 1947, 5 years before Christine Jorgensen's historic and very public sexual reassignment surgery. Micah related how she had first heard of Christine in 1965 at the age of 18 and something "just clicked into place." Not wanting to be "a freak," Micah shared that she figured if she joined the military, she could become "a real man." She joined the Air Force and served a tour of duty in Vietnam in 1967. This "flight into hypermasculinity" is a relatively typical attempt to evade discrimination and victimization based on transgender/gender-nonconforming identities and expressions (Hoy-Ellis et al., 2017). During this time there were no positive portrayals of transfolx in the media or other public discourse. Micah did not "see" herself anywhere and decided she needed to hide herself to survive.

*Action and Accompaniment*

Over the course of the ensuing weeks as our therapeutic relationship unfolded, we developed a loose collaborative plan. As we explored possibilities, it became clear that both internal and external actions were needed. Internally, Micah would benefit from working through internalized stigmas of heterosexism and cisgenderism. A part of this process included psychoeducation around how these "isms" were situated within societal structures of privilege and oppression. Externally, we explored what she wanted to do with her evolving sense of her gender identity.

Micah was in a heterosexual marriage. Initially her wife struggled with the idea that Micah was transgender. As a testament to the strength of their relationship, Micah's wife rather quickly concluded that she loved Micah, not Micah's gender. She supported Micah within their home around "typical" expressions of femininity (e.g., clothing, makeup). Micah shared her exhilaration at seeing herself more as a woman in the mirror. I also shared my knowledge of community resources with her. There was a local transgender organization that hosted weekly support groups for transgender/gender-nonconforming community members. Micah was interested in checking it out. At her first meeting, she presented as her then-typical masculine outside. With the group's enthusiastic support, she began experimenting with increasingly feminine presentation and over time presented herself as fully feminine. An unexpected benefit for Micah was group exploration of institutional heterosexist cisgenderism—the idea that one is either male or female as assigned at birth. During one of our individual sessions, she was able to name her experience, as a transgender woman, of heterosexist cisgenderism within the LGBTQ community.

As this process unfolded, I experienced (and shared with Micah) the pleasure that social workers tend to experience as we accompany our clients ever so briefly on their journey of healing. Periodically, we would take a step back and evaluate Micah's successes (and stubbed toes) during that journey. Micah critically reflected on her process over time and how she had come to know what she knew at different points in her life. Through this reflexive process she was empowered to construct a new, more meaningful narration of her lived experience (Bauer & McAdams, 2004). We knew it was time to start thinking concretely about closure.

### *Celebration*

While we had celebrated Micah's small successes along the way, our final session together was nothing less than triumphant. When I went to the lobby and called out her first name, an amazing woman stood up. In all honesty, I was a little caught off guard by the authenticity and poise of the woman I was seeing. We exchanged a brief chitchat as we settled into the office. She shyly opened her purse and took out two small items wrapped in tissue paper and handed them to me. She told me I should open the smaller of the two first; it held a small cocoon. She told me that several of the members of her support group had talked about the idea of caterpillars becoming butterflies only by spending part of their lives in cocoons. She nodded for me to open the other. I choked and got wet eyes as I looked down at the small, double picture frame and its contents—one an aged black-and-white photograph of her with her squad, dirty and unshaven in their military fatigues in Vietnam. The other taken by her wife the day before, looking every bit the authentic woman that I had the incredible honor to accompany ever so briefly on her path.

### CASE STUDY #2: DEREK

### *Engagement*

Derek (pseudonym), age 64 at the time (now in his mid-70s), came to see me for help with self-reported depression. Derek self-identified as a cisgender man; he also self-identified as gay and African American. In response to my follow-up questions Derek told me he was 16 when he realized he might be gay, and 22 when he first told another person. He was born and raised in the Midwest and had been employed there by a large corporation until the previous year. Derek had learned that Boston had a vibrant, racially integrated community of LGBTQ older adults and had planned to retire there. However, he was let go from his employment a year before he was eligible for the corporation's pension plan, so he would not be able to afford to live in Boston. He had moved to where we met 6 months previously and had not been able to make connections within the LGBTQ community. He was feeling isolated and lonely.

*Teaching-Learning*

Teaching-learning with Derek entailed both internal and external work. We explored unresolved internalized heterosexism and ageism. We considered how intersecting systems of oppression—such as racism, sexism, and ableism—are reflected not only in the broader society but also in the LGBTQ community (Adams et al., 2018). Ageism can be magnified within gay and bisexual men's communities. In most gay men's communities, typically, middle age is 30, and 40 is over the hill. Derek also taught me a lot about White supremacy, my own internalized racism, and the inherent racism within the LGBTQ community.

Derek vaguely remembered seeing something on television regarding the McCarthy Lavender Scare hearings when he was an adolescent. He didn't understand exactly what a homosexual was, but he knew it was terrible. He realized he was one of "those homosexuals" 4 years later and knew he had to hide who he was. At age 22, he told Ben (pseudonym), his best friend since third grade. Derek was devastated when Ben told him to stay away because he didn't want anyone to think he was queer too. Rumors began to spread shortly thereafter, and Derek moved to a large metropolitan area for anonymity. He stayed in the closet, occasionally finding anonymous hookups.

We talked about how painful it is to have to hide an important part of who you are. We also explored his gender socialization as a man, as it is not uncommon in our dominant culture to cast a gay man as "failed masculinity." Over time Derek began to realize that (as he jokingly put it during one session), "I guess it takes a real man to be gay in this world." I enthusiastically agreed.

*Action and Accompaniment*

Derek experienced the internalized stigma of ageism coupled with racism. Since arriving in the city, he had tried to make friends by going to gay bars. "You can tell when they [younger gays] just don't want you there," he commented on several occasions. Derek described how he had learned to deal with racism growing up in an African American family and community. He recalled the occasional hookups, primarily with White men, that he engaged in beginning in his early 20s. He described how they saw him as a sexual object, not a person. We considered how White supremacy has constructed African American men as sexualized brutes since the beginning of the European colonization of the Americas and continues to do so to this day (Nagel, 2003). The sexual objectification became less of an issue for Derek as he began to age, but the realities of racism persist.

Derek had tried other establishments where older adults would typically congregate; he said the people all seemed straight. We discussed the structural ageism within the city's gay community as there were no services or programs for older adults at the time. Then a magic moment happened. Derek said it was too bad people weren't treated like cars. Old cars can become vintage classics; old people are just tossed out. This led to uncovering that he had a passion for classic cars. There was a contingent in the city's Pride parade every year that featured a club of vintage car enthusiasts and their cars. Many of the club members were older and more racially diverse.

Derek was visibly brighter at our next session. He had contacted the club, and they had invited him to join them for their weekly Sunday brunch. I was struck when he reflected on what a powerful experience it had been seeing and being in the company of "people just like me, all of me, for the first time," not just in age and sexual orientation but also race. Over the next several weeks he had begun to develop friendships, including the "younger whippersnappers." He was engaging socially and declared that he never felt lighter in his life. At our second to last session, we did a major review of his journey. He acknowledged that while he still had a lot of internalized stigma to work through, he finally had the life he had dreamed of (though it had looked a little different in the dream).

*Celebration*

During our final session, we discussed what actions Derek would be taking to maintain and foster his newfound life. As we were finishing up, he asked me if I could step outside with him for a minute. As we stepped into the parking lot, he pointed and asked what I thought. There sat a gleaming red and black 1969 Mustang Mach II convertible. As I stumbled to find words, he smiled and said, "Well, if I'm going to drive in the next Pride parade with the rest of the gang, I have to have a car, don't I?" We all celebrate in different ways.

# Conclusion

As a clinical, contextual social worker, I continually look at the contexts and forces, current and historical, that shape our lives and communities. Contemporary populist politics have fueled racism, White nationalism, and heterosexism. Under the guise of "religious freedom," we are witnessing renewed calls for anti-LGBTQ legislation. Gains made by transgender and gender-nonconforming people are under attack. As social workers, we must honor the intersectional complexities of our clients' lives and resist racist, heterosexist, ageist, and cisgender systems of privilege and oppression. As one transgender person states, "I don't think this is theoretical; this is our lives" (Bauer et al., 2009, p. 348). For LGBTQ older adults and those who work alongside them, having a grasp of history and conditions in the 20th and 21st centuries is crucial. By attending to Just Practice principles, we can create a better future for today's and tomorrow's LGBTQ older adults.

## QUESTIONS FOR REFLECTION AND DISCUSSION

1. How might persons of differing intersectional LGBTQ identities (e.g., Latinx lesbian, White gay man) differentially experience the same historical contexts and events?
2. How might your knowledge of LGBTQ history help you understand power dynamics when working with LGBTQ clients? How might that knowledge open possibilities for practice?
3. How might social workers better meet the needs of LGBTQ communities and older adults?
4. What resources exist in your area to support the needs of LGBTQ communities and older adults? What advocacy efforts might you engage in to improve supports for LGBTQ older adults in your community?
5. What are your own ageist and LGBTQ implicit biases? How might your awareness or lack thereof of your own biases influence your work with older adults? LGBTQ clients? Older LGBTQ clients?
   a. If you don't think you have any of these implicit biases, I invite you to take the Age and Sexuality Implicit Association Tests at https://implicit.harvard.edu/implicit/takeatest.html.

## RESOURCES

For specific competencies and strategies when working with LGBTQ older adults, see Fredriksen-Goldsen and colleagues (2014), and (Hoy-Ellis, 2017 et al).

- National Resource Center on LGBT Aging: https://www.lgbtagingcenter.org/
- Diverse Elders Coalition: https://www.diverseelders.org/who-we-are/diverse-elders/lgbt-elders/

## REFERENCES

Adams, M., Blumenfeld, W. J., Catalano, D. C. J., DeJong, K. S., Hackman, H., Hopkins, L. E., Love, B. J., Peters, M. L., Shlasko, D., & Zúñiga, X. (2018). *Readings for diversity and social justice* (4th ed.). Routledge.

American Psychiatric Association (2013). *Diagnostic and statistical manual of mental disorders* (5th ed.). American Psychiatric Association.

Bauer, J. J., & McAdams, D. P. (2004, June). Personal growth in adults' stories of life transitions. *Journal of Personality, 72*(3), 573–602.

Bauer, G., Hammond, R., Traver, R., Kacey, M., Hohenadel, K., & Boyce, M. (2009). "I don't think this is theoretical, this is our lives": How erasure impacts health care for transgender people. *Journal of the Association of Nurses in AIDS Care 20*(5), 348–61.

Canaday, M. (2009). *The straight state: Sexuality and citizenship in twentieth-century America*. Princeton University Press.

Canaday, M. (2014). LGBT history. *Frontiers: A Journal of Women Studies, 35*(1), 11–19.

Carpenter, D. (2012). *The story of Lawrence v. Texas: How a bedroom arrest decriminalized gay America*. W. W. Norton.

Drescher, J. (2015). Out of DSM: Depathologizing homosexuality. *Behavioral Sciences 5*(5), 565–575.

Finn, J. (2020) *Just practice: A social justice approach to social work* (4th ed.). Oxford University Press.

Frank D., Boutcher, S., & Camp B. (2009) The repeal of sodomy laws from a world-society perspective. In: Barclay S, Bernstein M, Marshall AM (eds) *Queer mobilizations: LGBT activists confront the law*. New York University Press.

Fredriksen-Goldsen, K. I., Simoni, J. M., Kim, H.-J., Lehavot, K., Walters, K. L., Yang, J., Hoy-Ellis, C. P., & Muraco, A. (2014). The health equity promotion model: Reconceptualization of lesbian, gay, bisexual, and transgender (LGBT) health disparities. *American Journal of Orthopsychiatry, 84*(6), 653–683.

Hoy-Ellis, C. P. (2016, April). Concealing concealment: The mediating role of internalized heterosexism in psychological distress among lesbian, gay, and bisexual older adults. *Journal of Homosexuality, 63*(4), 487–506.

Hoy-Ellis, C. P., & Fredriksen-Goldsen, K. I. (2016). Lesbian, gay, & bisexual older adults: Linking internal minority stressors, chronic health conditions, and depression. *Aging and Mental Health, 20*(11), 1119–1130.

Hoy-Ellis, C. P., Shiu, C., Sullivan, K. M., Kim, H. J., Sturges, A. M., & Fredriksen-Goldsen, K. I. (2017, February). Prior military service, identity stigma, and mental health among transgender older adults. *The Gerontologist, 57*(Suppl. 1), S63–S71.

Krafft-Ebing, R. V. (1886). *Psychopathia sexualis* (C. G. Chaddock, Trans.). FA Davis.

Nagel, J. (2003). *Race, ethnicity, and sexuality: Intimate intersections, forbidden frontiers*. Oxford University Press.

Queer Nation NY (2016). Queer Nation NY History. Retrieved from https://queernationny.org/history

Silverstein, C. (2009, April). The implications of removing homosexuality from the DSM as a mental disorder [Letter]. *Archives of Sexual Behavior, 38*(2), 161–163.

# 4

# Just Practice in the Context of a Therapeutic Group Home

SARAH FIELDING, LCSW

> I just want to be a normal kid, not one who lives in a group home
> and gets dropped at school in a big white van.
> —Group home resident

---

**Overview**

In this chapter Sarah Fielding describes the challenges and possibilities of bringing the Just Practice framework to bear in a therapeutic group home for adolescent girls. She speaks to the power that systems of care often wield over youth and the ways in which personal and family histories are used as tools for judgment rather than as resources for understanding. Fielding presents the stories of three girls in her care who taught her why attention to meaning, power, context, history, and possibility matters. Fielding shows readers how she embraces the processes of engagement, teaching-learning, accompaniment, and critical reflection in her practice.

---

## Introduction

I have worked in the field of youth care for a decade. Most recently I have served as the lead clinical staff at River House, a therapeutic group home for adolescent girls. In this role, I oversee placement decisions and treatment plans, supervise youth workers, and provide direct individual and group therapy with girls in our care. In this chapter I bring the Just Practice framework (Finn, 2020) to bear in addressing the challenges and possibilities we confront every day in our work at the group home. I present the stories of Sophia, Amy, and Mary and show how they helped me appreciate the value of engagement, teaching-learning, accompaniment, and critical reflection in my social work practice.

## Context and History

River House is part of a youth-serving organization that has been providing out-of-home care for teens since the 1970s. The organization began as a basic group home with house parents, providing an alternative to institutionalization or incarceration of youth in need of care and supervision. It has evolved into a complex system of therapeutic care. In our organizational materials, River House is described as a six-bed, intensive-level therapeutic group home that serves 12- to 17-year-old girls with serious emotional disturbances stemming from family and victim issues. It is interesting to me that our organization names families as the source of "trouble" and frames the girls as victims of those families. The relentlessness of poverty, racism, gender oppression, and other forms of violence and violation that have taken their toll on their families and communities over time remains unmentioned. Many of the girls I serve have been removed multiple times from their birth, foster, and adoptive families, and they are now placed into the therapeutic group setting with the hope of "rehabilitating" them. Their histories have rendered them wary and distrustful. They and their families have lived the "cumulative effects of adversity" (Gupta, 2017, p. 453). They have experienced what Gupta (2017) describes as a "perfect storm of lack of supports, the tyranny of time-tables, and the absence of attention to socioeconomic and environmental factors" that constrain their lives (p. 454).

I bear witness to the ways in which multiple systems have repeatedly failed these girls, and yet my staff and I are expected to mobilize the magic of individual change efforts to help them become productive citizens and self-sufficient members of our society (Lohmeyer, 2017). I struggle with these contradictions embedded in our systems of youth care and my own complicity therein. Our group home is not immune to the pressures of neoliberal economic logic that emphasizes risk assessment and management, resource rationing, speed and efficiency, and personal responsibility over relationship-based work, nurturance of trust, social responsibility, and systems change (Lohmeyer, 2017; Rogowski, 2012). At the same time, I bear witness to the strength, resistance, and resilience of the girls in our care; they fuel my commitment to just social work practice grounded in relationship and resistance.

## Meaning and Power

Critical reflection on the meaning of family has been central to my work. During my years working with youth who have endured many traumatic losses throughout their lives, I have become intrigued by the complexities of human connection and how it can be formed and ruptured at the same time. A "culture of disbelief" about the motives of parents is pervasive in our systems of care (Gupta, 2017, p. 457). Blame is so often placed on parental failures rather than systems failures. We are quick to assume the family is at fault. The larger contexts of trauma and adversity in which families struggle are simply bracketed out of the assessment and intervention processes. And yet every day the girls with whom I work teach me through their words and actions that family connection matters deeply.

When youth enter into the foster care system the multitude of emotions they experience may vary, but the consistent theme is the longing for their families and grief over what they have lost. They may be removed from the physical context of home, but the meaning and power of family are woven into their histories and ever present in their hearts and minds. Parents love their children, and family is meaningful, even though that love and significance may be overshadowed by trauma, struggle, and the daunting daily realities of navigating nearly insurmountable barriers. This foundational parent-child connection often gets lost in translation due to the ways in which systems of care make meaning of family, adolescence, and "trouble." Systems of care often wield power over both youth and their parents, despite stated commitments to empowering practice. Further, systems of care too often draw on personal and family histories not as resources for understanding and inspiration, but as tools for judgment. The result is an approach to practice that is stripped of contextual understanding. In the following vignettes drawn from my work in the group home I show why attention to meaning, power, context, history, and possibility matters. I highlight ways in which I incorporated processes of engagement, teaching-learning, accompaniment, and critical reflection in my work.

## Sophia's Story: Engagement

When I first met Sophia, she was hiding behind the van that had just brought her from a residential care facility in a nearby state. She looked scared and disheveled. I had welcomed newcomers to the group home countless times during my 8 years there. I could see her pain, fear, and helplessness, but I also had a sense of her big heart. I had a long-term working relationship with Darren, her placing social worker, and we had established a mutual respect and trust. Darren was one of the best I had ever worked with, and he had been a strong advocate for Sophia's placement in our care. I told Sophia up front that I knew Darren and that he was a good man with her best interests at heart. I was attempting to ease some of her angst at being dropped off at yet another group home and, hopefully, help her see that we shared some points of connection, however tenuous they might seem to her. I was also telling her the truth. Honesty is always your best bet. Youth who have lived through trauma seem to have a sixth sense for detecting when adults with power over them are being less than candid. Their ability to pick up emotional inadequacies in adults comes from their long history of being responsible for everyone else's emotional states.

The context of Sophia's adolescent life had been largely contained in psychiatric facilities or therapeutic group homes. Her history had been told through child protective services reports, court records, and repeated clinical evaluations, where those in positions of professional power had repeatedly labeled Sophia as a problem. Sophia was described in the case records as a violent, withdrawn, and "difficult" child. Her current "problem" behaviors included using erasers to burn the skin on her face. After reading this, I had paused to wonder what this behavior might mean to Sophia. Had anyone ever asked her? If so, they did not note it in her records. In fact, Sophia appeared as no more than a voiceless bundle of pathology in the records. I thought of other girls I had worked with who had helped me make sense of their need for comfort and who had taught me about their unique and perhaps unorthodox ways of coping with their emotional pain. Perhaps Sophia's actions, too, would make sense as a soothing outlet for emotional pain. I made a note to ask her—but not right away. We would have to build our relationship together at the speed of trust (Covey & Merrill, 2006).

I have read many files over the years to determine whether the therapeutic program I was leading would be a good a fit for a particular girl. More and more, I have come to question what it means to be a good "fit." Are girls who are compliant, gender-conforming, and White perceived as a better "fit" within the unspoken meaning systems of our agency and predominantly White community? Were we honestly grappling with these questions at the group home? Or did the constant, everyday demands of the work distract us from these more foundational questions of meaning and power? Honestly, despite the review by our admission committee, and the conversations with social workers and therapists, the determination to admit a girl into the home has always felt a bit like gambling to me. It is hard to know whether she will benefit from the program. The odds are best when at least one staff member is able to build a genuine relationship. My decision to bring Sophia to the admission committee was based on my conversations with Darren and Sophia's therapist in her prior placement. They described her as capable, wicked smart, funny, and in need of love—so different than the depictions in her file, I thought. I was convinced that she would be a good fit. But another thought nagged at my conscience: What about the girls who don't get described this way, who don't have advocates who have built relationships with them, who aren't seen as something other than bundles of pathology? Where do they "fit"?

Sophia's power had been taken from her repeatedly—by the neighborhood kids who severely bullied her and the teachers who put her in "special ed" because she took her pain out on her desk and threw it across the room. She had seen case workers come and go over the years as her mother struggled with mental illness and the demands of parenting. She had been removed from her home multiple times since the age of 3 due to abuse and neglect. She was labeled early on as the problem child of a problematic mother. Sophia had been identified as "White" and had virtually no connection with her father and his Mexican family and culture. Her own voice had been squelched and distorted by the relentless pathologizing of clinical assessments. As a White social worker who was raised with my Mexican cousins and family by marriage in Los Angeles, I had an understanding of the importance of family and connection in the Mexican culture. Being able to connect Sophia to her Mexican culture could, I believed, potentially provide a different source of healing.

I was finally able to convince Sophia to come into the group home to see her room, and we began our journey of finding meaning through connection. I attempted to do an "intake" where we go over program rules and expectations, but then I realized that Sophia was overwhelmed and needed us to stop. So, we sat on the floor together and began some small talk. Sophia told me how she once had a cat, Beatrice, and she showed me her cat's collar that she wore as a bracelet. After her mother died following routine surgery, Sophia was brought back to her house by a social worker to grab a few items before going a children's shelter. She had no other family to take her in. Her cat was all she wanted. The social worker promised Sophia that she would be able to have the cat eventually and said the cat could stay at a friend's house. But in fact, the social worker took the cat to the local pound. After Sophia heard what her social worker did with her cat, she threatened to kill the social worker, which landed her in yet another psychiatric facility. As she fingered the collar-bracelet, Sophia told me she was not really going to kill her social worker. The grief of her mother's passing and the loss of Beatrice, her only friend, had just been too much. We talked about animals until I had to leave her room and start sessions with some of the youth returning from school. As a mother myself, I ached with Sophia's grief, and in that shared space of honoring grief and loss, a seed of relationship was planted. Eventually, Sophia began to engage the other staff and youth in the group home, to make a few, tentative friendships at school, and to find meaning in her circumstance. Sophia's list of losses was long and difficult to process, and yet she still yearned for the possibility of connection.

Sophia's story is not unique among youth in foster care. Many youth in care share histories of trauma and cumulative loss. They and their families have struggled with mental illness, addiction, poverty, homelessness, and systemic racism. Many youth we serve are not the first in their families to be in a group home. Both youth in foster care and the caregivers who have served them are bound together by a complicated history. Youth in care have long been targets of policies and practices of "detachment"—of removal from home, family, and community (Ghenie & Wellenstein, 2009). Ironically, they enter systems of care where, more and more, they are labeled as having disorders of "attachment," among other problems. Youth workers, on the other hand, are socialized to maintain boundaries and demonstrate appropriate professional "distance." We place restrictions on physical contact between youth workers and youth in care and provide training on the potential for harm that can come from physical touch. In effect, we train youth workers to take love out of the equation and to deny the urge to wrap their arms around a child, hold her tight, and tell her that you've got her. Perhaps we should ask why. Why does a profession committed to genuineness, relationship, and human dignity impose rules that run counter to the possibility of loving human connection?

## Amy's Story: Teaching-Learning

Amy was a tall Black girl who had been in group care since age 10. By the time she came to River House, she was 13. Amy described herself as Black on the outside but White on the inside. She was raised by her White stepfather and many other White caregivers, and lived in a mostly White community. Her only connection to her Black identity was her mother, and she hadn't lived with her since she was about 3 years old. She was removed from her home after revealing that her stepfather had been sexually abusing her for years. Amy had begun to unravel emotionally as she was shuttled from psychiatric facilities to foster homes, finally arriving at our therapeutic group home. Amy had a strong will, quick wit, and sense of style. She loved to shop. Over time, she became fiercely loyal to the group home staff. And Amy couldn't stand to be touched. She never asked for hugs, and she kept a good 2 feet distance from everyone.

I had been one of Amy's caregivers for about a year when she unleashed a fury that I feared would secure her another stay at the acute psychiatric unit. We were in the middle of Saturday "deep cleans," and I had told her to do a better job with her assigned chore. Amy yelled in my face, spitting tears and snot, screaming that I was not her mother and she did not have to do anything I had asked of her. She ran out the door in her stocking feet. Our policy at the group home is to call the police if youth run away and not chase after them. I waited at the door, my heart in my throat, unsure what Amy would do. She went to the end of the driveway and stopped. She was hysterical and cold, and I begged her to come back inside. She turned around, came back in the house, went to her room, and continued to wail. I followed her and found her slumped against the wall. I took a risk and put my arm around her; she melted into me. I held her, rocked her, and told her I was here for her. From that moment on, Amy began asking for hugs and began to find safety in touch again.

Amy was and continues to be one of my greatest teachers. She taught me that genuine relationship may demand resistance to rules about professional distance and boundaries. She taught me to look to social work's history and rediscover the deep value of relationship and the meaning of social work as a "special kind of love" (Perlman, 1979). I hear from Amy from time to time. Her nomadic ways have taken her to another city to find belonging and connection. I don't know where she will end up, but I know at the group home she was loved by those who cared for her for 18 months, and I know she continues to carry that love with her.

## Mary's Story: Accompaniment and Critical Reflection

As a youth care worker and clinician, I often found myself questioning the meaning and power of family. I spent time being angry at parents for their actions and their failure to act. I spent time being angry at the system for separating families and denying them the resources they needed to stay together. I struggled to make sense of the larger histories of colonization and oppression and the ongoing structures of power and inequality that continue to produce trauma for children and families.

Mary is an enrolled member of the Lakota Sioux. She came to us with a serious rap sheet. At age 13 she had hitchhiked over 500 miles to get back to her family after being placed in a White foster family. She had assaulted a number of staff members in a previous treatment facility and had more runaway tickets than most kids I had worked with. She had been living in and out of foster care since she was born and now, at 15, had come to River House.

Despite the passage of the Indian Child Welfare Act in 1978 to protect the rights of Indian children, families, and tribes and respond to the long and violent history of the systematic removal of Indian children from family and culture, racist practices of child removal have persisted (National Indian Child Welfare Association, 2021). Mary's record indicated that both of her parents had also been in and out of the child welfare system. What judgments had been made by White social workers, I wondered; what omissions and shortcuts had happened in court hearings and placement decisions along the way? Mary was resistant to being in yet another group home and with good reason. I was hesitant about having her at River House. Were we just one more White system perpetuating the cycle of removal that dates back to Indian boarding school days (Adams, 1995)?

I couldn't shake this notion of our complicity in this history of colonizing practice, so I started talking about it. I worked to raise consciousness of the youth care staff about the racist history of removal of Indian children. Together we began to examine ways in which racism infiltrated our society and affected our practice. We critically reflected on our own biases and considered the possible impacts of well-intentioned efforts that were informed by the privileged perspective of Whiteness. I strived to bring a sense of cultural humility to bear in my clinical work with Mary (Ortega & Faller, 2011). I was not always successful. Our early sessions consisted of Mary yelling at me about the various rules she was not going to follow. At first, I attempted to argue and help her understand why the rules were in place. That was a lost cause. I needed to find a way to connect.

Mary's mother had struggled with addiction and her own traumas. She had never gotten the support she needed to parent her children. Mary was angry with her mother and filled with the pain of broken promises. Mary's father had just been released from prison after serving almost 10 years for attempted murder. No one could tell me why Mary wasn't allowed to have contact with him. Eventually, I track downed his parole officer. I soon got insight into the systemic racism and interpersonal bigotry that marked Mary's and her father's lives. Her father had spent 10 years in prison for a bar fight. The person he hit did not die or suffer life-threatening injuries. Her father was not the violent man everyone on her child protective services team described. The parole officer asked me to keep Mary far away from her tribe in order to "give her an honest try." I took a deep breath, swallowed my anger, and started to ask the parole officer some questions. I asked him how removing her from her family was actually going to heal her. Where is the sense in ripping children from family, culture, and community? I told him that where Mary wanted was to be with her family. She had rebelled in the child protection and juvenile probation systems because she missed her family, her people. At the end of our conversation the parole officer agreed to allow contact as long as I facilitated all the communication. I agreed to the conditions and called Mary's father.

My conversation with Mary's father was initially difficult. He was apprehensive, with no reason to trust one more White woman telling him the conditions for contact with his daughter. I responded to his apprehension and acknowledged how wrong the processes had been that had kept him from his daughter. I acknowledged the power I had in the situation and promised I would do everything in my power to facilitate as much contact as possible. So began a relationship among the three of us that started from the honest recognition of systemic racism.

Mary and I continued our regular "therapy" sessions. These mostly involved phone calls to her dad to plan a reunion between them. I advocated with children's services to secure funds for her father to come for a weekend visit. As the time for the visit drew near, Mary's father became more reluctant. I called him the morning he was supposed to come and see her. He was a good 8-hour drive away, and his fears were getting the better of him. He was locked in a war with himself and his feelings of failure as a parent. He never showed up, and later that night Mary ran away from the group home. I stayed awake all night waiting for the phone call from my staff to tell me she had returned, and that she was safe. I never received that phone call, and I did not hear from her for 2 months. Mary had managed to make her way back to her father and had her own reunion, not one bound by rules about time and place with some White person watching all their interactions. Mary had been picked up and placed in lockup. She called the group home and asked us to send her glasses. I enclosed a letter with her glasses telling her to continue to fight and not to give up. While Mary was living at the group home some of our sessions involved making sense of her removals and the various Indian Child Welfare Act (ICWA) violations that had occurred. I had given her a book, *The Rights of Indians and Tribes* by Stephen Pevar (2002), and she had devoured it. She drafted a letter to the tribal judge and her case worker detailing all of her removals and how they did not follow ICWA. She was able to translate her anger into powerful, determined words in order to help herself and other Native youth. Mary taught me to be a stronger advocate for youth, to ask critical questions, and to talk back to powerful systems that have denied rights and voice for too long.

## Possibility

During our staff meetings we would often talk about possibility for the youth we were caring for. Success at the group home had many meanings, from daily tooth-brushing to making friends. My goal as the lead clinical staff was to help us transition from a problem-focused approach to one founded on relationship, resilience, strengths, and possibility. Over the years, we have made progress. We try to resist the managerial pressures that constrain genuine relationships with one another and the young people we serve. We try to give youth a chance to be kids again, to have fun, laugh, eat good food, have experiences in the natural world, and most of all to be loved and to love. I served over 100 youth during my time in the group home. Each one, whether they stayed 1 day or a couple of years, taught me this: We cannot survive trauma or loss by ourselves, we need each other, and connection is vital to our healing process.

## QUESTIONS FOR REFLECTION AND DISCUSSION

1. How do our own definitions of family impact our care for youth in the foster care system? How can we as social workers use critical reflection to examine how our own biases affect the work we do with families who have been impacted generationally by racism, poverty, and addiction?
2. How do we examine our own assumptions of success in relation to the success of youth in foster care? How might critical examination of "success" help us identify barriers that people impacted by systemic racism and poverty face?
3. How can we continue to support those we serve with a balanced notion of connection and advocacy? How do we accompany those with the highest risk factors and support our own challenges associated with limitations within the larger system?
4. How can we help those we serve to gain an understanding of how various systems disempower and continue to oppress them while also building their capacities for empowering action?

## REFERENCES

Adams, D. W. (1995). *Education for extinction: American Indians and the boarding school experience, 1875–1928*. University Press of Kansas.

Covey, S., & Merrill, R. (2006). *The speed of trust: The one thing that changes everything*. Simon & Schuster.

Finn, J. (2020). *Just practice: A social justice approach to social work* (4th ed.). Oxford University Press.

Ghenie, K., & Wellenstein, C. (2009). The well-being of children and the question of attachment. In L. Nybell, J. Shook, & J. Finn (Eds.), *Childhood, youth and social work in transformation: Implications for policy and practice* (pp. 145–168). Columbia University Press.

Gupta, A. (2017). Learning from others: An autoethnographic exploration of children and families social work, poverty, and the capability approach. *Qualitative Social Work, 16*(4), 449–464.

Lohmeyer, B. (2017). Youth and their workers: The interacting subjectification effects of neoliberal social policy and NGO practice frameworks. *Journal of Youth Studies, 20*(10), 1263–1276.

National Indian Child Welfare Association (NICWA). (2021). *About ICWA*. https://www.nicwa.org/about-icwa/.

Ortega, R., & Faller, K. C. (2011). Training child welfare workers from an inter-sectional cultural humility perspective: A paradigm shift. *Child Welfare, 90*(5), 27–49.

Perlman, H. H. (1979). *Relationship: The heart of helping people*. University of Chicago Press.

Pevar, S. (2002). *The rights of Indians and tribes*. Southern Illinois University Press.

Rogowski, S. (2012). Social work with children and families: Challenges and possibilities in the neoliberal world. *British Journal of Social Work, 42*, 921–940.

# 5

# A Very Good Day

*Just Practice and the Therapeutic Alliance*

ELIZABETH URSCHEL, MFA, LCSW

> I learned that connecting regularly in a safe space had a magical effect.
> —Jane S. Hall

---

**Overview**

In this chapter Elizabeth Urschel describes how the Just Practice framework guided her therapeutic relationship with "Cora," a 12-year-old girl diagnosed on the autism spectrum who had experienced severe abuse. Urschel recounts the emergence of their tentative relationship with Cora in the role of teacher. Accompaniment was central to their work together, nurturing trust over time. Action for Urschel also took the form of advocacy in support of Cora's right to express herself through her art. Urschel gives readers reason to celebrate as Cora finds both her voice and a loving family.

---

## Introduction

I first met Cora, a White girl diagnosed with autism spectrum disorder, when she was barely 13 and just beginning her journey in the foster care system. Hers had been an unfortunate childhood, with a history of maltreatment and abuse from caregivers starting from the age of 2. I am a White woman, mother, and writer who had embarked on social work as my career path in my 30s. I was a new practitioner working toward licensure at the time, my clinical experiences limited to grief therapy and the facilitation of therapeutic support groups. The agency I was working for focused on children and adolescents providing outpatient therapy, home support, case management, and therapeutic foster care. Because Cora's foster mother, Julie, had been licensed as a foster parent by our agency, we provided home support, case management, and individual therapy.

I had no clear therapeutic template in my new youth-focused practice beyond my emerging understanding of trauma and its effects. At times, I felt a mild panic, unsure that I was qualified to meet the needs of youth and families. On-site supervision, while supportive, was hands-off. I could implement any intervention I found useful. With a master's degree in creative writing in addition to an MSW, I was drawn to narrative therapy and artistic modalities. These seemed intuitively right to me but hard to quantify. I also subscribed to beliefs emphasized by Just Practice—namely, that all human experiences have a context, are embedded in history, hold a particular meaning for the individual and the environment, are embedded in power structures, and suggest future possibility (Finn, 2020). But it was unclear to me how these foundational beliefs meshed with mandated assessments and treatment plans required by my agency. I particularly struggled with the requirement that we assign a diagnosis to a child as the first step of their entry into our program. The diagnosis was essential to cover costs, typically paid by Medicaid, but it affected the child's care in unforeseeable and possibly permanent ways.

I eventually learned that the basic principles from Just Practice held true in the interactional work of clinical therapy. When I slowed down, the work became clearer, more fulfilling. I built trust, listened, and looked for simple, collaborative ways forward. I took baby steps. I stopped reading the stacks of papers that usually arrived before I even met the client, listing all the treatments that had failed in the past. I learned to view my clients with fresh eyes, to listen to their unique histories, and to recognize aspects of my own life in their stories. Although they might see me as a representative of a system that was shaping their lives, I could try to create a safe, warm space for my clients and encourage exploration. I learned to work with the person and to let the diagnosis, as well as the preconceptions that often accompanied a client, fade into the background. I am secure in this approach now. But I had to learn to trust it through trial and error, and I made many mistakes. I also had an extremely effective teacher. That teacher was Cora.

## Cora's Story

Cora's mother Trina had lifelong mental health challenges, and she struggled to parent effectively. Her first daughter had been removed by Child and Family Services (CFS), and now Cora was the only child at home. Many of the men Trina dated ended up hurting her or Cora. Trina, too, was prone to violent outbursts and frequently subjected Cora to harsh punishments. Just before I met Cora, Trina had recently remarried. She clung to her new husband, Bill, trusting in him to create a new life for her and Cora.

Bill was an intelligent and violent man with a criminal background who was rumored to have physically and sexually abused stepchildren from previous marriages. And Cora was particularly vulnerable to abuse. Diagnosed in early childhood with autism spectrum disorder (ASD), her communication and development seemed to stall out as she approached puberty. Cora disclosed to a teacher that Bill was abusing her. In making her disclosures, she used objects lying around the classroom to communicate the sexual nature of the violations. The teacher reported the disclosure to police and CFS. Cora was taken to a child advocacy center for a forensic interview. The results were conclusive for multi-episodic sexual abuse.

Trina fiercely denied her daughter's story, claiming that Cora was a manipulative child who wanted to break up the marriage. After Cora was placed in foster care, Trina and Bill began to harass the CFS social worker with threatening phone calls and office visits. It was only after experiencing her husband's violence firsthand that Trina came to believe Cora. Suffering from a breakdown that accompanied this realization, Trina entered a residential care facility and relinquished her parental rights.

CFS relocated Cora to a foster home several hours away from her parents, extended relatives, and community. When the CFS social worker took her to school to say goodbye, Cora's teachers presented her with a few small gifts, including a plastic model of a human skeleton. "She's into skeletons right now," one teacher said, with a smile. Throughout the long drive to the town where her new foster family lived, Cora's manner was flat, mute, and apparently untroubled. When she did speak, her voice was a whisper. Only rarely did she make eye contact.

Cora didn't seem to care much about her few possessions, but she treasured the skeleton, as well as a piece of folded paper. The "shuttle," as she referred to it, was a curious paper shape she held in her hand, modeled after a space shuttle—dirty, crumpled, and softened through much handling. It went everywhere with her. Although it was unclear to the social worker why the shuttle was important to Cora, she understood that it was. When she took Cora to her new home, she told the foster family that Cora should be allowed to keep the shuttle.

Cora's foster mom, Julie, lived in a small house with two of her own children, both younger than Cora, as well as a dog and several cats. Since this was a therapeutic foster placement, Julie was required to take Cora for weekly individual therapy and case management meetings. Julie soon began to complain about travel time and the cost of feeding and clothing Cora. Her list of concerns grew. Cora still wasn't talking. She silently refused to do assigned chores such as picking up after the family dog, who frightened her. Hoarding food in her room, she was prone to tearful, angry outbursts. Cora began scratching her neck and pinching her arms, leaving bruises. Julie became concerned that Cora might negatively influence her other kids.

Julie called the CFS social worker in tears about an incident that had occurred with Cora's shuttle. Julie had unintentionally ripped the shuttle. Cora became escalated, first flying into a rage, then spending several days in a tearful, near-catatonic state in the bed, covers piled over her head. When this passed,

Cora began making new paper shapes, insisting she take them everywhere. The situation in the foster home was deteriorating by the day.

Julie seemed increasingly reluctant to get Cora to her therapy sessions. She told the CFS worker she was willing to care for Cora a little longer, but she had come to believe that Cora's biology (autism) and history (sexual abuse) had made her a lost cause.

## Anticipating Cora

I had begun to assemble this partial history of Cora's trauma and family background through conversations with the CFS social worker and a review of her file. In addition to ASD, her past diagnoses included defiance and ADHD. Her prior medical or mental health providers rarely mentioned the connection between these conditions and her experiences of neglect, maltreatment, and abuse dating from the age of 2. As I searched the literature on ASD and sexual trauma, I was saddened to learn that children with developmental disorders are among the most vulnerable to abuse. However, trauma treatments aren't even attempted due to doubts that reparative relationships are even possible.

I wondered whether Cora might blame herself for the violence she had been subjected to. What did safety mean to her? Whom could she trust? Did she see herself as "unfixable"? It seemed Julie could only view Cora's behaviors as symptoms of pathology. Cora had experienced positive, protective relationships with teachers at her old school. What had enabled them to get close to Cora? How might these relationships lay the groundwork for other possibilities to unfold?

I had other questions, too, about the meaning of Cora's apparently odd behaviors. Could there be some glimmer of strength and self-assertion in what seemed, on the surface, to be compulsive actions? I wondered whether Cora was using language, or its withholding, as a way to reclaim some vestige of power. Self-defeating though it may have seemed to others, perhaps *no* voice gave her *more* voice.

I was also inundated with questions from our agency's case manager and in-home support team. Although none of us had even met Cora yet, these team members came to me with their questions and fears, wondering how we would work with her autism and apparent mutism and keep her foster placement from disintegrating. All I could tell my co-workers was that I needed to meet Cora in person before I had anything useful to contribute.

## Engaging Cora: The Beginnings

Cora sat stiffly beside Julie in the agency's small waiting room while her foster sisters played with a large dollhouse. I leaned over to introduce myself, but Cora was too busy clutching a paper object covered in tape—the shuttle, I presumed—to notice. She was thin and vulnerable looking, with big eyes and an unruly shock of brown hair. This dear girl, I thought angrily, had been treated like *that*?

Cora walked ahead of me to my office at the end of the hall. Once in my office she slumped to the floor with her legs tucked under her. In the silence that followed, I studied Cora. Her clothing was too small for her growing body. Her hair seemed a little greasy, her skin pale and covered with acne along her hairline. She remained hunched on the floor, not making eye contact, seeming to study her shuttle, occasionally holding it up to her ear. I had been told about Cora's silence, but it unnerved me. I wondered how I would fill this session.

To fill the silence, I began pointing out objects around my office—shelves crammed with toys and miniatures, an art easel, various books. She glanced up, looking at me like I was from Mars. Then she slumped over again. She still hadn't said a word. I got on the floor and slumped down beside her, feeling lost. All of my preparation, consultation, and reading meant nothing now. I tried to relax and tune into my own body. I looked out the window at the clear blue sky and a cherry tree in bloom.

"It's nice down here," I said. "This was a good idea."

Cora made eye contact. While excruciatingly brief, it felt like a precious glimmer of *her*. The silence wore on. I offered up a little sandbox I kept in my office, a tray of paint, miniature objects and figurines, and all manner of dolls. But I'd lost her again.

"Are your legs falling asleep?" I asked her. "You know, you're free to move into any position that feels comfortable to you."

I thought, well, this can't get any worse.

I recalled something the case manager at our agency had told me in passing: Cora had had an old sewing machine at home that she could take apart and put back together. At the time, I'd found that story sad in its suggestion that she hadn't been given toys. Now I heard that information in a new light: Was it possible she simply didn't like toys as much as objects she could dismantle and fit back together? I thought about the small model skeleton the teacher at her old school had given her. Perhaps she likes parts, bits of things, I thought.

I told Cora I'd be back in a moment and stepped out of the office. "I will leave the door open so you can see where I am," I said. I found some Legos in an old red tub in the conference room. I returned and dumped them onto my office floor. I winced at the clatter they made, remembering that someone had told me Cora loathed the sound of paper crumpling. But Cora did not seem bothered by the noise. Her gaze was fixed on the multicolored heap of Legos. The energy in the room had shifted.

I began putting pieces together, hoping she might follow my lead. She continued staring at the pile.

"I thought you liked building?"

Sitting cross-legged, hunched over the pieces, she stayed silent. I picked up a few pieces, sticking them together at random. We still had a long 20 minutes left in the session.

The office was quiet except for the sounds of birds outside the window and the clicks of interlocking Legos. I remember reflecting on how peaceful it was and how nothing was happening. But wasn't this "nothing" just an assumption? I wondered what presence and participation meant to Cora. And how about me? When had I last had the opportunity to just sit peacefully with another human being?

Cora pointed at something in the pile. I tried to figure out what she was pointing at. As I excitedly offered her one Lego, then another, she shook her head. *But we were communicating!* Cora seemed to be pointing at one specific blue Lego piece near the bottom of the pile.

"This one?"

She kept pointing.

"What is it, Cora?"

As she moved her finger closer to the piece, I finally got the right one. I tried fitting it to another piece, but she shook her head and kept pointing at the square of plastic. Finally, I saw it: The Lego had a tiny spot on it, some grit wedged between the raised circles.

"Ah!" I said. "Is it dirt?"

She pointed at another piece. This one was cracked, with a fine line down the center.

Impressed that she could see such detail amid the pile of pieces, I said, "Wow, you have an eagle eye, Cora!"

I saw a hint of a smile on her face.

"Do you know that expression? 'Eagle eye'? It means you can spot things from a long way away."

My tone was calm in a way it hadn't been earlier. Getting to know her felt good—and did not rely on an exchange of words. The next piece she found had small indentations on it.

"That's strange," I said, picking up the piece and looking at it. "I wonder what happened to that piece."

Cora began motioning toward her mouth. She was pretending to *chew* the Lego piece.

"Wait a minute. Are those bite marks?"

With a playful smile, she nodded and repeated the action.

"Why would someone chew a Lego?" I said.

Cora seemed to freeze. Oh no, I've upset her! Then I realized she was laughing! Her laughter was silent, her body shaking. Her mouth opened and her eyes squeezed shut. When she opened her eyes, I, too, was laughing. Cora spotted another piece with teeth marks.

"You're kidding me!" I said.

Soon, the pile of broken or dirty Legos was larger than the pile of clean, whole ones, and I was surprised to see that we were at the end of the session. An hour had passed.

"Wow, we have a lot of work to do next time, don't we, Cora?"

# Learning with Cora

We continued our search for flawed Legos over numerous successive sessions. I ran out of "new" broken Legos for Cora to find and began recycling the broken pieces by remixing them in the pile. At first, I worried about this, but Cora didn't seem to mind. I think what was important to her was not novelty but the pattern, the way it had become a system for us, a game that allowed us to communicate.

Session after session, Cora found the broken Legos, and we sorted them into piles. She still wasn't talking, but I noticed it less. I made jokes about what sort of person would chew a Lego, and she laughed. She smiled more, enjoying the sessions. I began to invent other scenarios, some of which drew on aspects of her history that I had read about in her file. Knowing that she feared dogs, for example, I brought up the possibility that a dog might have chewed the Legos. At this, she became serious and shook her head. Okay, I thought. No dogs.

I refrained from sharing our process with my colleagues. I wanted what was happening to develop organically. Also, part of me was worried that what I was doing wouldn't be considered "real therapy." Yet what was happening was important. I became convinced that Cora was developing her own treatment strategy. It was my job to learn how to utilize that strategy.

A few months into our work together, something miraculous happened: Cora spoke. Her voice was whispery, hoarse from disuse. At first, I had no idea what she was saying. A little impatiently, she repeated herself until I understood.

"Broke."

The Lego piece was *broke*.

After that, our game shifted. Cora would point to a broken Lego in the pile, and when I found the piece, she would yell, "Broke!" and we would both laugh. She laughed hardest if I was the one who yelled "Broke!" The louder I yelled, the harder she laughed. I'm sure our voices were audible all the way out in the waiting room, but I didn't shush her, sensing that a comment like that could squelch Cora's attempt to communicate, taking even more power away from her. In time, the words flowed more easily, and others came naturally as well.

In one of our sessions, Cora was bouncing on a giant ball and holding a miniature trash can while we talked. She looked thoughtfully at the little silver trash can.

"Bill said my voice is garbage," she said.

I felt I'd been punched. Was that why she didn't talk? Her abuser didn't like her voice? For the rest of the session, we repeated a gesture of throwing an imaginary Bill into the miniature garbage can. We also practiced pulling Cora's voice out of the garbage can and putting it back in her throat.

"Elizabeth!" she said, loudly this time. "My voice isn't garbage!"

Cora started talking for good. She used shapes and colors to represent moments from her life. It was a kaleidoscopic jumble, perhaps making it hard for the processing of everyday life. As we told stories about these moments, repeating them through playful dialogue, they became more orderly and appeared to be more in her control. Cora might say something that at first I didn't comprehend. But I had learned enough to simply hold on, waiting for the meaning of her words to clarify as time went on. As she disclosed aspects of her past through our games, I tried to respond in a way that showed that I was on her side, that she could trust me if she chose to do so.

I drew diagrams to illustrate her stories. I am not much of an artist—these were just stick figures and crude shapes—but it didn't matter. Cora was generous with me as I struggled to understand, to keep the game going with her.

"What would you do if Bill threw my voice in the garbage?" she might ask. Or "What if Bill bit this Lego?" Or "What if Bill threw you in the garbage?" "Spanked your bottom with a belt?" "Peed on you?"

As the safe adult in the room, I chastised her abuser: "Don't you bite that Lego!" or "Don't you dare throw Cora's voice in the garbage!" With the more serious material, I explained that it was hard for me to say those words or imagine anyone doing such things to hurt her.

Cora possessed an inner wisdom regarding what she needed to heal. She upended my sense of what therapy is. She taught me that people can learn what works for them and should be given the permission to explore these instincts toward healing. Cora taught me to let go of the need for control, especially when working with a child. She offered me lessons in benevolent curiosity; I learned that everything a client offers is worthy (Hall, 1998). And perhaps the single most important thing I can do is to approach it all with love and curiosity—to welcome it in the room.

One day, I thought to ask who rode *inside* the shuttle. I am not sure why this had not occurred to me before. Cora thought for a moment.

"I'm inside the shuttle," she said. "And so are you."

In that moment, I was overcome with gratitude. She had let me in. She had taught me how to talk to her, how to understand her, and she trusted that I was on her side.

## Action and Accompaniment

Cora and I were on a powerful journey together. I trusted that she had her reasons for the things she needed and wanted. But other adults in her life struggled to see her in this way. I tried to use my role to influence others, including Cora's foster parents (Julie and subsequent ones) as well as Cora's teachers and school administrators. My goal was to help them see that she needed space and time for healing and growth. They often saw her needs as unnecessary or nonsensical.

In talking with someone struggling to interact with Cora, I would point out that the origami creations she wished to carry with her were large, cumbersome, and sometimes dirty, but they weren't hurting anyone. Like imaginary friends, they played an important role in her life. They may be a nuisance, but should they be outlawed?

As Cora progressed through middle school special-education classes, then went to high school, moving homes several times, I talked to her successive foster parents about her needs as I saw them. I advocated to school administrators and teachers that these creations were her *right*. They were important to her healing, like any prescribed therapeutic intervention. They were like family members.

A surprising number of people in Cora's life did come to see her paper objects as coping tools. One of Cora's foster moms equipped her with a tote bag for her ever-growing collection of creations. Some adults joked and played with Cora in her language, the way I had learned to do. They learned there was nothing to fear in this approach. As Cora's problem behaviors diminished, my approach gained more traction. Cora experienced new things, built new relationships, and even tolerated the heart-wrenching stress of an ever-changing life in the foster care system. She grew taller, learned to swim, ran track, and progressed academically—all the while clutching her shuttle or other origami figures close to her.

Over time I developed a deeper appreciation for the role that art played in Cora's life. The objects served an important attachment purpose. The shapes talked to her, soothed her, and helped her process painful as well as joyous experiences. They helped her translate her inner life to the outside world. They signaled when she should feel a certain emotion, such as anger when a boundary had been crossed, or the need for love and support from family members.

At times, Cora shook the paper objects near her ear. Once, I thought to ask her if she might let me hear what her object was saying. She held it up to my ear. Why hadn't I thought of asking this before? I listened as she shook it against my ear. The sound was both rhythmic and spirited.

"She's talking, isn't she?" (All of Cora's creations were female.)

Cora nodded with delight.

"What does she say?"

Cora shrugged. "What do *you* think she's saying?"

"Is she saying she loves you?"

"Yes," Cora said. "That's what she said."

The paper objects signaled Cora's need for connection. They were there for her when so many others had failed to stick around or keep her safe. The paper objects were now my friends, too. I had to care for them as well, and treat them with respect to continue to earn Cora's trust. Over time, we experimented with clay, origami paper, tinfoil. I also learned about Cora's world of color. The color blue, for example, represented a key figure in her life: her abuser Bill. Colors were assigned to other people in her life, indicating her feelings about them. I was "rainbow." I took this to be a good sign.

One day, while we were working with clay in my office, I happened to say, "Cora, you are an artist, aren't you?"

Cora listened attentively. I could tell that she wanted to know more.

"Do you like art? It seems like you do. You have such an eye for color, and you make beautiful creations. I mean, maybe you would like to be an artist someday?"

After discussing more what it meant to be an artist, Cora became thoughtful.

"I already *am* an artist, Elizabeth," she said.

Soon we began telling people just that. By naming her emerging identity as an "artist," we enabled others to make sense of and honor her emotional engagement with her creations. Where adults in her life had considered her paper objects to be an obsession to be extinguished, now many of them developed a sincere respect for them. They no longer pathologized her creations. Cora felt increasing pride in her creativity.

## Celebration

Cora now has a loving, permanent home where she is encouraged to create sculptures. Some are delicate paper or tinfoil models, and others are cumbersome creations made of blankets tied together with string. Cora's parents, siblings, and others in her community greet her creations with a degree of humor, but always with appreciation. Cora's sculptures travel almost everywhere with her in her special tote bag, and she uses them for support in times of stress.

In her free time, Cora now seeks out images of interesting structures in the world, and she is encouraged to find her own meanings within them. A tunnel system in Turkey. A fair ride, whose joint-like shape is reminiscent of a skeleton. Her old friend, the space shuttle. An airport's vertebrae-like contours when seen from above. She replicates the designs with paper, clay, and other materials. Recently, Cora gave a school speech about herself as an artist, applauded by her family and new community.

Cora's soon-to-be adoptive mother, Susan, called me not long ago because Cora had begun acting up at home—an unusual occurrence these days. Cora was angry and defiant, talking about returning to a previous foster family. My conversation with Cora's mom turned on the issue of their needing to wait until Cora was 18 to officially adopt her so as not to risk losing access to certain essential services and supports, including therapy. Cora's mom said, "We love her, she is now our daughter, and we will take care of her forever. But I feel like maybe she doesn't believe us. I think we need to hold a ceremony, to show her our level of commitment."

Susan knew a district judge in their area, and a ceremony was arranged for the following month. I was honored to be invited. There was a large multigenerational crowd in attendance, members of Cora's new family, friends from school, teachers, and other important people in Cora's life. Cora approached the judge holding a small shuttle, crying and smiling from ear to ear while she hugged her parents, who were also crying and smiling. If anyone in the audience had dry eyes, I didn't see them.

"I'm not crying!" Cora said, tears streaking her smiling face.

Her mother read her letter of commitment, a beautiful document the very existence of which completely floored me. All I could think was this: There are happy endings sometimes, and we have to celebrate them.

The judge asked Cora how she felt, and she turned her face slightly to those of us watching.

In a clear voice, she said, "I think this is a good day. A very good day."

## QUESTIONS FOR REFLECTION AND DISCUSSION

1. What lessons related to assessment, diagnosis, and treatment do you take from this narrative?
2. If you were in this social worker's place, what would you write in a note to justify this approach at the point before any measurable change had been noticed?
3. What are some points in the narrative when the social worker departs from established practices or methodologies? What other choices might have been made at these moments? What might the outcomes of those choices have been?
4. Where do you see other possibilities for bringing Just Practice concepts and processes to bear in working with Cora?

## REFERENCES

Finn, J. (2020). *Just practice: A social justice approach to social work* (4th ed.). Oxford University Press.
Hall, J. (1998). *Deepening the treatment*. Rowman and Littlefield.

Part Two

# INTEGRATING SOCIAL JUSTICE IN NEIGHBORHOOD AND COMMUNITY CONTEXTS OF PRACTICE

# 6

# Just Process

*Determining the Location of a Homeless Shelter*

AMIE THURBER, MSW, PHD

> This process brought to realization something we had been professing, but I don't think we really understood: that the Poverello Center fully belongs to this community.
> —Eran Fowler Pehan, Poverello Center executive director (2007–2016)

---

**Overview**

Amie Thurber describes a contentious community process of determining a new location for a homeless shelter in this chapter. Thurber drew on the Just Practice framework (Finn, 2020) to explore the meanings that diverse stakeholders assigned to the shelter; contexts and conditions that informed perspectives on the shelter; power relations among stakeholders; ways in which the relocation process was shaped by individual and organizational histories; and possibilities for mutually beneficial partnerships. Thurber describes the processes of engagement, teaching-learning, and accompaniment that she and her team utilized in carrying out the community effort, which resulted in a new home for the homeless shelter that all parties could embrace.

---

## Introduction

Like many, I was drawn to Missoula, Montana, by the richness of opportunities within this vibrant valley.[1] For 19 years, I lived, studied, and worked in Missoula,

---

[1] A version of this essay was first published in *Reflections: Narratives of Professional Helping*, 22(2). See Thurber (2017). I am grateful to Mike Barton, Eran Fowler Pehan, and Dave Hadley for their contributions to earlier versions of this manuscript, and to the team of NCBI Missoula staff and volunteers, without whom this process would not have been possible.

much of that time directing a local chapter of the National Coalition Building Institute (NCBI), a nonprofit organization that provides training and facilitation to reduce prejudice and resolve conflict.[2] This case study examines one of the most challenging and rewarding conflict resolution processes I have participated in—helping find a home for a homeless shelter—through the lens of the Just Practice framework.

## The Poverello Center: Context and History

Home to some 67,000 residents, Missoula is a college town teeming with arts and cultural events. Bridging the Clark Fork river and tucked between the Lolo, Nez Perce-Clearwater, and Flathead National Forests, it is also an idyllic place for those who want to live close to the land. Yet, as local community organizers often say, "You can't eat the view." Members of Missoula's large rental market feel this squeeze the most: As reported by the Missoula Organization of Realtors (2019), almost half of all Missoula households rent their homes, and while incomes among renters have remained stagnant—and even dropped—in recent years, housing costs have steadily risen. Missoula has the highest percentage of unhoused persons in the state (Missoula Organization of Realtors, 2019). As is true nationally, there are stark racial disparities in housing access in Montana. Although the Census estimates less than 2% of Missoula's population to be Native American, 15% of the unhoused people in Missoula are Indigenous (http://mthomelessdata.com/2019/), inextricably linking issues of economic and racial justice. Missoula's unhoused residents are served by a single emergency shelter—the Poverello Center (the Poverello).

Since 2014, the Poverello has operated out of a modern, spacious building on West Broadway Street. But the move to this location was highly contentious, and for a time, the future of the Poverello was uncertain. Between 1981 and 2014, the Poverello operated out of a century-old house, tucked between residential and business neighbors on the perimeter of Missoula's historic downtown. In 2011, on the coldest night in January, temperatures outside dropped to −7 °F, and 111 people sought shelter inside. Far exceeding capacity of the 68 beds, many people spent the night on the cafeteria and hallway floors (Fowler Pehan, 2011). The Poverello Center was not only undersized, but the building was not ADA accessible and was fraught with electrical and plumbing problems. The Poverello's board of directors had long accepted that the old building was simply unmaintainable. For 3 years, the board had sought a new facility—twice nearly closing on a sale, only to have community backlash undermine the purchase.

---

[2] Now known as Empower Montana (EmpowerMT.org).

## Navigating Meaning and Power in Shelter Relocation

In May 2011, the local newspaper reported that the Poverello Center was nearing a deal for a new location in Missoula's Westside neighborhood, and had the support from Missoula's mayor, the United Way, and many people in the neighborhood (Szpaller & Cederberg, 2011). This was news to most Westside residents, especially some parents of children attending Lowell Elementary School, located three blocks from the proposed site. A controversy erupted. Within a week, members of the Lowell School parent-teacher association (PTA) formed a Facebook group titled "Poverello Not by Lowell School" (Facebook, 2011), and the local paper received a flurry of letters and anonymous online comments, overwhelmingly opposed to the move. Many posts conflated unhoused people with violent and sexual offenders, and a number of residents of this working-class neighborhood decried being shut out of process that they believed was orchestrated by downtown business leaders. In response to the outcry, the mayor asked the Poverello Center to pause the purchase in order to address community concerns.

The city contracted NCBI to design a process to engage a large number of people who hold diverse, divergent, and emotionally charged points of view in some form of public deliberation. Given the Poverello's urgency for a new building, the city gave NCBI 3 months to complete the work. I played the lead design and facilitation role, and 16 staff, interns, and volunteer facilitators assisted in the coordination, development, and implementation of the process. We designed a four-phase process. While recognizing that the Poverello's final decision rested with their board of directors, our primary goal was to provide community members with the opportunity to meaningfully inform that decision-making. We had two secondary goals. First, given the stigmatizing discourse that had surrounded the controversy, we hoped to leverage the public process to correct misinformation about homelessness. Second, given that the relocation decision had largely involved the city's political leaders and economic elites—some of whom offered to pay the Poverello Center to leave downtown—and left out both the residents of the Poverello Center and those of the surrounding neighborhood, we endeavored to equalize power among participants to the greatest degree possible.

## Phase 1: Engagement

To begin, a small planning team from the city of Missoula and the Poverello Center generated a list of stakeholder groups, including those who had voiced concerns about the new location. I invited all stakeholders to participate in a confidential one-on-one interview or a focus group. Fifty-two community members accepted this invitation, and over a span of about 3 weeks I met with Poverello clients, residential neighbors, business neighbors, city representatives, and organizational partners.

The assessment phase was critical to developing my understanding of the various meanings that differently situated community members assign to the Poverello Center. A group of current residents of the shelter shared their anxiety about being relocated farther from the bus line and needed social services, as well as their pain—as parents and grandparents—at being labeled a threat to children. Business owners described their discomfort—and that of their patrons—when they have to step around people sleeping in their doorways or negotiate human feces on the sidewalks downtown. One Westside neighbor haltingly described stepping out the front door with his children to find an unhoused man who had died in the night in their yard, and his fear that occurrences like this might become more frequent.

As a facilitator, hearing these various concerns, perspectives, and experiences provided critical context that deepened my understanding of the controversy. In addition, through the assessment phase I began to create relationships with the diverse stakeholder groups. As they felt listened to, valued, and supported by me as the facilitator, they increased their willingness to enter into a community process with others they did not yet believe would listen to, value, or support them. The assessment phase generated critical buy-in for the next step, which would bring people together in a public meeting.

## Phase 2: Teaching-Learning

On a warm summer evening in August, my co-facilitator and I welcomed more than 200 people into a large conference room downtown. After providing an overview of how the 3-hour meeting would be structured, the Poverello Center's executive director introduced the organization's history, mission, and need for a new facility. This was the first time the Poverello had made its case for a new shelter to the community at large, and it was critical to correct some misinformation about their services and clients. The bulk of the meeting, however, was reserved for attendees to teach and learn from one another. My co-facilitator and I directed participants to self-select into one of several predetermined break-out groups, including

- Poverello residents, staff, and volunteers;
- residential neighbors who welcome having the Poverello as a neighbor;
- residential neighbors who object to having the Poverello as a neighbor;
- business neighbors who welcome having the Poverello as a neighbor; and
- business neighbors who object to having the Poverello as a neighbor.

Each group generated answers to three questions: Why do you care about finding an appropriate facility for the Poverello Center? What are one to two key concerns to be addressed at any new facility? What do others not understand about your position? After caucusing in small groups, each team shared their answers to the large group.

Just as I had gained important context from the assessment phase, the teaching-learning process helped attendees deepen their understanding of one another's diverse—and at times divergent—perspectives related to the Poverello. Poverello clients, volunteers, staff, and board members described the center as a critical safe haven to those in need. Given the risks of exposure in Montana winters, several people expressed that the Poverello had literally saved their life. For residents who opposed having the Poverello as a neighbor, the center signified a place of risk and danger. At the time of the public meeting, many neighbors' fears were on high alert, as a known child sex offender was found "lurking" around Lowell school (near the site of the proposed relocation), and another man, living one block from the school, was arrested for a series of sexual assaults (Florio, 2011). For some of the Poverello's current business neighbors, the center had become synonymous with public drunkenness and aggressive panhandling downtown. Despite the divergent perspectives in the room, there were also significant areas of consensus.

Much to our surprise, nearly half of those in attendance communicated strong support for the Poverello *at any location*. In addition, a commitment to shelter the unhoused and ensure the dignity of those in need was unanimous. Despite some extreme differences in perspective, the sharing in this first community meeting was strikingly nuanced and respectful, particularly in contrast to the divisive tone that had permeated letters to the editor and social media in the months prior. Ultimately, the teaching-learning phase produced a broad set of community-generated criteria to be considered as the Poverello moved forward in selecting a new location.

## Phase 3: Action and Accompaniment—Group Work

Following the community meeting, NCBI established a work group to evaluate possible locations. Recognizing the ways that distinct stakeholder groups have differential access to *power*, the 12-member work group was diverse by design: The city of Missoula appointed three members (including a member of the mayor's staff, a member of the planning staff, and a police officer); neighborhood associations appointed three members (including a representative of the Westside neighborhood); the Poverello Center appointed three members (including a resident, a staff member, and a board member); and the business community also appointed three members. About half of these people entered the work group process with preformed opinions about where the new shelter should be sited—some strongly opposed to the move, and others strongly in favor—yet all agreed to apply the community-identified criteria to the vetting process, and to use a model of modified consensus.

As the facilitator and a nonvoting member of the group, I drew upon basic practices of accompaniment, including non-intrusive collaboration; modeling mutual trust and equality; and a focus on process, particularly in mediating discussion as needed (Whitmore & Wilson, 1997). The work group met over three afternoon sessions. The first session we toured the current Poverello Center. Nearly half the members had never been to the shelter before, and were shocked at the cramped quarters and crumbling infrastructure. We then refined a rubric—using the criteria generated at the first community meeting—that members would use to score possible locations. During the second session, work group members toured five potential sites. At the first stop, I turned to one member and asked, "You've lived at the Pov for almost a year. What is most important for you as a resident?" He quickly answered, "Access to personal hygiene. Food. A safe place to sleep that has a roof over it. Access to medical assistance. It's a simple fact . . . I am too old to sleep outside." Members then began deliberating with one another informally. The patrol officer talked about the relative accessibility for emergency vehicles. Neighborhood representatives pointed out the impacts of foot traffic to and from each site, and the business folks reflected on which types of businesses might be more or less affected having the center as a neighbor. Between the second and third meeting, each member independently scored each site. During the final session, members reviewed one another's scores, discussed and challenged one another's decisions, and in many cases revised their scores based on further reflection. In the end, the work group unanimously agreed that three sites sufficiently met the criteria to be recommended for further consideration, and the two remaining sites did not. Interestingly, the sites that remained were the most controversial locations: the current location downtown, and two in the Westside neighborhood.

Spirits were high the night of the work group's final session together. Members spoke with pride of their collective ability to overcome initial divides and work collaboratively, and they shared a deep respect for one another's contributions. Though they still did not all agree on which site they thought was the best for the Poverello, they had reached consensus about which sites were viable. They left the room with handshakes and high-fives, ready to bring their recommendations back to the community.

## Phase 4: Action and Accompaniment—Final Community Deliberation

The work group's final task was to present its findings to the community. More than 100 people attended the second meeting. The stated goals of this meeting were to update the community on the workgroup's process and to gather additional community input about the three potential sites. After a brief introduction, participants split into three smaller groups. Each group cycled through facilitated conversations about each of the potential sites. A team of four work group members was assigned to each site. The work group members summarized the strengths and challenges they had identified about the location, and participants had the opportunity to ask clarifying questions and add additional strengths and challenges. Following the breakout sessions, everyone reconvened for a final large group deliberation.

Overall, the meeting achieved its stated goals. However, now that particular sites were up for discussion, the tone of this meeting was markedly different from the first. Though there were fewer people at the first public meeting, for many this was their first engagement with the process. They had not participated in the teaching-learning, and they came to this meeting not to learn but to advocate. Some conversations were less respectful than in the first meeting. At one point, a man stood up in the back of the room and shouted that he didn't want to live by a bunch of sex offenders. My throat tightened as he began to speak, and my heart sunk as I watched three Poverello residents—seemingly distraught by the accusation—slip out a side door. Although I intervened, asking people to remember that there were Poverello residents in the room and that everyone was here because they wanted a safe place to live, those three residents did not return.

Interestingly, while the tone of the second meeting was more adversarial than the first, meeting evaluations were overwhelmingly positive, affirming the value of creating spaces where people feel heard, even when there are divisive issues at hand. That said, facilitators and members of the work group were left with lingering concerns about the emotional costs of such deliberations, particularly for those who are currently or formerly homeless.

## Critical Reflection on Process and Principles

In the months following the Poverello relocation process, NCBI's team of facilitators reflected on what we learned about the best practices in—and limitations of—deliberative processes to address community controversial issues. To anchor these learnings, I return to the three goals our team identified at the start of our work.

### MEANINGFULLY ENGAGE COMMUNITY MEMBERS IN INFORMING THE POVERELLO CENTER'S DECISION-MAKING PROCESS

As facilitators, our primary objective was to create a space for a broad cross-section of community members to give input on the shelter's future location and services. The process was largely successful in this regard. Hundreds of community members engaged in the deliberative process, and participant evaluations from both public meetings were overwhelmingly positive, with 83% of attendees recommending using this process for other divisive issues (NCBI Missoula, 2011).

Designing, implementing, and evaluating a process of this scale would not have been possible without a strong internal team. To maximize participation, we provided multiple avenues for community members to engage in the deliberative process within and between public meetings. During the meetings, we facilitated structured large and small group discussions and recorded notes. In addition, volunteers armed with clipboards circulated to record individual comments and concerns, and we posted flip charts around the room where attendees could write remaining questions, comments, and recommendations. In addition, the city launched an interactive online forum where people could post additional feedback. The multiple modes of engagement allowed broad participation and transparency and increased the credibility of the process as a whole.

Ultimately, this process offered a constructive alternative to predominant modes of political engagement, where people talk at, rather than with, one another. While it is true, as one group member reflected, that "the most extreme people stayed extreme," evaluations indicate that for most participants, the deliberative process shifted their thinking. That said, as discussed below, the process was not without limitations.

## CORRECT MISINFORMATION ABOUT HOMELESSNESS

The biggest challenge in the process was effectively addressing stigma toward people who are homeless. Although many people had the opportunity to hear directly from Poverello staff, clients, and volunteers throughout the process—and the chief of police presented crime data demonstrating that the Poverello Center clients do not pose an increased risk to the community—in the end, many faulty assumptions still circulated. For those most directly affected by homelessness—the current and former residents of the Poverello Center and their allies—there was an emotional toll to repeatedly encountering this prejudice in such a public process. As Eran Fowler Pehan, Poverello's executive director, reflected, "There seemed to be such powerful divides that factual knowledge could not address (personal communication, Dec. 12, 2012)." Untangling facts and feelings to create new meanings of the causes and consequences of homelessness takes time, and for many, the 3 months allocated to this community process was simply insufficient.

## EQUALIZE POWER AMONG PARTICIPANTS

Our team endeavored to democratize influence and participation through the overall design of the process—for example, by ensuring that neighborhoods and businesses were equally represented on the work group—as well as a variety of moderation techniques within public meetings, such as asking that no one speak twice until everyone has had the chance to speak. Ultimately, these strategies were valuable and yet only partially successful. One of the most difficult moments of the process occurred the day after the final public meeting, when the newspaper ran a letter to the editor written by one of the neighborhood work group representatives under the headline "Process to Choose Site for Homeless Shelter Insufficient" (Little, 2011). Fellow work group members expressed deep disappointment and anger that this member had seemingly betrayed their work. He openly professed pride in the group's process during the meeting, yet had primed a letter to appear in the paper the following morning that questioned the credibility of the process and delegitimized their collective efforts. I, too, was shocked by his letter, and yet also came to value his critique. Political theorist Iris Marion

Young reminds us to be suspicious of "deliberative processes within institutions that make it nearly impossible for the structurally disadvantaged to propose solutions to social problems" (2001, p. 684). As this work group member saw it, the low-income residents of the Westside neighborhood were structurally disadvantaged relative to the city and business owners. The city—in allowing only 3 months for the process—made it impossible to identify any new site alternatives. The five sites considered by the work group had been previously vetted by the Poverello board of directors, and no new suitable locations became available within the time frame allowed.

In addition, both the city of Missoula and many of the downtown businesses were funders of the Poverello Center and thus wielded a particular kind of power over the agency's decision-making process. Indeed, a number of business community members opted out of the deliberative process altogether, choosing instead to exert influence through financial incentives. For some Westside neighbors, it may be that their relative lack of political and economic power compelled them to cling to the stigmatizing narrative of "the homeless as sexual predators." They had found power in the emotive capacity of language, and it may have felt like the only power they had. Clearly, those with the least power in the process were the unhoused people who sought shelter at the Poverello Center. Although shelter residents participated at all stages of the process, their needs received the least amount of attention and appeared to be of the least concern in the public forums. It became clear to our team that just because we wanted to equalize power did not mean that we could.

Reflection on the successes and limitations of this process led our team to wonder how we might have created more formal opportunities to center the voices of Missoula's currently and formerly homeless in the work. We considered our decision to combine Poverello residents, staff, and volunteers into a single breakout group in the first meeting. We did so out of a desire to offer some anonymity to current residents. In retrospect, we wondered if we should have given residents the option to speak for themselves. Though a number of our team members had lived or were currently living in poverty, very few had experienced homelessness, and we wondered the degree to which we may have been paternalistic in our desire to "protect" residents. We also imagined what might have been different had we incorporated a panel of residents in one of the community meetings, a video montage of resident experiences, or a photo-voice exhibit from residents in the meeting hall. While not all misinformation can be dissolved in 3 months, and it is not possible to fully equalize power in a community deliberation, any of these strategies might have moved us closer to our aspired goals.

## FROM DELIBERATION TO DECISION-MAKING

Two months after the second community meeting, the Poverello Center announced its intention to build a new facility at the Westside location that had sparked the original controversy. While disappointed, the Westside neighborhood council announced that they would "do whatever we can to welcome them to our neighborhood" (Szpaller, 2011). The neighborhood council established a work group charged with maintaining open dialogue with the Poverello and drafted a communication plan that was adopted by the Poverello Center to improve engagement with the neighborhood. The PTA Facebook group that initially mobilized opposition to the Poverello relocation changed its name from "Poverello Not by Lowell School" to "Northside-Westside Community Forum" (Facebook, 2011) and shifted its focus to building community within the neighborhood.

In December 2014, the Poverello Center opened its new 21,000-square-foot facility. That winter was the first time in years that the Poverello had enough beds for all who sought shelter on the coldest nights—and the first time it had sufficient space to provide classrooms for GED test preparation and résumé building, on-site medical treatment, and semiprivate rooms for clients with special needs (Kidston, 2014). According to Eran Fowler Pehan, the community engagement process exceeded the organization's expectations in both cost and gain. It required a considerable investment of time—and there was also a significant toll of those participating in discourse that was infused with stereotypes and stigma—yet, she also believes the process yielded significant rewards. As she concludes,

> This process brought to realization something we had been professing, but I don't think we really understood: that the Poverello Center fully belongs to this community. We are of course free to make decisions about our future and our services, but without support and buy-in from the community, there is no way for us to successfully see this vision play out. (personal communication, December 2, 2012)

Before the Poverello could build a new shelter, the Westside neighborhood and the Poverello Center needed to build a foundation as neighbors. The community deliberation process served as a critical component of that foundation building.

Although this case study traces a particular controversy, similar conflicts erupt in big cities and small towns across the country. Neighborhood resistance can surface in response to the proposed siting of housing for people transitioning out of prison, addiction-treatment facilities, or group homes for persons with disabilities. While these controversies are often clouded by biases and stereotypes, they are also animated by community members who rightfully expect to be involved in decisions that affect their neighborhoods. There is a critical need for practitioners who can help communities navigate these disputes in ways that uphold all people's innate dignity and worth; create spaces for people to hear, teach, and learn from one another; and, where appropriate, meaningfully engage community members in informing decision-making processes. While there is no cookie-cutter model for community deliberation, this case study offers promising practices and lessons learned that may guide similar efforts.

## QUESTIONS FOR REFLECTION AND DISCUSSION

Consider the most pressing controversial or divisive issues in your community.

1. Who has "a stake" in this issue, and what is at stake for different sectors of your community on this issue?
2. Whose voices and perspectives seem to be valued most on this issue? Whose perspectives are valued least?
3. What might a deliberative process around this process look like in your community? If you were the facilitator, what would be your goals for the process, and why?
4. In designing a deliberative process in your community, what challenges might you anticipate? What strategies might you use to address these challenges?
5. Under what circumstances would a deliberative process on this issue be appropriate in your community? Under what circumstances would other strategies—such as advocacy, protest, or community organizing—be more appropriate?

## RESOURCES

Learn more about EmpowerMT at https://www.empowermt.org/.
Learn more about the Poverello Center at https://www.thepoverellocenter.org/.

## REFERENCES

Finn, J. (2020). *Just practice: A social justice approach to social work* (4th ed.). Oxford University Press.
Florio, G. (2011, June 3). DNA evidence links accused man to downtown Missoula rape. *Missoulian*. http://missoulian.com/news/local/dna-evidence-links-accused-man-to-downtown-missoula-rape/article_71728c5a-8d2f-11e0-af9a-001cc4c03286.html#ixzz1fp3MPky8
Fowler Pehan, E. (2011, August 10). *Introductory speech given at the August 10, 2011, Poverello Center community conversation*, Missoula, Montana.
Fowler Pehan, E. (2012, December 2). Personal communication.
Kidston, M. (2014, October 12). Soon-to-be-completed Poverello Center to offer expanded space, services to Missoula's homeless. *Missoulian*. http://missoulian.com/news/local/soon-to-be-completed-poverello-center-to-offer-expanded-space/article_d31f1e5c-5278-11e4-9188-fb-c8b45d00b6.html
Little, J. (2011, September 14). Process to choose site for homeless shelter insufficient. *Missoulian*. https://missoulian.com/news/opinion/columnists/process-to-choose-site-for-homeless-shelter-insufficient/article_bfd25a5e-dedf-11e0-9fda-001cc4c002e0.html
Missoula Organization of Realtors. (2019). *2019 Missoula housing report*.
NCBI Missoula. (2011). *Poverello Community process report*.
Northside/Westside Community Forum. (2011). *Home* [Facebook page]. Facebook. Retrieved March 3, 2021 from http://www.facebook.com/groups/151402144931616/
Szpaller, K. (2011, November 18). Poverello Center officials say shelter will move to Trail's End site. *Missoulian*. http://missoulian.com/news/local/poverello-center-officials-say-shelter-will-move-to-trail-s/article_619477b0-1189-11e1-8362-001cc4c03286.html#ixzz1fc8fnJEM
Szpaller, K., & Cederberg, J. (2011, May 29). Poverello nears deal on new site on West Broadway. *Missoulian*. http://missoulian.com/news/local/poverello-nears-deal-on-new-site-on-west-broadway/article_bfb036f6-89b5-11e0-80e9-001cc4c002e0.html#ixzz1fcBrU1PH
Thurber, A. (2017). Housing a homeless shelter: A case study of community deliberation. *Reflections: Narratives of Professional Helping*, 22(2), 28–38.
Whitmore, E., & Wilson, M. (1997). Accompanying the process: Social work and international development practices. *International Social Work*, 40(1), 253–260.
Young, I. M. (2001). Activist challenges to deliberative democracy. *Political Theory*, 29(5), 670–690.

# 7

# Just Practice for Housing Equality

KARA BYRNE, MSW, PHD

> Again, brought to tears. This amazing group. At the end of the
> focus group, I hugged J. My colleague. My co-researcher.
> —Kara Byrne, reflective journal excerpt

---

**Overview**

In this chapter Kara Byrne brings the Just Practice framework to bear to engage tenants with immigrant and refugee backgrounds in participatory action research to promote housing equality. Byrne argues that Just Practice provides a theoretical and practical orientation for participatory action research. She addresses questions of power and positionality within her research team; explores meaning making within refugee communities; speaks to the importance of history in understanding the experiences of people with refugee status; and considers the context of globalization in which local experiences of refugees and immigrants are entangled.

---

## Introduction

The Just Practice framework has provided a foundation for me as a social work practitioner and researcher. In this chapter, I describe my use of the Just Practice framework to guide a participatory action research (PAR) project titled "Community Voices for Housing Equality (CVHE)." I highlight questions of context, meaning, power, and history and speak to the possibilities of PAR in promoting social justice. I describe my background as a social worker, introduce readers to PAR, and describe the CVHE project. I examine the project through the conceptual lenses of Just Practice and describe my processes of engagement, teaching-learning, and critical reflection throughout. I conclude with a brief discussion of helpful skills and resources to engage with PAR as a form of social justice work.

## My Path to Community-Based Social Work and Research

I first became interested in social work as an undergraduate student working with individuals with refugee and immigrant backgrounds. What initially began as an ethnographic study of Rwandan refugees living in Manchester, New Hampshire, turned into weekly case management-type check-ins and support with families. A few years later, I was introduced to concepts of community-based, participatory action research during my MSW program. Some classmates and I engaged in action research aimed at raising community awareness regarding fair trade and integrating fair trade principles into city policy. I came to understand local and global impacts of policies and the importance of meaningful stakeholder engagement in policy development.

After graduating, I worked with families involved in the child welfare system. I witnessed firsthand how their voices were often silenced in the monumental decisions affecting them. I also witnessed the impacts of poverty, inequality, and structural violence and saw the need for policy change to redress inequities in health care, housing, employment, child care, and neighborhood security as part of child welfare work.

When I decided to pursue a PhD in social work, I wanted to engage in research that would strengthen community capacity and lead to action for policy change. My future dissertation chair, Rosemarie Hunter, offered me that opportunity. At the time, Dr. Hunter was the executive director of University Neighborhood Partners (described in more detail below) and engaged in community-based and action research projects with local immigrant and refugee communities on the west side of Salt Lake City, Utah. I became her research assistant and dove in to participatory action research (PAR).

## Participatory Action Research

PAR is an approach to research in and with communities in which social-justice–oriented action is woven throughout the research process. Community members directly affected by the urgent issues being investigated are actively involved as co-researchers. Trained researchers partner with community members to collaboratively study issues and take action through community-identified change strategies (Cahill, 2007; Fals-Borda, 2001; Freire, 1992).

A central component of PAR is recognizing and engaging with knowledge centered within the experiences of communities, rather than imposed upon communities by outsiders. Within PAR, we embrace research as a human right, amplifying stories and experiences of those typically silenced in social science (Cahill, 2007). We do this by targeting issues that are critical to a community and building community capacity to ask questions and critically engage with policies and practices that affect their lives. PAR is a strengths-based approach to learning and action in collaboration with communities affected by social, economic, and environmental justice issues (Collie, Liu, Podsiadlowski, & Kindon, 2010). For this project, we aimed to learn about the housing experiences of tenants with refugee and immigrant backgrounds. As I discuss below, core processes of *engagement*, *critical reflection*, and *teaching-learning* were key components of the research.

## Community Voices for Housing Equality

Community Voices for Housing Equality (CVHE) is a participatory action research (PAR) group made up of community leaders and social workers whose aim is to address inequality and injustice in housing by centering the voices of tenants. CVHE was born from collective work at the Hartland Partnership Center (Hartland), a center out of University Neighborhood Partners (UNP) located on the west side of Salt Lake City. UNP is a department of the University of Utah tasked with building university–community partnerships focused on leadership, capacity building, and educational pathways with west side communities. Hartland houses a walk-in center where an on-site social work team provides case management services to residents, including providing information about renters' rights and mediating with property managers.

As a graduate research assistant at Hartland, I spent about 20 hours per week organizing community leaders, overseeing practicum students, and providing direct case management to community residents, mostly individuals with refugee and immigrant backgrounds. Much of my work with residents was focused on mediation with nearby landlords. Additionally, I worked with community residents who were colleagues of mine at Hartland and leaders in their communities through the Hartland Resident Committee. The Resident Committee is a board of community leaders whose primary mission is to guide, prioritize, and inform the work happening at the center.

## Identifying a Community Concern

Housing and evictions were emerging as significant issues. As I worked with local refugee and immigrant tenants, I started to learn about and feel the urgency to address rapid evictions on the west side of Salt Lake City. I wondered if this could be a topic the community wanted to explore. I put together a one-page document describing community-based and action research and arranged a meeting with about 10 community and agency leaders. I asked if this was a project the community would find helpful and relevant, and if so, how should we proceed. The idea was received with enthusiasm.

I joined with a small group of partners to form our research team around refugee and immigrant tenant rights. And so began Community Voices for Housing

Equality (CVHE). The CVHE research team was comprised of four co-researchers: Abdulkhaliq, Gilberto, Ellie, and myself. Over the course of 2 years we formed the "glue" needed to dive into action research (Palermo, McGranaghan, & Travers, 2006). Abdulkhaliq was a partnership manager and social worker at Hartland. He had been involved with Hartland from a young age, was a tenant in the local neighborhood, and was a leader within his own Somali community. He resettled in the United States with refugee status over 20 years ago. Gilberto immigrated to the United States from Mexico. He had been a west side tenant for over 15 years and was a leader on the Hartland Resident Committee. Along with other members of the committee, Gilberto was instrumental in identifying tenant-landlord tensions as an important issue for CVHE to target. As Gilberto put it, "People are scared." Ellie was a social worker at a popular resettlement site in Salt Lake City, and I had worked with her for over 3 years at that time. Her impetus for engaging in the research came through her work advocating for individuals with refugee status at this resettlement site.

## Creating the Glue

Action research takes time. So does "creating the glue" within the research team (Byrne, Kuttner, Mohamed, Rejon Magana, & Goldberg, 2018). Creating the glue is a collaborative process of building trust and cultivating a sense of ownership within the team. We did this through many shared meals and conversations, whether over pizza at the Hartland Partnership Center or around the table at a local diner. We also retreated for a day in the mountains with the Hartland Resident Committee and families. This allowed for a fun release and gave us time to connect beyond work and into our personal and familial lives.

I began to keep a reflective journal as part of the research process wherein I considered the purpose of this collaboration and my role as a facilitator. For example, in one entry, I questioned my ability to facilitate this process: "I have begun to wonder what I've done wrong and determined that creating this glue is harder than I thought" (December 2013). I quickly learned that this amount of preparation into creating the glue and supporting engagement throughout the project was important to maintaining momentum along the way. I also reflected on "possibilities and strengths of people and communities" (August 2018) and worked to ensure that opportunities to engage with these strengths were ever present throughout the project.

## Developing an Action Research Plan

With shared buy-in and trust as a team, we designed a process that entailed 1-hour facilitated community dialogues with 48 tenants from refugee and immigrant backgrounds. We arranged eight sessions with six to eight people participating in each. Participants were low-income renters from a range of countries, including Argentina, Burma, Iraq, Mexico, and Somalia. We four co-researchers were not only facilitators, but also active participants in the dialogues, sharing our experiences and observations as points of departure.

## PAR and Just Practice

The five key concepts of Just Practice served as a guide for my interactions with community co-researchers, for developing the topics to explore in our community dialogues, and for building trust and capacity among us. Throughout the research process the research team continually engaged with questions of context, power, meaning, history, and possibility (Finn, 2020). I briefly consider each of the five key concepts in the following sections and provide examples to illustrate the grounding of the research process in the Just Practice framework.

### CONTEXT

The research team realized that a critical understanding of local housing experiences of refugees and immigrants must be linked to critical consciousness of the broader context of globalization. Participants had fled life-threatening wars within their countries of origins, which were initiated or perpetuated by global forces largely beyond people's control. A grasp of this context was critical to understanding both trauma and resilience in refugees' experiences. For example, when feelings of hopelessness surfaced in their descriptions of current housing situations, we were able to gently prompt participants to consider the powerful steps they had already taken to settle into new homes and communities despite past experiences. Additionally, an understanding of forces of globalization also helped us in considering how the political context in Utah could be approached to support stable and inclusive housing for low-income renters with refugee and immigrant backgrounds.

Individuals with refugee and immigrant backgrounds have a significant presence in Salt Lake City. Over 45,000 people have resettled in Utah, representing over 20 countries of origin. The number of foreign-born residents in Utah has greatly increased from 1990 to 2015, which has led some to describe the state as a "new American immigrant gateway" (Mai & Schmit, 2013, p. 207; Migration Policy Institute, 2017). Much of this growth is the result of immigration and refugee settlement, with residents arriving from all over the world, including many folks from Latin America, as well as Somalia, Sudan, Iraq, Burma, and Bosnia, to name a few (Mai & Schmit, 2013).

Over the years, Utah has had generally good political support at the state and local levels for welcoming refugee resettlement and immigration into Salt Lake City, as evidenced by our active immigration and resettlement agencies, outspoken political statements for encouraging immigration, and quadrupling rates of refugee and immigrant population growth (Migration Policy Institute, 2017). For example, the *Washington Post* published an article describing Utah's efforts to encourage refugee resettlement in the state with Governor Gary Herbert stating, "We empathize deeply with individuals and groups who have been forced from their homes and we love giving them a new home and a new life" (White, 2019).

While state resettlement policies encouraged refugee and immigrant resettlement, racism also threaded its way through policy, practice, and local discourse. For example, Cahill, Quijada Cerecer, and Bradley (2010) found that anti-immigrant values had a negative impact on west side Salt Lake City immigrant youth. I also uncovered multiple examples of racist, xenophobic discourse published in our local newspaper during the time of our project (e.g., McFall, 2016; Phibbs, 2016). Refugee and immigrant communities are acutely aware of these contradictions between promising public policies and anti-immigrant attitudes.

Consciousness of the local neighborhood context was also central to our work. The neighborhoods on Salt Lake City's west side are the home to most of the people with refugee and immigrant backgrounds in Utah (Mai & Schmit, 2013; Utah Department of Workforce Services, Office of Refugee Services, 2015). Home ownership rates are lower on the west side than in the rest of the city, and while rental housing may be more affordable, units are often poorly maintained (Salt Lake City Corporation, 2013). There has been little investment in or incentive for building more affordable housing. Overall, stable and affordable housing is difficult to come by in Salt Lake City, and many immigrant and refugee families have been quite transient around the city as a result (Downen, Perlich, Wood, & Munro, 2012).

This local-level context was also powerfully shaped by tenant-landlord policy. Broadly speaking, the policies favor landlord rights over those of tenants. For example, these policies encourage one-way communication paths that allow landlords to communicate directly with tenants, but they do not allow for parallel processes for tenants to respond or defend themselves when landlords may be unfair. We also recognized that tenant-landlord policies were not readily separable from landlords' attitudes toward refugee and immigrant resettlement, which then impacted the renting experience of individuals with refugee and immigrant backgrounds.

We brought a critical understanding of these contextual elements to bear in our analyses and in dissemination efforts. In our analyses, we pulled out elements of individuals' stories that highlighted barriers and strengths in tenant-landlord policy. For example, as tenants described the mechanisms by which landlords give warnings or evictions notices, the stories illuminated one-way communication strategies wherein tenants would be unable to defend themselves and would be forced out of their rental. We learned that the mechanisms in place for tenants to defend themselves, such as a day in court, made assumptions related to tenants' ability to find and hire a lawyer and make time to appear in court. Many tenants with refugee and immigrant backgrounds reported that the time frame required for responding to a landlord complaint was unreasonable (e.g., 3 days to put a response in writing) and oftentimes not feasible (e.g., securing a legal representative and taking a landlord to court over a $300 fine). In considering how context could be changed to support stable and inclusive housing for low-income renters, we focused on changing tenant-landlord policy to focus more on low-income renters' rights and facilitating outreach that amplified stories of resilience and challenged xenophobic or racist perspectives.

## POWER

Participatory research calls for ongoing consideration of power in the research process and concerted work to craft and support a context of reciprocity. Issues of power arose both in the research team's engagement with community participants and in my interactions with my co-researchers. The research team worked hard to build the capacity of community members as partners in examining and addressing questions of importance to the community. To that end, I facilitated ongoing research training to empower my colleagues to ask questions, challenge, and analyze the research process. We made all decisions regarding research design, implementation, analysis, and dissemination collaboratively.

Questions of power also permeated my relationships with my co-researchers and spurred me to further critical reflection. I had to examine my privilege and power as an academic researcher and White, middle-class young adult. Reflection on my own power helped me recognize how my own positionality as a resident of a neighboring affluent community may create barriers to understanding the lived experiences of residents of the west side with lower incomes than my own. This reflection was spurred by a colleague of mine, who questioned how my living outside of the west side community impacted my interpretation of residents' experiences.

As I became aware of my own ignorance in understanding the experiences of renters on the west side of Salt Lake, I turned to the research team for guidance. I asked, "How does my positionality impact my ability to learn from and understand experiences?" Given our glue of trust, we were able to have poignant conversations around the table, speak openly, and challenge each other. The team viewed me as someone they could be open with and someone they could challenge without jeopardizing our relationship. My co-researchers taught me how their everyday lived experiences, challenges, and choices contained elements that I may not fully grasp. As a result, the team as a whole became more invested in fully collaborating in the analysis of our findings.

I also had to grapple with power dynamics related to my positionality as a university-affiliated researcher. It seemed that the team deferred to me, and without my leadership and ongoing meeting preparation, the research group's work might have come to a halt. This was likely due, in part, to the challenges my co-researchers faced in undertaking research in the midst of busy lives. There was also a sense among my co-researchers that I, as a university researcher, knew best how to facilitate meetings, organize dialogues, and analyze findings. I posed questions to the group about this as well. In response, two of my co-researchers took ownership of the project at different points in time. At the same time, they helped me embrace the knowledge and skills I brought to the process as a university researcher. I did not need to give up my leadership role, but rather followed the guidance of the group.

I continually asked myself the following questions and regularly checked in with my co-researchers for feedback. How do my experiences shape my assumptions regarding research methods? Does my position of power as an academic researcher silence other co-researchers? Does my stable housing situation create unconscious biases as I contribute to analysis of qualitative findings? Answers to these questions helped guide how I interacted with my co-researchers and ensured that we all had opportunities to guide and own the process.

## MEANING

Participatory research calls for collaborative meaning making, which we integrated throughout the research process—from development of dialogue guides (a written document with open-ended questions to guide participant discussions) to co-researcher debrief discussions about content in the dialogues and in the formal interpretation of findings. Ever mindful of ways in which vulnerable voices are often silenced, we intentionally tapped into meaning-making processes within refugee communities We facilitated focus groups in participants' first languages when possible. In reviewing and analyzing transcriptions of the community dialogues, the team worked collaboratively to carry out context analysis and critically reflected on how we individually and collectively interpreted the data. For example, in one community dialogue, a participant spoke in detail about the ongoing work they put into their rental to keep it clean. When I first read this, I understood this to reflect a sense of hopelessness. My co-researchers challenged this interpretation and suggested that instead, participants may have felt a sense of pride in the amount of work they had invested into making their space a home. As a result, the analysis shifted from a central focus of hopelessness to the power participants harnessed in making the space a home.

As a research team, we continually explored questions of meaning in the development of the research project. We asked ourselves, what does "refugee and immigrant backgrounds" mean to us as co-researchers? To refugees and immigrants themselves? To the broader community? How do we make sense of our findings and communicate the findings effectively to diverse audiences? We realized that one of us may interpret a participant's statement through a deficit lens while others might interpret the same statement from a strength's perspective. Through our ongoing dialogue we came to more nuanced understandings of the issues related to housing and a sense of home. We moved beyond the limits of our individual interpretation toward a deeper shared understanding.

We centered part of our analysis on the meaning of home. We found that it is not just about defining "home" but also about how we make meaning of that home and who is involved in the process of making a home. The meaning of home is shaped by experiences of immigration and resettlement. "Home" may be temporary or permanent, place-based or centered around specific people or circumstances. Participants also described their homes with a sense of ownership and pride. For example, when dealing with unresponsive landlords, many took matters into their own hands using homemade remedies to eliminate pests or fix broken appliances.

## HISTORY

PAR provides opportunities for the writing or rewriting of one's own history. Individuals with refugee status are fleeing their own countries of origin as a result of war or natural disaster. Those who have immigrated from countries in Central and South America are often fleeing life-threatening living conditions in poverty and community violence. Attention to the histories and conditions from which one flees was critical to our work. The research team sought to frame questions in a way that drew out the strength and hope manifest in their histories. Co-researchers with lived experience of displacement or war framed questions that allowed participants to bring their own histories and lived experiences to bear. They helped us rethink received historical accounts of resettlement and displacement. For example, one researcher suggested we ask questions about personal experiences with resettlement and how individuals navigated the many seemingly impossible obstacles for making a house a home in a time of transition. As a result, we learned a lot about the weight of translating seemingly endless small print and signing misunderstood leases within hours of landing in the United States during resettlement.

The community dialogues also provided opportunities for participants to share accounts of how they had responded to situations with landlords in the past and what approaches had been successful. The sharing of personal histories of success in self-advocacy and action for tenant rights created another teaching-learning opportunity and contributed to individual and collective capacity building. Participants were invited to describe their beliefs and practices related to creating and maintaining a home. Their stories reflected their resiliency and strengths and challenged deficit-based thinking.

We also brought an understanding of historical trauma to bear in the research process. We identified historical encounters shaping current experiences today. People with refugee and immigrant backgrounds have experienced individual and collective psychological, emotional, and often physical injury over time. They have been victims of and witnesses to war, genocide, and other abuses. We could not understand current experiences of making a home without cognizance of historical trauma surrounding the loss of home. This cognizance deepened our appreciation of strength and resiliency as participants made this place a home.

## POSSIBILITY

Possibility is apparent in the "action" component of PAR. As discussed above, individual and community capacity building was a form of action built directly into the research process. We linked research findings to concrete actions for change. We developed postcards that captured findings from our community dialogues and listed recommendations regarding possibilities for policy change. We distributed the postcards at Utah's "March for Refugees" in 2017. People from around the state marched from downtown Salt Lake City to the state capitol, urging state and federal leaders to support refugee resettlement in our communities. The postcards initiative led to an invitation to speak at local housing meetings with fair housing advocates and landlords. We also testified against a bill that would take away a judge's ability to extend the time a tenant would be granted to respond to a landlord's eviction notice. Unfortunately, this bill did pass, but as a result of this CVHE became more engaged with local fair housing agencies.

Our final action component entailed hosting a fair housing exposition. The exposition was designed by the entire research team with input from the Hartland Resident Committee and other refugee and immigrant community leaders. It brought together fair housing advocates from the Disability Law Center, Utah Legal Services, and the University of Utah's pro-bono legal clinic to provide renters with an opportunity to learn more about their renter rights and to speak with a lawyer regarding any troubling circumstances. Both agency and tenant participants described this as an empowering experience.

## Conclusion

In sum, PAR offers an integrated approach to social justice work that incorporates micro, mezzo, and macro social work skills. Micro skills include active listening, engaging in power analyses, integrating a strengths-based perspective into all aspects of the research process, and practicing cultural humility. Mezzo skills include facilitating groups and developing collaborative partnerships. Macro skills include engaging in policy analysis, participating in advocacy, and identifying and amplifying community assets. Additionally, I had formal training in PAR and in qualitative and quantitative research methods. This was particularly useful to the research team as we designed our project and analyzed the transcripts from our dialogues. The training I received allowed me the opportunity to then train the community-based researchers in our PAR research group.

I believe there is a powerful intersection between the principles of Just Practice and those of PAR that have the potential to inform and transform social justice work. As I worked with my co-researchers on this PAR project, the lines between social work and action research became blurred as they merged into a social-justice approach to practice-informed research and research-informed practice. Taken together, the Just Practice framework and PAR offer critical, political, and transformative possibilities for engaging with individuals with refugee and immigrant backgrounds as partners in knowledge development, capacity building, and policy change in the pursuit of justice.

## QUESTIONS FOR REFLECTION AND DISCUSSION

1. Reflect on urgent issues in your community. If you were going to facilitate a community-based action research project, what issue(s) would you target, who would you invite as collaborators, and what action could you initiate? Think of an initial first step you could take to begin conversations with people in your community.
2. Reflect on your own positionality in the context of community-based research. How might your positionality affect the research process?
3. What social work skills are important in practicing PAR? Where do you see connections between the skills of Just Practice and those needed to carry out PAR?
4. Consider the current political climate. What role can PAR play in creating sustainable and social justice–oriented change?

## RESOURCES

Community Campus Partnerships for Health (CCPH). Check out their community-based participatory research (CBPR) curriculum. https://www.ccphealth.org/cbpr-curriculum/

The Public Science Project. I would encourage anyone considering facilitating an action research project in their community to engage with this group of action researchers. https://publicscienceproject.org/

## REFERENCES

Byrne, K., Kuttner, P., Mohamed, A., Rejon Magana, G., & Goldberg, E. (2018, August). This is our home: Initiating participatory action housing research with refugee and immigrant communities in a time of unwelcome. *Action Research*. https://doi.org/10.1177/1476750318790797

Cahill, C. (2007). The personal is political: Developing new subjectivities through participatory action research. *Gender, Place, and Culture*, 14(3), 267–292.

Cahill, C., Quijada Cerecer, D. A., Bradley, M. (2010). "Dreaming of …": Reflections on participatory action research as a feminist praxis of critical hope. *Affilia: Journal of Women and Social Work*, 25(4), 406–416. https://doi.org/10.1177/0886109910384576

Collie, P., Liu, J., Podsiadlowski, A., & Kindon, S. (2010). You can't clap with one hand: Learnings to promote culturally grounded participatory action research with migrant and former refugee communities. *International Journal of Intercultural Relations*, 34, 141–149.

Downen, J., Perlich, P., Wood, A., & Munro, S. (2012). University neighborhood partnership area: West side neighborhood profile. University Neighborhood Partners, University of Utah. https://partners.utah.edu/about-unp/neighborhoods/

Fals-Borda, O. (2001). Participatory (action) research in social theory: Origins and challenges. In P. Reason & H. Bradbury (Eds.), *Handbook of action research: Participative inquiry and practice* (pp. 145–155). Sage Publications.

Finn, J. (2020). *Just practice: A social justice approach to social work* (4th ed.). Oxford University Press.

Freire, P. (1992). *Pedagogy of the oppressed*. The Continuum Publishing Company.

Mai, T., & Schmit, K. (2013). Creating political and social spaces for transcultural community integration. In J. Hou (Ed.), *Transcultural cities: Border crossing and placemaking* (pp. 207–221). Routledge.

McFall, M. (2016, January 12). Where White People Meet billboard pulled after complaints. *The Salt Lake Tribune*. http://www.sltrib.com/news/3411271-155/where-white-people-meet-billboard-pulled

Migration Policy Institute. (2017). *MPI data hub, Utah*. Retrieved July 24, 2017, from http://www.migrationpolicy.org/data/state-profiles/state/demographics/UT

Palermo, A., McGranaghan, R., & Travers, R. (2006). Unit 3: Developing a CBPR partnership—creating the "glue." In Examining Community-Institutional Partnerships for Prevention Research Group (Eds.), *Developing and sustaining community-based participatory research partnerships: A skill-building curriculum.* www.cbprcurriculum.info

Phibbs, T. (2016, January 12). High school basketball: Minority coaches raise concerns about bias. *The Salt Lake Tribune.* http://www.sltrib.com/sports/3386720-155/boys-prep-basketball-minority-coaches-concerned

Salt Lake City Corporation. (2013). *Housing market study.* BBC Research and Consulting.

Utah Department of Workforce Services, Office of Refugee Services. (2015). *Refugee services division.* https://jobs.utah.gov/department/refugee.html

White, G. (2019, December 2). Trump gave states the power to ban refugees. Conservative Utah wants more of them. *The Washington Post.* https://www.washingtonpost.com/national/trump-gave-states-the-power-to-ban-refugees-conservative-utah-wants-more-of-them/2019/12/02/d8de7b00-1085-11ea-a533-90a7becf7713_story.html

# 8

# Just Practice for Water as a Human Right

ANN P. RALL, MSW, PHD

> We believe water is a human right and all people should have
> access to clean and affordable water.
> —People's Water Board

### Overview

Ann Rall addresses the role of the Michigan Welfare Rights Organization (MWRO) in the ongoing struggle for water as a human right in Detroit, Michigan, through the lens of Just Practice in this chapter. Rall examines the history of disenfranchisement through which people living in poverty in Detroit were systematically denied access to affordable water. She describes how local people built a powerful coalition—the Detroit People's Water Board—to challenge oppressive policies and demand access to clean, affordable, public water as a human right. Rall also highlights the power of arts-based activism to spark consciousness and expand possibilities for transformative change.

## Introduction

For the past 15 years, I have worked as a volunteer with the Michigan Welfare Rights Organization (MWRO). Active for over 50 years, MWRO is an all-volunteer organization that describes itself as a union for low-income people and calls for us to "fight poverty, not the poor." In the 1990s, in the face of severe cutbacks in public assistance, MWRO began noticing that low-income people in Detroit and Highland Park (a small municipality surrounded by the city of Detroit) were increasingly facing the disconnection of their utilities, including water. Water shut-offs were a particular cause for alarm because of the threats to human life and public health that they represent. Furthermore, unpaid water bills began to be placed on people's property taxes, which increased rates of foreclosures and evictions.

It became clear that water shut-offs were being used to force low-income people out of areas that had become desirable to wealthy people.

MWRO began to organize to bring public attention to this situation and to call for remedies. In 2009, MWRO was part of the formation of the Detroit People's Water Board coalition (PWB), which brings together environmental organizations, unions, and organizations concerned with economic justice and racism to advocate for three major goals: the protection and conservation of water; access to water as a human right; and the need to hold water as a public trust.

## Detroit and the 25-Year Struggle for Clean, Affordable Water

In 2013, Detroit had been accused of financial mismanagement and forced to accept the governor's appointment of an emergency manager (EM). The EM, a corporate bankruptcy attorney, promptly announced plans to declare bankruptcy on behalf of the city. Part of this process included massive water shut-offs. Many social justice activists believed this move was aimed at pressuring low-income people out of the parts of the city that wealthy interests were planning to "develop." Activists noted fact that some institutional customers owed thousands of dollars in unpaid water bills but were not having their service terminated.

In March 2014, Detroit Water and Sewerage Department (DWSD) announced plans to shut off the water of any household whose bill was over $150 or more than 60 days late. They hired a private contractor, Homrich Inc., whose trucks started going up and down streets, cutting off water from most of the houses on entire blocks. In June 2014, MWRO and the PWB called Detroit organizations and activists together to confront these threats. During a 9-month period in 2014, more than 30,000 households had their water shut off, affecting more than 80,000 low-income people. Through 5 years of efforts, MWRO and the PWB have had some effect on the lives of individuals and on local, state, and national policies. However, the struggle is ongoing—in 2018, the water department reported 16,000 shut-offs, which impacted over 44,000 people. In this chapter, I use the Just Practice framework (Finn, 2020) to examine key issues. I show readers how the MWRO and PWB brought processes of Just Practice to bear in advocating for water as a human right.

## Meaning

Initially, MWRO members grappled with how to understand the meaning of these shut-offs. The dominant understanding in our society has been that people who are unable to pay their water bills are at fault—they have failed to manage their money, work hard enough, or make the right choices. This narrative has been internalized by many people living in poverty, and they often suffer from feelings of guilt and shame. These feelings are compounded by fear of material consequences. For example, people who fail to pay their utility bills may lose Section 8 housing benefits, and lack of water may be interpreted as a sign of "neglect" by child welfare workers. MWRO encourages members to think critically about the root causes of poverty in general, and of the water shut-offs in particular, in order to redefine shut-offs as part of a systemic failure to support all people in our society.

Water and sewerage rates in Detroit and Highland Park are some of the highest in the country. At the same time, severe poverty made it impossible for many people to pay their bills. This contradiction became the basis for the term "water affordability." MWRO and its allies have insisted upon the importance of affordability as a basis for water policies.

MWRO, with our focus on water affordability, joined forces with environmental organizations concerned about water pollution and conservation. Employees of the water department and advocates concerned with corporate abuses were also challenging water privatization. In 2008, representatives of these organizations came together to share perspectives and search for common meanings and goals. During these conversations a focus on *water as a human right* emerged. We formed a coalition—the People's Water Board—and drafted a mission statement to express our shared understanding:

> *Water is life. The People's Water Board advocates for access, protection, and conservation of water. We believe water is a human right and all people should have access to clean and affordable water. Water is a commons that should be held in the public trust free of privatization. The People's Water Board promotes awareness of the interconnectedness of all people and resources.* (People's Water Board, n.d.)

The conceptualization of water as a human right is powerful. It places the responsibility for access to water on our society—people don't need to blame themselves for being denied something that is their right to have.

## Context

We began to learn about the complex interrelatedness of water affordability with issues of affordable housing, "development," and privatization of public resources. Detroit has been in the process of major transformation. After a period of deindustrialization and disinvestment that started in the 1950s, corporate powers unveiled new plans for profit-making in the city, in which poor people would be forced out of particular neighborhoods in favor of high-priced new or renovated homes, stores, and restaurants as well as the creation of large, open areas for capturing storm water run-off (Clement, 2013). MWRO and the PWB came to understand that water shut-offs were a key component of this effort to force low-income people out of their homes. We also became concerned that part of the reconfiguration of the city was being done with an eye toward turning Detroit's remarkable water system into a mechanism for selling water nationally and internationally.

## History

Since before the time of its founding by French colonialists over 300 years ago, Detroit has been a site of struggle over access to its rich resources and strategic geographic location. This history includes a long heritage of resistance by Native Americans, Black and Latinx Americans, and workers to capitalist efforts at resource extraction and labor exploitation. Access to water has been a key part of these processes. Detroit sits at a crucial place on the Great Lakes, which contain 21% of the fresh water in the United States and 84% of the fresh water in North America. The industrialization of Detroit and the establishment of its suburbs included the creation of a massive water and sewerage system that is the third largest in the United States (Miles, 2017; Rector, 2017).

Over the last 30 years, the state of Michigan has instituted a series of laws that enable the state government to impose emergency managers with increasingly autocratic control over local governments. In Detroit, emergency management has been used to dismantle the public schools and to take the city through a bankruptcy process that resulted in the sale of public assets and reductions in pensions and benefits of retired city workers. Moreover, Detroit residents have borne an unequal burden of water and sewer costs while suburban customers have paid fractional, wholesale prices. These processes, combined with the brutalization of low-income Detroiters through home foreclosures and water shut-offs, have created a climate of deep alienation and disaffection among residents.

In 2011, the state legislature passed a law giving emergency managers even more extensive powers, including the power to break union contracts. A revised version of this law was instituted despite massive public opposition. A few months later, Detroit's emergency manager filed for Chapter 9 bankruptcy on behalf of the city of Detroit, the largest municipal bankruptcy in U.S. history.

## Power

Detroiters have been living under increasingly autocratic conditions for the last 30 years. The placement of Detroit under bankruptcy "protection" took that autocracy to a whole new level, but it strengthened resistance as well. MWRO and the PWB coalition joined with thousands of activists from a wide variety of organizations to oppose the bankruptcy process (Schneider, 2017). Although many losses were suffered by Detroit's poor and working-class people—including the loss of union jobs, the slashing of the pensions and health-care benefits, and the sale of city assets to private companies—MWRO and the PWB continue to work hard to educate and empower grassroots Detroiters, to form alliances with advocates and activists on local, state, national and international levels, and to raise our voices to demand a better city and a better world for all people. We have gained a new appreciation for the importance of working on micro, mezzo, macro levels simultaneously, and of taking our efforts to multiple fronts—the legislatures, the courts, and the streets.

## Possibility

Amidst the pain of confronting an undemocratic and inhumane system, many of us in MWRO and the PWB have developed a sense of great possibility. Our ability to build on our heritage of social justice activism has helped us find new ways of acting in solidarity and maintaining our determination to survive and thrive. Coming together as a coalition has enabled us to see Detroit emerge as a leader in water struggles nationally and internationally. We have seen the concept of water affordability spread across the country and are witnessing growing concern with issues of pollution and privatization. The sense that Detroit and its water system are at the nexus of the interests of global capital is both a major challenge and a great opportunity for those of us working for social justice. In the following sections, I highlight how the work of MWRO and the PWB illustrate the processes of engagement, teaching-learning, and action in carrying out our work.

## Engagement

MWRO creates an environment where people can call or drop in and raise whatever issues they have related to survival in the harsh conditions that poor people face. MWRO's inviting, informal office space is staffed entirely by volunteers, many of whom are surviving on low incomes. If volunteers have brought any food that day, it is shared. Issues are viewed as interrelated, and the views of visitors are considered as seriously as those of office staff. People can get or share information on which agencies, organizations, or individuals offer assistance and how they can be navigated. Because MWRO is structured as a "union for low-income people," people are encouraged to pay a nominal annual membership fee (currently $30) to support the organization.

MWRO works to create an atmosphere in which people feel comfortable talking about the difficulties that they face and to enable them to overcome barriers of shame and self-blame. People are able to see that others are also struggling. They are able to share knowledge and make connections among the different issues that impact their lives.

The PWB uses similar approaches to engagement. The PWB holds meetings that are widely publicized, open to all, and held in a welcoming and accessible community space. As with MWRO, people often bring food to share. All are considered "experts" and can reserve time on the agenda or raise a hand and be recognized to speak. Wide-ranging discussions offer the opportunity to make connections among issues that might have seemed unrelated and to engage support from a wide variety of community members.

The PWB also combines attention to immediate needs with critical thinking, community organizing, and advocacy. In 2014, the coalition established a water hotline that people could call if they were being threatened with water shut-offs. We established "watering stations" at several churches and community centers where people could get water for free. Volunteers went door-to-door in low-income communities distributing cards with the hotline number that carried the slogan, "It's not your fault, but it is your fight."

Coalition members talked with people as they entered or stood in line at DWSD offices, turning the office into a place of engagement. We created fliers that combined information on assistance programs with information about the PWB and its meetings. We talked with people about their immediate concerns and encouraged their involvement in addressing the systemic roots of those concerns.

## Teaching-Learning

At MWRO and the PWB, the process of teaching-learning takes many forms. This process involves taking an in-depth look at a particular problem being experienced by an individual or a group and exploring how that problem connects to larger social forces. When new members join MWRO, they are assigned one volunteer with whom they will work closely. Volunteers listen and validate the experiences of new members. Many new members are dealing with the threatened loss of public benefits or child custody and lack of access to crucial resources such as utilities, housing, transportation, and employment. We take the time to explore all of these issues and their interconnections.

A second part of the teaching-learning process is learning what steps the member has already taken to address their situation. It is important to document the member's efforts, because they can be used to highlight the treatment that people are receiving from the water department. For example, members talked about trying to call the water department to discuss their bill and being placed on hold for hours, as well as having their water shut off without any prior warning from the water department. The water department denied these actions, but we were able to use our documentation to pressure the department to change its practices.

MWRO also engages in research as part of teaching-learning. Some members had received high water bills that didn't make sense. MWRO volunteers track down the answers. Sometimes members had plumbing leaks, but sometimes the leaks were in pipes that were the responsibility of the city. Sometimes members were expected to pay bills for which their landlords or previous residents were responsible. In several instances, we found that people's water had been shut off due to errors made by the water department or the private contractors hired to execute the shut-offs.

We have researched the actions and decisions of the water department and its private contractors in order to demand accountability. We have compiled annual reports and meeting minutes to understand how costs have been determined and distributed. We have used Freedom of Information Act (FOIA) requests to determine the numbers of shut-offs, get information on residential versus institutional shut-offs, uncover the histories of individual cases, and study patterns in the relationship between race and water policies statewide. Research is also being undertaken on the public health implications of shut-offs (Gaber, 2019).

One of the most powerful examples of the effectiveness of research was work that MWRO and the PWB did with water activist Maude Barlow and her organization, the Council of Canadians. We worked with their staff to write a report on the denial of access to affordable water in Detroit and submitted it to the UN special rapporteur on the human right to water and sanitation. Based on this report, the special rapporteur issued a statement asserting that Detroit's "disconnection of water services because of failure to pay due to lack of means constitutes a violation of the human right to water and other international human rights" (UN Human Rights Office of the High Commissioner, 2014). Their statement generated widespread attention from mainstream media. MWRO and PWB members provided countless interviews and documentation to media sources around the country and the world.

# Action

### CONVERSATIONS AND CONNECTIONS

MWRO uses its voice as an activist organization to put pressure on the water department to respond to the issues of individual members. For example, during the height of the water shut-off crisis in 2014, DWSD was so concerned about public criticism they were receiving that their deputy director met with MWRO volunteers and offered his direct contact information. This information became very useful in enlisting rapid responses from DWSD to the water shut-off crises being experienced by MWRO members.

Volunteers also work with members to make connections between their experiences and the experiences of others, and to show how those experiences are shaped by larger social forces. Conversations held in the office and at MWRO gatherings offer people a chance to share their stories and understand their common situation. New members are encouraged to think of themselves as leaders in the effort to change the system that creates water shut-offs. They are the ones who have seen firsthand how that system operates and can help others who are being hurt by the system to see the possibilities for creating change.

One example of the forging of connections between individual experience and social and political contexts is the visit from the UN special rapporteur on the human right to water and sanitation and the special rapporteur on the human right to adequate housing. During their 2-day visit, the special rapporteurs took a bus tour of the city, visited Detroit residents to learn about their experiences, met with activists, and questioned city officials. MWRO and the PWB also conducted a tribunal on the violation of human rights to water, sanitation, and housing. Hundreds of Detroiters gathered to listen and offer their testimonials regarding how they had been denied access to life-sustaining resources. The opportunity to speak and listen in such a setting helped many people overcome their shame and self-blame, to see the systemic roots of their issues, and to feel energized to take action. After their visit, the special rapporteurs issued a press release that was very critical of the policies and practices of the city. This statement brought increased national and international attention to the inhumane treatment of Detroiters. These efforts helped to shift the narrative in the broader society as well as to reshape people's understanding of their own situations.

## WATER JUSTICE JOURNEY

Another example of the PWB's integrative approach to working for change is the Detroit to Flint Water Justice Journey, which took place July 3–10, 2015. Initially conceived as a way of drawing attention to the interconnectedness of the issues of water affordability and access to clean water, the walk brought together hundreds of people, who walked or rode from Detroit to Flint, stopping for community education and celebration activities along the way. One account of the action was written by three Detroit-based activists:

> One of the major successes of the Water Justice Journey was the way it allowed for conversations among people directly experiencing water shutoffs and exposure to toxic water, who could share how their daily lives had been affected and discuss the state of their own health and wellbeing, while also speaking to their tremendous capacities to provide care and be cared for by family and neighbors. . . . The walk further developed solidarity between Detroit and Flint activists as we built new networks of social-justice oriented churches, organizations, and groups along the way. (Howell, Doan, & Harbin, 2017)

The Detroit to Flint Water Justice Journey exemplifies how MWRO and the PWB have worked to change public attitudes and perceptions in a way that combines community building with an analysis of issues that is both deep and broad.

## ADVOCACY

MWRO and the PWB have also engaged in legal and legislative advocacy for change. MWRO partnered with Michigan Legal Services to hire an environmental consultant who created a Water Affordability Program (WAP) that called for people to pay between 2% and 5% of their income for water and sewerage services and to restrict water shut-offs. Those suffering from the inability to pay increasingly large water and sewerage bills provided crucial testimony before the Detroit City Council. With the support of key allies on the council, notably the Honorable JoAnn Watson and a brilliant social worker named Maryann Mahaffey, the council approved this program as a resolution in 2005. Although the city government failed to implement the program, the WAP remains a key focus of the organizing activities of MWRO and the PWB.

MWRO members and others who suffered shut-offs traveled to Lansing (the state capital) and Washington, D.C., to testify on the urgency and importance of water as a human right that is being denied to people in poverty and threatened by privatization. In the Michigan state legislature, Stephanie Chang, a social worker who serves in the state House of Representatives, put together a coalition of representatives to create a slate of bills to protect access to clean, affordable water in the state. Nationally, the late John Conyers, who represented a Detroit district in Congress for 52 years, introduced the Water Affordability, Transparency, Equity, and Reliability Act (WATER) Act of 2017. Brilliant testimony in support of this act was provided by attorney and PWB member Alice Jennings.

## LEGAL ACTION

MWRO and the PWB coalition also brought a class action lawsuit against the city of Detroit to stop water shut-offs, restore services to residential customers, and institute a water affordability plan. This lawsuit presented testimonies of 10 residents who had suffered water shut-offs and other forms of abusive treatment from DWSD. It argued that shutting off the water of poor residents was a violation of not only their constitutional right to equal protection under the law (because poor residents were being subjected to shut-offs but institutional customers with unpaid water bills were not) but also their human rights and rights as beneficiaries of a public trust to water.

In presenting their case, the lawyers also relied on the testimonies of social workers and other advocates. For example, I provided an affidavit describing some of my experiences in working with people who were facing shut-offs, including stories that I had collected by recording conversations with people waiting in line at the water department.

## TAKING IT TO THE STREETS

The activism of MWRO and the PWB coalition is not limited to the courts. We also organized street demonstrations. One of the largest demonstrations took place in downtown Detroit on July 18, 2014. It was organized in conjunction with the National Nurses Union and coincided with Netroots Nation, a national conference of web-based activists and media makers. Over 1,000 protesters from Detroit and around the country marched to demand an end to the shut-offs, declaring that water is a human right and that lack of access to water creates a public health emergency.

MWRO has also connected the struggle for access to clean, affordable, publicly held water to other social justice issues. For example, we were part of organizing the Poor People's Campaign: A National Call for Moral Revival, an ongoing effort to raise public awareness of and opposition to the interlocking injustices of systemic racism, poverty, ecological devastation, and the war economy/militarism. MWRO also organized two International Gatherings of Social Movements on Water, which brought together hundreds of organizers from the United States and abroad to share their stories and strategize future actions. These gatherings fostered a stronger appreciation for the significance of water issues, a deeper understanding of the struggles for access to clean water, and a sense of the many possibilities for furthering the cause of water as a human right.

## ACTION RESEARCH

One member of the PWB coalition, an organization called We the People of Detroit (WPD), created a Community Research Collective that has taken information gained primarily through FOIA requests to create a "data visualization project." The collective published a book titled *Mapping the Water Crisis*, which addresses racial inequity of austerity policies and documents the relationship among water shut-offs, racial demographics, and home foreclosures in Detroit (We the People of Detroit, n.d.). PWB activists have also created an online timeline, which starts with the founding of Detroit in 1701 and documents the history of the Detroit's water system, serving as "an evolving research tool for individuals and communities working to establish and maintain equitable public water systems in Detroit and worldwide" (Bellant et al., 2014, p. 1).

## ARTS-BASED ACTIVISM

MWRO and the PWB have embraced creative arts as a source of expression, community building, and public education. Graphic arts are used extensively to create images for fliers, posters, banners, and social media. Sign and banner-making parties provide opportunities for creative synergy and community building. Musical projects have also been an important tool for consciousness raising and action. PWB member and longtime Detroit hip-hop artist and activist Will See created a song about the water struggle in Detroit titled "Water Power." See then worked with videographer and activist Kate Levy to make a powerful video of the song, which can be viewed at https://vimeo.com/304732944. PWB members created the Flowtown Revue, a singing group open to all that replaces the lyrics of famous Motown songs with poetry about water as a human right and performs at community gatherings of all sorts. One of their signature tunes is "Stop Shutting Water Off," sung to the tune of "Stop in the Name of Love, " with lyrics by Kim Redigan. It begins,

> Stop shutting water off before you kill us all
> Turn the taps back on, turn the taps back on.
> We've tried so hard, hard to be patient,
> Hoping you'll stop this abomination.
> But each day when we reach for the toothbrush
> The taps are dry and we can't even flu-ush.
> So next time before you leave us dry,
> Remember, people could die.

A remarkable example of the combination of research and creative endeavor can be found on the website DetroitMindsDying.com, created by Levy and her colleagues. This website provides a link to a 50-minute video about the water struggle in Detroit, titled *I Do Mind Dying*. It also contains a wide range of resources pertaining to the struggle for water as a human right in Detroit and Flint.

The efforts outlined above illustrate Just Practice processes and show how critical it is to bring these processes to life in diverse, creative, and collaborative ways. The work is rewarding and exhausting. It is full of moments of celebration and moments of frustration. We face persistent challenges in the form of individualizing and victimizing narratives and the increasing severity of poverty and economic inequality that shape the everyday lived experiences of our members. Low-income Detroiters and those who stand with them continue to be the targets of severe political repression. These structural challenges constrain our work, but they do not define us. Instead, they offer us growing opportunities to analyze, educate, and organize to overcome them and build a society that will work to meet the needs of all its people.

## Covid-19 Epilogue

In March 2020, Detroit became one of the most serious hotspots of Covid-19 infection and death in the United States. One of the causal factors in this development was the fact that thousands of residents did not have running water in their homes. In the face of omnipresent directives to "wash your hands," the PWB coalition put forth a call to the governor to marshal the resources to immediately restore water services to all Michiganders, noting that the mounting public health crisis provided concrete evidence of the longstanding claims of so many activists that access to clean water for all is fundamental to human life. In response, the governor and mayor quickly reversed the denials of any connection between access to water and public health made a week earlier (Kurth, 2020) and announced a program to reconnect households for a $25 monthly charge. However, in its initial form, the program proved to be remarkably ineffective; social workers played a crucial role in documenting cases in which people had been turned down for assistance. The PWB coalition put out an appeal to the governor, bringing attention to the failure of city's program and calling on her to bring the power of the state to bear on making the mayor's promises a reality (People's Water Board, 2020). The governor then issued an executive order requiring municipalities to restore water services to all households and allocating funds to help them comply with this order. However, as of January, 2021, 18,000 Detroit households were still struggling to keep water running despite Covid relief (Newman, 2021). The PWB coalition continues to work to supply bottled water to households without water, to document the failures of the DWSD to make good on its promises of reconnection, and to demand a permanent water affordability plan that will ensure access to water for all Detroiters long after the Covid-19 crisis has passed.

## QUESTIONS FOR REFLECTION AND DISCUSSION

1. What can social workers do to break through dominant narratives that blame poor people for being poor? Where do you encounter these blaming narratives in your community? How will you challenge these narratives?
2. Where do you see systematic violations of human rights playing out in your community? How can social workers respond in ways that directly name and promote human rights?
3. What new lessons in community organizing do you take from this chapter? Where do you see possibilities for bringing arts-based activism to bear to create change in your community?
4. How might insights from this chapter inform your actions to dismantle interlocking injustices of systemic racism, poverty, and environmental devastation in your community or state?
5. What can social workers and the people we serve do to resist and overcome increasingly autocratic power structures?

## RESOURCES

- A History of Detroit's Water Crisis web page with interactive timeline: https://cdn.knightlab.com/libs/timeline3/latest/embed/index.html?source=15XFgYsyw9sYVvc-V5pexEBTJqKVs_-WQv8zS8dpF4s4&font=Default&lang=en&initial_zoom=2&height=650
- Water history website: http://www.waterworkshistory.us/MI/Detroit/
- Detroit Water Stories (Wayne State University oral histories): https://detroitwaterstories.wordpress.com/
- Video of visit from UN Office of High Commissioner for Human Rights to Detroit: https://www.youtube.com/watch?v=39rpLE4fwLQ
- Video by Story of Stuff Project on bottled water: https://www.youtube.com/watch?v=Se12y9hSOM0
- Video footage of testimony of MWRO and PWB members to the state legislature: https://vimeo.com/129853822
- "A Burgeoning Crisis? A Nationwide Assessment of the Geography of Water Affordability in the United States" article: https://journals.plos.org/plosone/article?id=10.1371/journal.pone.0169488

- Report on water equity in Detroit: https://haasinstitute.berkeley.edu/sites/default/files/detroit_water_equity_full_report_jan_11_2019.pdf
- UUSC's "The Invisible Crisis: Water Unaffordability in the United States": https://www.uusc.org/the-invisible-crisis/

## REFERENCES

Bellant, R., Cabbil, L., Damaschke, M., Howell, S., Levy, K., & Orduño, S. (2014). *Detroit Water and Sewerage Department: A public timeline.* https://docs.google.com/document/d/1HgB5xG-UUDGD3Ge9sfusnwq-kVAFdoNrOoiHi3gPYy8/edit?pli=1

Clement, D. (2013). *The spatial injustice of crisis-driven neoliberal urban restructuring in Detroit* (Publication No. 406) [Master's thesis, University of Miami]. Open Access Theses. https://scholarship.miami.edu/discovery/delivery?vid=01UOML_INST:ResearchRepository&repId=12355216170002976#13355507860002976

Finn, J. (2020). *Just practice: A social justice approach to social work* (4th ed.). Oxford University Press.

Gaber, N. (2019). Mobilizing health metrics for the human right to water in Flint and Detroit, Michigan. *Health and Human Rights, 21*(1), 179–189. https://www.researchgate.net/publication/334065348_Mobilizing_Health_Metrics_for_the_Human_Right_to_Water_in_Flint_and_Detroit_Michigan

Howell, S., Doan, M., & Harbin, A. (2017). Detroit to Flint and back again: Solidarity forever. *Critical Sociology, 45*(1), 63–83. https://doi.org/10.1177/0896920517705438

Kurth, J. (2020, February 28). Detroit says no proof water shutoffs harm health. Get real, experts say. *Bridge Magazine.* https://www.bridgemi.com/michigan-health-watch/detroit-says-no-proof-water-shutoffs-harm-health-get-real-experts-say

Miles, T. (2017). *The dawn of Detroit: A chronicle of slavery and freedom in the city of the straits.* The New Press.

Newman, E. (2021, January 12). Coronavirus epidemic changes Detroit's water shut-off policy. Morning Edition. National Public Radio. https://www.npr.org/2021/01/12/955938725/coronavirus-pandemic-changes-detroit-s-water-shut-off-policy-

People's Water Board. (2020, March 16). *Appeal to Gov. Whitmer in light of COVID-19 water and sanitation needs.* https://www.peopleswaterboard.org/2020/03/16/appeal-to-gov-whitmer-in-light-of-covid-19-water-sanitation-needs/

People's Water Board. (n.d.). http://peopleswaterboard.blogspot.com/

Rector, J. (2017). *Accumulating risk: Environmental justice and the history of capitalism in Detroit, 1880–2015* (Publication No. 1738) [Doctoral dissertation, Wayne State University]. https://digitalcommons.wayne.edu/oa_dissertations/1738

Schneider, K. (2017, August 26). *Detroit water shutoffs resume: Bankruptcy lawyers and banks cash in.* Circle of Blue. https://www.circleofblue.org/2014/world/detroit-water-shutoffs-resume-bankruptcy-lawyers-banks-cash/

UN Human Rights Office of the High Commissioner. (2014, June 25). *Detroit: Disconnecting water from people who cannot pay—an affront to human rights, say UN experts.* https://www.ohchr.org/EN/NewsEvents/Pages/DisplayNews.aspx?NewsID=14777

We the People of Detroit. (n.d.). *Water.* https://www.wethepeopleofdetroit.com/water

# 9

# Just Practice in a Gentrifying Neighborhood

AMIE THURBER, MSW, PHD

*I feel so naked. So lost without my other people, and without my neighborhood. That is one of my concerns, that we do not lose each other, because we matter for each other.*
—Ms. T.K., resident of a gentrifying Nashville neighborhood

---

**Overview**

In this chapter Amie Thurber describes the Nashville Neighborhood Story Project, a community-based initiative to engage residents as agents of change in analyzing and acting on gentrification in their neighborhoods. Thurber shows how residents came together to explore the meaning of gentrification in their lives and then worked together to document the histories of their neighborhoods. Residents critically examined the power relations shaping decisions made by and in their communities. They created contexts of co-learning and mutual support to inform collective action. In addition, they discovered new possibilities through the re-storying of their neighborhoods and sharing those stories through diverse media.

---

## Introduction

Five months after the *New York Times* declared Nashville, Tennessee, the next "it" city (Severson, 2013), I moved there to begin doctoral study. Construction was at an all-time high (Sichko, 2019), job opportunities were increasing (Kotkin & Shires, 2015), and home prices were soaring. Yet, beneath a skyline broken by cranes and the ever-present din of construction noise, I heard a common refrain: "*Who is this all being built for?*" Indeed, entire neighborhoods were being rebranded and rebuilt to attract a wealthier, younger, and whiter market, and boutique businesses were moving in to serve these new residents. The city's longtime affordable neighborhoods were gentrifying, and fast. I was intimately implicated in this transformation, having moved my White family into a historically Black neighborhood. Over the next 4 years, I immersed myself in the study of gentrification. In the classroom, my peers and I grappled with theoretical perspectives on social and spatial inequities. In the community, I worked alongside residents, citywide organizing groups, and policymakers to respond to gentrification on the ground. Given my experience developing community-based programs, I wondered how I might best leverage my skills to assist residents grappling with gentrification and had a hunch I would end up designing some type of neighborhood initiative. But first, I became a student of the city, applying the Just Practice framework (Finn, 2020) in my reading of archival documents and news articles, in my conversations with longtime residents and city planners, and in my observations of my own and others' efforts to influence housing and community development policy. I trace that learning here, focusing on the development of what would become the Neighborhood Story Project.

## The Context of Gentrification in Nashville

Currently home to an estimated 692,600 residents, Nashville is an ethnically and racially diverse city, and among the fastest growing cities in the nation (Sharf, 2018). Unsurprisingly, the city's housing market is also booming. Yet the "it" city is not benefiting everyone. Nearly a third of county residents cannot afford the cost of housing, and the city reports a shortage of 18,000 affordable homes (Office of the Mayor, 2017). The housing crisis disproportionately harms Nashville's Black residents, who are twice as likely to live below the poverty level as their White counterparts (Metropolitan Social Services, 2016) and are also more likely to live in neighborhoods where housing costs are rising the fastest. For example, in Cleveland Park, one of the city's historically Black neighborhoods, housing costs went up 110% between 2002 and 2016, more than twice the county average.[1] Increased home values inevitably drove up rents and property taxes, pushing many people out of the neighborhood. According to the U.S. Census, the number of Black residents in the neighborhood decreased by 68% between 2000 and 2010.

As I began to grasp the context of gentrification in Nashville, I became convinced that the rapid development and concurring loss of affordable housing constituted a social injustice: The city's economic engine was being fueled, in part, by the displacement of low-income residents who were disproportionately people of color. But why were so many of Nashville's gentrifying neighborhoods among those with the highest population of Black residents? To learn more, I turned to Nashville history.

[1] To determine changes in housing values, I analyzed GIS layers provided by the Nashville Metro Planning Department (which include 2002 and 2016 tax assessor data and neighborhood boundaries).

## The Historical Significance of the Color Line

Black neighborhoods in Nashville did not evolve by chance. Before the start of the Civil War, just 4,000 Black people lived in the city, and most of them were enslaved (Lovett, 1999). However, after the Union army gained control of the city, a surge of freedom-seeking Black families migrated to Nashville, and in just 5 years the Black population tripled (Lovett, 1999). In exchange for lodging in one of three large encampments stationed around the city center, the army enlisted these formerly enslaved men and women to fortify the city (Kreyling, 2005). As the new residents were still considered someone else's property, the encampments were called "contraband camps" (Lovett, 1999). The camps offered little more than most basic shelter, and yet, after the war, it was here that these new Nashvillians formed the first Black business districts, opened the first Black schools, and erected the first Black churches. And it is here that an impressively large number of historically Black-owned and/or -led businesses, schools, and churches remain.

The racialization of Nashville neighborhoods—which can be understood as the practices that shape who lives where and the quality of those neighborhoods—continued over time. For example, between the 1930s and the 1960s, discriminatory practices in municipal planning opened up new amenity-rich neighborhoods in the suburbs to White families, while the banks offered subsidized home ownership opportunities to Whites only. Meanwhile, the urban renewal freeway construction of the 1950s–1970s gutted many Black neighborhoods. The city seized hundreds of homes through imminent domain, displaced businesses, and annexed previously thriving communities (Houston, 2012). Through each of these eras, Black communities organized, launched legal challenges and public protest to preserve their communities, and worked to maintain and when necessary rebuild the economic, cultural, social, and spiritual foundation of their neighborhoods. Organizing efforts accelerated during the civil rights movement, which won important victories against discrimination. And yet the racialization of Nashville neighborhoods also intensified during this period. As Nashville historian Benjamin Houston writes, "The dotted lines of roads now replaced the WHITE and COLORED signs of the past.... [A]n entire city was redrawn and reshaped in order to preserve the legacies of the past" (2012, p. 242). Indeed, though there have been disruptions over time, the persistence of the color line has meant that a number of Nashville's neighborhoods have been anchoring spaces for the Black community since the late 1800s. These neighborhoods are marked by deprivation and disinvestment from the city, and at the same time are sites of community-led industriousness, congregation, creativity, and resilience.

As my historical understanding deepened, I realized that any intervention in Nashville's gentrifying neighborhoods would need to account for the nuanced ways that the past laid the groundwork for Nashville's current housing crisis, as well as the significance of residents' historic ties to the place they live. I wondered how others were making sense of the rapid demographic changes taking place across the city.

## Meaning Making in a Gentrifying City

Although increasingly part of everyday nomenclature, the term "gentrification" is inconsistently used. Gentrification was first coined in 1964 by geographer Ruth Glass to describe the transformation of modest London homes into high-end residences serving the "gentry," or upper class (Glass, 1964). This remains perhaps the most common meaning of gentrification: the displacement of low-income residents. In the face of Nashville's rapid development, many residents—and at times, city officials—have taken up the discourse of gentrification-as-displacement. For example, in 2014 the Metro Nashville Planning Department commissioned a report on best practices for mitigating displacement (Thurber, Gupta, Fraser, & Perkins, 2014). The loss of affordable housing and increased resident displacement became a core issue for two citywide community organizing and advocacy efforts (Cannon, 2015; Smith, 2016). However, concurrent to this narrative is another argument: that gentrification is good for the city.

Proponents of gentrification essentially conflate revitalization with gentrification (Lees, 2007). They highlight the need for improved housing, infrastructure, and other amenities in declining areas; dismiss calls for housing market regulations; and shrug off concerns of widespread residential displacements (Vigdor, Massey, & Rivlan, 2002; Freeman, 2005). The conflation of revitalization and gentrification has had broad uptake and is reflected in a wide range of zoning practices, policies, and strategies that open up areas to development (Moskowitz, 2017). These include preemptive city- and state-level legislation prohibiting rent control mechanisms or barring policies that require developers to build affordable housing. Such preemptive prohibitions are currently in place in 42 states (www.nmhc.org), including Tennessee.

Perhaps unsurprisingly, in Nashville the gentrification-as-revitalization frame is most often used by developers and real estate companies. One of the most concerning aspects of these narratives is the racial coding that often accompanies the message. Aerial Development, one of the largest development groups targeting "transitional areas" in Nashville, casts itself as "dedicated to the full-circle revitalization of Nashville's urban neighborhoods." In a recent promotional film featuring a high-end housing development in a rapidly gentrifying East Nashville neighborhood, the camera pans over a modest single-family home while the narrator says, "Some bad news lived here before . . ." (Trageser, 2015). While the "bad news" remains racially unmarked, the cast of actors representing those here now—shown running, drinking lattes, doing yoga, and hosting rooftop dinner parties—is all White (or racially ambiguous). Messages like these make it clear that certain bodies are imagined to be *in place* in this changing neighborhood, and others are not. These messages do not just equate gentrification with revitalization; they essentially contend that the displacement of poor people and people of color is a *benefit* of revitalization.

Running alongside these competing narratives—the harm of lost affordable housing versus the benefit of removing undesirable people and homes—runs a third, albeit less prevalent, narrative. In community meetings and conversations around kitchen tables, I listened as long-term residents spoke with deep sadness about a loss of collective history in their neighborhoods. Some spoke of rising racial- and class-based friction, and the pain of being viewed as suspicious on the block where they were raised. Many spoke with pride of their efforts over time to create safe neighborhoods for their families and expressed outrage at the barrage of news articles crediting recent neighborhood improvements to newcomers alone.

The more I listened, the more I became attuned to the gaps between residents' expressed concerns and the city's response. To the extent that the city of Nashville had addressed gentrification at all, it was as a housing problem. Without a doubt, the loss of affordable housing was alarming. Yet, missing from this singular focus on housing was attention to other losses residents were experiencing. When areas gentrify, people may lose social ties, access to cultural and civic spaces, and/or a sense of belonging—and in this context, many people are fighting to keep more than just their homes (Thurber, 2017). I committed that any intervention I developed would honor the fullness of residents' experiences of neighborhood change.

## Powering Nashville's Response to Gentrification

It became increasingly critical for me to understand who was shaping Nashville's collective understanding of, and response to, gentrification. The city of Nashville was certainly playing an important role. In the 2016–2017 fiscal year, the city provided $15 million to the Barnes Fund, Nashville's affordable housing trust fund, and in September 2016, Metro Council passed an inclusionary housing bill designed to incentivize developers to build affordable homes for purchase. The city also leveraged its own stock of property to meet housing needs, donating 30 metro-owned properties to be developed as affordable housing. With these efforts, the city reported that more than 1,500 affordable and workforce housing units had been preserved, built, or were soon coming to market (Office of the Mayor, 2017). And yet, given that Nashville is on track for a shortage of 31,000 affordable units by 2025, many are concerned that these efforts, while important, are insufficient.

Meanwhile, the private sector has largely been unwilling to address what is now widely recognized as an affordable housing crisis (Garrison, 2015). Many affordable housing measures have been stalled by developers, the planning commission, and state legislators (Garrison, 2017). The final inclusionary housing bill was watered down due to developer pushback, and it now incentivizes but does not *require* the development of affordable homes. Further, the bill applies only to homeownership units, which does nothing to stem the rapid loss of affordable rentals. Nearly every week there are reports of private apartment complexes raising rents and evicting residents. Unsurprisingly, the rate of homelessness is rapidly rising: Between 2015 and 2016, the number of unsheltered homeless people in Nashville increased by 43% (Lowe, Poubelle, Thomas, Batko, & Layton, 2016).

In response, housing advocates and activists have ramped up efforts to protect people's homes and accelerate efforts to fund and build additional units. A number of tenant-organizing efforts across Nashville have won important site-specific victories. For example, a tenant organizing group within a public housing project that was slated for demolition pushed the local housing authority to commit to replacement of all affordable units onsite (Thurber, Collins, Greer, McKnight, & Thompson, 2018). However, few of these tenant organizing efforts have been sustainable over time.

It was evident from tracing the various responses to gentrification in Nashville that those able to hold sustained power in shaping and responding to gentrification were the policymakers at the city and state levels, as well as private developers, while the perspectives of longtime residents living in gentrifying neighborhoods were seldom heard. Traditional modes of city policymaking highly constrain, if not altogether block, opportunities for many residents to represent their own experiences. This is particularly the case for low-income people, people of color, young people, and elders. I determined that building residents' capacity to effect change in their neighborhoods needed to be at the heart of any intervention I designed.

## Reimagining Possible Responses to Gentrification

As I analyzed the ways that context, history, meaning, and power shaped gentrification in Nashville, I began to imagine alternative interventions, not in place of—but in addition to—efforts to build and preserve affordable housing. I wondered, what might be a way for people to address the injustice of gentrification in the present, with attention to the past struggles for justice in these same spaces? What processes can give voice to the more than material harms of gentrification—such as loss of social ties, spaces of cultural gathering, or shared place-histories? What structure is needed to engage and amplify the voices of longtime residents of gentrifying neighborhoods? Ultimately, I developed the Neighborhood Story Project, a 12-week facilitated program that brings a small group of residents together to conduct action research in their neighborhood.

Several practice traditions inform the design of the Neighborhood Story Project: group work, popular education, critical participatory action research, and public humanities. However, each provides distinct contributions to the project design (see Thurber, 2019). Among these is a shared commitment to centering local knowledge and expertise. In building a team of researchers comprised largely of members from within the community, the Neighborhood Story Project is predicated on the belief that all interested neighbors have valuable resources, skills, and experiences that will aid in and guide the group's work together. It is the residents of a place who know what is being lost as their neighborhood changes, what ought to be preserved, and what futures they want to build. This is not to say that long-term residents have a singular or unified perspective, but rather that there is an intimacy of place-knowledge held by those most deeply connected to a place, and that knowledge matters.

Between February and November 2016, I worked with small groups of residents in three gentrifying Nashville neighborhoods. To begin, I had a number of meetings with local leaders in each neighborhood to consider the goals of the Neighborhood Story Project, and my own interests as a scholar, practitioner, and White neighbor concerned about gentrification. In each case, leaders expressed enthusiasm about the project and suggested a number of possible participants with whom I followed up individually. I also attended area neighborhood association meetings to talk about the project and publicized the project through social media. In total, 28 residents joined one of three Neighborhood Story Projects. The participants were predominantly Black women who had lived most of their lives in their neighborhood. Although only a few miles apart from one another, the three neighborhoods were distinct, and participants in each project brought differing interests and concerns.

To ensure that the Neighborhood Story Project is tailored to the interests of its members, I developed a flexible curriculum organized in three phases of work. The first phase is focused on group formation and helping the group determine what they want to learn. Once members have established a guiding research question, in the second phase they determine the best methods to use and collect data. In the third phase, members plan a culminating event to share what they have learned with their neighbors and seed further action.

Concerned about fractured social ties and a loss of place-history in their community, one project collected oral histories, photographs, and artifacts and brought long-term and newer residents together at an interactive exhibition to learn from and about one another—and about their shared neighborhood. About 50 people came through the community center over the course of the 2-hour event, perusing materials, adding to a neighborhood timeline, and visiting with others. In an area where many residents feel like their neighborhood is changing without them, the event created space for long-term residents to see their place-history affirmed.

Another team was most concerned about the development-fueled displacement in their community and used the research process to educate themselves—and their neighbors—about ways to fight back. They produced a short video featuring interviews with neighbors to help activate the community and a report and comic strip explaining how residents can have a voice in the zoning process. Their culminating community event featured a showing of the film, the release of the report, and a social-action fair where attendees could connect with various organizations working against displacement. Members were very pleased with the turnout at the event, as well as the press coverage, which dramatically increased the reach of their project.

The third team centered their project on a local high school and countered the persistent stigmatization of the school with a feature-length documentary. Integrating more than 30 interviews and archival data, the film examines the ways that school segregation, busing, neighborhood disinvestment, White flight, and now gentrification have impacted perceptions of the school over time; it also invites neighbors to be part of shaping a different future for the school and community. More than 100 people, predominantly alumni and current students, attended the initial screening and participated in an animated feedback session with the team, and the film has since been viewed by several thousand others. Much as the Just Practice framework informed the development of the Neighborhood Story Project, the intervention mirrored that process, engaging each team of residents to consider the ways context, history, meaning, and power shape their neighborhoods, and to envision the possibilities for change.

As I have explored elsewhere (Thurber, 2019), participants in the Neighborhood Story Projects overwhelmingly viewed their work as successful, believing they had produced materials and experiences that were of value to their communities as they grappled with gentrification. They also reported gaining meaningful relationships, knowledge, skill-building, and experience in collective action that can be transferred to other initiatives. Study of these outcomes, along with limitations and lessons learned, have informed the replication of the Neighborhood Story Project across Tennessee.

## Insights From the Just Practice Framework

As noted at the outset, the purpose of this reflection is not to detail the specific design elements or outcomes of the Neighborhood Story Project, but rather to make evident how the Just Practice framework informed the program development process. For the purposes of conceptual clarity, in the preceding sections I teased apart the five Just Practice concepts and examined each in turn. In practice, the process was much more integrated. The Just Practice framework offered an orientation to practice that guided my exploration of how best to leverage my skills and resources in partnership with others to address a pressing community need.

Applying the Just Practice framework slowed me down. Faced with the urgency of many social problems, it is all too easy for practitioners to rush past or through the assessment phase, to prematurely diagnose community needs, and to unnecessarily narrow our interventions. In our haste we often reach for quick fixes, do what we have done before, or attempt to replicate the first decent-looking model we find online. The Just Practice framework encouraged me to look for multiple sources of knowledge: history texts and neighborhood elders, academic articles and meeting minutes, letters to the editor and conversations on street corners. It deepened my analysis of the problem, allowing me to understand the historic forces that shape the contours of the affordable housing crisis and to make sense of the intersections of race, place, and power in the city. Importantly, the Just Practice framework helped me to see the already existing resources in the city, particularly the many residents who were dedicated to their neighborhoods and determined to protect their communities. Ultimately, the Just Practice framework led me to imagine an intervention that might support and mobilize those residents to effect change within their own gentrifying neighborhoods and then to partner with my neighbors to see that possibility into action.

## QUESTIONS FOR REFLECTIONS AND DISCUSSION

Consider the place where you live.

1. How and what have you learned about the place where you live? What sources of information do you draw on? What and whose histories do you know, and not know?
2. What do you consider the most pressing issue where you live? Who or what is doing the pressing, and who or what is getting pressed? How do you know?
3. What resources already exist to address this issue? What is already being done, or has been done, to address this? What informal resources could be leveraged in the future? Where is additional resource most needed?
4. Begin to imagine a new community-based intervention to address the pressing issue you have identified. What form might an intervention take? What might be key elements of a program, initiative, or event designed to address this issue?
5. As a community-based practitioner, is there a particular population whose needs or perspectives you hope to center, whose voices you hope to amplify, whose power you would hope to build, through this intervention? What might this look like in practice?

## RESOURCE

- To learn more about the Neighborhood Story Project, visit the Humanities Tennessee website: https://www.humanitiestennessee.org/programs-grants/core-program-overview/neighborhoodstoryproject/.

## REFERENCES

Cannon, C. (2015, December 9). *Nashville group holds candlelight vigil before affordable housing meeting*. NewsChannel 5 Network. http://www.newschannel5.com/news/group-concerned-with-affordable-housing-options-in-nashville-holds-candlelight-vigil-before-meeting

Finn, J. (2020). *Just practice: A social justice approach to social work* (4th ed.). Oxford University Press.

Freeman, L. (2005). Displacement or succession? Residential mobility in gentrifying neighborhoods. *Urban Affairs Review, 40*(4), 463–491.

Garrison, J. (2015, October 29). New Barry office focuses on affordable housing, workforce. *The Tennessean*. http://www.tennessean.com/story/news/politics/2015/10/29/barry-office-focused-affordable-housing-workforce/74797504/

Garrison, J. (2017, February 7). Nashville affordable housing law under threat in Tennessee legislature. *The Tennessean*. https://www.tennessean.com/story/news/2017/02/10/nashville-affordable-housing-law-under-threat-tennessee-legislature/97744608/

Glass, R. L. (1964). *London: Aspects of change* (Vol. 3). MacGibbon & Kee.

Houston, B. (2012). *The Nashville way: Racial etiquette and the struggle for social justice in a southern city*. University of Georgia Press.

Kotkin, J., & Shires, M. (2015, June 4). The best cities for jobs in 2015. *Forbes*. www.forbes.com/sites/joelkotkin/2015/06/04/the-best-cities-for-jobs-2015/#8dbc92c7fa97

Kreyling, C. (2005). *The plan of Nashville: Avenues to a great city.* Vanderbilt University Press.

Lees, L. (2007). A reappraisal of gentrification: Towards a "geography of gentrification." *Progress in Human Geography, 24*(3), 389–408.

Lovett, B. L. (1999). *The African-American history of Nashville, Tennessee, 1780–1930: Elites and dilemmas.* University of Arkansas Press.

Lowe, E. T., Poubelle, A., Thomas, G., Batko, S., & Layton, J. (2016). *The U.S. Conference of Mayors' report on hunger and homelessness.* United States Conference of Mayors. https://endhomelessness.atavist.com/mayorsreport2016

Metropolitan Social Services. (2016). *2016 community needs evaluation.* http://www.nashville.gov/Portals/0/SiteContent/SocialServices/docs/cne/2016FullCNEfinal.pdf

Moskowitz, P. E. (2017). *How to kill a city: Gentrification, inequality, and the fight for the neighborhood.* Nation Books.

Office of the Mayor. (2017). *Housing Nashville report.* https://www.nashville.gov/Portals/0/SiteContent/MayorsOffice/AffordableHousing/Housing%20Nashville%20FINAL.pdf

Sharf, S. (2018, February 28). Full list: America's fastest-growing cities 2018. *Forbes.* https://www.forbes.com/sites/samanthasharf/2018/02/28/full-list-americas-fastest-growing-cities-2018/?sh=741bd17e7feb

Severson, K. (2013, January 8). Nashville's latest hit could be the city itself. *The New York Times.* http://www.nytimes.com/2013/01/09/us/nashville-takes-its-turn-in-the-spotlight.html?_r=0

Sichko, A. (2019, April 9). Boom! Metro approves record-smashing amount of construction. *Nashville Business Journal.* https://www.bizjournals.com/nashville/news/2019/04/09/boom-metro-approves-record-smashing-amount-of.html

Smith, D. (2016, February 26). *Suspensions are down in Nashville schools, but racial disparity persists. Nashville Public Radio.* http://nashvillepublicradio.org/post/suspensions-are-down-nashville-schools-racial-disparity-persists#stream/0

Thurber, A. (2017). Keeping more than homes: A more than material framework for understanding and intervening in gentrifying neighborhoods. In J. Clark & N. Wise (Eds.), *Urban Renewal, Community and Participation—Theory, Policy and Practice* (pp. 24–43). Springer. https://doi.org/10.1007/978-3-319-72311-2

Thurber, A. (2019). The Neighborhood Story Project: A practice model for fostering place attachments, social ties, and collective action. *Journal of Prevention and Intervention, 49*(1). https://doi.org/10.1080/10852352.2019.1633072

Thurber, A., Collins, L., Greer, M., McKnight, D., & Thompson, D. (2018). Resident experts: The potential of critical participatory action research to inform public housing research and practice. *Action Research Journal.* Advance online publication. https://doi.org/10.1177/1476750317725799

Thurber, A., Gupta, J., Fraser, J., & Perkins, D. (2014). *Equitable development: Promising practices to maximize affordability and minimize displacement in Nashville's urban core.* https://www.nashville.gov/Portals/0/SiteContent/Planning/docs/NashvilleNext/BackgroundReports/Housing_Gentrification_EquitableDevelopment_report.pdf

Trageser, S. (2015, November 13). Aerial Development Group vs. East Nashville: The push to rebrand, develop, and the push against. *The Nashville Scene.* http://www.nashvillescene.com/pitw/archives/2015/11/13/aerial-development-group-vs-east-nashville-the-push-to-rebrand-and-develop-and-the-push-against

Vigdor, J. L., Massey, D. S., & Rivlin, A. M. (2002). Does gentrification harm the poor? [With comments]. *Brookings-Wharton Papers on Urban Affairs*, 133–182.

# 10

# Practicing Social Justice Work in Refugee Resettlement

JEN BARILE, MSW, AND JESSE LITTMAN, MSW

> For me and my family, Missoula, and Montana in general, has not been a mere place to live in. Rather, it has been like a home to us here in the U.S. as the people there always made us feel as part of their wonderful community.
> —Mushtaq Alrashidany, who arrived in Missoula as a refugee in 2017[1]

---

**Overview**

In this chapter Jen Barile and Jesse Littman describe their work as resettlement director and caseworker, respectively, with a local office of the International Rescue Committee (IRC). They explore questions of meaning and power regarding access to housing, employment, health care, and social services for people of refugee status. They speak to the importance of history and the role of the IRC in community education around the histories of trauma that refugees have experienced. They address capacities of both refugees and community partners in crafting a sense of home. They show how engagement, teaching-learning, accompaniment, critical reflection, and celebration play out in their work.

---

## Introduction

On August 19, 2016, a family of six from the war-torn Democratic Republic of Congo (DRC) arrived in Missoula, Montana. They had been living in a refugee camp in Tanzania for many years, and all four children had been born there. They had waited almost 3 years to be resettled to a country like the United States where

---

[1] Quote from a letter to the editor of the *Missoulian* written by Alrashidany, November 18, 2019.

they would begin their new lives. The exhausted family was met at the airport by fresh-faced staff members and volunteers from the newly opened International Rescue Committee (IRC) Missoula office. We all shared a sense of trepidation and hope on this momentous day. Although we were unsure where this new journey would take us, we were committed to accompanying one another and learning side by side as we crafted a sense of home and belonging in Missoula. In this chapter, we introduce ourselves, present a brief history of the IRC in Missoula, and show how the Just Practice framework (Finn, 2020) informs our work.

## Meet the Authors: Jen's and Jesse's Stories

Jen and Jesse have been with IRC–Missoula since its inception. We are both White women and U.S. citizens. While we are both conversant in Spanish, neither of us speaks the first languages of those who comprise our new refugee communities. Jen joined IRC–Missoula as the caseworker in 2016, providing services and support to Missoula's newly arrived refugee families. In 2017, Jen became the resettlement director, managing the IRC team and programs. Prior to joining the IRC staff, Jen had been a child welfare social worker and a housing advocate with a local faith-based social justice organization. Although Jen had over 15 years of experience as a social worker before coming to the IRC, she found that welcoming refugees to a community that had not resettled refugees for years proved to be both challenging and rewarding in unique ways.

Jesse joined the IRC as an MSW practicum student in August 2016. After 8 months, she became the caseworker. Jesse picks up each family from the airport, ensures that families are connected to services, and is their main liaison for health, education, public benefits, personal documentation, and general support. Jesse is now the immigration legal representative and helps families with green card applications, family reunification, and travel documents.

## IRC Comes to Missoula

In 2015, the world watched in horror as Alan Kurdi, a young Syrian refugee child, drowned in the Mediterranean Sea as he and his family were trying to reach Greece by boat. For many, this devastating image brought much needed attention to the global refugee crisis. In Missoula, Montana, this image was a catalyst for action that sparked the formation of Soft Landing Missoula, a nonprofit organization established to support the resettlement process and the work of the IRC. Through their determined advocacy and consciousness-raising work over the course of the year, Soft Landing was successful in petitioning for an IRC office to reopen in Missoula.

Missoula had been home to Montana's refugee resettlement program in the late 1970s and 1980s when Hmong people from Laos were forced to flee their war-torn homelands. During this time, hundreds of Hmong refugees were resettled to Missoula by the IRC. When the original IRC office closed in 1991, it would be another 25 years before Montana would again participate in the U.S. Refugee Admissions Program.

Since August 2016, over 346 newcomers have resettled in Missoula from the DRC, Eritrea, Syria, and Iraq. The IRC office has grown from a staff of two to five full-time staff, MSW practicum students, Americorps leaders, and hundreds of trained volunteers. IRC staff work intensively with newly arrived individuals and families during their first few months in their new community. We support families in securing housing and employment, receiving economic assistance, getting medical care, enrolling children in school, learning English, and getting familiar with the social, cultural, legal, political, and geographic contexts of life in a mid-sized U.S. college town.

Resettling refugees to Missoula brought with it many questions. Would employers hire refugees who spoke little English? Would landlords rent to people with no rental or credit history? How would parents communicate with their children's teachers at school? Over the years, IRC and our community partners have worked hard to put infrastructure in place and reduce barriers for refugees resettling to Missoula. We accompany the people we serve in order to best meet their needs. Our programming continues to expand, and we have partnered with various agencies to offer financial literacy, advanced job placement, higher education assistance, and summer camp opportunities. In November 2019 our office became accredited by the Department of Justice (DOJ) to provide immigration services. Jesse is a DOJ-accredited representative who assists clients in applying for permanent residency, family reunification, and travel documents. As our office capacity has grown, we continue to engage the refugee population to express their voices on future programs with the goal of creating a refugee advisory board to empower refugee individuals in making the changes they wish to see in their community. In the remainder of this chapter, we bring the key concepts of Just Practice to bear in highlighting the work of IRC and provide examples to show how we enact Just Practice processes in our work.

## Considering Meaning, Power, Context, History, and Possibility

### MEANING

It was not until the Refugee Act of 1980 that the United States established a robust refugee resettlement program. Central to the 1980 law was the adoption of the definition of "refugee" from the United Nations' Protocol Relating to the Status of Refugees:

> The term "refugee" means any person . . . who is unable or unwilling to return to, and is unable or unwilling to avail himself or herself of the protection of, that country because of persecution or a well-founded fear

of persecution on account of race, religion, nationality, membership in a particular social group, or political opinion." (Ciment, 2001, p. 1313)

Adoption of the definition marked the first time that human rights language was used in a U.S. immigration bill, heralding a fresh approach to welcoming foreigners of all backgrounds. An intrinsic meaning to this designation is that the United States would be the new and safe home for persecuted peoples. By welcoming refugees to our communities, we would be welcoming them into our schools, our places of work and worship, our families, and our social circles. How this definition and subsequent programming has played out in reality varies across communities and political lines. In Missoula, the outpouring of support for refugees was louder and stronger than the opposition. Missoulians of all ages signed up to attend volunteer trainings to be a part of mentor teams assigned to new arriving families. Donations of bikes, clothes, and furniture poured in, and the city of Missoula passed a resolution declaring Missoula a Welcoming City in August 2016, as the city's first refugee families began to arrive.

Even though the community by and large supported refugee resettlement, the larger structural realities of life in Montana have posed challenges for families calling Missoula home. Missoula is a predominantly White and monolingual community in a relatively rural state. There are no ethnic food markets or ethnic community-based organizations that are common in larger cities. We do not have a mosque or Eritrean Orthodox church, and the majority of Missoulians do not speak any of the languages of our refugee families. Language was, and remains, a huge barrier, making communication and navigating resources difficult. Complex information on topics such as health insurance and rental agreements are explained via interpreters, but some of these concepts are new to some and can take hours to explain. The comfort of language and food have a strong impact on the meaning one can attribute to a place. In this way, refugees have had to make new meaning of their new homes in more ways than just moving to a new city. They are forging new associations with the aromas and sounds of Missoula and trying to form a safe space that they can truly call home.

Resettlement is not a linear process. It takes more than just a welcoming community to alleviate the stresses and painful adjustments refugees have to make when they come to the United States. As practitioners in the field of refugee resettlement, it is key to acknowledge the various forms of meaning making each party attributes to fostering a sense of home and also to understand the diverse social and cultural fabrics of the community and their role in providing a welcoming and safe space for refugee resettlement.

## POWER

Refugees come from deeply disempowering circumstances. Whether they hail from Eritrea, Syria, Iraq, or the DRC, refugees experience loss of homeland, access to land resources, education, and economic opportunity. Once they arrive in the

United States, the process of refugee resettlement itself exposes differences in power and can create a feeling of powerlessness for many. For example, many refugees we work with do not speak fluent English, making them dependent upon IRC staff members to help them make important decisions that affect their lives. The IRC team works hard to help refugees get their power back, taking the time to explain, in their native language, all of the complexities of adjusting to life in the United States. Even though barriers such as language can make it hard for refugees to exercise their power, the people who have resettled to Missoula have made tremendous strides in this area. For example, some of the Congolese families have started their own religious congregation to help preserve their culture for themselves and their children. Some have continued their education, learning English and going to college.

IRC is dedicated to an empowerment approach. However, we have learned that accompaniment must go hand in hand with empowerment as interdependent processes. Since many of our clients were not able to complete paperwork or schedule their own appointments due to language barriers, it was up to us to accompany them through these daunting initial processes and ensure they had access to resources and services. As social workers, we learn how to "do with" instead of "do for," in order to empower our clients. For example, completing a childcare scholarship application for a family with the help of an interpreter can take quite some time. It requires explanation of concepts such as co-payments, rights and responsibilities, and terms and conditions. It can be tempting to complete this paperwork on behalf of a client in order to save time. But to do so denies opportunities for teaching, learning, and building relationships. In order to assist refugees in gaining power over their lives, it is important that we provide means to ensure their full participation in all facets of resettlement so that they can successfully navigate their new circumstances.

## CONTEXT

Questions of power are intimately linked to those of context. As mentioned above, Missoula is a predominantly White, monolingual community in the Rocky Mountain West. The summer sunshine that greeted the first arrivals in 2016 is offset by long, harsh winters for which few newcomers are prepared. There was, however, a warm and welcoming social and political context in Missoula with strong support from the mayor as IRC opened its doors. Faith-based organizations, advocacy groups, and committed community members came together to support the cause. At the same time, a broader context of resistance and critique was occurring. Some politicians were using resettlement as a pawn during election campaigns, demonizing refugees, and admonishing their opponents for bringing "terrorists" to Montana. On the national level, the rhetoric was similar. During the 2016 presidential election, refugees and other immigrants became the target of political attack, influencing sentiment in Montana in regard to refugee resettlement.

Only a few months after the IRC–Missoula office opened, a new president was elected, and immigration policy began to change rapidly. The Trump administration started to implement travel bans, barring refugees and other immigrants from certain countries or faiths from entering the United States. In early 2017, there was also a temporary ban on all refugee resettlement to the United States for 120 days. To date, U.S immigration policy continues to turn its back on refugees, impacting the fragile contexts of safety and belonging that we are trying to nurture with the individuals and families we serve.

## HISTORY

There are currently 79.5 million forcibly displaced people worldwide, including 26 million refugees and 45.7 million internally displaced people (United Nations High Commissioner for Refugees, 2020). This population grows ever larger as civil war continues to rage in Syria and competing factions continue to displace thousands of individuals and families across the globe. It is estimated that 37,000 people are forcibly displaced every day as a result of conflict or persecution (United Nations High Commissioner for Refugees, 2019). While ever expanding, this global humanitarian crisis is not new to the world. Before the term "refugee" was even used in state language, displaced persons have historically fled war-torn and starvation-stricken countries to survive. As the political climate in the United States shifts toward more xenophobic attitudes, it is important to reflect on the laws and policies that have governed immigration and refugee affairs in the United States.

As a young nation, the United States encouraged immigration, and there were few barriers for newcomers who wished to settle in America. While there was fear among colonists that "the new immigrants' differences in speech, customs and antecedents would disturb the cultural unity of the American people" (President's Commission, 1953, p. 84), the fear was not great enough to stop the 750,000 immigrants who arrived from 1600 to 1770. Acceptance rather than a dissuasion of immigrants was the guiding force in the United States. By the 1800s, however, the United States turned to more restrictive policies, grounded in ideologies of White supremacy and concerns about those who could become an economic burden. By the early 1900s the country began to employ quota systems based on national origin, literacy tests, and other means to exclude those deemed "undesirable" (Cho et al., 2004).

Throughout the push and pull of U.S. immigration history, a common thread across generations is the issue of "self-sufficiency" and the "dangers" of a dependent population. The Immigration Act of 1882 first codified these fears by allowing authorized persons to board a ship and conduct examinations of the immigrants onboard. If officials found "any convict, lunatic, idiot, or any person unable to take care of himself or herself without becoming a public charge" (Immigration Act, 1882), they would have the authority to deny said person to land. The fear of immigrants becoming "public charges" remains very much a focal point of political argument today. The Trump administration made "public charge," or the receipt of certain government health, housing, and nutrition programs, a ground of inadmissibility, making it difficult or impossible for certain immigrant groups to obtain a green card, visa, or entry to the United States. In a White House press briefing discussing the public charge rule, Acting Director of USCIS Ken Cuccinelli, said that the government has

> issued a rule that encourages and ensures self-reliance and self-sufficiency for those seeking to come to, or to stay in, the United States. It will also help promote immigrant success in the United States as they seek opportunity here. Throughout our history, self-reliance has been a core principle in America. The virtues of perseverance, hard work, and self-sufficiency laid the foundation of our nation and have defined generations of immigrants seeking opportunity in the United States. (White House, 2019)

This justification echoes the sentiments of the Immigration Act of 1882 and illustrates the fraught history the United States has with immigration. This historic focus on self-sufficiency continues to the present as a primary objective required by refugee resettlement programs. To arrive in the United States, a refugee is allocated to a refugee resettlement agency such as the IRC. In turn, that agency is given federal funding to spend on the refugee's behalf within the first 90 days of arrival. This money is primarily used to secure housing, pay for a deposit (usually a double deposit due to a lack of credit and rental history), and hopefully cover a couple months of rent and costs of basic home furnishings. Refugees are also provided with a cell phone and pocket money for minor discretionary expenses when they first arrive. This federal funding is a one-time grant, and the expectation is that after 90 days a refugee is fully self-sufficient. Of course, the reality is much different. Refugees, like other low-income people, have to navigate complex bureaucratic systems to seek support and attempt to cover high costs of housing and health care while working jobs that may not pay a living wage. They also face significant language and cultural barriers. In sum, these long-standing attachments to the value of self-sufficiency continue to pose challenges for justice-oriented practice today.

At IRC, we have also turned to history as a tool for consciousness raising. Discrimination on the basis of race, ethnicity, and national origin has deep roots in U.S. immigration policy. Understanding the workings of quota systems and other restrictive policies from the past provides an important context for practice in the present. In developing our volunteer training, for example, we have actively incorporated lessons in immigration policy history to ensure that volunteers have a critical understanding of this history and its role in shaping public attitudes and sentiments regarding people of refugee status.

## Possibility

Looking back to 2016 when our office first opened, it feels good to reflect on how much we have learned and how far we have come. We have expanded staff and programming to support clients' needs, and yet there still is so much more we want to accomplish. We aim to offer more support to families in the areas of financial literacy and digital inclusion. We want to grow our workforce programming so that refugees can obtain better jobs. One year from now, the first round of arrivals to Missoula will be able to apply for naturalization to become U.S. citizens. We look forward to this exciting milestone, where refugees will be able to vote and become elected officials.

Fortunately, the IRC can provide additional case management for families beyond the first 90 days, and we rely on a myriad of community organizations to further support families in achieving both inter- and independence in their new community. For example, the local adult learning center offers free English as a second language (ESL) classes every day. As Missoula has continued to resettle more refugees, the center has expanded its curriculum and now offers vocational English classes, computer classes, and citizenship preparation classes.

We have also seen growth in the capacity of the local job service, which now has access to translation services and can serve not only refugees, but any non-English speaker who asks for help. The local public schools have hired local interpreters to help translate documents that go home with students and to interpret during parent-teacher conferences. As the IRC has grown in staff and capacity and the number of refugees continues to grow, so have social service agencies in Missoula increased their ability to serve refugees and non-English speakers.

During this process of program development and growth, we have also developed our commitment to cultural humility, which is the acknowledgment of the limitations of our knowledge and recognition of the unconscious stereotypes we employ in attempting to understand or explain cultural difference (Finn, 2020, p. 60). In acknowledging the limits of one's knowledge about another's reality, it is possible for new ways of knowing and seeing to emerge and productive dialogue to flow. This practice has led the IRC to pursue creating a refugee advisory board to help ensure that the programs we implement and the policies of other agencies best represent the needs of the clients we serve. Their voices must shape the roadmap and guide the future of refugee programming in Missoula.

On a larger scale, we hope to see U.S. immigration policy changes that allow more refugees to enter the United States, enabling families to be reunited with loved ones and to offer safety to those fleeing violence and persecution. With the creation of IRC's refugee advisory board, we hope that our clients reclaim their power to have more influence over the way resettlement occurs in Missoula. As we learn and do this work together, we hope to foster a sense of belonging for refugees in Missoula.

## IRC and the Processes of Just Practice

We highlight here some of the ways in which Just Practice processes of engagement, teaching-learning, action and accompaniment, critical reflection, evaluation, and celebration guide our work at IRC. In our work, *engagement* happens at many different levels. At the individual level, we engage with refugees daily, walking alongside them to support their needs. We welcome families at the airport, visit them in their homes, share food with them, and listen as they share their hopes and dreams. At the community level, we engage with partners in a collaborative way, bringing diverse stakeholders to the table to share successes and troubleshoot challenges. Together we set the stage for teaching-learning by sharing resources and educating the community about refugee resettlement. More recently, we have engaged with the University of Montana, balancing the interest in student community engagement and service-learning projects with education about refugee rights and the importance of nonintrusive, refugee-led approaches to interaction. We are also engaging people of refugee status themselves in this work as partners, staff members, interpreters, and community leaders.

As a small office of five full-time staff, it is imperative that we collaborate with and learn from other experts in the community to ensure a cohesive delivery of services. It can be frustrating at times when some in the community fail to appreciate the unique needs and strengths of our clients. However, as social workers we meet people where they are. This includes communities as well. Therefore, we often assume the role of teacher-learners in the broader community, sharing accounts of refugee experiences, educating others about the systems and support already in place, and continually learning how our organization can best utilize existing resources to engage our clients and the public in resettlement.

A teacher-learner perspective opens a space for co-learning where "the social worker and other participants in the process come together to share knowledge, pose questions, seek out new information, develop critical awareness of the situation, assess needs, strengths, and resources, and draw on their collective wisdom to inform action" (Finn, 2020, p. 223). This approach is fundamental to work with refugee clients. We are constantly learning from our clients. They teach us to see the world differently, which helps us provide a higher level of support and advocacy. For example, upon arrival, refugee clients may not know how to ride the bus, use a phone, or operate the stove or toilet in their house. While we teach them how to do these activities, it is through their lens that we hope to approach each activity. Our clients teach us what it looks like for them to prepare food, get to appointments, or communicate with family. Through our interactions we learn together and are better able to help one another make sense of how things work in this new community context.

Accompaniment is a core part of our practice at IRC and a key facet of our empowerment approach. In its most elemental sense, accompaniment means simply to walk alongside someone. For example, a lot of Jesse's work involves accompanying individuals and families to a variety of appointments. Sitting with someone at the Social Security office may not in itself sound like a very important thing to do. However, sitting at the Social Security office and watching refugee children interact and play with other children despite cultural and linguistic boundaries is in a way building a bridge across differences. Witnessing positive and encouraging interactions between providers and families and being there to validate those experiences is instrumental in creating a welcoming space. The immensity of new experiences confronting each family in their first 30 days is shocking. Not only are they grappling with the trauma of leaving everything they know behind, they are also expected to understand and grasp the nuances of American life. By sitting with a family as they wait for the doctor, sharing coffee with them in their home, or walking with them to the bus stop, we are showing a commitment to being part of their journey here in the United States.

Taking time to critically reflect on the work that we do is crucial to our success. One way we do this is by creating intentional space for reflection during our staff meetings. After each staff member gives their weekly update, we each share a story about connection. This can be an instance where we felt connected to our clients, to each other, or to our work in general. Setting aside this structured time to reflect reminds us to pause and remember why we do this work. Sometimes it can be hard to see the big picture when we are bogged down in the day-to-day logistics, and reflecting helps us to focus on what is really important. When we convene with our community partners, this is also a time for us to reflect on challenges and lessons learned, and we can share that knowledge with each other.

Evaluation and assessment are also important aspects of the work that we do. It is important for us, in this new office in a community new to refugee resettlement, to understand what we are doing well and what we can do better. In 2019, IRC partnered with the University of Montana social work faculty to form a research team that included representatives from the different refugee communities who have resettled in Missoula. This team worked together to create a community-based participatory research project in which a survey was developed and administered to all refugee adults living in Missoula. This project enabled us to get a better sense of what the resettlement experience has been like for the people we serve, and it gave us invaluable information about how the IRC and our community partners could be better attuned to the needs and strengths of our newest neighbors. One of the main themes that emerged from this research was the desire of our clients to have a greater voice in decision-making processes. Hence, the IRC–Missoula Refugee Advisory Board was born. This survey also enabled us to create a baseline of data so that we can more accurately measure our program outcomes moving forward.

Finally, we love to celebrate at IRC. Every year since we opened our doors in August 2016 we have had an anniversary and a holiday party. We invite every refugee family and our community partners and volunteers to join in the celebration. We see these gatherings as a way to express our joy and gratitude to the families and to the Missoula community for their graciousness and resiliency. It is a way for us to all come together to do something that blends and bridges cultural and linguistic diversity. We come together and we dance and sing and eat. And it does not matter that we do not speak the same language or listen to the same music. In these moments we are celebrating our common humanity and the hope we all have for Missoula and our continued desire to welcome refugees to this community.

## QUESTIONS FOR REFLECTION AND DISCUSSION

1. What do you know about the history of refugee resettlement in your community or state? Where might you turn to learn more?
2. What challenges and opportunities have you encountered in working across linguistic and cultural differences in your social work practice? What lessons have you learned?
3. What lessons can you draw from this chapter regarding the interplay of personal struggles and public policies?
4. Take time to consider the notion of "self-sufficiency." How has it become so central to discourses and policies regarding social and economic support in the United States? How might a focus on self-sufficiency limit our ability to imagine other possibilities for interdependence and social responsibility?
5. The IRC–Missoula office is celebrating 5 years in existence. If you were asked to help the IRC create a vision and plan for the next 5 years, how would you proceed?

## ADDITIONAL RESOURCES

To learn more about the work of IRC, visit their website at https://www.rescue.org/.

For perspectives from an IRC caseworker, visit this link: https://www.rescue.org/displaced-season-2/refugee-resettlement-perspectives-irc-caseworker.

Further accounts of displacement and resettlement can be accessed through the IRC podcast series titled *Displaced*: https://www.rescue.org/displaced.

## REFERENCES

Cho, E., Paz y Puente, F., Louie, M., & Khokha, S. (2004). *Bridges: Building a race and immigration dialogue in a global economy*. National Network for Immigrant and Refugee Rights.

Ciment, J. (2001). Refugee Act 1980. In *Encyclopedia of American Immigration* (Vol. 4, pp. 1313–1314). Sharpe Reference.

Finn, J. (2020). *Just practice: A social justice approach to social work* (4th ed). Oxford University Press.

Immigration Act of 1882. (1882). Act of August 3, 1882 (22 Stat. 214; 8 U.S.C.).

President's Commission on Immigration and Naturalization. (1953). *Whom we shall welcome*. U.S. Government Printing Office.

United Nations High Commissioner for Refugees (2019). *Global trends: Forced displacement in 2018*. https://www.unhcr.org/5d08d7ee7.pdf

United Nations High Commissioner for Refugees (2020, June 18). (2020) *Figures at a glance*. https://www.unhcr.org/en-us/figures-at-a-glance.html

White House. (2019). Press briefing by USCIS acting director Ken Cuchinelli [Press briefing]. https://www.whitehouse.gov/briefings-statements/press-briefing-uscis-acting-director-ken-cuccinelli-081219/

Part Three

# INTEGRATING SOCIAL JUSTICE IN SCHOOL SETTINGS

# 11

# Just Practice and Restorative Justice in Schools

JEN MOLLOY, MSW, PHD

> I think that's probably where [restorative justice] has been most beneficial . . . there's space now to humanize, not just the people within the system, but the system itself.
> —School administrator

---

**Overview**

In this chapter Jen Molloy reflects on her work with educators to implement a restorative justice approach in an alternative high school through the lens of Just Practice. Molloy engaged educators in exploring meanings of education, discipline, and restorative justice; considering their histories within the school; and examining the school as a context of support and resistance. Molloy addresses the tensions in implementing restorative justice and the importance of critical reflection on these tensions. As educators deepened their dialogue about the meaning of education and the history of power relations in the school, they discovered possibilities for changing the culture and practices of the school.

---

## Introduction

This case study shows how the Just Practice framework (Finn, 2020) can guide social work practice in schools seeking to implement restorative justice. It derives from a research project I implemented in partnership with an alternative high school in a midsized U.S. city in the Intermountain West. The goal was to understand the process of implementing restorative justice, including how educators learned, practiced, and responded to the shift in mindset. I give a brief history of restorative justice philosophy and practice, describe the school context in which we implemented the approach, and examine questions of meaning and power that played out in the process. I show how I brought processes of Just Practice to bear along the way. I close with reflection on the challenges and possibilities of implementing and sustaining restorative justice in schools.

## Schools and Discipline

Schools are complex systems, and social work practice in schools involves engagement with diverse stakeholders to tackle the social problems that interfere with students' ability to learn and thrive, including poverty, violence, racism, homelessness, abuse, and substance use. School social workers' overarching goal is to give all children the opportunities and resources to help them succeed academically and socially in a safe and healthy school environment. They support students contending with interpersonal challenges, struggles with belonging and difference, and ramifications of harmful disciplinary approaches. Exclusionary and punitive discipline practices and policies (i.e., suspension, expulsion, referral to law enforcement) are used disproportionately with some groups of students more than others, particularly Indigenous students, students of color, and students with disabilities (ACLU, 2018). Students who miss school as a result are less likely to graduate and more likely to become entangled in the criminal justice system (U.S. Commission on Civil Rights, 2019). These traditional behavior management approaches are deficit-based, punitive, and antithetical to social work values. The philosophy and practices known as "restorative justice" have gained attention as an alternative to harsh school discipline and as an approach for building community within the school environment. School social workers can play instrumental roles in promoting, developing, implementing, and evaluating restorative justice in schools.

## What Is Restorative Justice in Schools?

In educational settings, restorative justice includes equal emphasis on three components: building and maintaining relationships; repairing harm and transforming conflict; and creating just and equitable learning environments (Evans & Vaandering, 2016). Restorative justice is not a particular tool or program; it is a mindset or paradigm that guides interactions in the school environment that are rooted in values of respect, dignity, and mutual concern. Implementing restorative justice requires a culture shift in which relationships are prioritized over rules. It involves both proactive efforts to build a sense of community in the school as well as responsive efforts to constructively address conflict and harmful behavior. Examples of restorative practices used in schools include community-building circles, restorative questioning, and restorative conferencing. Community-building circles bring students in a classroom together in a talking circle to build relationships and develop communication skills. Restorative questioning entails question-posing after an incident of harm or conflict so students can learn from it and have an opportunity to process their thoughts and feelings. Restorative conferencing is a more formal process which brings a student who has caused harm together with the person harmed in a facilitated dialogue to discuss the impact of the behavior and consider ways to repair the harm. In terms of discipline, restorative justice seeks the root causes and needs behind individual and group behaviors instead of treating the behavior as an isolated incident or a "symptom" of trouble. The goal is to shift away from punitive disciplinary practices and school cultures based on social control to embrace intentional community, co-created values, accountability for upholding shared ideals, and an overall culture based on social engagement (Morrison & Vaandering, 2012).

## Understanding the Context of School Discipline

Most of us, myself included, have been raised within a punishment-based approach to wrongdoing. This paradigm is built into our institutions of education, through the patterned ways of speaking about and relating to students and the everyday ways in which values and assumptions translate into practice. For example, when a student breaks a school rule, the traditional response focuses on determining which rule has been violated, who is to blame, and what punishment to institute, which often results in isolation or exclusion of the student. Absent is a deeper exploration of root causes and needs or ways to resolve the issue and work toward a positive outcome for everyone affected. This process often places students in a very passive stance and teaches students that unless punished for behavior, it is not a problem. It does not teach students ways to problem solve, take accountability, or live in community. Further, these practices can also generate defiance, undermining students' sense of belonging and capacity to engage in the school community. Finally, these disciplinary practices are associated with negative short- and long-term consequences, such as student and teacher perceptions of a negative climate (Steinberg, Allensworth, & Johnson, 2015); reduced academic achievement and engagement (Perry & Morris, 2014); and juvenile justice involvement (Fabelo et al., 2011).

Teachers and administrators are asked to address bullying, violence, and other disruptive behavior; however, we must acknowledge that, as human beings, they see and interpret the behavior of their students through the prism of race, culture, and class. We all have implicit biases, and without critical reflection and intentional efforts to remain unbiased, Indigenous students, students of color, and students with disabilities experience punitive and exclusionary discipline at increased rates, oftentimes for less serious behavior than their White peers (Fabelo et al., 2011). These are highly contextualized social interactions, in which punishment becomes a reflexive response to perceived wrongdoing, and relatedly, not punishing becomes equated with doing nothing at all or "being easy on kids."

The implementation of a restorative philosophy demands, in most educational institutions, a major shift in thinking about discipline, its purpose, and practice. A school's underlying understanding of the purpose of restorative justice will determine the manner in which it goes about implementing schoolwide restorative justice. If restorative justice is implemented as another tool of social control, students may be suspended less, yet still not feel a sense of belonging or justice in the school environment. If restorative justice is implemented to support student engagement in the learning environment, systems that address misbehavior and harm will be created in a way that strengthens relationships. Administrators will develop more constructive and nurturing ways of dealing with behavior issues and classroom conflict. When implemented with fidelity to its underlying principles and values, restorative justice has been shown to decrease student misbehavior and school discipline incidents; improve school climate, culture, and safety; improve attendance and academic outcomes; and reduce racial disparities in disciplinary actions (Gregory & Clawson, 2016; Jain et al., 2014).

## Implementing Restorative Justice

In 2017, I partnered with an alternative high school in a midsized city in the Intermountain West to help implement a restorative justice approach and to help participants make sense of the process. I was involved at the school in multiple roles, but the role that most resonates with my experience is that of a "critical friend." A critical friend is "a trusted person who asks provocative questions, provides data to be examined through another lens, and offers critiques of a person's work as a friend" (Costa & Kallick, 1993, p. 50). In this role, I helped the school make sound decisions based on restorative values, challenged expectations and taken-for-granted procedures, alerted the school to critical issues, and helped them shape outcomes but never determined them. School social workers are often placed in this role, at once part of the school community and apart from it. Guided by social work knowledge, skills, and values, we approach the work of schools and the treatment of students from a relational and social justice orientation, which often diverges from traditional education's emphasis on curriculum and behavior management.

I must also acknowledge my positionality when considering my role of critical friend. As a White, educated woman, I was seen as a credible source coming into the school system, although my background as a social worker set me apart from educators. I simultaneously carried the power of an academic and the deficit of having not worked in the school system. I also carried my history of working as the director of a nonprofit whose mission was to provide restorative programming for youth and victims of crime in a community setting. In this position I had witnessed the power of restorative justice to transform individuals' experience of an event, their understanding of themselves and others, and their connection to the community. At the same time, I observed systemic barriers and labeling that impacted the potential for youth to experience healing, growth, and connection.

As I entered the school, I was challenged to let go of preconceived notions of what was possible based on my experience in the community context and to remain open to the potential presented by the school context. However, as a mother of two elementary age girls, I had seen firsthand the pressures and constraints presented by our educational system. I noticed school administrators purporting to use restorative justice when they demanded apology letters from students or had them clean the lunch room in isolation. These practices did not align with my understanding of restorative justice, although they were being accepted and promoted by others as restorative acts. So, in some ways, my involvement with the school was driven by a fear that something I loved (restorative justice), and saw profound potential in, was being co-opted. As I engaged with the school community, I continually had to consider the lens I filtered our work together through. In what follows, I discuss my experience with implementing restorative justice using the core processes of engagement, teaching-learning, and critical reflection and key concepts of Just Practice.

## Engagement

First steps in engaging the school involved partnering with the principal and restorative justice coordinator to develop a whole-school restorative practices implementation plan. This process was very relational in nature and involved listening deeply to their needs, past experiences with initiatives and "outsiders," and hopes for the future of students and the school. Through these interactions, we were defining the *meaning* of the partnership, which required us to also discuss and define *power* and ownership of the process and resulting products of the research component. Given the success of our initial partnership and the mutual trust we established, the principal granted me access to spend extended time in the school, observing how community was created and how restorative justice processes were implemented and experienced by teachers, students, and administrators, as well as trials and tribulations encountered by those enacting them. In addition to observing, I had many informal conversations with students, educators, and administrators, which allowed me to build relationships with the larger school community and explore possibilities for further dialogue and action.

During this initial period of engagement, I began to understand the forms of power present in the school and to understand the power I held as a perceived "expert" on restorative justice. I was wary of being placed in the "expert" role because there was potential to further embed hierarchical power structures and potentially devalue the wisdom of school personnel. Taking this concern into consideration, I made extensive efforts to elevate educators' knowledge and experience and create opportunities for them to learn from one another. These foundational observations and interactions provided me with *context* to consider next steps as we engaged deeper in the process of teaching-learning.

I also needed to consider that implementation was taking place within the nationwide political context of heightened attention on school disciplinary action related to the school-to-prison pipeline and school safety discussions resulting from numerous school shootings (Mediratta, 2012). In the specific state where this research took place, legislation had recently passed mandating that schools use alternatives (such as restorative justice) to traditional, punitive discipline methods for certain types of offenses. This alternative high school was viewed by the school district to be at the forefront of restorative implementation efforts. Although the school was only in year 1 of implementation, and research suggests it takes 3 to 5 years to fully embed the philosophy (Thorsborne & Blood, 2013), the school was put in the position of representing the district's restorative ambitions. As such, it received news coverage and mention at statewide administrator meetings, which placed pressure on the administrators to be able to report on the process and effectiveness of implementing restorative justice.

## Teaching-Learning

Over the course of a yearlong teaching-learning process, we considered varied meanings of education, discipline, and restorative justice. We explored educator and administrator histories within the school, past experiences with student discipline, the context of the school as a site of support and resistance, and the complex life circumstances of students. These various topics were explored in relation to restorative justice theory through *embodied, cognitive, and reflective* approaches.

Embodied approaches were more experiential in nature and involved participating in restorative practices (Sodhi & Cohen, 2012). For example, faculty meetings were held in a circle—a restorative practice used for community building where many values are communicated, including respect for each voice, equality of participation, empathy and emotional literacy, self-awareness, and shared leadership. This is in contrast to most traditional faculty meetings where administrators talk at faculty who are seated lecture style and passively participate. A cognitive approach to learning restorative justice was engaged through didactic sessions, in which faculty were provided with a foundational restorative justice overview including theory, principles, and values. Reflective approaches included individual and collective inquiry into assumptions made about what is normal and appropriate, in terms of both expectations of student behavior and educator responses to misbehavior. Critical reflection often took the form of small group dialogue sessions.

Engagement in embodied approaches allowed educators to experience firsthand the emotions and bodily reactions that can occur when witnessing and sharing stories in a circle format. Responses to this approach were mixed. Some educators felt that it allowed them to get to know their colleagues better, its intention; others felt that it took too long and did not go deep enough.

I encountered some resistance from teachers regarding the cognitive approach. I hoped that by engaging in theory, educators could actively bring their own grounded knowledge to bear to inform implementation efforts. Educators, on the other hand, were reluctant to grapple with theory. Instead, some asserted that they were already "restorative" in their orientation and others pushed for me to teach concrete techniques and skills of restorative justice rather than engage with theory.

## Critical Reflection

I turned to critical reflection to help educators connect cognitive learning about the theory of restorative justice with existing classroom practices and ways of being. Using examples from their experience, we unpacked how they reacted to students and how they were bringing restorative justice tangibly into the classroom. We also reflected on the competing and contradictory demands they faced within the education system and the challenges they faced in knowing what to prioritize. Critical reflection deepened our understanding of restorative justice and also created discomfort as we recognized the need to unlearn some learned behaviors and responses. Thus, learning restorative justice required an iterative and evolving process.

Educators struggled with a shift of *meaning* from restorative justice as a practice you *do* to students and toward a more philosophical understanding of a *way of being* with students. Educators had been socialized over time into the *habitus* of education—the myriad ways of being and doing that become ingrained and that simply go without saying in the context of school (Bourdieu, 1984). Thus, they exhibited a tendency to focus on individual student behavior rather than their relationships with students. This default position also required critical reflection to bring to light. As educators began to engage in dialogue about their understanding of restorative justice, they began to question ingrained assumptions about the education system. In particular, it was challenging for them to shift from a hierarchical to a relational orientation to their work with students. They clearly cared about students; however, they saw themselves as separate from the students and their social context, and they saw restorative justice as primarily impacting student—not educator—behavior. This paradigm shift proved to be an ongoing challenge.

Educators struggled not only with historical ways of being with students, but also with ways of being with each other. Group discussions were not always easy, as perspectives varied and power was continually at play based on history between individuals, position descriptions, and level of comfort with conflict. As a result, educators grappled with interpersonal conflict and power relations.

A deeper analysis of power in the school could have been beneficial, but that would have required deeper trust among the faculty, which we had yet to build.

To truly engage in a dialogue about the changes would require risk, courage, and vulnerability. Without a safe space, facilitated by a competent facilitator, with clear guidelines for communication, educators did not want to explore further their conflicting understandings of the purpose of education and their role within it. The creation of a restorative school requires an openness to different ways of relating. It requires a culture of forgiveness, creativity, risk-taking, and relationship among adults and between adults and students that is counter to the conditioning most of us have experienced in education and the workplace. We had not yet created the conditions and relations to take our analysis of power further.

While implementation of restorative justice may suggest that we are engaging students in new practices, much of the foundational work focuses on the adults involved and their relational abilities to practice restorative justice among themselves. Over time, implementation could extend into changes in the classroom, disciplinary processes, and schoolwide community-building activities. At this point, the next steps in implementation involved assessing existing practices and relational trust. Faculty spoke to the importance of appreciating existing restorative practices occurring within the school and the need for relational trust to support the capacity to change. In many of my informal conversations and observations, I would see practices used by educators to engage students that I would label as restorative: things like noticing that a student had not been in class for a few days and inquiring, recognizing that class content was not resonating with students and engaging them in creating a solution, or addressing sleeping in class from a place of concern. These existing practices could have been used as a foundation for creating a restorative environment schoolwide. However, some educators shared that they were still struggling to identify existing restorative practices. Instead, they wanted me to teach them something specifically labeled as "restorative."

Exchanges like this made me realize that we had missed an important opportunity to unearth existing practices and to demystify the restorative approach. Further, it demonstrated the power of labeling. Educators wanted me, the expert, to label their practices as restorative or to teach them specific practices that they could label as restorative; it seemed that they did not trust themselves to do this. The critical question that arose from this apparent lack of self-confidence was what supports educators' need to take the risk—to be vulnerable enough to share their practices with each other and to be open to being critiqued when they inadvertently fall back into traditional ways of working with and having power over students.

## Evaluation

Looking back on the implementation process to evaluate what worked and what could be improved was an important part in supporting the school to create a sustainable change effort. Since evaluation is an ongoing process, we had taken time throughout the year to reflect on the implementation process; however, as the year ended we turned our attention to the importance of and questions related to evaluation of the change effort as a whole. There is debate among restorative justice advocates over which goals and associated outcomes restorative justice should aim to achieve. Some advocates emphasize outcomes such as reductions in suspensions and expulsions, while others focus more on process-oriented measures of teacher and student satisfaction. This school was in the initial stages of creating an evaluation plan and likely will collect both outcome and process-oriented measures of "success"; the goal being to see decreases in school disciplinary actions, as well as increased connection and relationships in the school community. Evaluation efforts can further enforce the creation of a just and equitable learning environment by also assessing racial and ethnic disparities in disciplinary action, experiences of bias, and other measures of social justice. Including these measures in the evaluation process is critical to eliminating unjustifiable discipline disparities and related negative educational impacts and outcomes. Further, including students in the evaluation would allow the school to better understand students' experience with and response to restorative justice.

The close of the school year also provided me with an opportunity for self-evaluation. This implementation project was intended to be a catalyst for change—for myself, as I grew to greater self-understanding in relation to restorative justice and the implementation process, and for the school, as faculty engaged in critical reflection and schoolwide transformation. While I aspired to serve as a critical friend, at times I felt placed in the expert role and that I was supposed to have the answer to challenges we faced as a team. I questioned whether these expectations were externally placed on me or if I had placed the responsibility on myself. I am not sure of the answer. By the end of the year, though, I could acknowledge that we had gotten stuck in the forest and only by stepping back could we see, honor, and celebrate the progress we had made. As a way of wrapping up our partnership, we closed the school year in a talking circle in which we took time to collectively appreciate the learning we had gained together and the possibilities for further implementation in the coming school year.

## Conclusion: Just Practice and Restorative Justice

The Just Practice framework provides a guide to critical social work with the intent of translating the concept of social justice into a concrete practice. As this case study demonstrates, the Just Practice concepts and processes are in alignment with those offered by restorative justice. As such, I would argue that restorative justice is a prime example of a social justice practice that social workers could benefit from further implementing in their practice in schools and other social service settings. Stepping out of the school context and explaining more generally, as a starting point, restorative justice requires engagement of those most intimately involved in a conflict in the process of determining how to move forward. It is only through dialogue, or teaching-learning, that a full understanding of the meaning, history, and context of an event ascribed by individuals and groups involved can be discovered. Restorative justice practices provide opportunities for individuals to reflect on how their actions and beliefs are influenced by social, political, cultural, and institutional contexts, where power is constantly being negotiated. In these processes, those involved have an opportunity to name impacts, critique injustices, take accountability, have a voice in their community and in the repair of harms, and to take action to shift their community's perspective of the needs and meaning of justice. In these ways, possibilities for transformative social change are made tangible and social workers can pursue justice-oriented practice.

## QUESTIONS FOR REFLECTION AND DISCUSSION

1. How might restorative justice be relevant to other social work settings? How would you go about implementing it in your practice setting?
2. In what ways is this school's experience with implementing a new approach relevant to change efforts in other organizations and systems?
3. In what ways does this school's implementation process resemble a process you have been involved in? How did those involved navigate the challenges that come with learning and practicing a new approach?
4. What can we learn about the role of trust in change processes from this school's experience? How can trust be built?

## RESOURCES

Implementation guides:

- Chicago Public Schools Restorative Practices Guide and Toolkit: https://blog.cps.edu/wp-content/uploads/2017/08/CPS_RP_Booklet.pdf
- Oakland Unified School District Restorative Justice Implementation Guide: A Whole School Approach: https://www.ousd.org/Page/1054

Videos demonstrating restorative practices:

- https://www.healthiersf.org/RestorativePractices/

Books related to restorative justice in education:

- Boyes-Watson, C., & Pranis, K. (2015). *Circle forward: Building a restorative school community*. Living Justice Press.
- Brown, M. A. (2018). *Creating restorative schools: Setting schools up to succeed*. Living Justice Press.
- Evans, K., & Vaandering, D. (2016). *The little book of restorative justice in education: Fostering responsibility, healing, and hope in schools*. Good Books.

## REFERENCES

ACLU. (2018). *11 million days lost: Race, discipline, and safety at U.S. public schools*. https://www.aclu.org/report/11-million-days-lost-race-discipline-and-safety-us-public-schools-part-1

Bourdieu, P. (1984). *Distinction: A social critique of the judgment of taste* (R. Nice, Trans.). Harvard University Press.

Costa, A., & Kallick, B. (1993). Through the lens of a critical friend. *Educational Leadership, 51*(2), 49–51.

Evans, K., & Vaandering, D. (2016). *The little book of restorative justice in education: Fostering responsibility, healing, and hope in schools.* Good Books.

Fabelo, T., Thompson, M. D., Plotkin, M., Carmichael, D., Marchbanks, M. P., & Booth, E. A. (2011). *Breaking schools' rules: A statewide study of how school discipline relates to student's success and juvenile justice involvement.* Council of State Governments Justice Center and Texas A&M University, Public Policy Research Institute. http://knowledgecenter.csg.org/kc/system/files/Breaking_School_Rules.pdf

Finn, J. (2020). *Just practice: A social justice approach to social work* (4th ed.). Oxford University Press.

Gregory, A., & Clawson, K. (2016). The potential of restorative approaches to discipline for narrowing racial and gender disparities. In E. Skiba, K. Mediratta, & M. K. Rausch (Eds.), *Inequality in school discipline* (pp. 153–170). Palgrave Macmillan.

Jain, S., Bassey, H., Brown, M., & Kalra, P. (2014). *Restorative justice in Oakland schools implementation and impacts: An effective strategy to reduce racially disproportionate discipline, suspensions and improve academic outcomes.* Data in Action. https://www.ousd.org/cms/lib07/CA01001176/Centricity/Domain/134/OUSD-RJ%20Report%20revised%20Final.pdf

Mediratta, K. (2012). Grassroots organizing and the school-to-prison pipeline: The emerging national movement to roll back zero tolerance discipline policies in U.S. public schools. In S. Bahena, N. Cooc, R. Currie-Rubin, P. Kuttner, & M. Ng (Eds.), *Disrupting the school-to-prison pipeline* (pp. 211–236). Harvard Education Review.

Morrison, B., & Vaandering, V. (2012). Restorative justice: Pedagogy, praxis, and discipline. *Journal of School Violence, 11*(2), 138–155.

Perry, B. L., & Morris, E. W. (2014). Suspending progress: Collateral consequences of exclusionary punishment in public schools. *American Sociological Review, 79*(6), 1067–1087. https://doi.org/10.1177/0003122414556308

Sodhi, M., & Cohen, H. (2012). The manifestation and integration of embodied knowing into social work practice. *Adult Education Quarterly, 62*(2), 120–137. https://doi.org/10.1177/0741713611400302

Steinberg, M., Allensworth, E., & Johnson, D. (2015). What conditions jeopardize and support safety in urban schools? Influence of community characteristics, school composition and school organizational practices on student teacher reports of safety in Chicago. In D. J. Losen (Ed.), *Closing the school discipline gap: Equitable remedies for excessive exclusion* (pp. 118–131). Teachers College Press.

Thorsborne, M., & Blood, P. (2013). *Implementing restorative practices in schools: A practical guide to transforming school communities.* Jessica Kingsley.

U.S. Commission on Civil Rights. (2019). *Beyond suspensions: Examining school discipline policies and connections to the school-to-prison pipeline for students of color with disabilities.* https://www.usccr.gov/pubs/2019/07-23-Beyond-Suspensions.pdf

# 12

# Verbatim Theater and Social Work

*A Just Practice Approach to Trauma-Informed Education*

ERIN BUTTS, MSW, AND SARAH BUTTS, MFA

> Not everything that is faced can be changed. But nothing can be changed until it is faced.
> —James Baldwin

---

### Overview

In this chapter social worker Erin Butts and theater director/playwright Sarah Butts describe their collaborative effort to create a "verbatim theater" project with high school students and staff in a working-class community. Through the project, students shared their histories, described the contexts of their lives in and out of school, and identified what has meaning for them. Their stories became the basis for an empowering play written and directed by Sarah Butts. The play centered youth voices and created a context for teaching-learning. The play was performed before community audiences, sparking possibilities for critical reflection and community action.

---

## Introduction

*Converge*: come together or unite in a common interest of focus. *E pluribus unum*: Out of many, one.

At 7 p.m. on a snowy evening in February 2019, hundreds of community members filed into the historic auditorium at Great Falls High School. Just weeks ago, Great Falls High was staging an adaptation of S. E. Hinton's classic young adult novel *The Outsiders* on this very stage. Tonight, the audience is here to watch a different kind of play. This play doesn't tell a fictional story with characters like Pony

Boy, Johnny, or Sodapop. The play they are watching tonight, *Converge: E Pluribus Unum* (Butts, 2019), is about *them* and *their* community.

The original play was commissioned by Great Falls Public Schools and is a form of *documentary theater* called *verbatim theater* (*documentary* because it is about real events and real people; *verbatim* because it uses the precise words of actual people) (Odendahl-James, 2017). Stories and words for *Converge: E Pluribus Unum* were generated through a week of intensive interviews with over 50 Great Falls residents including youth, educators, parents, law enforcement, Indigenous community members, mental health professionals, and more.

The production was a citywide collaboration featuring a cast of student actors from all three of the city's public high schools. A professional theater artist served as both playwright and director for the production and conducted all interviews. While much of the script was written before rehearsals began, student cast members were active collaborators in shaping the play and generating content. A staff or faculty member from each high school worked on the production team as stage manager, assistant director, and technical director. A string quartet from the Great Falls Youth Orchestra accompanied the play featuring original compositions written by Great Falls Symphony Music Director Grant Harville.

Public performances of the play were followed by an audience talk-back led by members of the Great Falls Public School District. The play was scheduled to run for 3 nights; however, due to the positive community response, an encore performance took place in conjunction with *No More Violence Week*. In addition, a community forum titled *Converge: Listen, Plan, Act* was hosted by United Way of Cascade County, No More Violence Week, and Great Falls Public Schools. The goal of this event was to engage the community in devising action steps in response to the issues of trauma, struggle, addiction, violence, homelessness, exclusion, resistance, and resilience addressed in the play.

The process of developing and producing *Converge: E Pluribus Unum* reflected core social work values of honoring the dignity and worth of the person, the power of relationship, and the commitment to social justice. Project leaders and the production team were intentional about sharing stories and casting members representing diverse identities, communities, and lived experiences including people of color, Indigenous community members, individuals experiencing homelessness, individuals with disabilities, and members of the LGBTQ+ community.

So how did *Converge* come about? That is a story of social justice work. The authors of this chapter, social worker Erin Butts and playwright/director Sarah Butts, bring the Just Practice framework (Finn, 2020) to bear as they recount the process from initial idea through final curtain call and ongoing reverberations of possibility.

## Erin's Story

I began working as the mental health coordinator for Great Falls Public Schools (GFPS) in 2017. GFPS is the second largest school district in Montana. Fifty percent of our schools qualify for free and reduced lunch, the highest among any of the state's Class AA schools (those with a student body of 750 or more). Our homeless student population has increased annually since 2015, and in 2020, we had over 450 homeless students enrolled (Great Falls Public Schools, n.d.).

In brief, my role consists of collaborating with teachers and other school personnel to plan and implement prevention, intervention, and crisis response efforts so that students struggling with mental illness, behavioral disorders, and the relentless challenges of poverty, racism, homo- and transphobia, addiction, homelessness, and violence can stay in school and succeed there. Too often, given the high level of need for student support, this work plays out in a series of crisis-oriented, one-to-one efforts with individual children, and the connection to the broader contexts and forces shaping their lives and those of their families gets lost. Moreover, the magnitude of needs young people and their families bring to our schools are challenging and highly stress-inducing for teachers, administrators, and staff. Despite and because of the challenges, I believed that we could marshal the resources of the school district and the community to draw attention to those broader contexts and forces and begin to address them. The Just Practice framework provided a lens for critical thought and action.

## Bringing the Just Practice Concepts to Bear

The first step toward expanding possibilities for action was to step back and reflect on community context and history. Great Falls is a city of 60,000 affected by deindustrialization with a significant population of working poor families. Once a booming smelter town in the heyday of mining in Montana, the Great Falls economy is now more diverse, but good paying jobs are limited. The city is predominantly White, with a significant representation of American Indian and Hispanic residents. The city's overall poverty rate of 14.5% masks the reality that 46% of American Indian residents and 31% of Hispanic residents live in poverty. Racism runs deep in Montana, and the intersections of racism and poverty shape the life stories of many of our students. For too many students and their families, home is not a context of safety but of unpredictability. Students bear witness to and bear the brunt of everyday violence. They may be caring for siblings or couch-surfing through homelessness when not in school. Their backpacks are weighted with histories of trauma that they cannot simply check at their lockers.

Questions of meaning, power, context, history, and possibility are key here (Finn, 2020). What does school mean for these kids? What does safety mean? How can we support them in navigating the complex contexts of their lives? Where do they have a modicum of power? Where can their voices be heard? How do we educate children who begin the school day with no breakfast—or dinner the night before? How are children expected to learn if they have been removed from their house the night before and put in another stranger's home at the age of 8—for the ninth time? What do we expect from young people in schools if their caregivers are incarcerated or unavailable due to substance use? What happens when youth are questioning their gender identity, and the fear of rejection by family and community is so heavy that suicide is the answer to eliminating pain? How does the pain of everyday racism affect students' experiences in school? These questions challenged us to look beyond one-to-one interventions and consider broader possibilities grounded in collective engagement with young people at the center.

## Adversity Demands Collaboration

I (Erin) had learned a great deal about trauma and trauma-informed practice in my previous social work experiences. Now, I was witnessing the toxic ways in which trauma insinuated itself in the very fabric of our students' beings. Increasingly, youth-serving systems are incorporating evolving research on trauma and adverse childhood experiences (ACEs) to inform collaborative action and systems change (Felitti et al., 2019). At the micro level, collaborative work in neuroscience and social science is helping us better understand the malleability and interplay of the mind and the brain (Hanson & Mendius, 2009). At the macro level, links are being forged in the interdisciplinary study of well-being to understand and develop "skills that foster a thriving, resilient, and compassionate society" (Greater Good Science Center, n.d.). My experience in addressing trauma has also taught me about the power of resilience, resistance, and survival within children, families, and communities. That knowledge fueled me with an unabashed sense of hope and possibility that our schools and community could come together, bring diverse voices to the table, and respond to the challenges our young people face.

Through critical reflection on questions of meaning, power, context, history, and possibility, a seed of an idea began to emerge. What if we could capture the students' stories we heard every day? What if we could share their stories with the larger community? Might there be an opportunity to spark consciousness and collective action? I have a strong commitment to interprofessional collaboration, and a new sort of collaboration was coming to mind. What if we were to use the power of theater to communicate the realities of our students' struggles and strengths? I have just enough knowledge of theater to make me dangerous, but I had both read about the use of theater for social change and had witnessed the transformative power of theater many times in my life (JRI, 2007). But the most intimate influence was my sister Sarah, a playwright and director, who offered her knowledge and talents in bringing youth stories to the stage.

I initially proposed the idea for a play centering youth voices and experiences to the principal of Paris Gibson Education Center (PGEC). PGEC provides an alternative to traditional high school education. The principal, in turn, brought the idea to the superintendent of schools. As they embraced the possibility, they also provided me with important lessons in the power of effective, collaborative leadership (Brothers & Kumar, 2018). They engaged others in conversations with intention and purpose, and they fostered a mindset of openness, growth, and possibility as they formed a project leadership team.

Sarah Butts came on board as playwright and director. The scope of the project expanded from a focus on a single school to a district-wide collaboration that would engage students, faculty, and staff in all three local high schools as well as students and staff in the local detention center. The leaders realized that the stakes were high for potential criticism. They facilitated crucial conversations about vulnerability and risk in the interview and performance process. The leaders formed an interdisciplinary school-community team, which engaged in ongoing conversations about the physical and emotional safety of all involved. School leaders were also aware of the potential risk in presenting strong and challenging content to community members who may have little understanding of what we encounter in our schools today. The school-community team grappled with these questions through candid, ongoing dialogue and kept the commitment to youth voices center stage.

The team engaged in critical question-posing, a key facet of *teaching-learning*: Could the play inform the greater Great Falls community in a way they had not heard or been exposed to previously? Is it possible that, through theater, audience members could truly hear the stories of students' lives and come to a deeper consciousness of their strengths and struggles? Does knowing that these are voices from their own community spark audience members' empathy regarding what their neighbor might be experiencing on any given day? Could *Converge* counter assumptions made about those labeled "different" in our community? Could the play open space for dialogue about topics that have been seen as taboo? Could it deepen understanding of social and economic injustices in our community that are too often unacknowledged? Did *Converge* have the capacity to unite us as school-community partners? We approached the project with high hopes and a healthy dose of humility.

## Sarah's Story

I am a director and playwright with a long-term interest in theater as a medium for consciousness raising and social change. My introduction to verbatim theater came in 2011 when I directed an original play called *A Heart Without: Real Stories of Homelessness* in Billings, Montana (Obee & Dixon, 2010). The project was led by Daniele Reisbig, who conducted interviews with community members experiencing homelessness. Transcriptions of the interviews were adapted to monologues written by local playwrights. The goal of the project was to bring about community awareness and to personalize the experience of being homeless. The project made a lasting impact and led me to continue exploring this kind of theater.

In graduate school at University of California–Irvine I had the opportunity to expand my knowledge and practice around community-based theater in general and verbatim theater specifically. I studied the work of theater companies like Cornerstone Theater (https://cornerstonetheater.org), Culture Clash (https://cultureclashtheatre.com), and Tectonic Theatre Company (https://www.tectonictheaterproject.org; creators of *The Laramie Project*) and the work of artists like Anna Deavere Smith (Anna Deavere Smith, 2020) and Andrea Caban (http://www.andreacaban.com). I also participated in an intensive training workshop from Cornerstone Theater, one of the country's leading theater companies that focus on original community-based theater. Through this formal and self-led education, I adopted many of the values, ethics, and practices that guide the interview, writing, and production process of creating verbatim theater.

## From Interview to the Page

It was of high priority to all leaders of the *Converge* project that a broad and diverse range of voices be represented in the play. Erin Butts and PGEC principal arranged and scheduled the interviews with over 50 members of the Great Falls community. I (Sarah) viewed my role as interviewer primarily as an active listener and guide. I had a set of open-ended questions that helped guide the interview, but the goal for the session was determined by what flowed from the interviewee. I allowed space and flexibility for various twists and turns to occur. Often the most compelling and vulnerable bits emerged from a "tangent" unrelated to a specific question.

All interviews were audio-recorded, with consent of the interviewee, in order to accurately capture their words and allow for fully active listening on my part. Audio files were then transcribed and the words assembled into the script. While each individual story was not included in the play, I strove to include at least some of the words from everyone I interviewed.

Here is an example scene from the original play *Converge: E Pluribus Unum* (Butts, 2019):

---

### Coping

*Actual names have been changed to protect privacy of those interviewed. The stories weave and overlap slightly. The scene builds as the circumstances of their story build.*

MUSIC BEGINS.

**ADAM**

After my young brother was born my mom struggled with postpartum depression and bipolar really bad. She would sleep all day and my dad was at work so I would watch my siblings and feed them.

**BRANDON**

I am no stranger to death. When I was 5 years old, I lost my mom to a gruesome murder where I witnessed my father kill her then take his own life.

**CARRIE**

My family was messed up. I was often the one acting like the adult. I was in charge of taking care of my younger siblings. Getting them up in the morning, getting them to school and stuff. I am just a kid myself, ya know?

**ADAM**

I was in 5th grade the first time my mom tried to kill herself. Sometimes we would just be sitting around the kitchen table and she would say something like, "I just swallowed a bottle of pills."

**BRANDON**

My grandfather became my surrogate father and he passed away in high school. He took me on a vacation to Cancun and ended up passing away the day after we got there.

**CARRIE**

One summer, I was repeatedly molested by my brother-in-law. My family didn't believe me. My sister said it was my fault, that I made him do it.

**BRANDON**

My grandmother became my surrogate mother and she passed away during high school as well. There wasn't much of the family left after that. I have kind of just been on my own ever since.

**CARRIE**

I ran away from home. I was angry about what happened to me and no one believed me or seemed to care.

**ADAM & BRANDON**

I was angry.
MUSIC BUILDS THROUGHOUT. *Tension is building as the weight of the circumstances are building. They are losing control, becoming erratic.*

**ALL**

I bottled everything up.
I kept it inside.
It would build and build and then explode.

**ALL**

I didn't know how to cope.
I DIDN'T KNOW HOW TO DEAL WITH EVERYTHING...
*MUSIC STOP. A beat. A breath. MUSIC CHANGES.*

## Youth Influence on the Creative Process

Although I was the key author, youth actors played an active role in shaping the play during the rehearsal process. One example was a scene about today's never-ending news cycle and its influence on young people. The scene started as an outline, then was developed collaboratively with the student actors. We began by discussing the relentless impact of media on their lives. Students shared what their anxiety felt like and the images that came to mind when they thought of this "storm of input." These ideas inspired the physical movement and tone of the scene. Additionally, students generated a list of current-event "headlines" that felt most pressing or that generated anxiety for them, which we incorporated into the script. One of the headlines they chose was the recent killing of Laquan McDonald, a 17-year-old Black youth, by a Chicago police officer. This led to a discussion about racism between a group of White students and students of color. They listened to and made space for each other and stuck around after rehearsal to continue talking. The level of honesty, openness, and mutual respect they held for one another was striking. In this moment, adults became the learners, and the insights of students determined the direction of the scene. Furthermore, this turned out to be a moment in the play that audience members found most impactful. Young people have a lot to teach adults when we choose to listen.

## The Impact of *Converge* on the Directing Process

There is a phrase that gets frequently uttered in theater rehearsal rooms across the country: "*Leave it at the door.*" That is to say, regardless of what you are going through or what kind of day you have had, it is your responsibility to put it aside and be fully present to get the work done. In classrooms across the country, students are often held to a similar expectation. They are to step into the classroom ready to fully engage and do what is expected, regardless of what they are walking in with. The process of conducting the interviews and then writing and directing *Converge* led me to reflect more deeply on this phrase. Whether in the classroom or rehearsal hall, the idea of "leaving it at the door" does not make space to consider what students may be walking in with. Perhaps they slept in a car the night before and are not well rested or nourished. Perhaps the place they call home is one filled with chaos, abuse, addiction, or violence. Perhaps they are regularly bullied by peers or struggling with a major mental illness. I am sure that a person going through these kinds of struggles would love to be able to snap their fingers and put their struggles aside to concentrate fully on the task at hand, but it may not be that simple.

Additionally, "leave it at the door" puts all responsibility on the one walking in, regardless of circumstances. It asks nothing of the adult leader in the room. Inspired by interviews with dozens of students, educators, and mental health professionals, I found that a recurring call to action made its way into the script.

It is a call for teachers, administrators, and other key adults to approach their practices in education and student interaction with a bit more flexibility, to truly *meet students where they are at*, work in partnership *with* them, *accompany* them, and find approaches that respect their life circumstances. I felt it was only right that I, too, as the adult leading the rehearsal process for *Converge: E Pluribus Unum*, hold myself to that same call.

Throughout the rehearsal and performance process, our adult leadership team sought to find a balance between challenging students to grow and strive for artistic excellence while carving out space and flexibility to account for the needs, health, and safety of the students participating. We worked to foster a rehearsal environment where students felt supported, listened to, respected, and safe, and where they had creative ownership of the production we were building *together*. We took into account the experiences of the students in the cast, many of whom were living with the kinds of struggles mentioned in the play. We made space to allow conversation within our formed community so that students and adults could listen, empathize, and learn from each other.

One specific practice that we implemented was a daily check-in and 2-minute meditation. In the check-in, participants were given the option to briefly share "where they are at right now." This was an opportunity for the students to share what they were walking in with. Maybe they were really struggling that day, or stressed out, or unwell, or maybe they were very silent and not wanting to speak that day. This practice invites the community to engage with each other in a way that takes where we are at, at any given moment, into consideration. It also provides a way for students to ask for what they need. This practice also helped me manage my own expectations day to day and helped me avoid making negative assumptions or generalizations around what a student is bringing to the table on a given day.

Adjustments made to the rehearsal process were impactful but not dramatic. These added practices did not take a lot of extra time, nor did they compromise the quality of the performance. In fact, many audience members remarked on the high level of professionalism and the strong impact of the performances. Making space for a bit more patience, flexibility, and compassion go a long way, and it is my intention to continue embracing these values in my practice as a director moving forward. As a playwright and director, I have gained much from the deepened understanding of social work tenets that came from this collaborative and interdisciplinary project.

## Embracing Possibility

With the support of courageous and collaborative leadership, *Converge: E Pluribus Unum* came to fruition. As the purpose and vision was shared in the community, several Great Falls community members independently came forward to financially support the initiative. Tim Ljunggren, a local filmmaker, was also a critical member of the team. He participated in the interview process and created a film titled *Converge: Many Stories, One Voice* that captured highlights of the process and performance. Diverse community audiences were able to bear witness to stories by young people grounded in their histories, revealing the contexts of their lives in and out of school, and defining what has meaning for them. The play tapped into the power of youth voice and the narration of one's own story. Participants made meaning of the experience of schooling, the context of struggle in a largely working-class town, and the connection of personal history to broader school and community histories.

Student musicians from the school district partnered with the Great Falls Symphony to play music for the film and at live performances of the play. American Indian dancers and drummers joined the production team, adding crucial depth that is part of the complexities of context, history, meaning, and power in Great Falls. Since the live performances and community forum, school-community stakeholders who did not know each other previously became connected through this project and continue to work together. Great Falls now has a community action team called the Converge Action Team that continues to meet. A local nonprofit organization opened the Youth Resource Center in 2020 (Rice, 2019). Sarah has been recruited by other school districts in the state to engage them in a similar process of crafting a play that centers youth voice. Community members still speak about *Converge: E Pluribus Unum* and the stories that stick with them. We certainly do not claim that the play has solved the problems confronting so many children in our schools and families in our community. Rather, it has helped us imagine and create new ways of being and working together to tackle these complexities.

For the authors, the process of creating *Converge* confirmed our belief in the power and potential of bridging theater and social work to promote social justice and social change. Individual interventions can take us only so far. There is so much untapped potential in social justice work that embraces new ways of knowing, being, communicating, and acting. Verbatim theater offered a unique vehicle for bridging the gap between the life stories that unfold within a given school and broader community understanding of those stories. The community needed an opportunity to come to know such stories in a way that would not only be heard, but heard in a way that people would remember. We believe we have an increased chance of remembering when we are moved to tears because of tragedy, moved to tears because of hope, and moved to tears by the resilience and survival of youth and families who are resisting and transforming the structures of violence and oppression that constrain their lives. Hopefully, the story of *Converge* sparks the reader's imagination about the creative potential for social justice work.

## *Converge* and Covid-19

Although the performances were completed prior to Covid-19, perhaps in a gentle way the vision has contributed to how GFPS and the Great Falls community responded to the impacts of Covid on our school system. Empathy and compassion have been far-reaching. In the spring of 2020, Great Falls passed the school levy, something that has happened only twice in the past decade. The Youth Resource Center, opened in spring 2020, provides young people with access to hot meals, showers, health care, and more. PGEC has hired an individual to partner with the center to facilitate safe transportation, one of our students' greatest needs. Administrators continue to implement creative interventions to support students and the community through this time of tremendous loss, tragedy, and isolation.

## QUESTIONS FOR REFLECTION AND DISCUSSION

1. Where do you see possibilities for the use of theater and other forms of storytelling to address issues of concern in your community?
2. Can *Converge* influence how we think about the value of the arts in education, particularly when public schools across the nation continue to experience grave challenges of funding and budget cuts?
3. What inspiration do you take from this chapter that might inform your own approach to social justice work in schools?
4. Might policymakers be influenced in their understanding of social and economic injustice by watching a live performance of *Converge: E Pluribus Unum*?
5. What might be other examples of innovative interdisciplinary collaboration among social workers, educators, and artists?

## REFERENCES

Anna Deavere Smith. (2020, March 1). In *Wikipedia*. https://en.wikipedia.org/wiki/Anna_Deavere_Smith

Brothers, C., & Kumar, V. (2018, December 20). *12 habits of highly effective leaders*. https://www.chalmersbrothers.com/blog/12-habits-of-highly-effective-leaders

Butts, S. (2019). *Converge: E pluribus unum. A theatrical collage* (pp. 1–27). Unpublished manuscript.

Felitti, V. J., Anda, R. F., Nordenberg, D., Williamson, D. F., Spitz, A. M., Edwards, V., Koss, M. P., & Marks, J. S. (2019). Relationship of childhood abuse and household dysfunction to many of the leading causes of deaths in adults: The Adverse Childhood Experiences (ACE) study. *American Journal of Preventive Medicine*, 56(6), 774–786.

Finn, J. (2020). *Just practice: A social justice approach to social work* (4th ed.). Oxford University Press.

Great Falls Public Schools. (n.d.). *Great Falls Public Schools, fiscal year 2020–2021, fast facts*. Retrieved January 5, 2021, from https://www.gfps.k12.mt.us/Page/557

Greater Good Science Center. (n.d.). *Our mission*. Retrieved December 9, 2019, from https://ggsc.berkeley.edu/who_we_are/about

Hanson, R., & Mendius, R. (2009). *Buddha's brain*. New Harbinger.

JRI. (2007). *Trauma center at JRI*. http://www.traumacenter.org/initiatives/Trauma_Drama.php

Obee, J., & Dixon, A. (2010). *Project homelessness: A model for social impact through theater* (pp. 2–82). https://ci.billings.mt.us/DocumentCenter/View/24653/Manual_FINAL-PDF?bidId=

Odendahl-James, J. (2017, August 22). *A history of U.S. documentary theatre in three stages*. https://www.americantheatre.org/2017/08/22/a-history-of-u-s-documentary-theatre-in-three-stages/

Rice, S. (2019, December 9). New center will help homeless teens. *Great Falls Tribune*. https://www.greatfallstribune.com/story/news/2019/12/09/youth-resource-center-help-homeless-teens/4357273002

# 13

# Social Workers in Schools

*A Just Practice Perspective*

KATIE BAUMLER, MSW

> Waiho i te toipoto, kaua i te toiroa. Let us keep close together not far apart.
> —Māori expression

---

**Overview**

Katie Baumler uses the Just Practice framework to reflect on her experience as a school social worker in New Zealand in this chapter. Baumler shows how she brought the Just Practice framework to bear in supporting Aroha, a young Māori girl, as she reconnected with her grandmother. She describes her engagement with Aroha and the importance of accompaniment in the relationship. Baumler bears witness to the power of culturally grounded practices of healing and support. She reflects on her own experience as a White, U.S.-educated social worker and how her practice has been shaped by students such as Aroha and their families.

---

## Introduction

I am a White woman and U.S. citizen who has been practicing social work for 11 years, 2 as a child protective services social worker in the United States, 2 as a home-based support worker in New Zealand; and the last 7 as a social worker in schools in New Zealand. New Zealand is a diverse country with strong ties to the culture of its Indigenous people, the Māori, as well as heavy influences from the surrounding Pacific Island cultures. Social Workers in Schools is a nationwide government-funded service provided free to children and their families at qualifying schools (i.e., those located in an area serving a higher number of low-income families). The role is multifaceted, including individual therapeutic work with young people; developing preventative programs; and collaborating with teachers to support the social and emotional well-being of young people in the classroom. In addition, there is a large emphasis on supporting school staff, advocating for families to find other supports when required, and wider community development.

Regardless of the level of intervention, the role of Social Workers in Schools is somewhat unique in that it functions to support young people first and foremost, within the contexts of home, school, and community. Unfortunately, many systems are largely deficit-based and seek to change "problem" behaviors in young people. However, my experience suggests that the most effective interventions actually stem from simply walking alongside young people and seeking to understand what lies beneath the behaviors through a non-directive approach of listening and validation. The Just Practice framework (Finn, 2020) aligns very well with this approach and has provided a fundamental base of knowledge to my social work practice.

## Aroha's Story

Aroha is a Māori word with the simplest translation, "love." I first met Aroha when she was a 7-year-old at one of my schools where she participated in a few group programs. To the outside world, Aroha presented an outgoing and compassionate personality; however, underneath she was hiding a lot of anxiety related to historical and ongoing violence between her parents. By the time Aroha turned 12, her parents had separated and the exposure became less frequent. However, the years of witnessing violence had taken a significant toll and finally become too much to keep secret. The biggest clue to how Aroha was feeling came from her drop in attendance, which was odd as she normally loved being at school. Around this time, Aroha's class also participated in a pilot program for a violence-prevention organization called Jade Speaks Up, and Aroha finally found the courage to speak with a teacher about what was happening in her family. The reason she had been staying home from school was because she wanted to be close to her mother, whom she believed was at risk of harm from her father. Aroha had grown up believing that violence was normal and had been told to keep quiet and "keep it within the family." Her bravery, however, led her mother to finally seek support from the local women's shelter as well as police to put protections in place for herself and the children. It was at this point that Aroha's mother referred her for individual support with the Social Workers in Schools program.

## Engaging Aroha

My engagement with Aroha began simply by offering a safe and nonjudgmental space to tell her story. We started off with a few rapport-building activities, like playing "Getting to Know You Jenga" (a Jenga game with numbers on the pieces corresponding to get-to-know-you questions) and constructing a family tree. Activities such as these are non-threatening and help with getting to know each other in a fun and lighthearted way, planting the seeds of trust in a new relationship.

However, it quickly became apparent that what Aroha needed was to talk. So I listened. Week after week we met, and each time she told me a little more of her story—the things she saw, the words she heard, the places she hid. Aroha let me into her world, a place that at times could leave her feeling very powerless and confused about whom to trust. Despite the temptation to do so at times, I didn't ask questions or give advice; I just let her say whatever she needed to. I became a learner and Aroha the teacher, guiding me through her own world and experience. Aroha enjoyed doing arts and crafts activities; she said it helped to keep her hands busy so the words could flow. Every time Aroha left a session, she described herself as feeling "lighter," simply for having unburdened some of the load she had been carrying for so long.

Despite all the positive movement as a result of her speaking up and the relief from sharing her story, Aroha continued to feel anxious a lot of the time, which in turn led her to want to stay home from school as well as engage in risky activities like drinking and self-harm to "numb" the feelings. Aroha has always had a very strong conscience, however, and was embarrassed about turning to these activities. She didn't want to "disappoint" anyone—her family, the school, or me—which was adding an extra element of pressure and anxiety. I learned of some of the activities from her mother and the rest after the police caught her drinking with a group of young people. When I addressed this with Aroha, she was tearful and honest as well as apologetic about not telling me sooner. This opened a whole additional dimension to her story and also within our relationship. We were able to unpack the layers of trauma contributing to her current behavior and make connections to the strategies she was using for coping, especially when she put together that she had previously seen her father turn to drinking and her older brother to self-harm as coping mechanisms.

Aroha was also experiencing a sense of mixed loyalty toward her father and his side of the family. A police protection order had been issued preventing contact from Aroha's father. While this created some immediate relief from a safety perspective, the emotional aftermath was very tough as it polarized both the immediate and extended family, who effectively "took sides" with either mother or father. Meanwhile, Aroha felt responsible for all of it, adding additional anxiety and stress. Despite the events of the past, Aroha still loved her father and wanted connection with that side of her family, particularly because they represented the link to her Māori heritage. Aroha identified these as some key things she wanted support with and so we set about finding the best way to do that.

Validating Aroha's experiences and gently supporting her to find the feelings underneath her reactions to current situations helped Aroha begin to make sense of how her previous trauma was impacting her current state of being. It was incredibly important, though, that this come from Aroha herself, in order for her to accept and be able to use it. She acted as the guide and I accompanied her at her pace as we worked together, irrespective of time; the process took as long as it needed to, working at the "speed of trust" (Covey & Merrill, 2006). Aroha was making great progress when an unexpected phone call changed everything—for the better. Aroha's paternal grandmother, Wairua, contacted me to say that she would really like to support Aroha's journey. As there were legal protection orders in place, I made the necessary arrangements and gained consent from Aroha's mother to support the reconnection between Aroha and her grandmother, whom she had not seen in 5 years.

## Learning with Aroha and Wairua

Wairua began to visit Aroha for some of our sessions at school. While Aroha's anxiety had greatly improved, she was still struggling with the temptation of drugs and alcohol. Unfortunately, this can be quite common among young people and exacerbated through peer pressure and a sense of shared experience among other youth experiencing similar challenges. Wairua spoke with Aroha from a *whanau* (family) perspective and reminded Aroha of her culture and her strength as a Māori woman. She spoke of her own journey and facing similar challenges. She described that she didn't have a supportive team around her at the time and how much she wished she had had someone to talk, too. Most importantly she let Aroha know that she was so incredibly proud of her for speaking up and telling her story. Wairua introduced Aroha to a Māori model for health and well-being called *te whare tapa whā* (New Zealand Ministry of Health, 2017). The model is popular among social workers working with Māori people and has been widely adopted by the care and protection system as a best practice approach. The model held special significance in this case as it was also being led by a family member.

*Te whare tapa whā* is based on bringing into balance the four cornerstones of health and well-being: *taha tinana* (physical health), *taha wairua* (spiritual health), *taha whānau* (family health), and *taha hinengaro* (mental health). Over the next weeks, Wairua and I worked together to support Aroha in developing a plan with concrete steps to bring each of her cornerstones back to equilibrium. Not only did this effort provide motivation for change, it also offered the critical link back to culture and family that Aroha was missing. The plan detailed the ways Aroha would look after herself through playing sports, getting ready for and attending school each day, and completing her schoolwork. It also outlined how she would connect and spend quality time with various family members. The plan also included alternative strategies for managing her anxiety such as listening to music, writing in her journal, and talking to one of her key support people.

## Key Concepts in Action

The Just Practice framework translates very well into practice for social workers in a school setting, and Aroha's journey was no exception. The key concepts of meaning, context, power, history, and possibility are interwoven throughout her story.

## MEANING

Meaning refers to the way we make sense of our own circumstances and how that influences our perception of the world around us. Aroha's story is laden with meaning, as she struggled to make sense of her experiences in her family and her responses to those experiences. Through exploring the root causes for her distress, Aroha was able to identify what she needed to do to make steps toward positive change and bring herself back to balance. Part of Aroha's meaning-making process entailed fostering deeper connection to her Māori identity, family, and culture. Wairua played a key role in helping Aroha find this deeper meaning. In addition, Māori culture and identity are a significant part of the school curriculum in New Zealand. Aroha's school was particularly encouraging of youth learning the language, dance, and traditions of Māori and other Pacific Island cultures. Aroha participated in weekly *te reo* (language) lessons as well as in *kapa haka*, a performance art that blends song, movement, and chanting, as additional ways to foster deeper connection to her cultural identity.

Meaning is also important from the practitioner's point of view. In this story, there was a shared commonality of experience regarding risk-taking behavior. However, it was very important to use reflective practice and critical dialogue with other professionals to understand the crucial differences in two very different situations. When I was young, I also fell in with a group of people experimenting with drugs and alcohol. While my own reasons for being part of the group were much more related to peer pressure and "fitting in," I can look back now and see the very real struggles some of my friends were facing. Remembering this time in my life and those relationships, both with my friends and the people trying to support me at the time, helped me to both normalize and empathize with Aroha's situation. However, it was very important to understand that Aroha's story was not my story and to never assume I knew exactly what she was going through. Being able to unpack the situation through supervision was critical. Thus, while the shared experience did offer some space for understanding, it was important not to let my own journey as a White girl in the United States struggling with identity and relationships influence the way Aroha defined her path, which ended up being incredibly meaningful and unique to her.

## CONTEXT

Understanding context was an important part of Aroha's story. Cultural humility is a fundamental component to consider when looking at context for this situation. As a social worker practicing in a cross-cultural context, it was vital to acknowledge the importance of cultural difference in this situation, understand my own limitations, and discover ways to meet a critical need. It was clear that linking Aroha back to her culture was a key step toward change. I was also keenly aware of my own position as a White social worker who did not grow up in New Zealand. I was learning as much from Aroha and her grandmother as I was supporting them. I believe this genuine teaching-learning partnership contributed to our success. By working with Wairua to use a culturally driven model, we were able to achieve a plan that not only addressed Aroha's key goals, but also linked her back to her culture and her family.

As with meaning, another important aspect of context is to acknowledge that there is a high probability of shared experience when working with young people due to our own personal values around growing up and/or raising children ourselves. Being aware of this and how it influences our responses to the young people we work with is critical. The context of working in a school is also an important consideration. Social workers in schools are uniquely placed to support and understand the broader context of what children bring with them to school each day and how this is shaped by the wider context of their everyday lives, which can have a critical impact on their learning and functioning in the classroom.

## POWER

Power is a particularly interesting concept to consider as it can be viewed as negative or positive depending on the context. A common theme with school social work, and working with young people in general, is that many systems are designed to suppress the child's voice and "fix" problematic behavior. By focusing on the problem behavior, they fail to seek an understanding of the root cause of that behavior and how it serves as a signal that something is not right in the young person's world. This focus can then lead to multiple referrals trying to find the right service, which can create a complex interplay of many systems—school, government, psychological services, nonprofit organizations—that may further complicate rather than support a young person's journey. Advocating for the young person's voice to be heard becomes increasingly important, and sometimes very difficult, as more systems come in to play, but it is an essential part of good practice.

From a positive perspective, power can also be viewed in the context of collaboration. Caring adults can work together to hear the young person's story, validate their experiences, and help put words to their emotions, even if it isn't always possible to fulfill their wishes. This was very evident in Aroha's journey as there were multiple times when her immediate wishes were not possible due to court orders. For example, Aroha really wanted to spend time with her dad and his family on Christmas Day. We discussed her wishes around this, and she formulated a plan to talk with her care and protection social worker, who agreed to take Aroha's request to her supervisor and the courts. Unfortunately, the visit was not approved, but an alternative plan was developed whereby she was able to have a supervised phone call with him. Aroha talked about how she missed her dad and at times even considered she might like to live with him. During these times, it was crucially important to acknowledge both her sadness in missing her dad and her frustration over decisions that were beyond her control. I was deeply touched when Aroha acknowledged that, though her wishes might not be met, she felt better knowing the people around her could understand her and validate her frustration.

## HISTORY

The Just Practice model maintains that history is much more than an objective reporting of the facts and rather paints a picture of the past that varies based on the storyteller. History holds relevance to this situation given the cultural significance and impacts of colonization on Māori people, which forms a part of Aroha's heritage. New Zealand's history is marked by British colonization, which profoundly disrupted Māori culture. In 1840 British and Māori leaders negotiated the Treaty of Waitangi to establish a "foundation of biculturalism in the country" and to recognize the rights of Māori people (Staniforth & Noble, 2014, p. 178). However, those rights were systematically violated over time. In 1986 a government review documented widespread institutional racism in social welfare systems negatively impacting Māori people. The social work profession began to adopt practices that better aligned with Māori history, worldviews, and relationships.

Critical reflection on this history has opened social work to new possibilities. The Aotearoa New Zealand Association of Social Work (ANZASW) has since adopted a bicultural code of ethics and practice that honors the identity, history, and rights of Māori people (Aotearoa New Zealand Association of Social Workers, 2015). In addition, as of 2021 New Zealand will require every practicing social worker to be registered with the Social Workers Registration Board (SWRB). The SWRB has developed competency standards based on the code of ethics, many of which directly relate to practice with Māori and other cultures. In order to become registered, social workers must demonstrate understanding and commitment to ongoing professional development in these key areas.

It has been my responsibility, as a social worker in New Zealand, to learn and locate my practice within a critical understanding of this history. History is also particularly important from the more recent context of Aroha's family and the way her mother, father, and siblings view and respond to their family story. This can present a challenge when working with young people in the context of their families as sometimes the stories do not seem to align. However, more often than not, it is possible to understand the discrepancies in light of the way family members are making sense of their own stories. Family histories are complex blends of individual developmental trajectories, interpersonal histories, and stories located in the context of larger social, cultural, and political history. Navigating multiple, interwoven, and sometimes contradictory historical narratives can be challenging at times.

## POSSIBILITY

As important as it is to consider history, it equally important to move beyond the past and present to imagine realities for the future. This is a particularly exciting and important concept when working with youth because the possibility for meaningful change is generally quite high. However, in order to support young people on their journeys, it is critically important to spend time building rapport and gaining trust. Once this has been obtained, the possibilities are truly endless, and, as with Aroha's story, young people generally will find their own creative solutions. Including Wairua in my work with Aroha opened a whole new dimension of possibilities that I could not have accessed from my own position as a White social worker. The relationships for Aroha and her father's side of the family continue to evolve, ebb, and flow with time. Things are by no means perfect, but there is great potential for continued growth and development well beyond the scope of my work with the family.

# Highlights of Processes

## ENGAGEMENT

The process of engagement represents a particularly strong component of this case study as well as an important part of working with young people in a school setting. Engaging with youth in the wider classroom and school can be a very helpful way to establish relationships and support any future individual intervention. Young people can get to know you in a setting in which they are already comfortable, with their teachers and peers. This was the case with Aroha, who participated in small groups and classroom programs with me prior to our individual work together. With an existing relationship already established, the process of rapport building flowed much more freely and took less time. In the early stages, engagement with Aroha consisted of getting to know each other at a more in-depth level and gently supporting Aroha toward identifying the things that were important to her. The engagement process continues and develops for the duration of the relationship. For Aroha, there were significant ups and downs in her journey. By working through these obstacles together with openness and curiosity, our relationship continued to strengthen and allow for increasingly difficult conversations at times. The use of play, games, arts, crafts, and sensory objects in conjunction with talking therapy has proven especially effective for engagement with young people.

## TEACHING-LEARNING

The concept of teaching-learning is so important within Māori culture that it has a specific term—*ako*—which literally means both to teach and to learn. *Ako* recognizes the knowledge that both teachers and learners bring to learning interactions, and it acknowledges the way that new knowledge and understandings can grow out of shared learning experiences. Teaching-learning is a key feature of working with young people, and approaching relationships in this way can have significant positive effects. Similarly, by acting as a naïve inquirer and allowing young people to become the experts of telling their own story, as well as gently guiding them to come up with their own strategies, is incredibly empowering and much more effective than simply telling them what to do.

The use of the *te whare tapa whā* model with Aroha is a prime example of how teaching-learning can be a very powerful tool for collaboration and change. When I first began practicing social work in New Zealand, I felt somewhat intimidated about working with cultures that were new to me because I worried that my lack of experience could appear insensitive, even though what I wanted more than anything was to learn and improve. Being part of Aroha's journey has been a very profound part of my own journey as a social worker and has helped me realize how important it is to practice in a person-centered and strengths-based way. Through the power of respectful listening, genuine curiosity, and accompaniment, social workers can make meaningful connections with young people and in doing so strengthen their own practice.

## CHALLENGES AND POSSIBILITIES

Although Aroha's journey continues to have ups and downs, she is in a better space and better equipped to manage future challenges. Her story highlights not only the key themes of Just Practice, but also a number of larger challenges, and corresponding possibilities, relevant to social work practice. Unfortunately, many systems are largely deficit-based and seek to change "problem" behaviors in young people. Aroha's journey demonstrates that many effective interventions actually stem from simply walking alongside young people and seeking to understand what lies beneath the behaviors through a non-directive approach of listening and validation. A corresponding challenge is also the tendency of wider society toward suppressing children's voices. The role of Social Workers in Schools offers hopeful possibility by acting specifically to represent the wishes of the young person, with the understanding that these can't always be fulfilled, but that there is power in feeling heard and validated. Another key theme for this story is the importance of cultural humility. Through education and seeking cultural support when needed, there is even greater possibility for long-lasting and meaningful change.

### QUESTIONS FOR REFLECTION AND DISCUSSION

1. Trust building and engagement were a very important part of Katie's journey with Aroha. Can you think of any specific activities or strategies you might use in the engagement phase?
2. What additional considerations did Katie have to take when applying the Just Practice framework in an international context? Can you think of other considerations that might be important?
3. Discuss the benefits and potential challenges of how a social worker's personal experience can impact on their work with someone who is going through something similar. Are there things from your own past or present that might factor into your future work with clients? How will you manage this?
4. Where do you see common ground and important differences between school social work in New Zealand and in the United States? Where do you see further possibilities for applying in the Just Practice framework in the school setting?

## RESOURCES

Jade Speaks Up: Children Making Choices to Keep Themselves and Others Safe: http://www.jadespeaksup.co.nz/

Māori Health Models—Te Whare Tapa Whā: https://www.health.govt.nz/our-work/populations/maori-health/maori-health-models/maori-health-models-te-whare-tapa-wha

Social Workers in Schools Service Overview: https://www.orangatamariki.govt.nz/working-with-children/programme-and-forums/servicesinschools/

The Concept of Ako: https://tereomaori.tki.org.nz/Curriculum-guidelines/Teaching-and-learning-te-reo-Maori/Aspects-of-planning/The-concept-of-ako

## REFERENCES

Aotearoa New Zealand Association of Social Workers. (2015). *Codes of ethics.* http://anzasw.nz/wp-content/uploads/COE-for-website-chapter-3.pdf

Covey, S., & Merrill, R. (2006). *The speed of trust: The one thing that changes everything.* Free Press.

Finn, J. (2020). *Just practice: A social justice approach to social work* (4th ed.). Oxford University Press.

New Zealand Ministry of Health. (2017). *Māori health models—te whare tapa whā.* https://www.health.govt.nz/our-work/populations/maori-health/maori-health-models/maori-health-models-te-whare-tapa-wha

Staniforth, B., & Noble, C. (2014). Social work education in Aotearoa/New Zealand and Australia. In C. Noble, H. Strauss, & B. Littlechild (Eds.), *Global social work: Crossing boundaries, blurring borders* (pp. 171–184). Sydney University Press.

Part Four

# INTEGRATING SOCIAL JUSTICE IN THE CRIMINAL JUSTICE SYSTEM

# 14

# Social Justice Work in Jail

*Navigating Tensions of Care and Control*

DEANNA COOPER, LCSW

> No one makes it easy out there. The easiest thing is to quit and that's what they want us to do. Come back to places like this. The hardest thing to know is that life is uncomfortable.
> —Carl Clampett, Yankton Dakota, volunteer sweat lodge leader

---

**Overview**

In this chapter Deanna Cooper takes readers inside a jail-based substance use treatment program in New Mexico. Cooper describes the history and context in which the treatment program is embedded, explores the power relations therein, and shows the possibilities for fostering collaborative partnerships. Cooper addresses the significance of making racism and economic injustice talkable subjects with program participants. She shows how Just Practice complements intervention strategies such as motivational interviewing. She speaks to the possibilities and frustrations of creating change within systems of control.

---

## Introduction

This case study centers my experience as a White, middle-aged cisgender female clinical social worker overseeing the treatment component of a jail-based substance abuse program. In this retrospective reflection on practice, I draw on the Just Practice framework (Finn, 2020) as I untangle and identify the complex layers of social justice work within systems of oppression.

I had been a social worker for 20-some years when I became the clinical director for a jail-based treatment center located in the "Four Corners" area, where

Colorado, Utah, Arizona and New Mexico meet. Our primary program at that time was a model 28-day, mandatory jail-based treatment for first-time DWI (driving while intoxicated) offenders. When I came on board, the DWI treatment program was well established, with a strong connection to researchers affiliated with the University of New Mexico Center on Alcohol, Substance Abuse, and Addictions (UNM CASAA). I was responsible for overseeing programmatic content and clinical supervision of substance abuse counselors, social workers, case managers, and, as the program grew, practicum students and peer mentors.

The program emerged as a collective response to our state's dubious status of having the nation's highest per capita DWI fatalities in the 1990s (New Mexico Department of Health, 2014). Its model was based on emerging best practices for reducing DWIs through legal sanctions that utilized treatment (National Highway Traffic Safety Administration, 2005). The program was controversial for its tough stance. It combined punishment as a deterrent and treatment as a supportive intervention. The intent was for all first-time offenders to serve 28 days in a stand-alone minimum-security jail.

The program was funded through grants and required fidelity to evidence-based practices, including use of motivational interviewing, the community reinforcement approach curriculum in group work, and specific screening tools (Miller & Rollnick, 2013; Smith & Meyers, 1995). Administrators were committed to training in and implementation and monitoring of evidence-based practices. Program outcomes, measured by self-reports of reduction in problem drinking and reduced drinking-related offenses, were carefully tracked. The data showed promising results.

## Meaning, Context, History, and Power

To understand what it means to be a social worker in this jail-based treatment center, it is important to consider context, history, and power (Finn, 2020). The Four Corners area is primarily located on the Navajo reservation, the largest of the U.S. reservations. Our program, run through the county government, was in a reservation "border town," where the demographic makeup was roughly 40% identifying as White; a little less than 40% identifying as Native peoples, primarily Navajo, but including other tribes and pueblos; and 20% identifying as Hispanic, often with specific identification as Spanish or Mexican, in keeping with the state's historical colonization and immigration patterns.

People of color were highly overrepresented in the 28-day program. Further, those of lower socioeconomic status, regardless of ethnicity, were also overrepresented. Although the program was developed as a *mandatory* program for first-time DWI offenders, not every first-time offender was sentenced there. There were clear discrepancies between who was arrested for a DWI and who was sentenced to our facility. The state's 2014 DWI Offender Report noted these disparities but offered no explanation for them.

The American Civil Liberties Union (ACLU), however, directly addressed the systemic racism behind these disparities, embedded both formally and informally throughout the New Mexico criminal justice system, from decisions made at the point of arrest to sentencing and incarceration determinations. The ACLU recommended that the state "invest in evidence-based interventions at the local and state levels to reduce racially disparate treatment and overreliance on incarceration, while improving public safety throughout our communities" (ACLU, New Mexico Voices, 2017).

Sitting on the border of the Navajo Nation, the county had a lengthy history of overt racism and hate crimes, which had been exposed on a national level in the 1970s. A series of murders and a legacy of assaults on people of color had warranted a U.S. Civil Rights Commission investigation, with the resulting advisory committee findings stating that "Native Americans in almost every area suffer from injustice and maltreatment" (U.S. Commission on Civil Rights, 1975).

A new advisory committee to the U.S. Commission on Civil Rights revisited the area 30 years later to see what improvements had been made. In their 2005 *Farmington Report*, the committee noted improvements but also reported that there was clear evidence of continued overrepresentation of Native people in the criminal justice system. The only reference to the state's model DWI program was the following statement:

> As an example, Commissioner Chavez expressed incredulity at the high number of Native Americans in the county's DWI facility: It's kind of (peculiar) I guess when you look at the makeup of our population here in San Juan County within our DWI facility as well as our DWI treatment center. The majority of the population is made up of Navajos or Native Americans right now. You can't tell me that only Indians drink in this town. (New Mexico Advisory Committee, 2005)

That the state's model project for jail-based treatment garners this one mention of overrepresentation of Native peoples reflects the larger power relations in the criminal justice system as a whole. This is a common theme in reservation "border towns" and is representative of a larger history of racism, colonization, historical trauma, and ongoing structural violence. However, when I brought up these issues with administrators, I was consistently met with the response that our facility "works with whoever was sentenced to us." The message was that (1) judges who sentenced clients were supportive of the program and had clients' best interests at heart and (2) the program needed the judges' support. This administrative rationale was not to be questioned.

## Reflection on Positionality

As a social worker, I struggled with the irony that the only supportive treatment we could offer clients and their families was tethered to this punitive context. Our program reflected both deep systemic oppression and the complacent acceptance of these patterns and practices by county officials. I felt we needed to offer clients the truth and acknowledge the overrepresentation of people of color in our program and the disparities within the criminal justice system as we worked with clients, families, and community partners to effect realistic change.

Let me offer readers a disclosure on positionality here. My husband and children are enrolled tribal members. I am White. Our experiences in the community differed greatly. For example, I was aware that the experience I had in the local supermarket was often vastly different than that of my family. This was a frequent topic of family conversation at home. I was made aware of these very different experiences by my family. From my blinkered perspective as a White person, I had not "noticed" these differences on my own. That my family commonly experienced racial tension and at times outright racism in our community helped sensitize me to own my privilege and hone my ally skills. I was able to draw on these hard and humbling lessons learned in the context of my family to inform and transform my practice as a social worker.

## Engagement

As I entered this world of jail-based practice, I resolved to support my staff and to work with detention partners so that we could provide high-quality treatment for our clients. The first step to successful engagement called for building trusting collaborative partnerships with the jail-based team. I worked very closely with the lieutenant of detention. Together we embraced a preventative and responsive approach to intervention, balanced support and accountability, and modeled a willingness to engage in critical conversations aimed at keeping clients in treatment. Perhaps most importantly we modeled reciprocal trust and respect, which are foundational to engagement. We often met as a team with clients whose behaviors were undermining their treatment progress or presenting a threat to their physical and emotional safety and engaged clients as partners in problem-solving.

I was fortunate that the lieutenant in charge of detention staff was willing to engage with me. The lieutenant had a long history of employment as a detention officer and was one of very few Navajo women in a leadership role within the county detention system. Her positionality, convictions, and lived experiences led her to working in the treatment realm. She was dedicated to respectful treatment of all "inmates" and had a critical understanding of how people of color, specifically Native people, were overrepresented in our facility. We developed both a strong working relationship and close friendship, despite not always agreeing. Our shared goal of helping people exit the criminal justice system and move forward in their lives was a powerful bond, which produced a side effect of strengthening the relationships and engagement among detention and counseling staff. It also, at times, placed us at odds with top administrators, who prioritized policies and procedures over cultural considerations for Indigenous populations.

Successful engagement with clients needed to begin at intake. Clients arrived wary and exhausted after a lengthy jail booking process. Initially, our intake process was an unwieldy group endeavor consisting of an overview of treatment expectations and completion of numerous consent forms and inventories. Basically, it was antithetical to the trust and rapport building of genuine engagement.

My office was across the hallway from the intake room. I would listen to our paraprofessional staff review the forms and answer questions, and I would be ready when called to come introduce myself and say a few words about treatment. By that time, most clients were either half asleep or really in need of the restroom. This was not engagement. And it was not the fault of the staff assigned to intake duty. As I listened and thought about this first impression to treatment, I began to recognize a significant missed opportunity.

Clients were mainly interested in what to expect in treatment and when and how family visits occurred. It was my job to convey how we "rolled" as treatment providers, clarify expectations, and communicate respect for clients and their families. I acknowledged how hard it was for families when their loved ones were incarcerated and how important families were to client success. I took on the task of anticipating and responding to resistance while asking court-mandated clients to engage in treatment. I discovered an opportunity to engage clients in conversation about what these forms really meant for them and their treatment experience. The forms became the starting point for talking about privacy and confidentiality in the criminal justice context, about stigma regarding substance use disorders, and about supporting their successes in behavior change.

Perhaps my biggest realization was that by shifting the intake process to one of genuine engagement, I, as one of the few White people in the room, could directly acknowledge that the system was not a level playing field. I began telling clients the following: People of color and people who cannot afford a private attorney are overrepresented in this program. We need to recognize it. We need to discuss it. We will have groups on how this over-incarceration of people of color and without funds for legal representation has happened, how it is being challenged, and how not to offer yourself up to an unfair system. We can have this discussion. And we also need to have you willing to look at your own story for landing here, examine your relationship to substances, and be active in plans to get you through probation successfully.

## Expanding the Program

Just as New Mexico was lowering its numbers of DWI fatalities, our region was experiencing the spread of methamphetamine abuse, and the resulting impacts on individuals, families, and community. In the mid-2000s our county had seen a proliferation of child welfare cases related to methamphetamine-impacted parents, mostly women. New Mexico was truly "breaking bad," and our county was feeling it. A grassroots movement made up of community members, law enforcement, judges, child welfare workers, and treatment providers came together to secure funding for intervention. Our program, already a model for the state in addressing DWI, was selected to start a grant-funded pilot project to address methamphetamine use with women involved in the child welfare system who were at risk of losing parental rights.

Initially, this 60-day program was based on a voluntary approach. Clients agreed to participate as part of their child welfare case requirement, since family court could not mandate sentencing to the facility. However, the voluntary aspect proved to be a barrier to successful treatment. Given the profound pull of cravings and triggers, common in severe use, many clients chose to leave when the work of sobriety and recovery became too much for them. Unfortunately, a client's decision to leave treatment often provoked moralizing judgments about drug-involved parents, especially women, on the part of some of our partners and some in the broader community. These judgments ignored the science of the addictive process and the power of trauma and cravings and led to further stigma (Mate, 2010; Volkow, Koob, & McLennan, 2016). In response, the program switched to a court-ordered model, where clients were sentenced for substance-related offenses and the program served as an alternative to lengthy jail stays, prison, and revoked parole.

Given that most clients had children in state foster care, or in kinship care with grandparents or other family members, we honed our skills in providing and expanding inclusion of families in treatment. The program also evolved in its understanding of the polysubstance use pattern of many clients. As prescription opioids initially became popular drugs of misuse, followed by black-tar heroin, this pattern was identified and treatment was adapted to address it. Interestingly enough, the racial makeup of this program roughly mirrored that of the general population, with about an equal representation of White, Native, and Hispanic women. The proliferation of "illicit" drug use and the criminal sanctions for these substances appeared to result in less disparity in sentencing. The programs also differed philosophically. While the 60-day program was conceived as an alternative to prison, the DWI program required jail-based punishment along with treatment.

## Teaching-Learning

The treatment staff and I had to open ourselves up to the humbling process of ongoing learning. Fidelity to motivational interviewing (MI) requires systematic training and careful attention to the specifics of a conversational approach that promotes change. Research has shown that many of those trained in MI, when actually observed, are not using the skills properly. Effective MI demands ongoing practice and feedback to learn how to listen for "missed opportunities" and recognize those moments when we actually "hear" the client and witness the impact for the client of being genuinely heard. Clients, especially those in systems of containment and control, are not used to being heard. When one is truly heard and when the practitioner can truly reflect and clarify what she is hearing, the effect can be profound. Thus, part of our practice included review of taped sessions and ongoing coaching for all members of the treatment team, myself included. As you might imagine, this could engender some resistance from staff, which, I hoped, could enhance their empathy for their clients (Miller & Rollnick, 2013).

I had learned from my mentors in MI to position myself as a learner. I taped my own sessions and used myself as the role model for "bruised-ego survivor" in terms of missed opportunities. The staff and I were co-learners and teachers, building our practice skills together. We were also very candid with clients, letting them know about the staff requirement to tape interviews as part of our ongoing learning. Most clients were quite open to signing consents. I would also ask permission to tape sessions when I met with clients who were having trouble in treatment. I would explain that my goal was to get better at listening and be more helpful in problem-solving. Although clients always had the right to say no, nearly all agreed; they liked knowing that someone was overseeing treatment. Many shared comments such as, "I have had a lot of crappy counselors. I am glad my counselor is learning new things." Our staff, initially resistant to exposing their skills, became increasingly comfortable with the teaching-learning process. They also became more conscious of how their vulnerability paralleled that of their clients.

## Action and Accompaniment

### THE ROLE OF CASE MANAGERS

Part of my role included supervision of case managers. They were a crucial part of the program, working with clients, family, criminal justice partners, and treatment staff during and after inpatient treatment. Our best case managers maintained a delicate balance of support and accountability. A practice of "compassionate compulsion" was often the crux of their success to help clients navigate the complexities of the court system. If clients experienced recurrence of use, they would walk through an analysis of what happened with their case manager, get credit for what they did right, and then pick up the phone, which at that point weighed about a hundred pounds, to call their probation/parole officer and self-report the situation. This approach often worked in the client's favor with the probation officer and began to increase the range of options for working with clients around recurrence beyond imposing punitive sanctions such as jail time. Case managers provided important role-modeling for new staff and criminal justice system partners. They reported satisfaction in their work in that they got to share in the "possibility" of client outcomes.

### STRENGTHENING TRANSITIONAL SERVICES

As the 60-day pilot project began to show promising results, we identified the need for expanded transitional services for clients and their families to enhance success. We designed an intensive transitional phase upon release from jail-based treatment, which clients attended daily. Treatment groups were part of the services, and so was a robust schedule of activities, including family potlucks and sessions where children, caregivers, and clients could come together to identify what was working in reintegrating their loved ones back home and clarify expectations and triggers for them in this process. We introduced a practice of *accompaniment* involving peer mentors, most of whom were graduates of the program. Peer mentors helped clients complete crucial tasks that are often not recognized as barriers to successful reintegration. These included practical support in obtaining birth certificates, Social Security cards, and food stamps, and applying for Medicaid as needed. Clients practiced asking for help from peer mentors and navigating healthy boundaries in the process. After families, peer mentors were the first to be aware of recurrences. Part of their accompaniment also included accountability by conveying to clients that their support did not include keeping secrets.

Both programs also included family involvement, incorporating community reinforcement family training (CRAFT), an approach for involving concerned significant others that has been shown to improve family mental health (Meyers, Miller, & Smith, 2001). The CRAFT approach helps family members strengthen their coping skills by changing their responses and communication around their loved one's use. As family members and concerned significant others build new skills, they experience less stress and anxiety related to their loved one's use, and their loved one is more likely to engage in treatment. Our programs, which incorporated family involvement by requiring attendance at CRAFT sessions in return for in-person visitations, included children as well.

We initially anticipated resistance from family members regarding participation in CRAFT. We found instead that most were desperate for information, open to participation, and found the sessions very helpful. The sessions validated their need to give voice to the impact their loved one's behavior had on them and their children. Our family facilitators often included Navajo-speaking staff, who welcomed all in attendance, shared their own stories of recovery or support of a loved one, and translated concepts and constructs around treatment into culturally relevant examples and language. Loved ones and clients alike would report back after weekend visits on how new ways of communicating provided hope and improved relationships. The CRAFT sessions culminated in a graduation ceremony, which created time and space for celebration of client successes and family support.

## CULTURALLY GROUNDED ACTION: THE SWEAT LODGE

As the clinical supervisor, I made a concerted effort to recruit Indigenous treatment staff, some of whom were also traditional practitioners. Utilizing the Wellbriety model, which promotes culturally based healing, treatment staff were able to indigenize treatment approaches. Wellbriety is a holistic approach that addresses the physical, cultural, emotional, and spiritual realms. It has been shown to support recovery and address generational trauma for incarcerated Indigenous people, and it was very popular with clients, including non-Natives (West, 2014; White Bison, Inc., 2002). Sweat lodges have been incorporated as part of the Wellbriety approach.

Sweat lodges were originally part of the DWI program but had been discontinued several years before I came onboard. There were two main barriers to this crucial practice. First, the cultural appropriation of sweat lodges by for-profit White "healers" had resulted in the deaths of paying clients in a Sedona, Arizona, "treatment center" (Gumbel, 2009). As a result, liability insurance was now required for traditional Indigenous practitioners to be compensated for providing sweat lodges. Recruiting local traditional leaders by requesting they obtain insurance was a nonstarter. The second barrier was jail accreditation standards. Despite these barriers, the social justice and treatment implications supporting traditional sweat lodge practices were worth the effort. Thus ensued a lengthy advocacy process with administrators, who had varied levels interest in and support for this practice.

With the support of an administrator with a background in theology and advocacy on the part our partners in detention, both Native and non-Native, we were able to renew the sweat lodge. Sweat lodge leaders agreed to volunteer their services, bypassing the need for insurance. The male leaders, from different tribes, were fulfilling pledges within their respective affiliations of traditional practices and were not Navajo. The female leader was Navajo and a treatment team member. The male leaders worked with our female leader and the local sweat lodge community to gain support and approval for providing a sweat lodge that was intertribal and at the same time honored and acknowledged the local tribes and pueblos. Clarifying the intent of the jail-based sweat lodge as an intertribal approach to recovery served as a unifying practice among different tribal traditions in the correctional setting (Grobsmith, 1994). The sweat lodge leaders initiated and encouraged sharing of songs, prayers, and traditions within the sweat lodge. As sweat lodge leader Carl Clampett describes,

> First thing we do is humble ourselves, crawl through that door on our hands and knees.... We sit around the rocks and realize we're all equal, no one's better than anyone else.... You can't tell who's a counselor or who's in treatment.... Sweat lodge is about being uncomfortable. No one makes it easy out there. The easiest thing is to quit and that's what they want us to do. Come back to places like this. The hardest thing is to know that life is uncomfortable. It's not just about being sober. It's being well. When we close that door, it's gonna be hot. It's gonna be dark. There's going to be songs, we're going to talk. It's going to be uncomfortable, mentally, physically, spiritually. That's how we pray because that's how we live....
>
> The sweat lodge setting, starting with being around the fire and rocks, brings out good memories, even for the non-Natives. They start

recalling the smells and gatherings around campfires or sweats that connect them to good things in their lives. Inside the sweat lodge, traditions are reclaimed and shared, maybe experienced for the first time. There is support for one another to make it through each round, and personal reflection that supports healing. It brings closeness to the elements and each other. They offer up prayers in ways that have meaning to them. (C. Clampett, personal communication, June 2, 2020)

Client surveys consistently demonstrated that the sweat lodge was one of the most valuable experiences in treatment. In order to expand and enhance the practice, I had to invoke the Native American Religious Freedom Act (1978) with our administration and advocate alongside the lieutenant for specific sweat lodge considerations, such as providing shade for clients, moving the port-a-potty that had been placed right next to the lodge for "security reasons," providing ground cover so clients and lodge weren't muddy during the rain, and allowing food and drinks to be brought in for communal sharing and fluid replacement post-ceremony. Detention officers, some of whom were initially hesitant, became staunch defenders of the sweat lodge. They supported these requests and embraced additional duties involved in overseeing client involvement in the upkeep and preparation of the sweat lodge grounds. Detention officers offered to be rock carriers and were included in the communal post-sweat thanks. Native treatment staff began asking to be mentored in sweat lodge leadership.

## Critical Reflection

I close with three stories of practice moments when I felt I could have done more and when our persistent efforts paid off. Early on in my position, I questioned why our clients had to wear jail garb. It felt counterintuitive to our treatment approach. The administration responded that taxpayers wanted to see punitive consequences for offenders, a reminder that jails are institutions of social control. I questioned why we trained staff to comply with HIPPA regulations, yet required clients to be shackled as they entered and exited the treatment facility. Again, administrators pointed to the need for punishment, and the "walk of shame" continued. It was painful to see client reactions, with some laughing nervously and teasing each other as they started out and others looking somberly at the ground. The shame felt by clients was palpable, but I could not convey that to administrators. Looking back, I see that lack of empathy on the part of administrators may have reflected their distance from actual clients. Detention staff, the majority of whom were Navajo, generally shared what Miller and Rollnick (2013) term "accurate empathy," revealed in their statements of "I feel bad for them. I know it is embarrassing." In retrospect I wish I had explored ways to connect administrators more directly with our clients so that they could bear witness to their humanity and honor their dignity.

The success of the sweat lodge was threatened when new administrative leadership came on board. Staff relayed to me that administrators were making offensive comments about the "bad smell" of burnt cedar and sage that lingered after a sweat, a beloved and valued aroma to many Indigenous peoples. Administrators placed fragranced "odor removers" in doorways leading to the sweat lodge grounds. A senior administrator told a Native treatment team staff that they "couldn't . . . imagine crawling into that dirty, dark hole." I was told these things in confidence and asked not to bring them up, for fear that the sweat lodge would be shut down. As a White ally, I respected the request even as I struggled with the profundity of White racism reflected in these remarks. I did not feel I could usurp the reality of Native staff's experiences and concerns. At the same time, I felt complicit in not challenging my White leaders. My Native colleagues provided me with perspective. One of the sweat lodge leaders shared with me, "We don't expect them to make it easy. That's how we've survived. And that's what they [clients] are up against every day, inside and outside. They [the administration] don't get it and don't want to. Sweat lodge is resistance and resiliency."

As the facility gained jail accreditation status, the setting felt more restrictive and less treatment-oriented. A "No Public Bathrooms" sign was placed in the front lobby, denying access to outpatient clients and family members. I expressed concern to our administrator that this sign contradicted the spirit of motivational interviewing. When I was told the sign would stay, I argued that people had traveled from the reservation or across town and needed a restroom for relief or a diaper change. I was told no. I argued that as the person responsible for maintaining fidelity to our evidence-based approaches, I could not in good faith say we were practicing them. I was told that if someone had an urgent need, they could request to use the bathroom. I argued that the sign did not encourage people to ask; it just denied access. Still no. I began to go to the lobby on a regular basis and invite those who needed to use the bathroom to do so. The lieutenant joined in, regularly checking to see if anyone needed a restroom. The woman at our front desk began to check with visitors to see if they needed the restroom or a drink of water. She put a sign in her window, "Got Questions? Just Ask!" with a big happy face. As this progressed, I reported back to the administrator. I shared that an elderly Navajo couple had entered the lobby after a very long drive to visit their grandson. When I asked if they needed to use the restroom, they said they didn't think they were allowed to and pointed to the sign. I welcomed them to get water and use the restrooms. The administrator finally agreed to take the sign down.

Over the years I learned I was not alone in grappling with jail-based policies. Ensuring fidelity to an empowering treatment was limited within a restrictive incarceration setting. This reality was a constant struggle. I learned to choose my battles carefully, convey a healthy respect for others' scope of practice, and find common ground, especially in our commitment to treating clients as individuals deserving of dignity and respect. I give thanks to all those, staff and clients, who supported these efforts.

## QUESTIONS FOR REFLECTION AND DISCUSSION

1. What new learning do you take from this chapter that informs your thinking about the possibilities of social justice work within systems of control, such as the criminal justice system?
2. Have you faced similar challenges in terms of administrative barriers to social justice work in your practice? How have you navigated those barriers?
3. What do you see as some of the challenges and possibilities of bringing about justice-oriented change from below and within organizations?
4. What other possibilities do you see for challenging stigma and racism and promoting human dignity and rights within the criminal justice system?

## REFERENCES

ACLU, New Mexico Voices. (2017). *Racial and ethnic bias in New Mexico drug law enforcement: A summary of preliminary findings and recommendations*. https://www.nmvoices.org/archives/9229

Finn, J. (2020). *Just practice: A social justice approach to social work* (4th ed.). Oxford University Press.

Grobsmith, E. S. (1994). *Indians in prison: Incarcerated Native Americans in Nebraska*. University of Nebraska Press.

Gumbel, A. (2009, October 22). Death Valley: Two weeks ago on a retreat with new age guru James Arthur Ray, three people died in a sweat lodge. What went wrong? *The Guardian*. https://www.theguardian.com/world/2009/oct/22/james-ray-sweat-lodge-death

Mate, G. (2010). *In the realm of hungry ghosts*. North Atlantic Books.

Meyers, R., Miller, W., & Smith, J. (2001). Community reinforcement and family training (CRAFT). In R. Meyers & W. Miller (Eds.), *A community reinforcement approach to the treatment of addiction* (pp. 147–160). Cambridge University Press.

Miller, B., & Rollnick, S. (2013). *Motivational interviewing: Helping people to change* (3rd ed.). Guilford Press.

National Highway Traffic Safety Administration. (2005). *A guide to sentencing DWI offenders*. https://one.nhtsa.gov/people/injury/alcohol/DWIOffenders/index.htm

Native American Religious Freedom Act, 42 U.S.C. § 1996 (1978).

New Mexico Advisory Committee to the U.S. Commission on Civil Rights (2005). *The Farmington report: Civil rights for Native Americans 30 years later*. Create Space Independent Publishing Platform.

New Mexico Department of Health. (2014). *New Mexico substance abuse epidemiology profile*. https://www.nmhealth.org/data/view/substance/474/

Smith, J., & Meyers, R. (1995). The community reinforcement approach. In R. K. Hester & W. R. Miller (Eds.), *Handbook of alcoholism treatment approaches: Effective alternatives* (pp. 251–266). Allyn & Bacon.

U.S. Commission on Civil Rights. (1975). *The Farmington report: A conflict of cultures. A report of the New Mexico Advisory Committee to the United States Commission on Civil Rights*. http://crdl.usg.edu/id:tmll_hpcrc_1859456

Volkow, N., Koob, G., & McLellan, T. (2016). Neurobiologic advances from the brain disease model of addiction. *New England Journal of Medicine, 374*(4), 363–371.

White Bison, Inc. (2002). *The red road to Wellbriety: In the Native American way*. White Bison Org.

Williams, J. (2014, May–June). Walking the red road in the iron house. *American Jails*. https://narf.org/nill/documents/2014_MJ_Williams_Red%20Road.pdf?_ga=2.264532940.2135860770.1593384533-918506878.1593384533

# 15

# Diane's Story

## *From Incarceration to Social Justice Advocacy*

VICKII COFFEY, MSA, PHD

> I saw broken spirits. I saw women that needed help....
> And I tried to give it.
> —Diane

---

**Overview**

In this chapter Vickii Coffey allows readers to accompany Diane, an African American mother of four, on her journey through addiction and abuse to incarceration and, ultimately, to post-prison social justice advocacy as manager of a prison ministry program. Coffey introduces readers to transcendental phenomenology, a social justice–oriented research approach that situates participants as co-researchers. Coffey details the context and history of Diane's life leading to incarceration, examines the power relations through which Diane was "compelled to crime," describes how Diane navigated questions of meaning and power in prison, and reflects on the possibilities Diane embraced in her life beyond prison.

---

## Introduction

I am an assistant professor of social work at Governors State University in Illinois. I am interdisciplinary trained with a master's in social work administration and a doctorate in criminology, law, and justice. Over the course of my career, my practice, research, and scholarship have focused in two areas—violence against women and the re-entry experiences of formerly incarcerated persons. My focus on these issues, as an African American woman, is compelled by the profound overrepresentation of African Americans in the criminal justice system and the consequent social, economic, and political deprivation caused by the dual forces of violence against women and mass incarceration in Black and Brown communities.

During my tenure as the executive director for a nonprofit workforce development program, I became interested in the topic of re-entry and employment success among formerly incarcerated persons. The mission of the program was to help unemployed and underemployed persons reach their full potential through learning and the power of work.

Persons who were disadvantaged and marginalized due to physical and mental disabilities and citizens returning to the community from prison made up a significant portion of the approximately 1,500 annual participants in the program. Of that number, formerly incarcerated persons comprised roughly 30% of the agency clients. The vast majority of the persons returning home from prison had served lengthy sentences, and they were looking forward to opportunities to find legitimate work and turn away from crime. Frequently, the applicant waiting list was 2 to 3 times greater than the available program space. Once accepted into the program, participants received 3 weeks of intensive case management and training, which covered life skills, computer literacy, general equivalency diploma (GED) test preparation, financial literacy, interviewing, résumé writing skills, and information and referrals for employment, housing, substance abuse treatment, and health services.

Upon program completion, clients participated in graduation ceremonies, where we recognized their achievements and awarded program certificates. As executive director, I handed out certificates similar to the conferring of degrees. Participants often joyfully expressed how they felt renewed and regenerated by their new life possibilities. However, within a few weeks or months, rumors would filter in from the community—stories of dashed dreams and faded hopes. All too often, participants experienced demoralizing application and interview processes that led nowhere and left them feeling wounded by rejection and filled with mounting hopelessness and desperation. Few obtained employment, and for those who did, the employment was often transitional, short term, and low paying, with few options for financial independence and long-term economic security.

On the other hand, I routinely collaborated with a group of colleagues who had also experienced incarceration but somehow broke through enormous barriers to achieve exceptional employment success. Not only did they find jobs, but they also built careers and became professionals in an industry designed to help others overcome the life adversities caused by the stigma of incarceration. Some individuals were employed by my agency; others worked for network agencies that served formerly incarcerated persons, including policy, corrections, housing, substance and mental health treatment, legal advocacy, and educational services. I became intrigued by the successes of this group of individuals and curious about lessons that could be learned from their experiences.

Motivated by my observations, I developed a research agenda aimed at exploring re-entry and employment success among formerly incarcerated African Americans. Specifically, I wanted to learn how these men and women survived histories of struggle, moved beyond the disempowering context of incarceration, gave meaning to their experiences, found new forms of power within themselves and with others, and created transformative possibilities for their lives.

## A "Just" Research Approach

In order to learn about the employment successes of formerly incarcerated persons, I developed a qualitative study using "transcendental phenomenology" (TP) as my research method (Moustakas, 1994). While the terminology sounds complicated, the method is ideal for social justice–oriented research. A distinct and empowering feature of TP is that research participants are acknowledged as "co-researchers" (Moustakas, 1994, p. 103). TP's methods for situating participants as co-researchers and teachers honors participants' knowledge as primary and creates a nonhierarchical, collaborative, empowering research process, centered on respect and mutuality—all core principles of *Just Practice* (Finn, 2020). The process of TP allowed me, through shared power, learning, and collaboration, to honor another's lived experience and promote human dignity—a sharp contrast to the top-down process and coercive power of incarceration.

In this chapter, I introduce my co-researcher and teacher Diane, a formerly incarcerated woman. Diane shares her incredible experience of surviving incarceration, domestic violence, and substance abuse, and her achievements and life chances. Through excerpts from an in-depth qualitative interview, Diane teaches us about human agency and resilience and about key moments and possibilities for social work action in support of human dignity and social justice.

## Diane's History

Diane (pseudonym) is a 48-year-old African American woman. She is the mother of four children (three adult sons and a teenage daughter). She has been married twice. Upon reflection, she describes her younger self as a rebellious and resentful teen whose father suffered from addiction and was absent from her life. She dropped out of high school at 17 and left a stable home in Chicago, where she had resided with her mother and her stepfather, and moved to Kansas. She did not elaborate on her living arrangements in Kansas but recalled returning to high school without completing her senior year. Shortly after leaving school, she returned to Chicago and married her first husband.

Diane was "compelled to crime" (Richie, 1996, p. 9) and addiction in her first marriage at age 19. Her husband was a gang-involved criminal, wife abuser, and the father of her four children. He was constantly in trouble with the law and did not hesitate to exert his power and control over Diane through verbal, emotional, and physical abuse. Diane expressed deep concern about the long-term effect on her children due to what they witnessed:

> I want them to . . . not take on that curse. . . . Cause sometimes it's a hereditary curse . . . their father through addiction, me through addiction,

incarceration... We have to look at what our children see... They think it's normal to do certain things... Those are my worries for my children. I want them to be happy.

Diane credits her mother and stepfather for their ongoing support and help in "taking care of her children while [she was] going through the storm." She also acknowledges that they tried to protect her from the bad influences of her husband and frequently bailed her out of jail.

## Power Over: "Like a Chain Reaction . . ."

Diane described the powerful pull of her relationship to her first husband and how it led to her incarceration:

> He was constantly in and out of something... He was in jail more than we were together. I was in an... abusive relationship... He had some substance abuse issues [and] just a lot of controlling... When he went to jail, I got pulled into [his] cases. The very first time... I was in trouble with the law... he was trying to state that he was working.... So I created a document [from her stepfather's business] and doctored up the paper saying that my husband worked for [his] company. My first incarceration was a case with him.... After that first time... things started like a chain reaction. It's like once my name was written down on some kind of court police paper—it started as to being a chain reaction all my life... Things were just so easy for me to be caught up with something else again.

As Diane's experience teaches us, women are more likely to become engaged in crime through their relationships with men, and a vast majority are compelled to crime by the men they love (Leverentz, 2006; Richie, 1996). Far too often, women who are involved in crime experience what feminist criminologists refer to as "gender entrapment" and the "triple threat" of incarceration, domestic violence, and substance abuse, which extracts an enormous toll on their mental health, coping abilities, and relationships with family and children (Richie, 2001; Arditti & Few, 2006). Further, Diane teaches us about inequality in treatment for women who commit crimes. Statistically, women tend to commit nonviolent offenses, such as property and drug-related offenses, yet they are subjected to the same harsh penalties as men who commit serious offenses (Covington & Bloom, 2003).

Diane was convicted for six offenses, four of which involved her husband. Despite difficulty in recalling the dates of her arrests, Diane vividly recounts the scenarios and events involved with each case. All but one of her convictions were for nonviolent crimes, a pattern consistent with trends in the incarceration of women and girls (Sentencing Project, 2020). Further, the stigma of her record, race, and gender increasingly positioned her for physical and sexual victimization and powerlessness in an unforgiving and unjust criminal justice system (Sentencing Project, 2020). In three of the six cases, she was innocent, unjustly arrested, and convicted. Diane recounted being coerced into bringing drugs into a jail by her husband and a corrupt guard who tried to seduce her, framed for a robbery committed by her husband and another woman, and arrested for unlawful possession of a weapon that she took from a man whom she feared would harm her.

She described how she became entangled in an intricate system of prison corruption involving the collusion of guards and her husband:

> I'm going to visit him [husband] at the time when the situation happened with me entering drugs in the penal institution. When I came in the evening . . . I only did it . . . I think maybe twice. . . . I drop it, they pick it up, and they take it in the prison . . . because the drugs in there was going for much more than what it went on the outside. So they making money, the guards and everybody else is running the real money inside the prison. There was a whole system of it that was involved.

Diane's involvement in smuggling drugs left her vulnerable to sexual harassment by a prison guard whom she rebuffed during one of her prison visits. Sexual harassment and abuse by corrections staff is a consistent theme in the narratives of incarcerated women (Willingham, 2011). Below Diane describes a particular incident after visiting hours when the guard tried to lure her into his car, a block away from the prison entrance.

> I wouldn't get in the car with the guard, and the guard told me "I'm gonna get you next time . . . you . . . [sexually explicit] teaser." So the next time I came out there, he said I had drugs on my baby [which was a lie]. And I was taken into custody. . . . They arrested me. I had my children. My children saw that process.

Diane recalled her total disbelief and the emotional pain of being arrested in the full presence of her children for a crime she didn't commit. Because Diane did not have the funds to hire a private attorney, the court appointed her one. Diane describes the attorney's disregard for her innocence and his failure to advocate for her best interests.

> The lawyer [said] . . . it's your word against the officer. You plead guilty to this . . . and this will be over. You can go on and live your life. . . . I wish I really would have fought it to the end. . . . That's on my record. That's something that people look at . . . as cases got bigger, as things I was involved in later. . . . Oh, you have this . . . a plead guilty is still on my record. . . . It was piling on to future cases.

Diane was defenseless and feared the risk of leaving her children parentless and wards of the state. That was simply too great a price to pay. Diane did what any mother would do for her children. Disregarding her own innocence, she pled guilty and received 2 years' probation. Diane's experience exemplifies the "structural forces" (competence of lawyers, costs, bail issues) and "psychological biases" (skewed inequality of bargaining and punishment) that significantly and often harmfully influence plea bargain outcomes (Bibas, 2004).

## Contextualizing Diane's Story

Diane's story is not unique among women in the criminal justice system. Over 61% of women entangled in the criminal justice system are mothers (Schlafer, Duwe, & Hindt, 2019). In 2008, nearly 1.8 million minor U.S. children had parents serving time. Profoundly, Black children were 8 times more likely to have a parent incarcerated than White children (Bureau of Justice Statistics, 2008). In recalling the memory of the emotional pain of being arrested in the presence of her children, Diane teaches us about the mechanisms of structural violence, gender oppression, abuse, and inequalities that permeate the criminal justice system. Most importantly, we learn of the system's capacity for exacting coercive power and control over the lives of Black women and their children.

The third case in which Diane was implicated for her husband's wrongdoings was for an armed robbery charge.

> I had an armed robbery. They broke it down to a robbery, but it was not me. That was . . . my husband and another female . . . and they charged me. . . . He did eventually get charged . . . and he got 20 years. . . . I was like, "Tell them who it was" . . . but he didn't really wanna say nothing because it would give him a rap. He said, "You know you didn't do it.". . . But they charged me with it. I end up getting probation on that.

After her husband was sentenced to prison, Diane continued to engage in survival crimes, mostly to support her addiction. She received two additional convictions, the first for unlawful possession of a weapon and the second for forgery.

> I was with a guy who had a gun in his car. I saw the gun. I took the gun. . . . They took us both into custody. They dropped the charges . . . with him. They held me with the gun because . . . it was in my purse. And it was loaded. . . . I was in my active addiction at the time. And it was a matter of just trying to get safe, because I didn't know exactly what he was going to do.
>
> My last experience ever with the criminal history was forgery . . . That was when I was writing bad checks . . . . I had a—drug habit.

The forgery charge did not result in her imprisonment. She received a 2-year prison sentence for a technical violation of the conditions of bail bond. Diane's recounting of her pathway to incarceration teaches us how race, gender, and poverty matter in the allocation of punishment for technical violations. Consistent with literature on ethnic and racial disparities in probation revocation, Black probationers consistently experience higher revocation rates than their White counterparts and women are more likely to be committed to prison for a technical violation than men (Jannetta, Breaux, Ho, & Porter, 2014).

It is important to further situate Diane's experience in the context of mass incarceration in America. The United States incarcerates more people than any other country in the world. Close to 6 million people in America are under correctional supervision. Over 1.4 million persons are in state and federal prisons, and another 4.5 million people are serving time in their communities on probation or parole. Incarceration in America is deeply racialized. Although African Americans comprise 13% of the U.S. population (U.S. Census Bureau, 2019), they make up 31% of the total adult prison population (Bureau of Justice Statistics, 2020). The imprisonment rate for African American males in 2018 was 5.8 times that of White men (Bureau of Justice Statistics, 2020).

The incarceration of women and girls is deeply disturbing: The rate between 1980 and 2017 increased by more than 750% (Sentencing Project, 2020). Close to 111,000 adult women are doing time in America's prisons, and approximately 13% of adult women in the total corrections population are on parole. African American women comprise approximately 18% of the female prison population (Bureau of Justice Statistics, 2020). Black females are nearly twice as likely to be imprisoned as White females (Bureau of Justice Statistics, 2020) and young Black girls are disproportionately subjected to gendered violence through intensified police surveillance and racial discrimination by state agencies (Gross, 2018). A Georgetown study (Epstein, Blake, & Gonzalez, 2017) details the theory of adultification of Black children. The study found that young Black girls ages 5 to 14 are viewed more adultlike than their White peers, and this adult perception leads to harsher disciplinary sanctions and disproportionate treatment and punishment within juvenile justice and child welfare systems.

## Finding Meaning and Power During Incarceration

Diane grappled with questions of meaning and power during her incarceration. She used her time in prison for critical reflection, healing, and positive transformation. She described her own critical reflective process as one of "rewinding the tape":

> I had just come out of the Illinois Department of Corrections . . . [I] had been clean [not using drugs] for 5 years, and [I] went back into the atmosphere [addiction, then prison]. And it was like this is not where I supposed to be. It [incarceration] gave me a glimpse of the things that's around me and the things that I need to be out there focusing on. It made me feel that I had to be on top of doing some changing for me. . . . I saw young and I saw old there. . . . I didn't want to be old coming out of

prison... Most of them were frequent flyers, they came back and they came back. They was conforming to the circumstances. I didn't want to partake in the conforming.... I got a vision to see what's around me that needs to be helped. I saw broken spirits. I saw women that needed help. I saw women that needed some direction. And I tried to give it. We don't have church, but let's start one. And we started church in the gym.... I [had] been trained for the prison ministry.

I knew I was going home and I was going home a little different than what I came in.... I was ready for change... It was like each time God took something away... until it was all, let me surrender all.

Incarceration for Diane meant a time for critical reflection, revelation, and acceptance to change. She teaches us that her religion, faith, and spirituality helped her to make sense of her incarceration and to find power from within to cope with and survive her imprisonment. Her faith was her essential source of transformative power over a prison system that sought to confirm her identity as a criminal other. Historically and culturally, faith and spirituality have been at the center of the struggles for justice and equality for Black people. The centrality of faith and spirituality as essential coping mechanisms for incarcerated women has been a consistent theme in literature on overcoming and surviving imprisonment (Stringer, 2009).

## Changing Contexts: Life After Incarceration

While her faith was a catalyst for power from within, Diane once again faced the power of stigma attached to her identity as a formerly incarcerated person. She described her struggles in finding employment after incarceration as "the hurting time":

It was very difficult to attain employment. So when they asked, "Have you been convicted of a felony?" my stomach would [do] butterflies and turn around, because I didn't know how to answer the question... Do I answer yes or do I answer no? Do I just not answer it? And I really didn't know how.... I would stand on that part for about 20 minutes and be acting like I'm still filling out the application, 'cause I need to go back to that question. And I didn't know how to present that question, because it's like if I do this, they're gonna say no.

I had one interview.... And she said "I need you to come back for a second interview, 'cause – you're qualified for the job. I wanna hire you, but I gotta go through some other people to see if we can get you in." And then she said, "I tried everything I can, but your background... We can't hire you." I was like, Lord Jesus, I just need to get in the door. And it kept hurting. That was the hurting time.... "Have you been convicted of a felony?" That's the thing that's on the application that really tears people down.

Applying for jobs and facing rejection is difficult for most people. For many formerly incarcerated persons the application process is frequently an anxiety-ridden experience, tantamount to being blind-folded in front of a firing squad—not knowing when the trigger will be pulled. Hopes are dashed in an instant, as a result of retributive rather than rehabilitative collateral consequence laws and punitive employment policies. Black women are particularly vulnerable to employment discrimination and rejection due to the stigma of their race, criminal history, and societal perceptions as of them as loose, fallen women and bad mothers (Chesney-Lind, 2004).

Diane also faced daily challenges in the context of family life after incarceration. "I'm a mother, a wife, and a daughter all in one house, so I get pulled in all different directions . . . and I am constantly pouring out."

Diane is also the mediator in a violent relationship between her adult son and daughter-in-law; the caretaker for her elderly father; the support line for an incarcerated son and an unemployed son; and the disciplinarian for a rebellious teenage daughter. And, for the past 2 ½ years she has been "trapped" in an abusive second marriage:

> Verbally, it's certain gestures and certain things that he would do . . . like the biting of the tongue or biting your bottom lip, like anger, like you mad or something, or even drawing your fist to even acting like you wanna hit . . . He was like, 'yeah, your family told me how promiscuous you are' . . . [He] didn't even let me know that [he] owe[d] back child support and they took all of the [tax return funds].

Employed as a security guard, Diane's spouse has a license to carry a gun. She describes his intimidation:

> I trust God that it will be safe . . . He walks around with his gun on his hip all day long. And I was like, that ain't necessary. You ain't . . . Robocop...that's not necessary in the home . . . .My father feels intimidated by him . . . He's never threatened me.

Diane has found power from within to reclaim her dignity, leave her abuser, and take back control of her life.

> I'm gonna just go ahead and file for divorce and just move on, because it's obvious that it's not gonna get better . . . I have not told him yet. I'm waiting to speak to my lawyer to know—what my rights are so I know what I have, since he's been paying half of the rent and he's been staying in the house.

Diane's situation is complicated, and although she admits that her spouse has never threatened her with his gun, her situation bodes danger. As she has sensed, it is important that she take extra precautions to be safe.

## Possibility

Diane was fortunate to find full-time employment as the manager of a prison ministry program. She worked for the program for 10 years, and she was affiliated with the church that runs the program for more than 16 years.

> I told the pastor that I had just came from incarceration, and he told me you're gonna run my prison ministry . . . once I got home I needed to get grounded in a faith-based organization. I needed to be connected spiritually. That was the thing that was missing from me . . . The criminal background didn't affect me in getting a job because the prison ministry was . . . helping formerly-incarcerated individuals.

Diane believes that her distinction in finding work at the church was that the job "received" her. For once, she feels she is employed at a place where her past did not resurrect to block her opportunity for meaningful work. She describes her job as spiritually rewarding and an empowering passion.

> Helping others [doesn't] feel like work . . . the passion of helping someone else . . . it's a gift to be able to give to others what was so freely given to me . . . it's—such [a] reward . . . .to be able to see a person's life change, to be able to see them obtain the jobs, to be able to see them get the housing and build the relationships back with families that sometimes were broken because of . . . incarceration . . . I want to help other people build their life.

In our last meeting, Diane reflected on her life experiences. She described her most important and meaningful achievements: "[being] in my children's lives, clean and sober with a right state of mind . . . [being] a role model . . . showing my family I finally got it . . . [and] helping other people to build their life."

A few months after our interview, Diane suddenly passed away. Diane's life was a testament to her strong faith, resilience, and perseverance against overwhelming odds. She was a remarkable woman who gave her all to positive change and new possibilities in her life. She openly shared the tragedy and suffering in her life to give meaning and hope to others. She used her power from within to teach and help others find power over the barriers of incarceration and addiction and to inspire other formerly incarcerated persons to return to their families and communities whole. The one constant in her life was her enduring faith and hope for parity and social justice for persons involved in the criminal justice system. It is in that spirit that she shared her power with me to be an agent of social change.

## QUESTIONS FOR REFLECTION AND DISCUSSION

1. How does Diane's story contrast with common preconceptions about incarcerated women? How does stigma serve as a powerful barrier to possibilities for positive transformation and new life chances for formerly incarcerated African American women?
2. What does Diane's lived experience teach us about the intersections of intimate partner violence and structural violence in the lives of Black women? How do abuse, addiction, and poverty converge as pathways to incarceration for Black women and girls? What were missed opportunities for social work intervention and advocacy for Diane before her imprisonment?
3. What does Diane's life course teach us about the interlocking systems of racism, gender inequality, and mass incarceration? What resources did Diane use to overcome the barriers to her freedom, employment and re-unification with her family? How does Diane's experience and advocacy inform social work practice with people returning home from prison?
4. What does Diane teach us about the importance of accompaniment, engagement, and empowerment in the process of social work research and practice?
5. How might you draw on Diane's story to inform how you bring the Just Practice framework to bear in your own work?

## REFERENCES

Arditti, J. A., & Few, A. L. (2006). Mothers' reentry into family life following incarceration. *Criminal Justice Policy Review*, 17(1), 103–123.

Bibas, S. (2004). Plea bargaining outside the shadow of trial. *Harvard Law Review* 117(8), 2463-2547. http://dx.doi.org/10.2139/ssrn.464880

Bureau of Justice Statistics. (2008). *Parents in prison and their minor children (NCJ 222984)*. U.S. Department of Justice. http://www.bjs.gov/index.cf(2008)m?ty=pbdetail&iid=823

Bureau of Justice Statistics. (2020). *Prisoners in 2018 (NCJ 253516)*. U.S. Department of Justice. https://www.bjs.gov/content/pub/pdf/p18.pdf

Chesney-Lind, M. (2004). Beyond bad girls: Feminist perspectives on female offending. In C. Sumner (Ed.), *The Blackwell companion to criminology*, 255–267. Blackwell Publishing.

Covington, S. S., & Bloom, B. E. (2003). Gendered justice: Women in the criminal justice system. In B. E. Bloom (Ed.), *Gendered justice: Addressing female offenders*, 3–23. Carolina Academic Press.

Epstein, R., Blake J. J., & González, T. (2017). *Girlhood interrupted: The erasure of black girls' childhood*. Georgetown Law Center on Poverty and Inequality.

Finn, J. (2020). *Just practice: A social justice approach to social work* (4th ed.). Oxford University Press.

Gross, K. (2018). Policing Black women's and Black girls' bodies in the carceral United States. *Souls* 20(1), 1–13. https://doi.org/10.1080/10999949.2018.1520058

Jannetta, J., Breaux, J., Ho, H., & Porter, J. (2014). *Examining racial and ethnic disparities in probation revocation: Summary findings and implications from a multi-site study*. The Urban Institute. https://www.urban.org/sites/default/files/publication/22746/413174-Examining-Racial-and-Ethnic-Disparities-in-Probation-Revocation.PDF

Leverentz, A. M. (2006). The love of a good man? Romantic relationships as a source of support or hindrance for female ex-offenders. *Journal of Research in Crime and Delinquency*, 43, 459–488.

Moustakas, C. (1994). *Phenomenological research methods*. Sage Publications.

Richie, B. E. (1996). *Compelled to crime: The gender entrapment of battered women*. Routledge.

Richie, B. E. (2001). Challenges incarcerated women face as they return to their communities: Findings from life history interviews. *Crime and Delinquency*, 47(3), 386–389.

Schlafer, R., Duwe, G., & Hindt, L. (2019). Parents in prison and their minor children: Comparisons between state and national estimates. *The Prison Journal*, 99(3), 310–328.

Sentencing Project. (2020). *Incarcerated women and girls*. [Fact Sheet] https://www.sentencingproject.org/publications/incarcerated-women-and-girls/

Stringer, E. C. (2009). Keeping the faith: How incarcerated African American mothers use religion and spirituality to cope with imprisonment. *Journal of African American Studies*, 13(3), 325–347. New York: Springer.

United States Census Bureau. (2019). *QuickFacts*. www.census.gov/quickfacts/fact/table/US/PST045219

Willingham, B. C. (2011). Black women's prison narratives and the intersection of race, gender and sexuality in U.S. prisons. *Critical Survey*, 23(3), 55–66.

Part Five

# INTEGRATING SOCIAL JUSTICE IN UNIVERSITY CONTEXTS OF PRACTICE

# 16

# Healthy Market

## Addressing Food Insecurity at an Urban College Campus

SONYA CRABTREE-NELSON, PHD, LCSW,
MARISSA CIRILO, LCSW, AND
ERIC CRABTREE-NELSON, LCSW

> I get kind of embarrassed thinking like, "Oh I'm walking out with a bag of food and I don't know how people are going to be thinking of me," but at the same time . . . you feel kind of grateful. And then afterwards, you go home and you're going to get to eat and not starve, and that feels kind of good.
> —Harold, Washington College student

---

**Overview**

In this chapter Sonya Crabtree-Nelson, Marissa Cirilo, and Eric Crabtree-Nelson describe a collective effort to raise consciousness concerning hunger and food scarcity among urban college students. The initiative resulted in a partnership with a local food depository and establishment of a free healthy market for students and staff. The authors show how the group broadened the meanings associated with being a college student and challenged power structures that failed to see the complex histories and contexts of urban, often first-generation, under-resourced college students' lives. The authors describe how teaching-learning and critical reflection were central to their campus change effort.

---

## Introduction

The authors highlight the grassroots movement of a small group of students, administrators, staff, faculty, and counselors to bring awareness concerning hunger and food scarcity among urban community college students, ultimately resulting in a partnership with a food depository and a free healthy market for students and staff. This example takes place at Harold Washington College (HWC), one of seven City Colleges of Chicago. It is located downtown with access to transportation and serves approximately 13,000 diverse, mostly first-generation college students. The concerned group initially focused on challenging and broadening the meaning associated with being a college student. They centered their efforts on the education of staff, faculty, and administrators in order to challenge the power structures that have historically sought to educate students without considering the broad and complex context in which urban, often first-generation, under-resourced college students are seeking advanced schooling. Over the course of 2 years, this group expanded and deepened the college's understanding and commitment to the whole student and built a partnership with the local food depository. Together they have created a permanent healthy market on campus for students and staff to receive free food and healthy cooking ideas and pairings. In this chapter we outline the process and show how it is grounded in the concepts of Just Practice.

## Recognizing the Need

The concept of the Healthy Student Market was initially conceived by the Student Success Council (SSC) in 2015. This college-wide committee consisted of faculty and representatives from the Department of Student Services and Academic Affairs. Student representatives from the Student Government Association (SGA) also joined meetings when they were able. The purpose of this group was to address basic needs that students reported during their academic endeavors. The SSC, headed by the associate dean of the college, contacted the Greater Chicago Food Depository to begin discussions about how a program could be implemented within HWC. As the SSC attempted to address these needs without a formal institutional structure, the Wellness Center was also in the beginning phase of clarifying its role within the broader school setting. The Wellness Center team began to take part in the larger discussion around students' needs. These needs, and possible solutions, were informed by the broader work toward understanding stigma within mental health centers and thinking through the way that people were currently given distributed food. It was decided that the best, least stigmatizing way to distribute food was to imitate the way that people shopped for food. The recipients made decisions that were right for their diets, health, and cultural needs, and available in the market. These decisions were backed up in discussions with the Greater Chicago Food Depository staff.

In fall 2016, the Wellness Center assisted with the first pop-up market for students at HWC. It was called the Healthy Student Market. The pop-up occurred once monthly for 2 hours during which students and employees could shop for food items from the Greater Chicago Food Depository right on campus. The Wellness Center staff managed this event with the assistance of volunteers who were faculty and staff employees within HWC. In order to promote access and visibility, we marketed it as "free groceries for the entire community." We intended the program to be an inclusive space where both campus employees and students who experienced food insecurity were welcome. The administration at the time was supportive of the pop-up market, which operated between 2016 and 2017. Our efforts included a monthly calendar that provided employees with time off to volunteer when the pop-up operated. This volunteerism ensured that the program was accessible. Additionally, these efforts supported the management of the Healthy Student Market so the community could utilize this resource consistently. However, toward the end of 2017, the SSC dissolved amid a time of difficult transition across all city colleges. The colleges experienced an overhaul of upper administrators due to the appointment of a new chancellor over all seven city colleges and thus new administration at each campus.

During this time of unrest and change, the Wellness Center director, Eric Crabtree-Nelson, made the decision to take over management of the Healthy Student Market, due to the departure of Associate Dean Cerrentano, who had initially championed the idea. Eric tasked the new Wellness Center coordinator, Marissa Cirilo, with the transition of the pop-up. Eric, a licensed clinical social worker, had a unique and informed perspective on the role the Wellness Center would play in managing the Healthy Student Market. He was able to ensure the survival of the program by including it within the Wellness Center's core services. Dr. Anna Zettel, Wellness Center staff psychologist, was also an integral part of managing the original pop-up market and its transition to a permanent program.

In spring 2018, the new president of HWC was officially confirmed. The president met with Eric to discuss the future of the Healthy Market and transitioning it to a permanent space within HWC. We were aware that the success of this effort would require collaboration by multiple stakeholders to ensure its viability. The initial planning began with establishing monetary funds, finding a physical space for the program, and creating a name indicating the project would be a permanent part of the HWC campus. Eric initiated the planning of the permanent program. In spring 2018, the operational planning and partnership with Greater Chicago Food Depository began to solidify with training on management of a food program.

In honor of one of the founding members of the HWC Student Success Council, Associate Dean Arlethia Mayes, who had passed away, the program was named the Arlethia G. Mayes Healthy Market. Our Wellness Center team secured part of the former campus cafeteria, which had been underutilized due to the profusion of places to find food in our downtown location, to house the Healthy Market. It officially opened at the beginning of the fall 2018 semester. The former cafeteria location was an optimal space for food storage, washing, and marketing purposes due to its visibility and accessibility. Students were able to utilize the exterior space to eat and socialize given the large number of tables and chairs in the location.

The Greater Chicago Food Depository's team worked closely with our team to discuss hours of operation and the delivery schedule of food items from their warehouse. Due to staffing constraints, the program started with a twice-weekly schedule plus an additional day to receive the bimonthly delivery. It was important to create access for students and employees during morning, afternoon, and evening hours. We were able to hire students through the federal work-study program to help staff the market. Marissa, Eric, and Dr. Zettel invited social work, counseling, and clinical psychology interns and externs to participate in managing the program. These decisions created access for student stakeholders to be at the table with faculty, staff, administration, and other students. Through these efforts the Healthy Market became a permanent program for the college.

## Connection to Key Concepts of Just Practice

The SSC group at HWC initially focused its efforts on challenging and broadening the *meaning* associated with being a college student. Because of their positions in classrooms and various student-facing offices within the college, SSC members had an understanding of student needs regarding hunger, food insecurity, and access to basic health and hygiene supplies. Students reported that inadequate access to basic necessities had a profound effect on their overall academic success. This was counter to the often-held and outdated belief that most college students have the means to be in college and thus do not struggle with basic needs such as food and water, shelter, and safety.

In fact, the Hope Center's Real College Survey of City Colleges of Chicago revealed that 44% of students reported experiencing food insecurity on some level during the previous 30 days (Goldrick-Rab, Looker, Coca, & Baker-Smith, 2019). Based on what we knew from students' personal accounts and other literature, we needed to advocate for the Healthy Market to include not only food items, but also hygiene supplies such as safer sex barriers, deodorant, toothpaste, and shower items.

At the very beginning of this process, the SSC would take up a collection once per year for these various items to give to students. But this "charity" approach did not address the social justice issues at stake within the college environment. Therefore, the SSC simultaneously centered their efforts on the education of staff, faculty, and administrators in order to challenge the *power* structures that have historically sought to educate students without considering the broad and complex system in which urban, often first-generation, under-resourced college students are seeking advanced schooling.

These educational efforts facilitated the contribution and support from staff and administration at HWC. In fact, they revealed the alarming truth that not only were students often in precarious economic situations, but some staff and faculty of HWC were also in the same situations. Oftentimes, these employees were the sole income earners for their large extended families. As our team came to understand the extent of food insecurity on campus, we worked to create a larger, more stable solution.

The reader can imagine the volatile bureaucratic *context* within a city entity. Invariably, changes can be frustrating at times within an institution that is both a college and an organization funded by and overseen by the City of Chicago. We often felt that the fate of the Healthy Market initiative was at the mercy of the individual occupying the position of chancellor or HWC president. Concerned with how precariously positioned the Healthy Market was, Eric pushed the administration to allow it to reside as a program within the Wellness Center, thus ensuring its long-term success. In essence, he utilized the power of his position in a time of transition to advocate for and ultimately protect the nascent food program. This proved to be a helpful and strategic move.

There was no *history* of providing ongoing help for students' basic needs at HWC or at any of the other six city colleges. In addition to this severe deficit, the Wellness Centers throughout the city colleges generally operated solely for the purpose of providing counseling and case management to students. While the Wellness Centers provided resources and referrals for basic needs, the actual meeting of those needs had historically been left to other institutions outside of the schools' orbit. This move to respond more directly to students' needs was a deliberate choice that entailed developing additional internal resources for the student body.

Over the course of 4 years, the SSC and our team expanded and deepened the college's understanding and commitment to the whole student and built a partnership with the local food depository. Together we have created a permanent healthy market on campus for students and staff to receive free food and healthy cooking ideas and pairings. The Healthy Market, as well as the process of implementing such a program, has created a shift in the way administration conceptualizes the needs of students. This in turn has created *possibilities* now and hopefully in the future for all institutions of higher learning and how they develop student services.

Currently, Marissa supervises interns entering their foundational year in graduate-level programs and HWC students participating in the federal work-study program who help run the Healthy Market. The Healthy Market specialists reported that many students were unaware of what to do with some of the food items in the market. The team members therefore decided to make easy recipes with the items available and offer samples to students around the college. Through this targeted outreach, students could be introduced to an item, taste it, and obtain a recipe that was easy to put together. This also generated engagement that led more students to visit the Healthy Market to take advantage of a service they previously did not know existed.

## Using Just Practice Processes

As social justice-oriented social workers, both Eric and Marissa continually engage in *teaching-learning* and *critical reflection* as they carry out their work with the Healthy Market (Finn, 2020). First, they position themselves as learners, attending to students' accounts of their lives and the multiple demands they face both on and off campus. Second, they learned about the pervasiveness of food insecurity from recent surveys and from students, staff, and faculty. Third, they examined the power dynamics of the university and strategized ways to best use the power they had at hand to protect the market and to bring other stakeholders into the process. Fourth, they mobilized critical education efforts with the larger campus community to challenge myths and expose the realities of the everyday struggles for food security that affected members of the campus community. Finally, they have instituted teaching-learning as an ongoing practice among Healthy Market volunteers and employees to ensure that the services they provide responded to the expressed needs of anyone who utilized the program. Basically, a large part of how they thought about their work with the Healthy Market process was in relation to the examination of power dynamics, collaboration, and education.

In addition to the role the students in the SGA had in the initial Healthy Market planning, an integral component to increasing student involvement was the inclusion of work-study students and first-year graduate-level interns who participated in the Healthy Market as their foundational social justice practicum internship. In integrating a social justice lens for this program, our Wellness Center team believed the embodiment of student involvement began with student leaders managing the day-to-day operations. This concept perhaps creates an atmosphere of safety and trust for the individuals who are accessing this food program. If students felt less stigmatized because other students were serving them, they would be more apt to use the Healthy Market in a more affirming way.

## Social Workers' Positionality and Impact on the Process

Throughout this process we also had to critically reflect on our positionalities in relation to the process of gaining a Healthy Market at HWC. Eric recognizes that his various areas of privilege played a role in the process. For example, due to the history of top-down administration at HWC, Eric's years of experience as a social work administrator played a positive role in how his ideas and requests were viewed. Eric came to HWC in fall 2015 with approximately 15 years of social work administrative experience. He immediately found that his opinions and views were taken seriously in college meetings. In addition, he is a White male in a society that tends to lend credence to and privilege his views above others (Mizrahi & Greenawalt, 2017). Thus, Eric found that when he approached administration, including the newly appointed president of HWC, in spring 2018 with a proposal to take over the operation and expansion of the Healthy Market, they were all too happy to agree. He utilized his experience level, male privilege, and education level—including research findings to back up his ideas—and found that all were quite happy to allow him to take over the operations. In contrast,

Marissa, Wellness Center coordinator, is a Latinx, cisgender, female-identified social worker and recent MSW graduate. She and Eric doubt that the administration would have supported the plan in the same way had she been the one to approach them.

Politics and timing also played a role in the events. The new president of HWC knew that an external survey of the student population was underway and would most likely highlight food insecurity as a significant issue. Eric and the Healthy Market team were able to use their persuasive power to show how HWC could be seen as an innovative leader of the city colleges. Eric also convinced the president that the media attention would benefit the college (Meredith & Monsell, 2018). In fact, the grand opening of the Healthy Market in fall 2018 included five media events (NPR on-line spread, reporting by two popular television news channels, and coverage by two local radio stations). Both the executive director of the Chicago Food Depository and the chancellor of City Colleges were present for the event. The Healthy Market gained visibility because HWC was the first of the city colleges to implement a permanent food program serving a community that was not typically associated with experiencing food insecurity. In the first month of operation, following its grand opening in September 2018, the Healthy Market served nearly 400 individuals and over 100 families. In addition, of the 393 individuals who used the program, 112 were also shopping for people with whom they shared a residence. This inferred that there were significantly more people who benefited from the program (Goldrick-Rab et al., 2019).

In addition, this process has expanded the consciousness of the Wellness Center staff. Eric, Marissa, Anna, and the Wellness Center interns now see the importance of ensuring that the center is a space for students to receive holistic care. Eric has embraced the idea that the counseling center can both meet the concrete needs of the students as it simultaneously attends to their mental health needs (Flanigan & Salm Ward, 2017; Parke, Meireles & Sickora, 2019). The Wellness Center staff have become advocates in the college counseling center space for the importance of seeing and meeting the needs of the whole student. In sum, they have embraced a social-justice–oriented practice that sees the intimate connection between personal struggles and the broader contexts of student's lives. They bring the best of their clinical skills along with their roles as advocates and educators to bear every day in their work (Hoefer, 2016).

## Challenges

The collective efforts to establish and sustain the Healthy Market was not without challenges. We had to be closely attuned to the shifting political landscape at HWC and the implications for the market's viability. Once we determined that the food program would flounder unless the Wellness Center, or some school entity, stepped up and charted a course for it, we made a commitment to act.

We recognized that the Wellness Center was the best informed and best positioned entity to provide these resources for the school community, but we alone could not sustain it. We had to build partnerships and relationships that could support the Healthy Market. We worked tirelessly on multiple fronts with various departments in order to find space, furniture, grant funding, and employees to run the Healthy Market. The biggest lynchpin to success was ensuring the partnership with our local food resource agency, the Greater Chicago Food Depository. They were willing to provide a monthly food grant budget and deliver it to our location, so that we could work on developing methods to efficiently distribute the food aid. We constantly drew on our social work knowledge and skills of engagement, relationship-building, and collaboration as we nurtured the development of the Healthy Market.

We also faced challenges regarding the disconnect between students' lived experiences and the assumptions of administrators. The initial excitement in the student body was not fully understood by privileged, upper-level college administrators, who seemed a bit surprised about the numbers of students, and staff, who were utilizing the Healthy Market. Even the name of the space became difficult for administrators. They persisted in calling the space "a pantry." This highly stigmatized language evoked ideas of food that was thrown together and "leftovers" destined for those of little means. Instead we envisioned the Healthy Market as a place where food-insecure students and staff could "shop" for food that would round out their budget. They could seek out food to their liking, and not simply be given a set of food items that did not fit their tastes or their dietary needs.

The team intentionally chose the name Healthy Market, as opposed to a name that included words such as pantry, food bank, or soup kitchen. The Wellness Center team's focus was to provide students and employees experiencing food insecurity with an aesthetically welcoming space that advertised the purpose of the program in an affirming way. The mission of the Healthy Market, "Addressing food insecurity and hunger on our campus and in our communities," appears on a banner with a colorful background of fresh produce and is the first thing people see as they enter the space where the program is located. The marketing and advertising put forth by the Wellness Center team is consistent with the mission statement. However, HWC's public relations team still refers to it as a "pantry program" when sending out notifications and events related to the Healthy Market. So there remains a great deal of education that needs to occur.

Further barriers that span to the present day include the challenges around providing the array of food and non-food options that many participants have requested. Our goal is to provide a wide variety of basic food options, which include shelf-stable, refrigerated, and frozen items, that allow clients to choose what they see as fitting to their household needs. Without additional funding, the Healthy Market's permanent program is limited in terms of what we can offer our customers. The Wellness Center staff have worked with the Student Government Association (SGA) to secure an additional monthly budget to purchase items not offered by the Greater Chicago Food Depository. Items such as toilet paper, paper towels, safer sex barriers, and other various food and non-food products are being considered for monthly purchase and distribution. The SGA also provided funding to purchase a deep freezer for the program, which allows for purchasing of foods that could last indefinitely and provide greater variety, creating sustainability for client use. This funding was the first to be offered outside of the Great Chicago Food Depository's monthly grant.

## Possibilities and New Insights

Each of the seven city colleges is a unique environment due to its culture and physical neighborhood. HWC is unique for its downtown location. Students often report holding at least one job, supporting others in their household, and contributing financially or otherwise to keep their households running. Since the beginning of the fall 2019 semester, students and employees have been able to access the Healthy Market twice per month. For some visitors, it would be a benefit to have the Healthy Market as an option at least three times a month in order to have enough food for their households. We hope to be able to expand access over time. We have also observed that many students are not interested in shopping, but are simply looking for snacks. They need something quick to get them through class. Our team is looking for ways to provide more healthy snack offerings. The stigma of utilizing food programs still exists and is a crucial part of the educating people about why supports like this are needed.

The Wellness Center team recently received student feedback that there is a need for low-sodium, diabetic-conscious, gluten-free, and vegetarian and vegan food options. After purchasing a deep freezer, we can better meet these needs with frozen vegetables, proteins, and other freezer stable items, whereas before participants relied heavily on canned protein foods and vegetables. The Wellness Center team see themselves as a link in the healthy food process for students. They also connect students with the Illinois LINK program for food resources outside of the Healthy Market. In closing, we are proud of the collective efforts that brought the Healthy Market to fruition, and we are eager to embrace new possibilities as our efforts expand and evolve.

## Covid-19 Postscript

In March 2020, the Healthy Market began its transition to temporary closure due to Covid-19. Our team quickly made pre-bagged kits following the CDC's guidelines. The HWC campus remains closed with the exception of essential employees (e.g., security and engineering team). The temporary closure of the Healthy Market, as well as the Wellness Center moving to virtual operations, has severely impacted how we address food insecurity. We have provided case management training to clinical interns and externs so they can assist students in locating current food programs in neighborhoods and communities using the Greater Chicago Food Depository's website. During the fall 2020 semester, all seven CCC Wellness Centers coordinated 10 to 15 outreach events with the Illinois Hunger Coalition and Near North Health Service Corporation, focusing on assisting students in applying for SNAP benefits as well as Medicaid, Medicare, and the Children's Health Insurance Program (CHIP).

While our efforts provide support, all seven Healthy Markets have been closed from March 2020 to the present. In October 2020, Eric and Marissa organized a small-scale pop-up opportunity to provide additional bags of shelf-stable items for individuals who were working or attending classes on campus. In addition, Eric stocks a cart at Harold Washington with shelf-stable food when he goes to campus twice per month. Students are able to access the building to utilize this food option. The Wellness Center team is continuing these efforts throughout the spring 2021 semester at and working toward a safe reopening of the Healthy Market in the latter part of 2021 if conditions allow.

## QUESTIONS FOR REFLECTION AND DISCUSSION

1. What sort of food resources are available on your campus, and who has access to them?
2. What would you need to know about your students, or staff, in order to serve them in the best way possible?
3. Who on your campus would be best situated to be involved in the development of food resources? Who might be a gatekeeper? Why?
4. Why did the team at Harold Washington choose to eschew the description of "food pantry"? What does a "food pantry" connote versus a "healthy market"?
5. How might you bring the concepts and processes of Just Practice to bear to address an issue of social and economic justice on your campus?

## RESOURCES

https://www.feedingamerica.org/
http://onenorthside.org/
http://www.ccc.edu/Pages/default.aspx

## REFERENCES

Finn, J. (2020). *Just practice: A social justice approach to social work* (4th ed.). Oxford University Press.
Flanigan, A., & Salm Ward, T. (2017). Evidence and feasibility of implementing an integrated wellness program in northeast Georgia. *Health & Social Work, 42*(3), 143–150.
Goldrick-Rab, S., Looker, E., Coca, V., & Baker-Smith, C. (2019). *City Colleges of Chicago #RealCollege Survey*. The Hope Center.
Hoefer, R. (2016). *Advocacy practice for social justice* (3rd ed.). Lyceum Books, Inc.
Meredith, J. C., & Monsell, M. E. (2018). *Lobbying on a shoestring* (4th ed.). Massachusetts Law Reform Institute & Massachusetts Continuing Legal Education, Inc.
Mizrahi, T., & Greenawalt, J. (2017). Gender differences and intersectionality in community organizing. *Journal of Community Practice, 25*(3/4), 432–463.
Parke, K. A., Meireles, C. L., & Sickora, C. (2019). A nurse-led model of care to address social and behavioral determinants of health at a school-based health center. *Journal of School Health, 89*(5), 423–426.

# 17

# Using Just Practice to Structure Learning in Field

LAURA DRESSER, MSW, PHD

> To hope is to give yourself to the future, and that commitment to the future makes the present inhabitable.
> —Rebecca Solnit

---

### Overview

In this chapter Laura Dresser describes the use of Just Practice to frame her yearlong MSW weekly field seminar for students in policy and administration placements at the University of Wisconsin–Madison. Students come together to reflect on work in the field, support one another, solve problems together, and develop a group project focused on social justice and macro practice. In the first semester, the *Just Practice* text provides a unifying frame of refence for students in diverse placements. In the second semester, the class works together on a key social justice issue wherein they directly apply Just Practice concepts and processes.

---

## Introduction

What is social work?[1] What is macro practice? What is social justice? These foundational questions are neither easily nor permanently answered. In my journey through teaching and my work with students and social workers, I often encounter these questions. Perhaps, more honestly, I consistently see incomplete or inadequate answers to these questions, limiting our ability to grapple with what this

---

[1] This chapter draws especially on work with the students in the most recent field seminar (the 2019–2020 cohort) and is reflects our work together. I'm grateful to each member of the class: Katie Amelse, Shayne Gerberding, Amelia Gonzales, Haley Ingersoll, Eunji Lee, Kadijha Marquardt-Davis, Elizabeth Primo, Caroline Pyon, Aaron Reilly, Sam Van Akkeren, Nerissa Vogt, and Sakara Wages.

profession should mean not only for social workers themselves but also for the people we work with and for, and for the broader society as well. Understandings of professional knowledge, identity, practice, and ethics are defined and framed by the way we take on these more fundamental questions. Whether you are just starting out in social work or have been practicing in the field for decades, it pays to visit and revisit these questions.

*Just Practice* (Finn, 2020) centers these questions and, indeed, the very practice of posing questions and provides a foundation for probing these questions, both for myself and with students. Over the past 3 years, in teaching both field seminars and macro practice courses, I've had the privilege of rereading *Just Practice* and learning from and reconsidering the text with dozens of students. Each journey through the book has been unique. To be sure, my understanding has evolved, but more important, each class grabs onto different aspects and themes, generating new insight and emphasis.

The text and its framework speak to students placed at huge state bureaucracies and tiny service driven nonprofits. It provides analytic insight to students with deeply considered radical politics and also to those who have not been exposed to or embraced a political worldview. It fuels thinking for students with a background in theory and those coming to theory for the first time. And, critically, the framework speaks to justice at every level of practice, blurring the false and dangerous distinction between micro and macro practice. At its most destructive, this distinction is used to locate social justice and system change in the *other* (macro) part of the profession, a safe distance from the spheres of influence that so many social workers toil in.

In this chapter I offer highlights from my MSW field seminar, which I have structured around *Just Practice*. I show how we bring key concepts and core processes to bear in both classroom and field. I return to the opening questions and offer some reflections from my own practice history as an economist and social worker. I make the case that a "just practice" approach enables social workers to move beyond a false dichotomy of "micro" and "macro" toward an integrated practice of social work that truly centers social justice.

## Just Practice Field Seminar

I teach the field seminar in policy and administration for students in their final year of the MSW program at the University of Wisconsin–Madison (UW). Each student is placed in a setting for both semesters of the year, working there with a site supervisor to develop and demonstrate advanced practice skills. Students participate in a yearlong seminar with others in similar practice settings. Students working in macro placements—those dealing with advocacy and system change; research, policy, and program design and evaluation; and organizational development and administration—are in the field seminar that I teach. In teaching,

I draw on my graduate training both in social work and economics and my experiences of more than 2 decades of research and policy work on the structure, policies, and organizing strategies for improvement of low-wage jobs that I have done with union, community, policy, and program leaders. This work is not at the heart of common understandings of social work practice. But just as *Just Practice* helps students see their own way into social justice work, the book has provided me with a bridge back into thinking about social work after my many years focused away from the field. Each year, along with a new class, I reread the text and discover new applications, interpretations, and insights.

From September to May, we meet each Monday morning to share what we're learning, doing, and facing in field placements. We support each other, solve problems together, and develop collective projects. *Just Practice* is our primary text for the fall semester, and we read it from cover to cover. The framework creates a common language for our discussion of diverse placements and issues. We consider the text on its own and in direct relationship to the issues that students are facing in their field placements. We bring questions of meaning, power, context, history, and possibility to bear as we examine social work's history, values, ethical principles, and theoretical bases writ large and in relation to the specific settings in which class members are practicing. Over the course of the year, we also develop and implement a collective action project that takes on some key structural issue identified by the class. In this project, we apply, evaluate, and refine Just Practice concepts and processes as we seek to make lasting change in the world.

The structure of our engagement with the book is straightforward and supports the creation of community in our seminar. Because we will be together all year, and because trust is essential in the context of exploring problems and addressing challenges of practice, we spend time early on developing a sense of community. We get to know each other and learn about the placements where students will be spending some 18 hours each week. We develop ground rules for our time together using a process that Laurie Frank, a friend and experiential learning expert, shared with me. In small groups, students identify as precisely as possible what has made their worst classes bad, with attention to who has power over what made the class bad—the professor (e.g., readings), the class (e.g., hogging discussion time), or external factors (e.g., flickering lights). In small groups, we then flip the question: If these aspects made for the worst class ever, would the opposite make for the best? This year one student group identified the White male hegemony in readings, discussions, and assignments as one aspect that made for the worst class ever. The group argued that for the best class, we should center Black and Indigenous women in our work, readings, and discussions.

The discussion around this, early in the semester, was challenging and rich. Black women in the class were at the forefront of describing how this approach would strengthen conversation as well as our approaches to practice. Together, the class agreed to the challenge, committing to center the experiences and insights of Black and Indigenous women through our discussions, changing our supplementary readings, and bringing a new perspective to our presentations and discussions. (I should note that as a White woman teaching this class, I have no doubt that I fell short of fully realizing the challenge we embraced together in our first weeks of class. But the explicit statement of the goal, the shared commitment to it, and the leadership of the class, especially Black women in it, allowed us to consciously and effectively create a space where discussion about race, racism, White supremacy, colonialism, and the need for decolonizing social work and social services was consistent and expected.)

Alongside these foundational conversations, we dig into the early chapters of *Just Practice*. The first chapters open the gateway to a new way of thinking about the meanings of social work and social justice, the importance of critical reflection, the history of the profession, the interplay of personal and professional values, and the contested nature of codes of ethics. By the time we get to the chapter on theory, the discussion is especially rich, as students have grown into a common language, found challenges in the book and their placements, and embraced a more critical view of social work that had not been named or discussed before.

Once we get to the chapters addressing the core processes of social work, we slow down. We spend 2 weeks on each chapter. For the first week, a team of three students leads discussion on the chapter, identifying key issues and engaging the class in exercises to apply, clarify, question, and reflect on the processes. In the 2nd week, class members critically reflect on the implications of the chapter for their work in their field placements. A few students start the conversation with presentations connecting concepts in the chapter with approaches and practices they see in their placements. Positive connections—ways that their placement shows evidence of key ideas from the chapter—are easiest, but we also work to identify critical ideas that suggest challenges or shortcomings at the placement and needed new directions. For many students, critique can be much harder. In these conversations, then, we devote serious time considering the importance and challenge of critical reflection.

Throughout the year, we translate theory into collective action by developing and implementing a class project that contributes to justice in the world. In the 2019–2020 year, for example, the class worked to extend and amplify learning from the UW School of Social Work's annual Social Workers Confronting Racial Injustice Conference. In 2020, Michelle Alexander was the keynote speaker, closing out a day of more than a dozen workshops and panels covering issues from the intersection of climate and racial justice to restorative justice and the mental health impact of historical trauma faced by Indigenous people. Our collective action project was to develop materials for the web and events for the social work community that would help social workers move the learning from the conference into anti-racist action.

I continue to find ways to create an environment for teaching and learning founded in true engagement and relationship with students. In striving toward the ideal of teaching-learning, I find that I am trying to listen more carefully, to structure space to engage all students in discussion, to bring materials and ideas in response to student interests, to co-structure processes for securing broader insight, to allow critique and redirection, and to have the humility to follow the lead of students at key moments. The class's ground rules process, described above, aligns with principles of engagement from *Just Practice*. When we read that chapter, we reflect not only on our placements but also on how we established relationships and community as a class. When we talk about teaching-learning, we consider our relationships with supervisors, clients, and each other. We explore the chapters through the lenses of our field placements, our work with communities, and our experiences in class.

We use decision-making strategies described in the action and accompaniment chapter. Through an iterative nomination and voting process, we pick the book that we will read together in the second semester of class. (This past year, we selected *Emergent Strategy* by adrienne maree brown, which connects in many ways to Just Practice themes. In hindsight, this was also a perfect book as the world moved into the Covid-19 pandemic in spring 2020.) We consider the importance of celebration in our placements and discuss strengths and limitations of approaches to celebration there. During check-in, we name and celebrate successes in placements and life. At our best, we remember to celebrate each other. At the end of the year, we host a brunch to celebrate our community and to thank our site supervisors.

The collective action class project is the place where we apply the Just Practice framework and social justice ideas in our community. Using participatory planning strategies, we select and develop our group project. We explicitly embrace the challenging reality that each one of us has different capacity to contribute to the project. Some have more time and will be able to lean into our collective project. Some will need to contribute less. We admit that there is no "fair" way to think about the work and its distribution. Instead we focus on designing a project that everyone sees as important, then each individual contributes what they can. The structure challenges notions of what is fair and equal and also helps students see how they might relate to social justice work in the future. Some can step into leadership roles while recognizing that they are not more important or committed as result. Some will support the effort in more contained ways. These students have the hard work of finding ways to understand, without guilt, the importance of their contribution and the constraints on it. Students tend to be more forgiving of their classmates than themselves. This, too, is considered in designing the project and in our participatory evaluation that we do as a class at the end of the year.

It is exciting to see how students and the class as a community incorporate and question the concepts and processes of Just Practice as they grow in their understanding of and commitment to social justice in social work over the course of the year. Three key ideas from the text—problematizing, power, and possibility—are especially important to students and class discussion.

# Problematizing, Power, and Possibility

## PROBLEMATIZING

Seminar discussions around *problematizing* (part of the work of exploring meaning) are, for some students, a critical gateway into the ideas in Just Practice. Early in the year, the Just Practice framework can feel unwieldy to students who are used to more "practical" ideas and directive writing. For these students, the first step is to become open to the challenge of definitions and the slippery nature of words and social agreement. The practice of *problematizing*, a critical exploration of meaning, offers a good starting point that opens a new way of seeing. The very idea that words can be interrogated and that creating meaning is a complex and contested process is, for some students, novel and revelatory. Even for students more familiar with the intellectual process of problematizing, the focus on problems in social work practice brings new insights and energy. We explore social work values and ethics as resulting from ongoing and contested processes. We bring concrete examples from field placements to bear in our discussions. We explore in detail the idea of "problematizing" our conceptions of what is presumed to be "normal" or standard.

One student noted the impact of this approach on her own thinking. The concept of problematizing was new to her and provided her a structure for critique of common social work approaches that she had learned in other classes. In class, she noted that problematizing should be more regularly applied throughout the field and she brought the concept of problematizing to her placement working on community economic development issues. This resonated with many students in the class for whom problematizing was a gateway concept that made the Just Practice framework more concrete. In her placement, Nerissa used insights from all key concepts in bringing a social justice perspective to more traditional economic development programs.

## POWER

The emphasis on seeing, questioning, and building power is another theme to which we constantly return in discussion and analyses of work in field placements. *Just Practice* centers the critical nature of questions of power from the start and encourages readers to continually consider forms and relations of power in social work practice. There is tension in this understanding of power. Power certainly exists, and many social workers can quite easily identify their own *lack* of power. For example, students point to the chronic underfunding of services and programs, the resulting relatively low wage in many social work jobs, and the intense occupational hierarchies in some social work settings, such as health care. But this is a very partial view of power.

The framing of power by Mexican academics and activists in terms of power over, power from within, power with, and power to do (Townsend et al., cited in Finn, 2020, p. 26) makes discussions of power both more accessible and challenging for students. Examining power in this multifaceted way allows for exploration of the contradictions and tensions within the word and within our work, which is a necessary foundation for social justice work. It challenges social workers to move beyond a perceived sense of powerlessness and to recognize the significant, and sometimes coercive, power that social workers have over clients. This power is rarely seen and discussed, but it is so essential for understanding practice and how to approach it. This challenge is a deep one—to understand the complex and contested nature of our own power, the power of the people we work with and for, and the power of the systems we work inside. As we make power a talkable theme in class, students come to see and understand multiple forms of power, to recognize their own power, to use the power they have to challenge oppressive practices, and to support the power of the oppressed.

We are dealing with questions of power across the entire year. These questions are so central to our human and professional relationships—with professors, classmates, supervisors, and the people we work with and for. The abundant inequities, in resources and respect, are easily seen. First, conversations tend to focus on the powerlessness that students feel—as new interns inside organizations and students in the university. But students also grapple with differences in power even in those settings. Students identify and question the White, heteronormative, and ableist structure of these settings. They also identify the power relations inside the organization as manifest in the structure of work with "clients." Seeing that power differential opens more clarity on the "power over" aspects of social work and brings forward the question of coercive power that the history chapter lays bare.

In our second semester, we continue to grapple with questions of power. A few examples help make this clear. One student led a discussion on colonization and decolonization in social work and nonprofits. Drawing on material from her own reading of Black feminists and material on anti-oppressive practice from *Just Practice*, she challenged us to consider how "colonialism" works, to name systems of oppression in social work, and to recognize and challenge how the profession tends to talk about families, especially Black families, in child protection work. She has applied the Just Practice lens in her own research and practice with Black families by rooting her work in the strengths of Black mothers. Another student led a discussion on women of color and intimate partner violence. Drawing on the NASW Social Justice Brief on Intimate Partner Violence, she challenged us to consider the unique experience of women, especially women of color, and reflect on how work in our placements might be more attentive to these realities for clients. We discussed the complex and multilayered structures of oppression and the unique reasons that women of color resist turning to the state (e.g., police) in the context of intimate violence. She closed with a class discussion challenging us to consider how social workers could play a greater role in domestic violence awareness, prevention, and intervention.

These are just two important examples. Throughout the year, the complexity of power, in its myriad oppressive and anti-oppressive manifestations, is central to our discussions and critical reflections on practice.

## POSSIBILITY

Freire reminds us that "history is made by us, and as we make it, we are made and remade by it" (Freire, cited in Finn, 2020, p. 27). Thus, as human actors we continually create history and possibility. For me, possibility is where hope presents itself and requires action of us. Imagine the Just Practice framework without possibility. It would provide all the tools to understand limitations, interrogate shortcomings, and develop devastating critiques of previous practice. But possibility calls us all to also see the brilliant steps forward in the past in spite of those myriad limitations. More importantly, naming possibility emphasizes that going forward requires us to be active contributors to the project of creating a stronger society. In *Hope in the Dark*, Rebecca Solnit (2016) writes, "To hope is to give yourself to the future, and that commitment to the future makes the present inhabitable" (p. 4).

This sense of history making, of moving into the future you hope to create, is so clear in the quotes from Freire and other Latin American thinkers drawn on throughout *Just Practice*. Eduardo Galeano lays out the right to dream as the foundational right for all other human rights, reminding us that "without the right to dream and the waters that is gives us to drink, the other rights would die of thirst" (Galeano, cited in Finn, 2020, p. 343).

This imagining of "possibility" holds in it a requirement to act. Our collective action project is how we honor this call to action as a class. This year's project sought to extend and amplify the impact of our annual Confronting Racial Injustice Conference. This popular event draws 500 participants from the school and community. It is easy to be inspired by the event, but it is harder to move antiracist principles into practice. Students committed to translating the learning from the conference into action and supporting others to do the same. Across the spring semester we disseminated information, hosted discussions, and organized antiracist practice events. We also carefully documented our work together and collectively evaluated our processes and outcomes. We hope to make the ideas we pursue this year sustainable in the future as well. In this work, we learn from the challenges of diverse priorities and disagreement, the friction of hard timelines and uneven ability to take on projects, the satisfaction of completing successful events, and the deepening of relationships in planning and doing the work. As we move into action together, we practice the core processes of Just Practice collectively.

## Foundational Questions, Collective Answers

As you can see, I have a pretty deep connection to "macro practice," but I find I don't really like the term. Outside the field of social work, few grasp its meaning. Big is clear. But beyond that, it's just hard to understand. Those who know I'm an economist (yes, both an economist and a social worker) often think that I must be teaching macroeconomics—exchange rates and federal reserve policy—to students. But the problem with the term is worse inside the field. Inside social work, we have clarity about "micro practice," and many students seem to have a strong sense that micro practice is what they're about. But "macro practice?" That's the thing they won't do. For many, and most distressing, macro practice is understood to be not only the thing they won't do, but also the nexus of the social justice imperative of the profession. The micro/macro distinction is comfortable and familiar; it is a way to divide social work into two camps with maximum distance between them. This distance generates an all too common "I don't do that" impulse in response to engagement at the systems level.

The Just Practice framework challenges the distinction between micro and macro practice and invites social workers to integrate social justice in every aspect of practice. It calls on us to continually reflect on questions of power and positionality, to approach our work with humility, and to see social justice as both a destination and a way of moving toward that destination. It reminds us that social justice, whatever our level of practice, can be found in our own processes, interactions, and relationships. The work of social justice is not easy and requires us to ask, learn, grow, see mistakes, and try again.

With democratic institutions showing stress across the globe; economic inequality on the rise; and the earth, its climate, and resources stretched past the breaking point, social workers need a framework focused on social justice. We need new ways of seeing what is going on globally and locally, and new strategies for building solidarity with oppressed communities, shifting relations of power, and pursuing social justice at every level of practice. We also need the humility to recognize that our pursuit of social justice must always be evolving, that we will make mistakes, and that we must learn, grow, and keep trying.

I've come to understand this in conversation with students. As we learn together, we become more aware of the challenges, clearer on the necessity of theory, and better able to move theory into practice. As we learn together, everyone gets more comfortable with a critique of easy answers in social work and better able to pose questions and learn and disagree in the development of new answers that this field and our world need.

## QUESTIONS FOR REFLECTION AND DISCUSSION

1. What challenges have you faced in incorporating Just Practice concepts and processes in your field placement?
2. In your placement, do you see assumptions—for example, assumptions about ways of working or about the people you work with—that could or should be problematized?
3. What possibilities have you discovered as you bring Just Practice concepts and processes to bear in your field placement? Do you think a sense of hope or possibility changes the way people work in your placement?
4. In what ways have you been able to challenge the dichotomy between micro and macro practice in your field placement? Do you see staff at your field placement grappling with issues of power in their work at either the micro or macro level?
5. What are some examples of ways in which you integrate micro and macro practice in your work or field placement? How do you bring Just Practice concepts and processes to bear in doing so?

## REFERENCES

Finn, J. (2020). *Just practice: A social justice approach to social work* (4th ed.). Oxford University Press.
Solnit, R. (2016). *Hope in the dark: Untold histories, wild possibilities* (3rd ed.). Haymarket Books.

# 18

# Just Practice for Disability Rights

AMY CAPOLUPO, LCSW

> While complaints by individual students and legal actions can incrementally improve access to higher education, there is no substitute for comprehensive and effective policies that are implemented and enforced at the highest levels by university administrations.
> —Marc Maurer, president, National Federation of the Blind

---

**Overview**

In this chapter Amy Capolupo describes how the Just Practice framework guided action in response to an Office for Civil Rights (OCR) suit brought against her university for failure to provide accessible education to a student who is blind. The complaint outlined the multifaceted nature of inaccessibility from poor quality of scanned documents to inaccessible features of online course supplements, and inaccessibility of the university's online course registration system. Capolupo used the Just Practice framework to help guide the university through a process of changing assumptions and practices in ways that recognized and honored students' right to an accessible education.

---

## Introduction

In May 2012 a student group, the Alliance for Disability and Students at the University of Montana (ADSUM), filed a complaint with the United States Department of Education Office for Civil Rights (OCR) alleging that the University of Montana (UM) was discriminating against students with disabilities by using educational technologies that were not inherently accessible (University of Montana, 2014). The students were able to file this complaint because of the guidelines set forth by the Americans with Disabilities Act of 1990 (ADA). The ADA is a national civil rights law, which guarantees that people with disabilities should be free from discrimination and that disability-related accommodations must be made in employment settings, in commercial and public facilities, in telecommunications, and in any institution or entity receiving federal funds. UM receives federal financial assistance from the U.S. Department of Education, is a public entity, and is therefore subject to the requirements of the Act. The OCR is charged with enforcing the ADA and investigating allegations of discrimination in public educational institutions. Sanctions for noncompliance with the ADA can range from resolution agreements requiring a corrective plan of action to loss of federal funding. In other words, the university faced serious consequences if it did not adequately address the complaint. I was the interim director of the Disability Services for Students (DSS) office at the time of the complaint. In this chapter I show how the Just Practice framework helped guide the university through a process of changing assumptions and practices in ways that recognized and honored students' right to an accessible education.

## Ability, Access, and Discrimination

The complaint filed by the student group specifically addressed electronic materials used in academic courses, university websites, and online learning platforms. The complaint alleged that faculty were posting inaccessible class assignments and materials on the campus's learning management system. It also stated that the "live chat" and "discussion board" functions in the learning management system were inaccessible. In addition, the complaint alleged that the university's websites and web pages hosted inaccessible documents, including uncaptioned videos. Further, the university's online course registration system, which was the only means for students to register for courses, was inaccessible. Finally, the "clickers" being used by faculty as course participation tools were not accessible. Interestingly, at a time when the university was strongly encouraging faculty toward greater integration of technology into the teaching-learning process, those very technological "advances" were not designed for accessibility and thus contributed to an educational equity gap for students with disabilities. A wide range of students, including those with learning disabilities or limited mobility, individuals who are deaf or blind, and those with physical and mental conditions that limit their ability to view printed materials or hear the spoken word, were thus disadvantaged in their educational experience. The burden was on them to request access to these materials through DSS.

Let's consider how this inequity played out. At the start of the semester, nondisabled students could simply go to the campus bookstore or an online store, purchase their textbooks, and read them. In contrast, students with disabilities seeking accessible print material would have to first purchase the books, then go to the DSS to submit a request that their course materials be converted into a format compatible with a screen reader. Disability Services staff would then have to seek copyright permission from the publisher to convert the material into an accessible electronic format. While our office tried to fulfill these requests in a timely manner, the process would still take anywhere from 3 to 14 working days to complete. Thus, students with disabilities could find themselves behind on course readings from the start of every semester. Likewise, the process for making class handouts and videos accessible was equally problematic. Students were typically responsible for going to the campus library to access scanning equipment in order to translate printed handouts into a format that could be read by a computer. For videos, DSS would have to contact course instructors prior to the start of the semester to get a list of videos to be shown in the class, seek permission for captioning from the video production company, and add the captions. These processes, too, often resulted in delays for students and placed the burden on students to gain access to required course materials.

These request processes were standard operating procedure at UM in 2012. DSS had an electronic formats specialist to convert the printed materials, an assistive technology trainer to provide training and assistance with screen reading programs, screen reading programs that students could download and use, self-scan stations in the library so students could convert printed materials themselves, and the most advanced screen reading technology available. Despite the fact that DSS was relatively equipped to translate materials, students with disabilities faced a time-consuming and at times stressful process that was not the experience of their non-disabled peers.

I had worked for DSS for 10 years, starting as an MSW student. As a person with a learning disability, I had direct experience with the frustrations and challenges of accessibility in higher education. After reviewing the complaint, it was clear to me that we could no longer expect students with disabilities to be the ones responsible for ensuring access to their educational materials. They had a right to those materials. Students were asking for educational products that were "born accessible," a core facet of universal design (National Disability Authority, 2020). "Born accessible" means that a document, website, book, or presentation doesn't have to be converted or adapted to be accessible; rather, it is created in accessible formats to meet the needs of users (RTC: Rural, 2015). In practice, this means that a person who uses a screen reader (an application that reads words out loud in addition to describing images on a computer screen or mobile device) can simply access the electronic material just by logging on to their computer, rather than have to request someone else to modify what is on the screen in order to read it. In other words, students with disabilities could access course materials just as easily as their non-disabled peers.

## From Allegation to Action

The UM president's office initially received the complaint in August 2012. The president, in turn, notified the university legal counsel, who decided to form a task force to investigate and, hopefully, resolve the complaint. In September 2012, the Electronic Information Technology Accessibility (EITA) task force, comprised of information technology staff; legal counsel; DSS staff, including myself; faculty members; UM online staff; and UM students, was formed. Our charge was to explore each of the allegations, discover the cause of the allegation, and then, if warranted, plan to resolve the complaint through specific actions. Students wanted simply to access their materials without having to come to the DSS office first. They wanted to be treated like their peers without barriers to educational materials. The complaint prompted me to critically reflect on the work my office was doing. It became clear that my office, and the services we provided, *attempted* to provide access, but that access was neither reasonable nor timely. While our efforts were well-intended, they were not effective in terms of educational equity.

Additionally, because the complaint named issues of visual access, it was of interest to the National Federation of the Blind (NFB). The NFB is an organization that focuses on the full inclusion of blind people and promotes the economic and social welfare of its members. It is the largest organization of blind people in the United States. When necessary, the organization will defend the rights of blind people through legal means (https://www.nfb.org/). The NFB legal team contacted UM and offered to work with the university to resolve the complaint. If we agreed to adopt several of their best practice guidelines and standards, they, in turn, would contact the OCR and encourage them to accept any finding and the resolution agreement that UM will have created with the NFB. It is also worth noting that several of the students who filed the complaint were also members of the NFB and welcomed the NFB's active role in the process.

From my perspective, the complaint presented UM with an opportunity to hold national technology companies responsible for creating products that are accessible to all individuals. I thought about ways to obtain buy-in from UM administration, faculty, and staff in making the changes needed to successfully resolve the complaint. I believed that we had an opportunity for consciousness-raising here. I created the following sets of "pre-complaint" and "post-complaint" assumptions for UM leadership and faculty to critically reflect upon to promote engagement with and deeper understanding of the key issues.

Pre-complaint assumptions:

- The student with a disability has to request the modification for accessible text and is responsible for knowing how to troubleshoot accessibility.
- Captioning for publicly available material will be provided to students when requested.
- Having an accessibility clause in software procurement is a standard practice and is sufficient to ensure access.

Post-complaint assumptions:

- The student with a disability has a *right* to an accessible environment. All documents and websites must be accessible without additional modification.

- All videos used for educational reasons must be captioned.
- All software procured on the UM campus must be evaluated for accessibility prior to implementation.

In explaining the pre- and post-complaint assumptions to campus members, I stated that the pre-complaint set of assumptions was rooted in the belief that major technology companies either could not or did not produce products that are natively accessible. I asked questions of campus members and of myself, such as "Are the materials and technologies we use to educate students what they want?," "What is most beneficial to students?," "Are we simply obtaining what is available?," and "What makes us feel that certain products are better than others?" This process of critical question-posing helped shift consciousness on campus from a view of accessibility as a student responsibility to one of accessibility as a student right. We engaged in campus-wide discussions about why major technology companies were creating inaccessible educational products and what our legal responsibility under the ADA entailed to ensure access in a digital age. Students with disabilities played key roles throughout the process. Not only were they represented on the committee and part of the critical conversations, they also organized collective action in solidarity with those who brought the complaint. For example, UM had recently launched a new logo with the catchphrase "Thrive." Student participants had T-shirts made with the new logo and the word "Survive" to depict the campus experience for students with disabilities.

## Using the Just Practice Framework

As a person with an invisible disability, I have experienced the barriers that exist in terms of physical, programmatic, and attitudinal access. I have benefited from the civil rights and social justice movements that have created access for people with disabilities, most notably the ADA and section 504 of the Rehabilitation Act (U.S. Department of Labor, n.d.). These disability rights laws, and the various intersectionalities that exist in myself and those I work for, inform my core values of equity and inclusion. Those values are central to my practice as a social worker.

In my experience, social workers are not always well received by people with disabilities. Those seeking services may view social workers as gatekeepers to vital services who promote models of dependency that maintain, rather than challenge, systemic inequity. Those not seeking services may see social workers as supporting people who are "leaning on the system" and who "need to be more self-sufficient." Such attitudes may be based in previous interactions with social workers or grounded in misunderstandings or partial understandings when only limited knowledge can be shared with the public due to issues of privacy and confidentiality. I have often encountered both of these attitudes and assumptions in my experience as a social worker in higher education.

As DSS director, and as a licensed clinical social worker, I recognized that my first obligation was to listen to people across the belief spectrum, pose questions about the various perspectives presented, and make sure that I communicated effectively as an EITA task force member. It was through critical, perspectival listening that we could come to a deeper understanding of underlying assumptions and concerns. Only then could we create strategies to drive effective change. To do that, we used the Just Practice framework (Finn, 2020) to examine the meaning, context, power, history, and possibility related to the complaint to create a more accessible and equitable educational environment for students with disabilities. We also relied heavily on the core processes of critical reflection, teaching-learning, accompaniment, and action. In each decision we made, the EITA task force challenged the assumptions of what is possible and asked what could be possible. In the following section, I show how we brought the framework to bear.

## The Meaning of "Accessibility"

An initial step for the task force was to agree on the meaning of "accessibility." Defined broadly, the term means to be able to use or benefit from a service or product. Pre-complaint processes for providing access to printed materials did that, by providing reasonable accommodations such as human readers and alternative format conversion. However, the complainants argued that such accommodations were no longer considered timely and therefore did not provide access in an equitable manner. Further, the practices did not reflect a rights-based orientation. The task force, through a deliberative process of reflection and teaching-learning, developed the following definition:

> "Accessible" means that individuals with disabilities are able to independently acquire the same information, engage in the same interactions, and enjoy the same services within the same timeframe as individuals without disabilities, with substantially equivalent ease of use. (University of Montana, n.d.)

UM's new definition opened the door to addressing the bigger question of what was possible in terms of technological access and inclusion.

It is also important to consider the meaning of the complaint. What were the students trying to achieve by filing it? What was the NFB trying to achieve in assisting UM in resolving the complaint? Both the students and the NFB stated that they wanted UM's agreement to be groundbreaking and, ideally, used as a model for national change. Our attempts to resolve the issue needed to be aimed at the goal of national change if they were to be successful. The EITA task force recognized this. The committee sought to have open, honest conversations with the students who filed the complaint and the members of the NFB, who had specific requests that the university would need to adopt if we were to successfully resolve the complaint. As a result, OCR agreed to accept the resolution agreement that UM brokered with the NFB rather than conduct their own independent investigation, saving UM and OCR time and additional monetary resources.

## History of Accessibility at UM

The task force and I also turned to history as both warning device and source of inspiration for addressing the complaint. The DSS office at UM was formed in 1989 in response to the growing number of students who were self-advocating for access and accommodations. Initially, DSS had one half-time director. At that time, the office's mission was to "ensure that programs at the University of Montana are accessible and usable by students with disabilities." Then and now, the office has been a resource for all faculty, students, staff, and campus patrons. Carrying out such a mission is a complex task, however, and not work accomplished by one office. Access at UM, therefore, has always been addressed through a collaborative approach.

Shortly after the DSS office was formed, the ADA was passed, giving people with disabilities the right to file a complaint when a business or entity covered by the law was not following statutory guidelines. Achieving access, therefore, has historically been a complaint-driven process, and, as a civil right, it must be fought for and pursued. This means that one role of the DSS office has been to educate students with disabilities about their rights under the ADA. DSS has approached this role through a combination of teaching-learning, accompaniment, and advocacy. The ADA also states that access must be timely and effective, protect a person's privacy, and allow for the greatest degree of independence possible. As we have seen, *timely*, *effective*, and *independent* are relative terms that change over time. Thus, our practices to ensure students' rights to an accessible education are dynamic and evolving with changing technologies. By reflecting on history, the task force was able to see the value of a collaborative approach, understand the complaint as a legal means for change, and recognize the need to continually evaluate efforts at accessibility in light of changing technologies.

The task force was also able to draw lessons from past complaints. In 1990, a UM student filed a complaint with the OCR alleging that the DSS office could not provide timely and effective services given that it was open only 20 hours per week. This complaint prompted UM to hire additional DSS staff and grow services. After this complaint was filed, the university hired a coordinator to work with students with disabilities to ensure that reasonable accommodations were made. These included enabling testing accommodation, allowing note-takers, hiring sign language interpreters for students who were deaf and hard of hearing, and hiring scribes for blind or visually impaired students and those with physical disabilities. The hiring of these staff members started the process of creating and institutionalizing access for an entire group of people with disabilities that had not always existed. This history provided a helpful context, as the impetus for the 1990 and 2012 complaints were primarily the same. In both cases, students sought equal access to services that would allow them to complete their college education as independently as possible. As new technology emerges, what is considered timely and effective has changed dramatically. In understanding the history of how accessibility has been achieved, we found it easier to understand the reasons for and the importance of the 2012 complaint and how successful resolution was essential to DSS's mission.

## Context for Accessibility

When looking at the context of the complaint, DSS staff had to examine UM's makeup. In 2012, as a state university, UM had a student population of 13,000. DSS had 12 staff to serve 1,100 students: two full-time and one three-quarter-time coordinators, four sign language interpreters, one testing coordinator, one e-text producer, one assistive technology coordinator, one receptionist, and myself, the director. Our resources were spread thin. Our campus context was also nested within a broader community context. Both student and community members of NFB were actively engaged in the process and in scrutinizing the university's efforts to respond to the complaint. They would be holding UM publicly accountable.

The task force was also navigating a complex legal context. ADSUM and NFB wanted to ensure students' rights to access educational materials, and they understood their rights under federal law. They also had a keen interest in demanding accountability from the large educational technology companies to create products and systems that are "born accessible." However, there is no law against developing inaccessible products. Those seeking change through legal action against companies producing inaccessible products must sue, or file complaints with the Office of Civil Rights or the Department of Justice against, the entities that fall under ADA and that purchase and use these products. This legal context set the stage for the complaint against UM for its use of technology commonly found on most college campuses.

There was also an important technological context to consider here. For a disability accommodation to be considered lawful under the ADA, it needs to be *timely* and *effective*. Timely and effective are both relative terms, however. With the advent of 4G, smartphones, and video streaming services, the task force grappled with questions such as "Is it still timely for students to wait 2 weeks for an electronic textbook?" And, given that technological advances had by 2012 enabled all films to be captioned from the outset, was it effective to give students video transcripts in instances where UM did not have permission to caption? In light of changing technologies, what were our legal and ethical obligations to students with disabilities? As the task force considered the campus, community, legal, and technological contexts of the case, we also faced questions of power.

## Scope of Power Regarding Accessibility

In thinking about power, it is helpful to critically reflect on the power each person or entity has, as well as what the complainant or aggrieved party is trying to accomplish. In cases where power dynamics aren't entirely clear, it is important to consider the power each group has to resolve the issue, in addition to the mission or goals of the group or entities. In the case of the OCR complaint, ADSUM had the power to file the grievance; the ADA and the U.S. government, meanwhile, served as conduits for the exercise of the group's power. The NFB had the power to further its goals of creating a more equitable society for blind individuals. The OCR had the power to leverage costly fines against the university, furthering its mission to ensure that people with disabilities are not subject to discrimination.

UM had the power to fight these entities by defending the status quo. UM did not have the power to directly change the technology used for student accessibility—that was the purview of outside technology companies that developed curricular materials and learning management systems. However, the task force came to realize that UM had the power to attempt to resolve the complaint by recognizing the potential impact the school's purchasing decisions could have in forcing large technology companies to make their products more accessible. UM had the opportunity to push for change on much larger scale to ensure that the products that UM purchased were to be "born accessible" and not require modification.

Over the course of a year, the task force grappled with questions such as "Do we have the capacity to meet the standards sought by the NFB and ADSUM?" That question was complicated by the fact that many companies did not at that time follow accessibility standards that the NFB and students were asking UM to set. The question before the task force was really about power. Did our group have enough collective power to set a national standard for information technology accessibility? To fully embrace this type of collective power, UM would have to admit fault for accepting the status quo and put itself forth as a role model in terms of willingness to change. It is a very humbling experience to be told that the years of work you put into something has to be redone. It is even more humbling to have to tell hundreds of university employees, who are protected by a variety of collective bargain agreements, that their teaching practices and the tools provided by the institution are, in fact, discriminatory. The task force had to recognize the power it had to use the complaint to enact changes on micro, mezzo, and macro levels and to acknowledge the challenges they would face. UM had the power to set the standard that we would no longer procure technology that did not follow certain accessibility guidelines. The university would now have to independently check every information technology product to ensure accessibility prior to purchase and implementation. Taking the manufacturer's word that a product was accessible was no longer an option.

In the end, UM settled on standards that would dramatically change not only UM's institutional practices but also the practices of institutions nationwide, and, ultimately, change the way companies created their products by insisting that they be accessible from their inception. UM now requires, as part of requests for proposals from web-based technology companies, that bidders meet high accessibility standards (WCAG 2.0 Level AA) to ensure that all websites and associated content are fully accessible. UM also informs all faculty and staff about their obligations to ensure electronic accessibility and provides training and resources to assist in meeting those obligations. UM has established and maintains a university website dedicated to accessibility and provides tools and information on training for the campus community.

## The Possibilities of Electronic Information Access

With respect to the possibilities that exist in terms of technological access, they are truly limitless and continually evolving. In response to UM's settlement with the OCR, National Federation of the Blind President Marc Maurer said,

> While complaints by individual students and legal actions can incrementally improve access to higher education, there is no substitute for comprehensive and effective policies that are implemented and enforced at the highest levels by university administrations. This agreement, which is the most comprehensive of its kind to date, represents a thorough and systematic approach that will benefit University of Montana students for years to come and serve as a model for university policies and practices across the nation. (National Federation of the Blind, 2014)

In March 2020, UM abruptly shifted to remote learning, primarily through Zoom, for all students, in response to the COVID-19 pandemic. Many courses and programs continued to operate remotely through the 2020–2021 academic year. Interestingly, the university's born accessible technology was not only critical in providing equal educational access for students with disabilities, but it also benefited all students. Moreover, as faculty embraced a broader range of technological access for all students, such as administering tests online and allowing flexibility in attendance and assignments, students with disabilities have benefited from greater educational equity and inclusion. As Zoe Beery (2020) states, "For some of the 61 million Americans with disabilities, the ability to work, learn, and socialize from home has been an unexpected expansion of possibility."

## Looking to the Future

The resolution agreement between UM and OCR and associated policies essentially have no end date. As technology continually evolves, so, too, must access to that technology. Since the agreement between UM and OCR was finalized in 2014, this comprehensive approach to accessibility of electronic material has been adopted by many institutions. And, due to the work of numerous disability advocacy groups, the overwhelming majority of major technology companies now follow the standards set forth in the agreement.

Moving forward, universities will face complaints and legal action if they adopt technologies that discriminate on the basis of ability or if they are slow to adopt technologies that allow for greater independence. If full access and inclusion for students with disabilities are to be achieved, universities must continuously examine their practices and procedures. Social workers located in institutions of higher education are well-positioned to serve as advocates for students and as catalysts for systems change. The Just Practice provides a framework for thought and action to support students' rights to an accessible education.

### QUESTIONS FOR REFLECTION AND DISCUSSION

1. Take time to reflect on access in your community and identify barriers to equal access. What are these barriers? Are they programmatic, physical, attitudinal, or all three?
2. Using the Just Practice framework, how would you go about resolving one of these barriers?
3. Where do you see possibilities for creating change on your campus or community? Who would you involve in the process?
4. What are the short- and long-term effects of allowing an inaccessible environment to persist?
5. Considering the intersectional nature of disability, what are the possibilities that exist when access and inclusion are considered core values and are at the forefront of decision making?

### REFERENCES

Americans With Disabilities Act of 1990, Pub. L. No. 101–336, 104 Stat. 328 (1990).
Beery, Z. (2020, August 24). When the world shut down, they saw it open. *New York Times*, D3.
Finn, J. (2020). *Just practice: A social justice approach to social work* (4th ed.). Oxford University Press.
National Disability Authority. (2020). *What is universal design*. http://universaldesign.ie/What-is-Universal-Design/.
National Federation of the Blind. (2014, March 19). *National Federation of the Blind applauds groundbreaking agreement on equal access in higher education*. https://www.nfb.org/about-us/press-room/national-federation-blind-applauds-groundbreaking-agreement-equal-access-higher
RTC: Rural. (2015, November 3). *Born accessible*. http://rtc.ruralinstitute.umt.edu/born-accessible/
University of Montana. (2014, April 19). *UM news*. http://news.umt.edu/2014/03/031914disa.aspx
University of Montana. (n.d.). *Accessibility*. Retrieved March 3, 2020, from https://www.umt.edu/accessibility/implementation/policy/default.php
U.S. Department of Labor. (n.d.). *Section 504, Rehabilitation Act of 1973*. Retrieved March 3, 2020, from https://www.dol.gov/agencies/oasam/centers-offices/civil-rights-center/statutes/section-504-rehabilitation-act-of-1973

Part Six

# INTEGRATING SOCIAL JUSTICE IN ORGANIZATIONAL CONTEXTS OF PRACTICE

# 19

# Just Practice

*Lessons from the East Side Clinic*

DIANE KEMPSON, MSW, PHD

> They can't just close the clinic. Where will we go for care? We can't let them do this. We have to do something!
> —East Side Clinic client

---

**Overview**

In this chapter Diane Kempson uses the Just Practice framework to examine the history and power relations behind a decision to close a university-affiliated community health clinic, which left clients without access to psychiatric or medical care. Kempson, who served as clinic director, describes the clients' organizing and advocacy efforts in response to the closure. Although they were unsuccessful in reopening the clinic, Kempson and clinic clients discovered empowering possibilities as they came together to challenge injustice. Kempson reflects on her own transformation through this challenging process.

---

## Introduction

"You have to be kidding me—you can't seriously turn 1,200 psychiatric clients away from the clinic with no place to refer them!"

"The clinic is to be closed in 2 weeks," Peggy replied. Peggy was the dean of the College of Health Sciences at my university, and someone whom I had considered a respected colleague.

"But, Peggy, you are a psychologist. You know as well as I do that this is unethical."

"Refer them to the mental health clinic in town," Peggy continued.

"But they referred people to us—they don't have enough staff to see the people seeking services from them."

"*Refer* them back to the mental health clinic," she adamantly stated.

I could not contain my anger and frustration. "Peggy, listen to yourself. 'I am only doing what my commander told me to do; it's not mine to question.'"

After a long silence, Peggy replied, "This is not negotiable."

I was rendered stunned and silent. Over the next 3 weeks, my colleagues and I at the federally subsidized East Side Clinic were forced to close the doors and terminate services to 1,200 mental health patients.

In this chapter, I tell the story of the East Side Clinic. I draw on the concepts of Just Practice (Finn, 2020) in reflecting on the clinic's history and context; the power relations in play in its establishment, operation, and demise; its meaning to patients, staff, and the broader community; and the possibilities we discovered through its existence—and perhaps more surprisingly, through and after its closure. I consider some of the lessons in engagement, teaching-learning, action, and accompaniment I gained through my experience at the clinic and after its closure. In closing, I show how the experience provided me an opportunity to critically reflect on my own history as a clinical social worker and gain further insights to shape my teaching and practice in the present.

## East Side Clinic

The East Side Clinic was the first of its kind in my blue-collar community of roughly 50,000 located in the frontier West. In rural health care, the notion of "frontier" generally refers to an area with a population density of six or fewer people per square mile. So, our town was the "big city" for a large rural area. The development of the clinic reminds me of the movie *Field of Dreams*, in which Kevin Costner hears a voice, saying, "Build it and they will come." Those of us who launched the effort to establish the clinic didn't know exactly what we were getting into, but we knew that we wanted an interprofessional clinic that could provide services to those who had no resources and a place for interprofessional education, an effort that was just beginning to flourish in this area of the country in the early 2000s.

We were a model program in what is now called "integrated behavioral health," and we were proud of it. We created a welcoming place where family nurse practitioners, psychiatric nurse practitioners, nurses, social workers, and students of those disciplines gathered to offer integrated services to persons who were un- and underinsured. We became a kind of "drop-in" space for folks who lived on the street or who were alone—or felt alone. We became a safe haven for those who had been labeled as "the underserving poor" or "mentally unstable." For example, there was John, who, in his psychotic state barely managed by medication, still came by every week day for a smile and a cup of coffee. He knew he was welcome at East Side—and there was always time for him here.

There was a synergy among us as we engaged in this exciting new partnership joining the university health profession programs and a federally subsidized community clinic. The endeavor evolved over the course of a year or so. We established an interprofessional team in which a nurse practitioner from the nursing program, a physician in charge of overseeing the clinic and its operations, and I, a social worker interested in community well-being, along with several other community-minded individuals, met regularly to bring our vision of integrated community health to life. The sense of possibility was palpable. We set up the clinic in a new storefront building in the poorer area of town. We offered medical and behavioral health services and had plans in the works for a dental clinic as well. I believed I had found my dream job—working as part of a team, building a program from the bottom up, and responding directly to the needs of many forgotten members of the community.

Over the course of 2 years, the clinic grew to the point where we were serving about 2,000 medical and 1,200 psychiatric/behavioral clients, many of whom had overlapping needs. I was unaware of it at the time, but there were also tensions and power struggles simmering behind the scenes. The physician in charge also had oversight responsibilities for other clinics in the region. Over time, he turned the billing and financial management of the clinic over to an administrative officer. His presence at the clinic and contact with his administrative officer grew sporadic, and he did not respond to our efforts to contact him. Finally, we received news that he had resigned, but we received no explanation.

Over the next year, the politics of the situation became more evident, and tensions between the East Side Clinic and the administrative officer increased. As the story unfolded, a conflict of interest with the administrative officer became obvious. Her husband, a counselor in town, wanted to take over the psychiatric operations of the East Side Clinic. We made efforts to engage him in working with us, but to no avail. The administrative officer then contacted the university president and told him the clinic was in financial and legal jeopardy due to illegal billing. There was no validity to her accusation, but that was of little consequence. The president, rather than responding with an investigation into the accusation, reacted with a knee-jerk decision to close the clinic.

We, the staff, were stunned. Our efforts to challenge the decision were ignored. Instead, we had to begin the arduous task of informing our clients. To say that there was upset is an understatement. Our clients felt powerless in the face of these key power players. I recall John's reaction. He, more than anyone else, had difficulty making sense of what had happened. His agitation was palpable. Communication with him was often problematic around even simple things; there was no understandable explanation for something of this magnitude—the sudden disappearance of his safe and welcoming community space. Our clients, collectively, were at a loss. But for some, doing *something* was squarely on their agenda. Several clients wanted to call the local newspaper and voice their concerns publicly.

I, too, felt helpless. As an employee of the university, I could say nothing about the decision without risking my job. Then it came to me: I also had a part-time private practice. While I could say nothing as a university representative, I could say plenty as a private practitioner. I announced an open meeting for clients of the clinic who wished to convene and plan a response. Many clients attended, and a group of about 10 key people became spokespersons for the clinic population. I offered to call a news conference, and I worked with the spokespersons to invite media representatives from the local paper, TV station, and radio stations.

The media showed up in force at the East Side Clinic. I made the announcement of its closure and then turned the news conference over to the client representatives. They spoke powerfully about their distress over the clinic closing and what it meant to lose their mental health services and providers. They also demanded town hall meetings with political leaders in the community to address the medical and behavioral needs of un- and underinsured citizens of the community. Our collective efforts were not successful in stopping the clinic closure at the time. However, our failure to prevent the closure did not signal the end of possibility. In the next section I reflect on the East Side Clinic story through the lenses of Just Practice and the unexpected trajectory of our collective struggle.

## Just Practice Analysis

### MEANING

The need to make meaning of life events is part of the human condition. Our perceptions of the impact of events and how we deal with those events influence the stories we tell about our lives. Moreover, the narratives we tell to others of who we are influences the way we think about and encounter the future. The beauty of narrative in everyday life or as a therapeutic endeavor is that it is rife with opportunity for focusing on the strength of how we live or have lived our lives. We can tell and retell our stories in ways that allow us to be the authors of our lives, as well as the authors of the retelling of our lives. There is enormous power in that—in being our own agent.

In the closing of the East Side Clinic, the "politics of memory" was significant to the people who were impacted by this event and the meaning they attributed to their handling of the situation. "Politics of memory" is a term used by Patricia Deegan, a leader in the psychiatric survivor movement, to describe the historic layering of power relations that have played out in naming, confining, "treating," and oppressing those labeled "mentally ill" (Deegan, Strecker, & Krauss, 2004). It speaks both to the disempowering ways in which those with "expert" power have named and defined collective understandings of mental illness and to the ways in which people living with diagnoses of mental illness have resisted imposed meanings and have struggled to claim and name their own experiences. The closing of the clinic was not only a loss for clients at the level of individual well-being, it was also a blow to the collective well-being in that persons labeled "mentally ill" were not viewed as worthy of care by those in power.

But there is merit to a "good death." Although the clinic closed, the clients were, in the end, the victors in ascribing meaning to their experience. They refused to be labeled and dismissed as a disposable population. Instead, they brought their individual and collective voices to bear in describing what the clinic, and its closure, meant to them. Their voices and actions mattered—to themselves and to others in the community. They challenged the official narrative of the university, offered a powerful counter-narrative, found strength in their collective advocacy, and were exuberant in having their voices heard.

My own experience mirrored that of the clients. I, too, found new meaning in my work as my role shifted from clinician to advocate. I, too, experienced the adrenaline rush of self-efficacy as I joined my clients in naming the injustice of the clinic closure. I found new meaning in my social work practice through the integration of clinical practice and advocacy. I came to realize that we humans, more often than not, have little control over the circumstances that impact our lives. But the existential importance of integrity and action in the face of wrongdoing triumphs. And I am able to sleep at night.

## CONTEXT

As I have described, the clinic closure played out in the context of our relatively small community. The clients whom the clinic served did not have options in terms of access to care. The local mental health center was already overburdened. Clients did not have the resources or wherewithal to simply relocate to a more resource-rich locale. I understood at a theoretical level the pivotal nature of context in social work—our professional uniqueness is grounded in the "person-in-environment" approach. But what did these questions of context mean at a practical level in terms of the lived experiences and care needs of the clinic's former clients, and what was my responsibility as a social worker?

As is often the case in such a circumstance, finding their voice led some to be willing to be more vocal. Several clients joined together to call for town hall meetings that they orchestrated within the community. I also invited several of these clients to speak to health-care students about their experiences with self-advocacy and to share their personal accounts of how symptoms sometimes protected them or how their diagnoses did or did not define them. Others fell through the cracks without adequate services. One man with a serious psychiatric diagnosis had maintained moderate stability as long as he had the support of the clinic. After the close of the clinic, I learned from his wife that he sexually assaulted his stepdaughter and ended up in prison—a reflection of multiple system failures. I wonder how he survived that experience. Loss of hope is hard to navigate.

Once the clinic closed, I expanded my private practice and continued to see several clients whom I had seen for a long period of time. In addition, there were a handful of clients who came to me with a self-diagnosis of dissociative identity disorder (DID, or what is more informally referred to as multiple personality disorder), about which I knew virtually nothing. However, they asked me to work with them post-closure of the clinic because the local mental health center had turned them away. The mental health center had labeled their diagnosis as a form of borderline personality disorder and would provide crisis intervention services only to persons with that diagnosis. Thus, the community and organizational contexts of the clinic's closure and its aftermath placed me in a clinical and ethical quandary. I lacked experience with DID, but, given the direct request for help, I couldn't not act.

In order to respond to the contextual challenge, I took a *teaching-learning* approach. I had to start from a place of not knowing and a position of curiosity. I invited my clients to be my teachers and guides. In exchanges with my new clients, I came to a profound appreciation of their strengths and my own shortsightedness. I learned so much from them, in large part due to the context in which we were operating. I also drew on my own strengths and skills that I had honed in the context of my earlier work in the clinic. I had developed a good reputation in town for my work with people diagnosed with borderline personality disorder, and I was willing to work with them on an ongoing basis, not just in crisis. Further, I accepted Medicaid and Medicare payment options, which made care accessible for former clinic clients. I was clear with new clients that I knew virtually nothing about DID but that I was willing to sit with them, learn from them, and accompany them on their journeys.

And so we began. I even started a group for about four women with this diagnosis. As I heard their stories over time, I came to a sudden realization of the protective nature of DID. One of the women said to me, "Don't mess with my DID. I like it just the way it is—each of my personalities has a hand in keeping me safe." My clients led me to a new understanding of the protective function of what we, as professionals, refer to as "psychiatric symptoms." I developed a newfound respect for the protective nature of symptoms. My clients not only informed my practice, but they transformed it. I now operate from the perspective of restraint—encouraging folks to go slowly in making changes with an eye on what will be lost when they give up a "symptom" and how will they take care of what has been protected by that symptom.

The frontier context also shaped my practice. Being from the East Coast, I had always had access to emergency psychiatric assistance. In the frontier context, I was the emergency psychiatric assistance! For a while in my private practice, I carried a beeper for emergencies and attempted to be on call 24/7. But that was not sustainable. I explained to my clients that we needed to find a different approach. We agreed that we could work together as long as we had a verbal contract that we were both working on the side of life for them. Given my lack of access to backup, I had to be assured by each of my clients that they would go to the emergency room if they had a dire emergency. Further, if they could wait until the next day, I would manage to see them before the day was over.

Our verbal contracting approach was successful. I discovered the power in transparency, authenticity, collaboration, and trust with my clients. I learned to trust the strengths of my clients, even in the most acute, life-threatening episodes of depression or psychosis. In those contexts, I would gather my most "take-charge" mode with gentleness, authenticity, and clinical skill, and deliver a clear message that they must let me be in charge for this brief period when they need someone to oversee their well-being. And as soon as their situation stabilized, they would again have full control over their lives. These contextual understandings also taught me about power between my clients and me.

## POWER

Initially, the closure of the clinic was deeply disempowering for me. I was processing my own shock and anger and still trying to be present and professional with our clients. However, by bearing witness to the individual and collective actions of the clients, I came to recognize that with consciousness and voice comes power—the power to speak one's truth regardless of whether opposing forces like it or accept it. I also gained critical consciousness of factors in one's life that lead to a diminished sense of power—such as being other than a White male, being poor and disenfranchised, or bearing a diagnostic label that shrinks one's personhood.

I came to a deeper appreciation of the power dynamics that operate between me and my clients—always there and in need of acknowledgment. I hold power because I am White, grew up in a home that nurtured me, and I have an education and adequate income. I can name what I see, and it is generally accepted. In the mental health realm, I have the power to label and pathologize and the all-too-easily accepted power to situate my client's future depending on what I see in my "crystal ball" of prognosis. My clients, more often than not, have far less privilege and power. Clients frequently have to contend with systems that are less than supportive of them or less than user-friendly. There is, as Lavitt (2009) posits, the multidimensional problem setting with which clients have to contend and without realizing the complexity of it all. Unfortunately, we, as social workers, in these contexts often end up contributing to the oppression of the very group of marginalized people with whom we work and profess our commitment to serve.

It often feels as if my clients and I have little power within the larger systems in which we operate. But we do have the power to name. We can speak to lived experiences and struggles that others seem unable or unwilling to see. By naming we can illuminate what is not always obvious and what gets hidden from popular view. We have the power to name the structures of violence and systems of inequality that are often the real pathogenic forces in our clients' lives. By naming these external pathogens we can offer a powerful counter narrative to clients who blame themselves for what has happened. The naming that ensued with the closing of the East Side Clinic reflects this power. The collective response to the clinic closure also demonstrated "power with" and "power to act" (Townsend et al., 1999). Together, my clients and I tapped into horizontal power fueled by our shared expertise, complementarity, and solidarity. It is that horizontal power that now shapes my approach to clinical practice.

## HISTORY

The making and telling of history is deeply interwoven with power. The history of the East Side Clinic as told from the perspectives of the powerful was that the clinic was billing illegally, therefore it had to be shut down, and ample service options were available. Those in power did not count on the less powerful finding their voice. The "master narrative" was mightily challenged when those on the receiving end of services talked back, challenged the truth of those in power, and offered an alternative history.

I was proud to be part of that history. I was also moved to deeper critical reflection on my own professional history as I considered our service users' challenge to received "truths." I had been a young social worker in a New York City child and adolescent clinic in the 1970s. The clinic was part of a psychiatric teaching hospital. I remember accepting the espoused wisdom of the day about the origins of autism in children. We all "knew" that autism was the result of "cold mothers." We did not doubt our certainty. I participated in that ascription of cause and carried out my social work practice accordingly. I believed this professional truth over the accounts of mothers struggling to connect with their children, and I responded accordingly, subtly judging mothers for "rejecting" their babies. The moral of this story is this: Remember humility because today's truth is tomorrow's fallacy. We need to draw on history as both warning device and source of inspiration. We need to continually reflect on the "truths" that shape practice past and present. Perhaps my work today is, in part, a redemptive process for inadvertently harming another in the past. Perhaps through individual and collective redemptive effort we can aspire to a transformed world that is socially just.

## POSSIBILITY

As one of my students so eloquently put it, "Possibility is the asterisk at the bottom of a coupon that says 'subject to change.'" Possibility emphasizes agency and hope and reminds us that external forces do not wholly control our actions and decisions. Things do not have to happen the way they have always happened. Indeed, the forces that decided the fate of the East Side Clinic did not define the fate of the clients of the clinic. The clinic's closing set in motion imagination and a creative force—a lubricant to the wheels of personal agency—that allowed for participants to soar like eagles. They were proud of what they accomplished in bringing light to the service needs that they experienced. They were proud that they were successful in being heard—and of being remembered. I was proud of them. I quickly moved to the wings of the stage so that they could be front and center. They managed to stay vocal and visible for quite a long time. Even when their struggle faded from the public eye, the remembrance of what they had accomplished stayed with them.

These folks joined the ranks of those whose rebellion is a statement of power that they have taken back. It is power that comes from within—not power bestowed by someone else. Theirs was a statement of the power and possibility of the collective. Theirs was a reflection of the gestalt, of the potential when energy comes together in a cooperative context. The whole truly is greater than the sum of its parts. The collective energy was far bigger than the sum of each of those persons added together. The gestalt of the experience was inspirational and without limits. That collective effort brought out the very best of each person involved.

## Postscript of Possibility

A few years ago I ran into the woman with the DID diagnosis who told me to leave her DID alone, because she liked it just the way it was. After we exchanged hugs, she told me with excitement and pride that she was no longer on Social Security disability and had been working at the same place for a couple of years. She also described the successes of her children, both of whom I had seen for brief periods when they were adolescents. Her son was a Marine, and her daughter was married and had two children. We don't often get to see what has happened with our clients. And we don't often know the impact of our words or actions. But I like to think that I touch the life of another, not because of my professional expertise, but because I value the person I see who reflects back to me who I am. These connections contribute to the gestalt of the positive collective—to a positive creative force of endless possibilities.[1]

### QUESTIONS FOR REFLECTION AND DISCUSSION

1. Take a few minutes and discuss in small groups the point in time where each of the seven core processes of Just Practice—engagement, teaching-learning, action, accompaniment, evaluation, reflection, and celebration—are manifest in this account.
2. What are some of the potential—and perhaps, probable—ethical dilemmas within the process of the clinic's closing (beyond the obvious one of leaving clients without adequate services) and the movement toward advocacy?
3. Often, we find that the client's presenting concern is the least complicated aspect of the larger picture when we consider the multidimensional nature of the problem setting from micro to macro. This includes the social service agency, its community context, its funding sources, and the broader political climate. Lavitt (2009), in explaining the nature of the multidimensional problem setting, suggests that determining the focus of intervention is as important, if not

---

[1] I wish to footnote this entire chapter with a reference to Janet's *Just Practice* book. She and the book have been instrumental to providing an organizational structure to my thinking and to my legacy as an instructor of social justice practice at the University of Wyoming, particularly as she and the book have informed *meaning, context, power, history, and possibility* for me in the writing of this chapter.

more so, than actually solving the problem. Identify the contextual considerations of the multidimensional problem setting that set the stage for what later happened regarding the East Side Clinic.
4. Considering the multidimensional problem setting, including the partnership of a federally subsidized health clinic and a university, identify crucial processes that were in motion relative to the five key concepts of the Just Practice framework: meaning, context, power, history, and possibility.
5. Given the complexity of this case study, what are the potential conflicting roles that challenge the social worker? Discuss the process of deciding which role takes priority in a given moment.

## REFERENCES

Deegan, P., Strecker, T., & Krauss, A. (2004). *The politics of memory [DVD]*. SeaRose Productions.
Finn, J. (2020). *Just practice: A social justice approach to social work* (4th ed.). Oxford University Press.
Lavitt, M. (2009). What is *advanced* in generalist practice? A conceptual discussion. *Journal of Teaching in Social Work, 29*(4), 461–473.
Townsend, J., Zapata, E., Rowlands, J., Alberti, P., & Mercado, M. (1999). *Women and power: Fighting patriarchies and poverty*. Zed Books.

# 20

# Bringing Just Practice Into a Corporate Law Context

KAO NOU L. MOUA, MSW, PHD

What we practice at the small scale sets the pattern for the whole system.
—adrienne maree brown

> **Overview**
>
> In this chapter Kao Nou Moua shows how the processes of engagement, teaching-learning, action, and accompaniment played out to create change within a large law firm. Moua had been hired by a national law corporation to assess, implement, and evaluate policies and practices related to diversity, equity, and inclusion. She describes how she supported a group of employees in creating policy change related to accessibility that challenged the top-down decision-making culture of the firm and opened spaces of possibility for organizational change. Moua provides insights on interdisciplinary practice and the possibilities of embedding social justice work in a corporate context.

## Introduction

There is well-documented collaboration among social workers and lawyers (Coleman, 2001). The most often featured structure of interprofessional collaborations involves social workers and lawyers who work on multidisciplinary teams addressing clients' cases involving family problems, social and economic problems, and health and medical problems. We find social workers involved in legal aid; joint MSW and law degree programs highlighting child welfare experiences; law clinics focused on providing not only legal services to vulnerable clients, but mental health, housing, and economic resources; and social workers and lawyers working together on cases related to family law, drug courts, and youth justice (Coleman, 2001; Galowitz, 1999; Taylor, 2006). However, we know that generalist social work practitioners are trained to work beyond individuals and families; they develop and enhance practice skills that easily transfer to other levels of practice such as groups, organizations, communities, and policy.

This case study presents a professional experience of mine as a social work practitioner hired within a national corporate law firm to research, evaluate, and implement organizational policies and practices related to equity, diversity, and inclusion. In this case study, I use Finn's (2020) Just Practice framework to analyze the *history* of law firms and social work and the *context* of decision-making within law firms; describe how *power* is viewed and exercised in law firms and the *meanings* of equity, diversity, and inclusion for staff and attorneys; and discuss the *possibilities* for collaborative decision-making and empowering others. I show how the core processes of the Just Practice framework informed the steps of organizational change. Before I discuss the case through the Just Practice framework, however, I want to share more about myself and provide some details about the case.

## Positionality

Most of my professional social work experiences have been in mezzo and macro practice. As a result, how I understand social work practice—particularly social work clients, interprofessional collaboration, and the planned change process—is different. In my experience, my "clients" might be community partners, funders, an executive board or board of directors, or the entire organization. I collaborate with multiple people from various professional backgrounds and with different and competing goals and objectives. And how I perceive the process of engagement, intervention, and termination with my clients may vary greatly from conventional understandings.

Additionally, and perhaps most significantly, these practice experiences have been in secondary settings, in which social workers are not the primary professionals, social work principles do not guide ethical decision-making, and social work values do not underly organizational policies and practices. This has been challenging in that it can be isolating being the only social work practitioner; however, I have learned important skills in working on multidisciplinary teams, articulating my ideas, and finding common ground on difficult topics.

Lastly, my positionality, particularly my social identities, also plays a role in my professional experiences. Some of my most salient identities include being a Hmong American woman and being a mother of a child with a genetic disorder. My work related to equity, diversity, and inclusion is not a matter of professional obligation or even personal choice, but a matter of survival. If I want communities, organizations, and policies to better support and include me and my child,

I must be engaged in this work. My work related to equity and diversity has included both professional and volunteer experiences, including coordinating and facilitating after-school programs focused on diversity, teaching cross-cultural social work practice courses, and serving on local school district committees focused on equity.

## Accessibility Checklist

My specific responsibilities in the law firm included researching and implementing best practices related to hiring, retaining, and promoting diverse staff and attorneys, and conducting program evaluations to assess current organizational practices to create a more welcoming and inclusive work environment. In my capacity, I worked with various individuals within the firm, including attorneys and staff, and with various departments ranging from human resources (HR) to marketing to executive leadership.

Following a professional development workshop on ability/disability in the firm, a group of attorneys and staff were interested in developing an accessibility checklist. This checklist would be used when anyone associated with the law firm organized a firm-sponsored meeting or event. The form included items such as ensuring that the building or room was accessible; providing parking instructions with information on accessible parking spots; and establishing protocols for providing materials prior to the event for individuals with visual impairment or individuals who are deaf or hard of hearing. While the idea of an accessibility checklist may appear as ordinary or even routine in some organizations, organizational change can be more challenging in other settings, especially in a national organization with multiple offices and different individuals leading those offices.

Using Finn's (2020) Just Practice framework, I analyze how organizational change is conceptualized within a law firm and highlight how Just Practice concepts inform the process of organizational change.

## Conceptualizing Organizational Change Through Concepts of Just Practice

### HISTORY

The development of law firms in the United States is often correlated with industrialization and the emergence of large corporations. Law firms, as opposed to lawyers in solo practices, are organizations that are identified by several key components, including use of a team system for handling clients' cases, a hierarchical structure for decision-making and management, and a partnership model that outlines ownership and promotion within the law firm. While the law firm develops its own policies related to membership, professional associations and state and federal policies also regulate lawyers in terms of ethical practice and standards and legal practice within jurisdictions (Klegel, 2016). In many ways, law firms are similar to social work organizations, especially with their attention to teamwork and professional standards.

Additionally, law firms are highly dependent on their clients. As their clients shift their priorities, law firms also adapt in order to meet their clients' needs and compete with other law firms. One important shift among corporate clients is their attention to diversity, specifically the demographic diversity of the lawyers who handle their matters (Institute for Inclusion in the Legal Profession, 2011). With this change, law firms are becoming more aware of equity and diversity within their organizations and are making greater efforts to address these concerns from their clients.

When I was hired at the law firm as part of the inclusiveness and diversity team, the law firm had in place a longtime commitment to and practice of diversity and inclusion, even before corporate clients started to draw attention to diversity in the late 1980s (Institute for Inclusion in the Legal Profession, 2011). However, the law firm had not formalized these practices until recently. In the early 2000s, the firm hired a director for its national inclusion and diversity initiatives, began collecting demographic statistics to demonstrate their efforts to clients, and institutionalized their employee resource groups (ERGs), or affinity groups.

Months prior to my hiring, the firm started to offer quarterly professional development workshops. These workshops were designed to create dialogue among lawyers and staff and bring attention to different issues related to inclusion. The workshop on ability/disability sparked not only dialogue but also action. The group of attorneys and staff who came together to develop the accessibility checklist had various expertise and experiences that motivated their involvement. Many of these individuals shared both personal and professional connections to the challenges that oftentimes impact individuals with disabilities in the workplace. Several shared in planning meetings about how industry and organizational policies and practices had limited the full participation of individuals with disabilities in activities and events. These experiences ranged from meeting in inaccessible spaces to not having technology and software to access documents and policies that negatively impacted those with chronic illnesses and invisible impairments. Additionally, several people shared how the responsibility is often on the individual with a disability to inform and inquire about accommodations. Developing a checklist for firm-sponsored events would ensure that the responsibility for accessibility was on event coordinators to create inclusive spaces using principles of universal design (Ward & Baker, 2005), to allow for the greatest number of people possible to participate in firm-sponsored events regardless of ability.

## CONTEXT

Social workers and lawyers have a long history of interprofessional collaboration (Coleman, 2001). This collaboration is often necessary because both professions work closely with vulnerable populations; sometimes lawyers and social workers share common clients, and sometimes these professionals work on opposing cases. In both situations, lawyers and social workers bring different approaches and perspectives to their work. These differences are a result of different academic training and professional expectations, including "specialized standards of confidentiality, ethics, and legal obligations" (Galowitz, 1999, p. 2135). In fact, much of the scholarship on the collaboration between social workers and lawyers has primarily focused on the misunderstanding between these two professions (Coleman, 2001; Galowitz, 1999). Despite some major differences, however, both professions share important professional values, including an obligation to their clients and an adherence to a professional code of ethics.

When I was hired at the law firm, it was not necessarily because I was a social worker. At the time, I was completing my PhD in social work and was primarily known as a researcher with professional experiences related to issues of equity and diversity. Regardless, I brought to this position my academic training, including the professional values of social work and the Just Practice framework (Finn, 2020). As a social worker, I had developed strong skills in listening, organizing, and research. I was able to utilize these skills to listen to different perspectives; organize, strategize, and plan for next steps; and research and analyze information from multiple sources. This training and practice would be beneficial as I navigated the law firm's organizational culture and worked with different individuals within the firm.

As previously mentioned, law firms have a hierarchical structure. The law firm is composed of attorneys and non-attorney staff. The attorneys include partners, who are shareholders and joint owners of the firm; associates, who are early career attorneys and have the potential to become partners; and counsel, who are similar to independent contractors. The non-attorney staff include paralegals, administrative assistants, HR personnel, information technology (IT) staff, and other miscellaneous positions. Because this was a national law firm, each office had a managing partner; these managing partners, in addition to a chairperson and vice chairperson, made up the executive committee, who made all the decisions for the law firm.

Most non-attorney staff worked at the local level with specific offices and attorneys and had little engagement at the national level of the firm. However, the inclusiveness and diversity team was unique in that we were part of the national staff. We worked very closely with the executive committee, and through our work with affinity groups and professional development workshops, we had also built relationships with local attorneys and staff. While this unique position allowed us to easily engage with individuals throughout the strict hierarchy of law firms, navigating these relationships was a different matter. Fortunately, I was aware of the nuances of these relationships, especially as a social worker familiar with concepts of person-in-environment, positionality, and Just Practice.

## POWER

At this point, it should be fairly apparent how power works in a law firm, especially who has power. The partners, particularly the managing partners, have incredible power. In some aspect, this power is warranted: They are shareholders and joint owners of the firm, so they are invested in the success of the firm. However, what makes this hierarchy challenging is how decisions are made. In a typical manner, when there is a change in the organization, it has been discussed, developed, and voted on by the partners and sent to the executive committee for a final vote. Some decisions, particularly decisions related to human resources, are discussed and decided on only at the executive committee level. Regardless of how the decision is brought to the executive committee for approval, once the committee approves a decision, the chairperson will send the decisions in an email to the entire firm, and staff and attorneys are expected to follow the new protocol. Oftentimes, the new protocol is adopted in each office, and staff and attorneys follow the protocol because this is the culture of law firms. Sometimes, though, there is little buy-in from staff and attorneys, and so the implementation of new protocols is inconsistent, especially in a national law firm with multiple offices.

Another important aspect of power in this case is the concept of secondary settings. As previously described, secondary settings for social workers are settings in which social work is not the primary profession. For social workers in secondary settings, we must learn to navigate and negotiate. For example, schools and hospitals are secondary settings for social workers. In schools, the primary goal is education, and in hospitals, the primary goal is health. For social workers in these settings, we must adapt our practices so that we can support our clients to meet those primary goals. Sometimes social workers can easily adapt their practices and skills, and other times it can be more challenging.

In this case, the primary goal was to develop an accessibility checklist for firm-sponsored events. However, the individuals involved in developing the checklist wanted broad support for the checklist to ensure its consistent implementation across the firm's offices. They knew the importance of this checklist for creating a welcoming and inclusive workplace and wanted to engage in a different decision-making process that would ensure its consistent implementation. So, rather than develop the checklist themselves and present it to the executive committee to approve and send to its offices, we worked with the group to strategically widen its stakeholders. Our team identified specific individuals throughout the law firm to be part of the different phases of the checklist. This included bringing more administrative assistants and individuals from HR and IT into the initial development of the checklist; asking more individuals to assist with reviewing subsequent drafts; and finally, requesting those individuals to present the final version to their specific offices and among staff whose work would be impacted by the checklist.

## MEANING

The firmwide professional development workshop on ability/disability had sparked interest and conversation. Through these conversations, participants decided to develop a concrete way the firm could demonstrate their commitment to equity, diversity, and inclusion around the issues of ability/disability. For them, the law firm needed to intentionally plan and organize accessible events rather than make individuals who required accommodations to request those accommodations beforehand. Interestingly, some offices had already implemented a version of an accessibility checklist. However, the group wanted a firmwide and more complete checklist. When I assisted the group to widen its stakeholders, we were able to include potential allies. These individuals may not have a personal connection to disability but were aware of how inaccessible the law firm was and wanted to be part of addressing that inaccessibility.

The individuals who developed the accessibility checklist had various expertise, experiences, and personal connections to the issue of accessibility. These diverse perspectives were helpful in creating a more complete checklist, including considerations for accessibility that were not previously incorporated, such as providing location-specific instructions for accessible parking and requiring other organizations hosting events, in which the firm was a paid sponsor, to maintain the same accessibility standards.

## POSSIBILITY

The group wanted to ensure that the checklist would have firmwide support and consistent implementation throughout its offices. We knew we had to engage in a different decision-making process. This included bringing more people into the process to move the checklist from the ground up rather than the usual top-down approach. We could not imagine all the possibilities—when the group shifted away from the traditional decision-making process in the law firm, not only did it mean we could include more people in a collaborative process, but we would empower and inspire others to come forward with new ideas to create a more welcoming and inclusive work environment.

Some of these new ideas included professional development opportunities that were not only informational, but motivational and transformative. Through future professional development workshops, we hoped that more individuals would be inspired just as the initial group was inspired to create organizational change. In addition, we saw the importance of allyship, and many affinity groups moved to expand their affinity group membership. Lastly, several affinity groups shifted their approach and were not merely networking groups now. They saw themselves as working groups, planning and developing opportunities for learning, engagement, and organizational change across the law firm. These changes included reviewing and adopting policies related to remote work, benefits for same-sex partners, paid firm holidays, and pay equity.

## The Process of Organizational Change: Core Processes of Just Practice

### ENGAGEMENT

Several individuals who initiated the conversation following the workshop eventually became members of the Individuals with Disabilities and Their Family Members Affinity Group. In addition to these individuals, we also worked with administrative assistants and HR personnel. The engagement with both attorneys and staff helped us to consider multiple aspects of accessibility from external considerations, such as parking and ramps, to internal considerations, such as seating and microphones, to accessible files and documents. This kind of engagement also highlighted the importance of all the contributors, regardless of position (and power) within the firm.

### TEACHING-LEARNING, ACTION, AND ACCOMPANIMENT

The group took a teaching-learning approach, seeking feedback from staff and attorneys throughout the firm and incorporating new information. Their collaborative effort drew on employees' diverse expertise, experiences, and personal connections to ability/disability. Additionally, I researched best practices related to universal design in other industries, highlighting the significant changes that other industries were making related to accessibility. Knowing that law firms are highly dependent on clients and shaped by their external environment, this research was another supporting factor related to approving the checklist for firmwide use. By the time the checklist was considered by the chairperson and executive committee for approval, several offices in the firm were already using it. When it was sent via email to the entire firm for implementation, there was significant buy-in from individuals whose responsibilities would be impacted by the new protocol, including managing partners, office administrators, administrative assistants, and IT professionals.

The most surprising and rewarding impact of the checklist was the interest from others who wanted to share their own ideas for creating a more inclusive law firm. The checklist inspired other affinity groups to consider how they might want to create organizational change. These ideas included hosting annual activities to celebrate and commemorate events, providing monthly meetings to network across the firm, and continuing to offer quarterly professional development workshops related to inclusion and diversity.

## New Insights

Finn's (2020) Just Practice framework offers important approaches for social workers not only in conventional social work practice settings. Through the discussion of the Just Practice framework in this case study, I have also highlighted the transferability of social work skills between levels of practice when engaged in Just Practice, particularly at the mezzo level. Additionally, Just Practice can inform interprofessional collaborations, especially for social workers in secondary settings. I offer some additional examples.

The Just Practice framework moves us beyond the traditional planned change process and offers the seven core processes: engagement, teaching-learning, action, accompaniment, evaluation, critical reflection, and celebration. These processes allow social workers to transition between micro, mezzo, and macro levels of practice with ease. In the traditional model of the planned change process, the language of intervention and termination make it challenging for macro social workers to articulate their practice to non-macro social workers *and* to non–social workers in macro settings. What does *intervention* entail for policy advocates? What do *action* and *accompaniment* entail for policy advocates? What does *termination* mean for community organizers? What does *critical reflection* and *celebration* mean for community organizers? The language of the seven core processes better reflect the various practice settings in which we find social workers.

Just Practice also informs social workers in secondary settings by expanding how we critically assess complex problems. Finn (2020) asks us to consider the following questions: "How do different positionalities of participants shape engagement? What forms of power need to be addressed in the engagement process?" (p. 178). These questions can be asked by a social worker in child welfare or by a social work researcher in a law firm. The Just Practice framework is a valuable approach as social workers transition between levels of practice and various practice settings and engage increasingly complex problems.

## QUESTIONS FOR REFLECTIONS AND DISCUSSION

1. A law firms relies on clients, and its practices are greatly shaped by external changes. Can you identify examples of how external factors have changed social work practices?
2. What other secondary settings might you find social workers? Consider how social workers might navigate these settings. How might the Just Practice framework guide their navigation?
3. How are decisions made in your practice setting? How would you shift the decision-making process to increase collaboration and participation?
4. This case study illustrates the possibilities of creating change from within an organization. What might be an example of a change you would like to make within your practice organization? How would you proceed?

## ADDITIONAL RESOURCES

American Bar Association Disability Rights Commission: https://www.americanbar.org/groups/diversity/disabilityrights/

American Bar Association Accessibility Toolkit: https://www.americanbar.org/content/dam/aba/administrative/mental_physical_disability/Accessible_Meetings_Toolkit.pd

## REFERENCES

Coleman, B. (2001). Lawyers who are also social workers: How to effectively combine two different disciplines to better serve clients. *Washington University Journal of Law & Policy*, 7(131), 131–158. https://openscholarship.wustl.edu/law_journal_law_policy/vol7/iss1/9

Finn, J. (2020). *Just practice: A social justice approach to social work* (4th ed.). Oxford University Press.

Galowitz, P. (1999). Collaboration between lawyers and social workers: Re-examining the nature and potential of the relationship. *Fordham Law Review*, 67(5), 2123–2154. https://ir.lawnet.fordham.edu/flr/vol67/iss5/16

Institute for Inclusion in the Legal Profession. (2011). *The business case for diversity: Reality or wishful thinking?* http://www.theiilp.com/resources/Documents/IILPBusinessCaseforDiversity.pdf

Klegel, A. J. (2016). The firm as a nexus of organizational theories: Sociological perspectives on the modern law firm. *Annual Review of Law and Social Science*, 12(11), 459–478. https://doi.org/10.1146/annurev-lawsocsci-110615-085217

Taylor, S. (2006). Educating future practitioners of social work and law: Exploring the origins of inter-professional misunderstanding. *Children and Youth Services Review*, 28(6), 638–653. https://doi.org/10.1016/j.childyouth.2005.06.006

Ward, A. C., & Baker, P. M. A. (2005). Disabilities and impairments: Strategies for workplace integration. *Behavioral Sciences and the Law*, 23(1), 143–160. https://doi.org/10.1002/bsl.631

# 21

# Social Justice and the Triple Bottom Line

*Integrating Social, Environmental, and Economic Sustainability*

KATHERINE DEUEL, MS, MSW

> We are beginning to follow the guidance of our elders . . . by standing together for the benefit of all. We are remembering what they said, that all flourishing is mutual.
> —Robin Wall Kimmerer

---

**Overview**

In this chapter Katherine Deuel describes a Just Practice approach to creating meaningful, empowering work while linking the goals of social, environmental, and economic sustainability at Home ReSource, a retail building materials reuse center. Deuel addresses the history and community context of Home ReSource and its commitment to fostering a sustainable, inclusive economy and community. She details the organizational commitment to hiring, training, and supporting people experiencing barriers to employment, such as histories of mental health struggles, incarceration, trauma, and addiction. Deuel and her team practice accompaniment, teaching-learning, and ongoing critical reflection in their work with program participants to ensure their sense of belonging and dignity.

---

## Introduction

Michelle's hair is pink this week. When she comes to work at the retail building materials reuse store, which is the bread and butter of Home ReSource, her demeanor is as quiet as her hair is loud. But it's not her words that capture our attention. It is the work that she does diligently and the difference it makes to the full-time employees. Michelle makes sure things are put away in the right place, creates new signs to direct customers and display prices, and helps manage the general chaos that is our store. Michelle, a young White woman, started as a youth intern in the spring of 2018 and has since been hired at Home ReSource in a permanent position. What we notice these days is her increased confidence—evidenced by the regular appearance of her tentative yet genuine smile, her increasing willingness to opine on everything from her food tastes to the best teachers at the local alternative high school she attended, and her willingness to join in discussions and make suggestions for improving our operation.

Michelle's story is not uncommon here at Home ReSource, a nonprofit community sustainability center. Our integrated approach to sustainability is based on the "triple bottom line" business model, which attends equally to ensuring positive social, environmental, and economic impacts. We believe that these legs of the sustainability stool—social justice, sustainable use of resources, and community and economic vitality—truly work only when all three stand together equally. We recognize the potential of people, community, and materials in our strategy, activities, and organizational structure and operations. We are committed to raising awareness, propagating the model in our community and region, and leading our community in the transition to a more just, sustainable world. In this chapter I tell the story of Home ReSource and show how the Just Practice framework guides our practice and makes this vision possible.

## The Beginnings

It was 2003, and two bold, young University of Montana students wanted to change the world. They saw incredible amounts of functional but unwanted, resource-rich materials headed for the landfill every day from homes and the building industry. They believed that keeping those materials in the loop of the local economy instead of the landfill would bring value to the community. They recognized the value of the materials and realized that people donating and purchasing those reused materials both physically and fiscally demonstrates that value. They understood that accepting, sorting, and stocking materials requires people to handle them, that people need work, that businesses need employees, that thriving economies need local green businesses, and that providing quality, affordable reused materials benefits everyone, especially those with the least.

They may not have recognized all of this at once, but they had an instinct for what they wanted to create and saw the opportunity to create a culture of reuse as an important economic player in their community. They launched Home ReSource as a 501(c) with this mission: to reduce waste and help build a more vibrant and sustainable local economy. They tapped into the pulse of the community.

The founders started by collecting materials in a garage. At first, no one got paid, but then people did. Soon, they moved Home ReSource into a commercial space and became known for selling affordable materials that everyone needs: lamps and ceiling fans, solid wood doors, buckets of nails, PVC pipe, and all sorts of cabinets. They struggled to make payroll, and they battled the demons of "just throw it away." But community members continued to show up with materials to donate and were ready to work. The building materials reuse center grew and flourished.

Ten years down the dusty road of slinging affordable materials, Home ReSource had moved to an even larger location, with a professional-grade wood shop, a regular store staff of 10, a couple of administrative staff, and a deconstruction service employing four others. The founders created an organization that was highly prosperous, mostly profitable, and known and loved throughout the community. And they were tired. Dynamic organizations must reinvent themselves periodically, and Home ReSource was ready for the next chapter.

## Katherine's Story

I came to Home ReSource with a background as an educator, ecologist, and relatively newly minted MSW. Before my MSW, I had spent little time directly considering my White, middle-class privilege, the challenges of being a female leader in a male world, the insidious, systemic power of racism and gender oppression at play in our culture, or the almost insurmountable adversity created by chronic poverty. However, I have long understood, deep in my bones, the divides and discriminations that our society has institutionalized with structures and systems that reward some groups while denying others. My career has spanned education, environmental history, large-landscape wildlife conservation, climate change, family counseling, and divorce mediation. This eclectic mix has provided me quite a perspective on the cultural landscape of the intermountain West. I had grappled with the White male privilege rife in wildlife conservation. I had learned from ranchers and loggers how climate change threatens land and livelihood. I had worked side by side with some of the poorest tribes in North America as they fought for sovereignty, recognition, and the ability to manage their own lands and resources while living with significant and enduring historical trauma. I had seen people dying of cancer from exposure to toxins in the course of employment that was their source of dignity, income, and contribution to community, too poor to pay their healthcare bills and too proud not to. These people and experiences had taught me much about the power of finding strength in difference, the human capacity to persevere and overcome, and the necessity of working across demographics to build the kind of society that supports us all.

When I started as executive director at Home ReSource in 2013, people noticed. I was particularly intrigued by the steady stream of White males who asked polite but pointed questions like, Really—you are the director at Home ReSource? What skills do you have to do that? Do you know anything about tools? Do you know anything about business? What wasn't said, but implied, was, Are you qualified? And why would you want this job, anyway?

What is a woman, a mother, an ecologist-conservationist-poet-idealist, a softhearted, quiet-spoken, mediator–social worker doing running an $800,000/year nonprofit retail hardware store and construction firm? I asked myself that a couple of times as well. I had my doubts, for sure, but I also saw a well of possibility for what this organization might mean to our community that I was determined to draw on.

I was entering a job that was raw in power, meaning, and possibility, but familiar, in many ways, in history and context. It was time to leverage the organization's history and strengths within the context our community and the pressing social and environmental issues of our time. It was time to make new meaning from the work already being done and to turn possibility into change-making action. I started with these questions: How do we maximize environmental benefit? How do we engage social justice in every aspect of our everyday work? How do we show that doing both of those things is possible, necessary, and a benefit to the community?

Just as the organizational founders did, we saw possibility. Using the Just Practice framework (Finn, 2020), we expanded on the vital work of reducing waste, welcoming all, and demonstrating the potential of a green business to impact the whole community. We keep tons (about 2.5 tons, to be exact) of material out of the landfill every day and are leading our community to zero waste. We are key players in implementing the city-adopted "Zero by Fifty: Missoula's Pathway to Zero Waste" plan, and we run our homegrown, award-winning fifth-grade educational adventure known as ZWAP!, the Zero Waste Ambassadors Program. We accept and accommodate volunteers of all abilities and hire people experiencing barriers to employment in a range of intentionally designed, skill-building, temporary or permanent positions. We went from subsidizing a sporadically offered deconstruction service to launching a successful for-profit business that manifests the monetary value, social benefit, and practicality of reusing materials. We have inspired the creation of at least three other zero-waste service businesses, demonstrating the need for and value of just, green businesses in developing a thriving local economy.

## The Just Practice of Home Resource

The Just Practice framework (Finn, 2020) serves as both a planning tool and conceptual lens for our work at Home ReSource. In this section I describe how we developed our new vision of "a just and vibrant world based on the principles of sustainability where the potential of people, community, and materials is realized (Sward & Lundquist, 2020)," enhanced our community impact, and crafted a suite of intersecting programs with Just Practice principles guiding all our work.

## HISTORY

Let's start with *history*. History teaches us a lot; we can see things in retrospect that we couldn't see in real time. History helps us understand the trajectory that our current decisions can launch for us. I outlined the history of Home ReSource above and spoke to the intentions of the organizational founders. What I didn't mention were some of the practices that brought their intentions to life. For example, Home ReSource is inclusive, with customers, supporters, and employees from across the socioeconomic-political spectrum. There is always work to be done, and when someone is willing to do it, regardless of their position or personal history, they are welcome. Our woodshop came into being to allow folks to use and share tools and perspectives that might not otherwise be available to them. Home ReSource was founded on a principle of self-sufficiency—the belief that a truly successful, green business is one that pays its people and its bills from its earned revenue. And it always has, until Covid-19 taught us that in times of crisis, maintaining the services and providing affordable materials might mean asking for cash donations so that we keep our doors open though a time of uncertainty. We did not reject that history; we embraced its intention adaptively. Equally, we embrace that every pivot and adaptation we make now for Covid-19 (for example, how do we connect in a genuine way to accompany program participants from 6 feet away and with masks?) is making history and establishing patterns that become a part of our culture.

At Home ReSource, we recognize that in order to move forward, we must first stop, honor our history, and learn from it. We honor the values that have defined the organization and its practices over time. We honor the important social contract we have with our community. Personal histories inform us as well: My personal history with the conservation movement taught me that doing good work is no guarantee of practicing justly, and movements will not succeed if people are left out. Michel, a Blackfeet tribal member who worked at Home ReSource for years, was shaped by his history, which then shaped the organization's Work Programs and those who knew him. Though he battled alcoholism and homelessness as long as I knew him, he was a gentle and principled man with a keen sense of humor. He taught us all, over and over, what a tough battle addiction is, and that everyone has their enduring gifts. Through all of his challenges, Michel continued to connect with us, always offering a genuine smile and quiet insight. He never strayed from his values of caring for family and making the best of life in the moment. I suspect that he never knew how many folks he touched and inspired with his gifts of kindness, perseverance, and wisdom, but those who encountered him will never forget.

## CONTEXT

The *context* that guides and defines Home ReSource includes the place we live, the people we serve, the larger social trends of the day, and the position of our organization therein. If what we choose to do does not match the needs of our time and place, address critical social and environmental issues, or recognize the culture in which our daily lives are circumscribed, we cannot generate effective social change. We can neither simply accept the context as immutable nor try to push issues beyond the scope of community culture. We must find that edge that is relevant, real, and changeable, using our understanding of context to determine what we can control and influence and what we cannot.

When I started at Home ReSource, the organization was still recovering from an expensive relocation during the economic downturn of 2008. Wages were low, and benefits were minimal. The store was making money, but many services and opportunities—such as the wood shop and deconstruction service—were underutilized. Further, many people who worked at Home ReSource needed more mentoring and support. Technology was transforming the world and the way we do business. On a larger scale, climate change, and its underlying causes, including unsustainable use of resources, was coming into mainstream awareness. And the divide between those with the most resources and those with the least was widening every day. We had to examine and address each of these contexts that defined both our place in the community and possibility for change. Our original strategic plan did just that with goals of providing staff development, improving communications, building educational programs, and grabbing marketing opportunities to address global issues at a local scale.

## POWER

When I have taught organizational leadership to 2nd-year MSW students, I often notice a deep discomfort with *power*. Students readily identify abuses of power and power that corrupts. Of course, they understand there is power with, and power to act, as well as power over, but often they are most comfortable giving power away or shying from it altogether. I, too, have been uncomfortable with power. But what I have learned is that change cannot happen without power. Power may corrupt, but that is not inevitable. Power collected, held, and wielded with others, with humility, and in service of a clear mission is the only thing that will change the world. It is important to get comfortable with power and use it well.

At Home ReSource we asked ourselves these questions: What is the organization's power in the community? Where does it come from? What power do we have, who do we have power with, who needs power, and what can we use it for? What do we have the power to affect and what do we not? If we don't have power to make the changes we need to make—say we want to raise wages, and we don't have the money (and money is power, right?)—then what do we do about it? If we are afraid to seek the kinds of power we need to make change, then we will struggle to have impact. And if we hold our power too tightly, we will, ironically, lose it. As we work to genuinely empower others, the impact of our work expands.

## MEANING

To make social change, our work needs to be meaningful—not just to the board of directors and staff of Home ReSource, but to the whole community. Our work needs to make sense to enough people, in enough different ways, that it carries itself forward on the winds of many voices. I am a great one for making meaning: My mind can jump from a concept to a vision of impact without lifting a finger. But the work of Home ReSource is to create meaning through action. We must do work that engages, inspires, and empowers people. Our work touches lives and makes a difference. A customer with broken plumbing finds the materials and receives needed tips to fix it themselves. Staff members earn a living wage and are respected for what they contribute. We make business purchases from local vendors even though it costs more. Customers donating a lamp, hose, or door understand that those actions mean more than just cleaning out their garage, that they are part of the give and take of community where our collective actions mean that we are lightening our load on our natural resources, promoting decent working environments, providing affordable materials, and building a vibrant local economy. The meaning we create is collective and cumulative. It is the work of many.

## POSSIBILITY

Possibility is the impact we are having into the future, and our belief that we are not only doing just work right now but that the work we do is leading us to better tomorrow. We invest our hope in the actions we take and the people we work with. We trust in the ripples we create because we believe in our collective ability to fully realize ideas that today are only a concept.

Zero waste is a prime example. At Home ReSource, we say that the technical definition of "zero waste" is "zero waste or darn near"—approximately a 90% diversion rate. We know zero waste is practical, doable, and tangible. We take steps every day to get us there. It may not be possible to live a zero-waste lifestyle today, but it is our guiding principle. Zero waste envisions the possibility of living in a world that sees all facets of our complex human and material systems as valued, not as things to be discarded.

Home ReSource keeps 900 tons of material out of the landfill each year. The compost pickup service inspired by our zero waste work keeps out another million pounds. Through our work with city operations and local schools to reduce, reuse, compost, and recycle, we hope to double that number. Possibility inspires us and reminds us that while we may not actualize our ideals today, we believe that we have the courage and collective will to get there.

# Bringing the Core Processes to Bear

The core processes of Just Practice also guide our work at Home ReSource. I highlight a few examples.

## ENGAGEMENT

Engagement is a key process to all our work. It is the stance we use with our staff, customers, work program participants, students, community partners, and external stakeholders. Whether we are working with a customer or leading a ZWAP! class, our goal is connected interaction that engages folks with the organization, the materials, the larger concepts, and the needs of their community. In the store, the materials available and their locations may change day today, so we help customers find things and figure out projects. We direct, but we also engage; we get to know them. Our zero waste and educational programs are all about community engagement. Every job description that we post at Home ReSource states that employees must be able to "engage with everyone where they are at."

## TEACHING-LEARNING

We believe everyone has something to offer—whether a skill, a personal history, a perspective, or a vision for the future—and we want to learn from it. We are educators, constantly teaching the skills and practices of waste reduction and sustainability. If we aren't continually learning as we teach, we will not be able to effectively understand and meet the needs of the community.

Sometimes learning is simply listening to a customer or work program participant. But we also cultivate a culture of reflexivity and lifelong learning. We encourage professional development, provide regular feedback, and share concepts and ideas. When we try a new program, we do a pilot first. For example, we first taught ZWAP! to a modest audience of two fifth-grade classes. Through ongoing, solicited feedback from students and teachers, we have revised and improved the program so that in 2018–2019 we reached almost every fifth grader in the Missoula area with a solid and well-grounded program. The input from teachers and graduates means that our educational adventure is also replicable and scalable. This year, teachers as far away as Bozeman, Montana, and Grand Junction, Colorado, are sharing our fun and empowering version of Sustainability 101 with their fifth-grade classes.

When we developed "Zero by Fifty: Missoula's Community Zero Waste Plan," we started with four community listening sessions to learn from those who care about—and ultimately will have to execute—living in a zero-waste Missoula. We work with university interns and AmeriCorps service members every year, sharing knowledge and skills with them and learning from their youthful vantage points and fresh ideas. Our youth participants are clever, challenging, and vital. They are the future leaders who will solve problems we have not yet envisioned. The back-and-forth of the teaching-learning process keeps us all on the cutting edge of the change we want to make, at whatever scale.

## ACTION AND ACCOMPANIMENT

We are all about doing! At Home ReSource, we create meaning and impact through the accretion of many small actions over time. Everywhere you turn at Home

ReSource, we have things to do. From sweeping the parking lot for nails to greeting customers and treating them with respect, to making public presentations, the many actions that constitute Home ReSource align with our values and connect us to our community.

Accompaniment is a fundamental process in Home ReSource's work programs. We bear witness to participants' experiences. We acknowledge their strengths and struggles, walk beside them, and treat them with dignity and respect. We cannot solve every challenge, and we do not intervene. But we are present, providing tasks to do and teaching work skills, such as staying off the cell phone, safely handling materials and tools, and problem-solving. Not everyone gets there, but if program participants are seen and appreciated for what they give, that has value.

We are also clear that we don't provide housing, food, mental health counseling, or other services. But we will accompany folks to the local food bank, mental health center, or homeless shelter. We will go with a participant to a bike shop to get a needed part for a key mode of transportation.

One participant who made a lasting impression on me came to Home ReSource after making many moves throughout the Northwest. Matt, a sturdy White male in his late 50s, had some carpentry skills and did his tasks daily with neither complaint nor particular enthusiasm, but expressed a genuine gratitude for having a job. I would see Matt occasionally on my way to work. I would wave "hello" and ask how he was. One day he told me that he really appreciated that gesture of connection. After 4 months on the job, he was suddenly off again—he wasn't sure where he was going, but he left feeling he'd done his work well and was respected in the process.

## CRITICAL REFLECTION

All the Just Practice processes come together when we take the time to critically reflect. As we engage, teach and learn, act, and accompany, we are always asking ourselves if we achieved our goals, how we could have done things better, what we can and cannot control, and what we should be celebrating. We debrief everything. At Home ReSource, we have built in time at staff meetings for check-ins dedicated to personal and organizational reflection. For example, when the 2019 global climate strikes came around, we debated whether to shut our doors and participate in solidarity for a cause that is critical to our mission. Ultimately, we stayed open but put things in place to ensure that those staff who wanted to participate could, while those customers who rely on shopping and donating at Home ReSource as their personal climate action could reliably access us as well. The decision was made through considerable critical reflection, acknowledging both the image we want to project and the reality of serving a diverse clientele—and, ultimately, what our core values meant in this particular case.

Finally, *celebration!* We have structured times and channels to celebrate people, successes, impacts, partners, and transitions. Our annual events, which include a building contest and a fundraising auction where we raffle off the winning creations, are big public celebrations of creativity, reuse, possibility, generosity, and the amazing community we live in. And yet, despite the structure we have created, too often we forget to celebrate our small successes. Perhaps it is human nature to move on more quickly from success than failure, but we do so at our peril. Celebration is a form of gratitude. It generates positivity and connection and reminds us of what we have accomplished and who we cherish. It keeps us moving forward together to create the just and vibrant world that we envision.

## EMBRACING POSSIBILITY

When Roger, a young Crow man, was released from the penal system, his case worker suggested that he apply for a youth apprenticeship through our work programs. He applied, was accepted, and began his apprenticeship. Later on, this apprenticeship opened doors to a roofing job that could support his growing family. However, just weeks after the birth of their baby, his girlfriend left. When his roofing job proved inconsistent and his boss unsympathetic, Roger returned to Home ReSource looking for a permanent position. Downtrodden, he could barely look us in the eye as we coached him through a job interview. We gladly supported his success in a permanent position where he received not only a paycheck and mentoring, but piles of hand-me-down baby clothes, help in securing child care, and perhaps too much well-meaning parenting advice. Then, after 7 months of solid work, he missed several days without calling in. Typically, this would be grounds for termination, but when Roger showed up, we encouraged him to continue work. Then it happened again. Weeks passed with no word from Roger and no response to our efforts to contact him. Then one day Roger called back. He said he valued his connections at Home ReSource too much not to let us know what was happening, but that he just could not be around those he respected while in such a difficult space. But he hinted at his hope for a better future and promised to keep in touch. Just a few weeks ago, out of the blue, Roger showed up, announced, with his head up and looking us in the eye, that our intake department was "a mess," and spent 4 hours of his free time helping clean it up.

At Home ReSource, we know the world is full of challenges, pain, achievements, celebration, and simple joy. There is so much we cannot change. We have been deeply challenged by Covid-19—endeavoring to run our programs safely, to meet community needs, and to work through the fear and exhaustion that so many have experienced. But we have heard from the community that they need us now more than ever. The Just Practice concepts and processes keep us grounded and engaged in reciprocity. They ensure that we consider diverse perspectives that enable us to navigate relentless change, implement previously unthinkable practices, and build stronger connections across what often feel like widening gaps. They help guide our organizational culture as we integrate justice and sustainability and inspire others into the future.

## QUESTIONS FOR REFLECTION AND DISCUSSION

1. What new learning do you draw from this chapter to inform your thinking about the relationships among social, environmental, and economic justice?
2. What work is being done in your community to address the nexus of social, economic, and environmental justice? What role do social workers play?
3. Where do you see possibilities in your community to expand the presence of social workers and the practice of social justice work beyond traditional social work settings?
4. How does the Home ReSource story inform your thinking about social justice work as an organizational practice?
5. Does your community have a sustainability and building materials reuse store or center? If so, visit it and see what elements of Just Practice in action that you can identify.

## RESOURCES

Home ReSource: www.homeresource.org
Zero by Fifty, Missoula's Pathway to Zero Waste: http://www.ci.missoula.mt.us/2087/Zero-Waste
The triple bottom line: https://sustain.wisconsin.edu/sustainability/triple-bottom-line/

## REFERENCE

Finn, J. (2020). *Just practice: A social justice approach to social work* (4th ed.). Oxford University Press.
Sward, H., & Lundquist, S. (2020, June 5). Sustainable Missoula: Nurturing the zero waste leaders of tomorrow. *Missoula Current*. https://missoulacurrent.com/opinion/2020/06/zero-waste-leaders-tomorrow/

Part Seven

# INTEGRATING SOCIAL JUSTICE IN INDIGENOUS AND INTERNATIONAL CONTEXTS OF PRACTICE

# 22

# Just Practice in Indigenous Communities

ASHLEY TRAUTMAN, MSW, JD, AND
MARILYN BRUGUIER ZIMMERMAN, MSW, PHD

> If you have come to help me, you are wasting your time. But if
> you have come because your liberation is bound up with mine,
> then let us walk together.
> —Lilla Watson, Aboriginal Murri artist, activist,
> and academic

---

**Overview**

Ashley Trautman and Marilyn Bruguier Zimmerman describe how the core concepts of Just Practice guide their work with tribal communities through the National Native Children's Trauma Center in this chapter. The histories of federal policies and practices have had traumatizing impacts on tribal communities. In their work with tribes, Trautman and Zimmerman explore meanings of this history, impacts on present-day contexts, and possibilities for intervention that incorporate their unique cultures and traditions and honor tribal power and sovereignty. Trautman and Zimmerman explore their positionalities in relation to their practice in tribal communities and describe the centrality of engagement, teaching-learning, accompaniment, and critical reflection to their work in Indian country.

---

## Introduction

The National Native Children's Trauma Center (NNCTC) is a treatment and service adaptation center within the National Child Traumatic Stress Network (NCTSN). The focus of the NNCTC is to increase service providers' and child-serving systems' ability to respond to the trauma-related needs of American Indian/Alaska Native (AI/AN) children and youth in culturally appropriate ways. The NNCTC is primarily funded through grants from the Substance Abuse and Mental Health

Services Administration (SAMHSA), the Office of Juvenile Justice and Delinquency Prevention (OJJDP), and private contracts. We partner with tribal communities across the country who invite us to support trauma-informed systems change efforts. Though each tribal community we work with is unique, for the purposes of this chapter, a "typical" case for us would be responding to a request for training and technical assistance (T/TA) from a tribal child-serving agency. This request may start as a desire to learn more about trauma, how it manifests in the clients served by the agency, and techniques to better serve children and families.

What may begin as a training could develop into broader systems-change efforts. The NNCTC would collaborate with the agency to determine both immediate and long-term goals for trauma-informed change and create a T/TA plan. Project activities may include trauma screening and policy or tribal code analysis to determine if change in language would support trauma-informed practice. Trauma screening is the process of using standardized assessments to determine what symptoms a young person may be exhibiting as a result of experiencing trauma. An example of how trauma screening and policy change come together could be in recommending that a tribal court adopt a policy where all youth involved in the justice system are screened for trauma symptoms and referred to appropriate mental health services. Importantly, because many youth who have experienced trauma are involved in multiple systems, our T/TA seeks to promote cross-system collaboration by inviting representatives from local schools, juvenile justice, child welfare, law enforcement, and courts into trainings and program implementation.

## Using the Just Practice Framework

While certain frameworks for building trauma-informed systems help guide our work, which we will discuss in more detail later, the substance of our approach is grounded in the concepts of Just Practice (Finn, 2020). In each T/TA activity we provide, we consider the impact of a tribe's *history*, how the tribe makes *meaning* of their history, how that history impacts the current *context*, what *power* dynamics are at play which we must attend to, and importantly, what *possibility* exists in our work with that community. We expand on these concepts below.

### HISTORY

Research suggests that AI/AN youth are at increased risk of trauma, depression, and PTSD as a result of grief and exposure to violence. When exposure to traumatic events occurs frequently, or when traumatic stress is left unaddressed, children may be susceptible to relationship problems, drug and alcohol abuse, violent behavior, suicide and depression, problems in school, and bullying and victimization. Indigenous communities have the added consequences of historic and intergenerational trauma, which can intensify the impact of personal trauma. NNCTC, therefore, must understand the historical contexts of Indigenous people as we are invited to come alongside providers and tribal community members to support AI/AN children and families through trauma-informed approaches.

Historical trauma is defined as "collective trauma experienced over time and across generations by a group of people who share an identity, affiliation, or circumstance" (Mohatt et al., 2014. p. 128; Brave Heart & DeBruyn, 1998; Evans-Campbell, 2008). For Indigenous people, the traumatic events were the consequence of colonization of North America by Europeans. The U.S. government enacted federal policies meant to annihilate or assimilate tribal nations. The policies included removal of tribes from their ancestral homelands, introduction of diseases as instruments of genocide resulting in pandemics that wiped out entire nations, removal of generations of Native children from their families and communities and placement in boarding schools, and ultimately the prohibition of tribal spiritual and cultural practices (Stannard, 1992; Thornton, 1987). The intergenerational aftermath of historical traumatic experiences is often manifest through individuals and families living contemporary lives while struggling with persistent poverty, addiction, and interpersonal violence contributing to poor health outcomes (Gone, 2012).

Perhaps most devastating to the well-being of tribal people and communities was the removal of their children to boarding schools in order to "civilize" them. During the boarding school era, Indigenous children were taken far from their homes in order to ensure that parental and community influence was completely removed. The schools were administered by government and later religious organizations. The foundational teaching consisted of instruction in Christianity and Western European mores. The children experienced deprivations of food, medicine, and human comfort. Punishments for rule violations were harsh and physically abusive. The long-term impact on the tribal communities meant that generations of AI/AN people experienced the loss of wholesome traditional parenting practices and community nurturing roles, along with the knowledge of language, culture, and ceremonial and spiritual ways of knowing and being (Cross, Earle, & Simmons, 2000). The children returned home not knowing their languages, their ceremonies, or their social and cultural roles, and were often were marginalized in their own families. The painful historic experiences are well known among tribal members.

During the 1950s to 1970s, state child welfare and courts were removing Native children from their homes and reservation communities at alarming rates. In 1974, Congress conducted a study that revealed 25%–35% of Native children had been removed and placed in non-tribal member homes or institutions off their reservations. Once again, generations of Native children were lost from their families, and most failed to develop strong tribal identities. As a result of the study, Congress passed the Indian Child Welfare Act (ICWA) in 1978 to ensure that a Native child's tribal community (and court) has full jurisdiction over that child even when the child does not reside on their reservation. Despite passage of the ICWA more than 40 years ago, Native children continue to be removed from their families and tribal communities at disproportional rates compared to their non-tribal peers.

## CONTEXT

This very brief overview of historical and intergenerational trauma is what anchors the work of NNCTC. It is critical to effective work alongside Indigenous people to understand *historical context* of their lives in *contemporary societal context*. The challenges they face and the resilience they continue to demonstrate contribute to our work and their own community development.

Early in the founding of the United States, the government dealt with tribes as it did with foreign nations. Through treaties, a federal trust relationship was established between the United States and tribal nations. To explain this relationship in very basic terms, we would describe the history as a time when the United States overcame tribes, and tribes, in an effort to survive as nations, ceded tribal lands to the U.S. government in exchange for a designated homelands (reservations), education, and health care. The federal government began a campaign to terminate the federal-tribal trust relationship and treaty rights, rescind rights to designated lands, and pressure tribal members to relocate to urban areas. Today, the highest population of American Indians are living in urban settings and not on reservations. Thus, NNCTC adjusts from working in homogeneous reservation communities to heterogeneous urban contexts with many unique tribes represented in the communities. Whether in a rural or urban tribal community, the collective historical experience and impacts for tribal peoples are always at the foundation of our contextual understanding and work.

## MEANING

We are keenly aware of how we make *meaning* of our own experiences through our gender, ethnic, and cultural lenses that we bring to this work. However, what may be more important is engaging in cultural humility, which allows us to respect tribal spiritual ways, gender roles, and cultural values. We must accept the notion that the Western worldview is not superior to Indigenous worldviews and that Western scientific thought is not more valid than Indigenous ways of knowing and validating their origins and existence. When we are able to lean into Indigenous ways of knowing, we open ourselves and our work to possibilities that current social work practice as yet does not recognize. When we visit tribal communities and meet with tribal leadership, elders, and community members, they are quick to describe the resilience of their people and the medicines and ceremonies that have healed their people's physical and psychological wounds for thousands of years. They often ask if our evidence-based interventions to treat complex trauma were developed for American Indians. We walk in cultural humility and admit that although the interventions were not developed for American Indians, we have adapted the models to better fit the community and we have found that evidence-based practices (EBPs) do support healing for American Indian children and youth impacted by exposure to complex trauma.

The adaptation of EBPs to better fit the needs of tribes is critical. If the process of the intervention conflicts with a tribal value, we change the intervention to one infused with tribal values. If the tribe does not have access to master's-level clinicians, we change the model to a curriculum to be utilized by a cultural or spiritual leader. The tribes are looking for ways to bring healing and well-being to their children and families. They are very open to using some of the therapeutic models we employ to support and heal their families. We have also changed from solely using EBPs to address system change. Helping to create a trauma-informed agency or program that focuses on client engagement with trauma-informed approaches to care has been a better fit for tribal communities. Once we have permissions (such as tribal resolutions or memoranda of agreement) that honor tribal sovereignty, we begin working in the community. We are never prescriptive when working with tribal programs; we are humbled and grateful when the tribal agency or program is able to infuse their tribal language, values, and ceremonies into their practice.

## POWER

To effectively work alongside tribal nations, it is important to understand power. We understand the history of colonization as the federal government's attempt at annihilating tribal nations through exertions of extreme governmental power. We can also identify everyday examples of coloniality, which we understand as the deeply engrained hierarchies our country holds relative to race, the ways our society privileges Western forms of education and thought, and how social systems work to undermine efforts at decolonization (Almeida, Rozas, Cross-Denny, Lee, & Yamada, 2019). These processes to exert *power over*, as defined in Just Practice, are ones the NNCTC critically reflects on in practice to ensure we are not complicit in perpetuating historical traumas (Finn, 2020).

Our center has been honored to bear witness to tribes who have asserted their power of tribal sovereignty in promoting the well-being of their communities. An example of this is a trend across the country of tribes contracting with the federal government to take control of funds normally distributed to Indian Health Service (IHS). Rather than IHS, a federal agency, providing health-care services to a tribal community, tribal governments are able to direct funds and administer programs in ways they determine are best for their citizens. In practice, this means tribes develop and deliver medical and mental health services that are responsive to the unique cultural and health-related needs of their people. This is an important example of tribes' inherent *power within* (Townsend et al., 1999).

## POSSIBILITY

Possibility reminds us to honor history while considering the future (Finn, 2020). At NNCTC we embrace possibility by engaging in innovative problem-solving that brings to bear the wisdom of the past. We meld meaning, context, history, and possibility by supporting discussion on resilience. We define resilience as the existence and use of protective factors despite the experience of significant hardship (e.g., historical trauma) and ongoing stress (e.g., high rates of chronic poverty; Wexler, 2014). For Indigenous communities, this means that despite years of attempted assimilation and annihilation by the federal government, tribal culture, values, and traditional ways still exist and remain an important pathway to healing for many people (Wexler, 2014).

To honor this, our T/TA supports centering Indigenous ways of knowing into programming. This might include cultural adaptation of an evidence-informed practice, development of new curricula that is culturally informed, or introduction of a cultural connectedness tool. For example, a tribal juvenile diversion program created a trauma-screening tool that included culturally relevant images and concepts as a way of simultaneously teaching youth about their tribe's culture while assessing for trauma symptoms. Ultimately, we remain open and follow the tribes' lead in exploring ways to utilize T/TA efforts that encourage infusion of culture as a mechanism of resilience.

## Using the Core Processes

The NNCTC begins each relationship by *engaging* in a process meant to understand the needs of the agency and community. Our T/TA activities begin only after we have received an invitation to partner from the tribal community, which honors tribal sovereignty. The development of genuine relationships with agency staff and community stakeholders is crucial to the work. This means traveling to the community to observe processes and dialoging with those working in the system about community resources, strengths, and challenges. *Teaching-learning* is also central to our work. We do not enter tribal communities as the experts; we come as co-teachers and co-learners who put cultural humility at the forefront. We understand that our work is permitted and led by the community. We use both formal and informal assessment methods. If appropriate for the setting, NNCTC staff may use formal organizational assessments to evaluate existing trauma-informed practices and an agency's attitude toward trauma-informed change. In cases where formal organizational assessments are not possible, needed, or appropriate, we utilize informal methods to understand needs. We then work with agency staff to determine necessary adaptions of tools and curricula to ensure responsiveness to needs and culture.

The specific T/TA we offer varies depending on setting but includes common elements such as an introduction to trauma (which includes an overview of historical trauma, adverse childhood experiences [Felitti et al., 1998], and the impact of trauma on child development), discussion of trauma screening options, policy or code review, and secondary traumatic stress mitigation. As a member of the National Child Traumatic Stress Network (NCTSN), many of the resources we use are developed by the network. This includes curricula on trauma-informed approaches appropriate to different systems and populations, such as child welfare, juvenile justice, and resource parents. All of our T/TA work goes hand in hand with learning from our tribal partners. We describe our relationships and the work we do with any community as coming alongside the tribe rather than leading any particular initiative. This approach to *accompaniment* necessitates that we *critically reflect* on our positionalities as a way to ensure that each phase of our work, from initial relationship building to process mapping and implementation, honors the objectives each community has identified. The core processes are deeply anchored into our work and reflected in our practice.

## Considering Positionality

When considering positionality, it is important to recognize the different ways we as a center and our individual staff relate to the work we do. Some NNCTC staff are tribal members, some are not, and ultimately, we are all a part of an institution of higher education. Each of these social locations impacts the ways we engage with the tribal communities we work alongside. The following section contains brief reflections from these perspectives as a way to illuminate the complexities of the work.

### POSITIONALITY AS A SOCIAL WORKER IN AN INSTITUTION OF HIGHER EDUCATION

Our center is located within the College of Education at the University of Montana. As such, we are attentive to what a university may represent to tribal communities. We are mindful of the ways in which the research enterprise has betrayed tribal communities through misuse of data, exploitation of the research process, and failure to meaningfully collaborate on research projects (Tuhiwai Smith, 2012). In recognition of this history and in response to contemporary perspectives, our center follows certain principles when beginning work with any community. At the start of every major project, we seek permission from tribal leadership to work within the community. At regular intervals, we ask to appear in front of tribal council to update community leaders on each project. In addition, depending on the nature of the work to be accomplished, our center will engage with the tribe's institutional review board to ensure that any data collection or study is appropriately reviewed. In all cases, we clearly communicate that all data collected is the property of the tribal community.

Finally, we are thoughtful in each component of our work to bring to bear the NNCTC's core belief that tribes know the consequences of trauma in their communities and are intensifying their efforts around community healing as a response (NNCTC.org). In practice, that means we listen to understand needs, adapt any curriculum or intervention to respond to those needs, and remain flexible when changes occur in any given agency or community.

## POSITIONALITY AS AN AMERICAN INDIAN SOCIAL WORKER: MARILYN'S STORY

Growing up in my tribal community influences my perspective in the work that I do today. Being a member of a particular tribal nation means that I am as much an outsider as my non-Native colleagues when I am working in tribal communities that aren't my own. Tribal nations share some particular ways of being in the world, but we have unique languages and cultures. Native societies in America share the history of colonization and assimilation policies that negatively impacted generations of Native people. It is knowledge of this history and my own life as an Indigenous person that allows me a depth of understanding perhaps not available to my colleagues who are not tribal members. I am able to bear witness to the realities facing tribes as one who has familiarity with those realities.

As I have worked in a variety of tribal communities, I now know that utilizing an evidence-based therapeutic model to treat the symptoms of toxic stress may work in one tribal community setting but may be difficult to reproduce in another. Engaging tribal agencies, working with tribal leadership, and becoming members of larger community collaboratives looks different in every tribal community. The fact that I am a tribal member is helpful but does not guarantee that I will be successful in building relationships with every tribal community.

It is my academic journey that has helped me understand historical trauma, a history that I was not taught in elementary or high school. Today, it remains true that teaching tribal history in public schools does not occur. So, it is through an academic lens that I encountered historical trauma theory. I studied it by reading peer-reviewed articles, texts, and novels and through attending classes, seminars, and conferences. At one point it occurred to me that while growing up, I had experienced the effects of historical trauma, a concept I had yet to define. I found myself at a university deliberating the implications of historical trauma from an almost purely academic perspective. However, it is the understanding of lived experience that I hold close today. When working with tribal community providers, trauma is not academic. They are striving to be a conduit for healing for their children, their elders, and their community. Through my historical trauma learning journey, I have been honored to have been shown tribal healing processes through natural medicines, sacred songs, and tribally specific ceremonies. I have come to understand and value the resilience of my own tribe, both as individuals and as a community. Today, I have overwhelming hope that tribes have the answers for health and well-being within their own families and communities.

## POSITIONALITY AS A LATINX SOCIAL WORKER WORKING ALONGSIDE INDIGENOUS COMMUNITIES: ASHLEY'S STORY

Working in tribal communities as a non-Native person often means grappling with fears of replicating past abuses committed by White social workers during the disproportionate removal of Indigenous children from their communities, by non-Native researchers who exploited tribal communities, and by systems designed for the presumed benefit of tribal communities but which have contributed to ongoing collective trauma. As a non-Native social worker employed by an institution of higher education, I am critically aware of how the systems of which I am a part have perpetrated harm against tribal communities.

My positionality is also informed by my socialization as a biracial person, with one parent who is White, and one who is Latinx. I identify most closely with my Latinx ancestry but am mindful that a part of my identity is also as a settler. Therefore, my positionality as it relates to my work alongside tribal communities is often complex. At times, I have observed how similar, yet different, experiences of oppression and discrimination help inform my engagement with Indigenous colleagues and project partners. While this component of my identity may allow me to connect with the people and communities I work with, there are limits to this shared experience. As part of a family whose history contributed to the process of colonization, I hold certain privileges that contribute to my social location. This has, of course, led to cultural mistakes that have been some of the most powerful learning experiences of my personal and professional life.

As my work alongside tribal communities continues, I strive to develop an understanding of the ways my positionality impacts my practice and how the context I work within shapes this in return. To do this, I continue to deepen my practice of cultural humility, including how to repair mistakes when the burden of that repair is mine and not of the person or community in which I may have harmed. I value reflexivity, the process by which we constantly evaluate our perspectives, the perspectives of others, and the context we work within, and I have found that dialogue and *critical reflection* with colleagues to be imperative to this process (Finn, 2020). Finally, I continue to explore my own culture, the strength and complexities my identities bring to my practice, and the places of privilege I can leverage to be an ally in the work toward social justice in tribal communities.

## Challenges and Possibilities

Many of the challenges we experience in the work of the NNCTC are largely a result of the stressed systems that can exist in tribal communities. As in many human service systems, lack of access to sustainable and adequate funding levels is an ever-present reality for many tribal programs. What is unique in tribal communities is the fact that many of the existing funding structures are based on the historical relationship between the federal government and tribes. Known as the "trust responsibility," the federal government is obligated to fund many of the essential programs that provide health care to tribal members (Pevar, 2012). However, because funding for many of these programs are a part of yearly congressional appropriations processes, underfunding is a common and chronic problem (National Congress of American Indians, 2019).

This problem is present in the social service systems the NNCTC regularly works alongside. In general, nearly all of the funding sources for child welfare systems in tribal communities are administered through discretionary programs and implemented through the Bureau of Indian Affairs (BIA). These funds vary from year to year and place certain restrictions on which tribes can receive funding. The result is that many tribes are without BIA social service programs and many others experience unstable funding (First Kids 1st, n.d.). It is not uncommon, then, that tribal child-serving agencies apply for competitive grants to supplement these inadequate funding streams. While this funding can result in positive program development, it may also require tribal programs to use interventions or implement programming that is not consistent with tribal cultural values and practices (First Kids 1st, n.d.).

Federal funding levels and structures pose challenges to building and sustaining trauma-informed initiatives. Funding instability may result in understaffed social service systems with high caseloads and turnover, loss of institutional knowledge, and a practice approach geared to crisis management rather than development of new initiatives. For those child welfare agencies that do begin implementation of trauma-informed practices, many face challenges when attempting to refer to mental health providers because there may not be an adequate number of clinicians in the community.

Covid-19 has posed tremendous challenges over the past year. The pandemic has had devasting impacts to tribal nations across the country. As noted in data collected on the disproportionality of Covid-19 infections, confirmed cases among AI/AN people are 3.5 times that among non-Hispanic White persons (Hatcher et al., 2020). As the pandemic has progressed, we have observed how already challenged infrastructures within many tribal communities have been strained. In an effort to protect their communities, tribal nations have closed borders and shifted many program functions to remote modalities. In response, our team began delivering T/TA remotely. This has created challenges for our work. For example, engagement is difficult when we cannot be physically present within each community. Efforts to provide T/TA have also been challenged by barriers to internet accessibility and access to technology within some communities.

Despite connectivity issues and barriers to relationship building, we have also uncovered new possibilities. Through our T/TA relationships, we have learned about creative strategies communities are employing to respond to the unique context of the pandemic. Perhaps most notable is the leadership role many Native youth have taken in providing technology know-how to ensure provision of necessary services such as food distribution. For our part, the NNCTC has worked to convert content into an online format and created resources specific to the unique experiences of grief and loss many youth in particular, but tribal communities more broadly, are experiencing due to the pandemic. In all we do, the NNCTC seeks to embody the Just Practice framework and core processes by being constant in our flexibility to the priorities of the tribal communities we are honored to accompany on their journey to trauma-informed system development. These experiences have reaffirmed our commitment to a well-used phrase at the center: In all we do, we must keep a "rigid state of flexibility" (M. Zimmerman, personal communication, 2011).

## QUESTIONS FOR REFLECTION AND DISCUSSION

1. Why does an understanding of history, as described in this chapter, matter for micro-level social work practice with Indigenous individuals?
2. How can the concept of resiliency as it relates to Indigenous people, community, and tradition be incorporated into your work? How might you bring the Just Practice framework to bear in strengthening your approach to social work in and with Indigenous communities?
3. What is our responsibility as agents of change to work toward decolonization?
4. What does a decolonizing practice mean to you? How might this resemble or deepen your current practice?

## RESOURCES

National Child Traumatic Stress Network: https://www.nctsn.org
Indian Law Resource Center: https://indianlaw.org
National Indian Child Welfare Association: https://www.nicwa.org
National Congress of American Indians: https://www.ncai.org

## REFERENCES

Almeida, R. H., Werkmeister Rozas, L. M., Cross-Denny, B., Kyeunghae Lee, K., & Yamada, A. (2019). Coloniality and intersectionality in social work education and practice. *Journal of Progressive Human Services*, *30*(2), 148–164.

Brave Heart, M. Y. H., & DeBruyn, L. (1998). The American Indian holocaust: Healing historical unresolved grief. *American Indian and Alaska Native Mental Health Research*, *8*, 60–82.

Cross, T. L., Earle, K. A., & Simmons, D. (2000). Child abuse and neglect in Indian country: Policy issues. *Families in Society*, *81*(1), 49–58.

Evans-Campbell, T. (2008). Historical trauma in American Indian/Native Alaska communities: A multilevel framework for exploring impacts on individuals, families, and communities. *Journal of Interpersonal Violence*, *23*(3) 316–338.

Felitti, V. J., Anda, R. F., Nordenberg, D., Williamson, D. F., Spitz, A. M., Edwards, V., Koss, M. P., & Marks, J. S. (1998). Relationship of childhood abuse and household dysfunction to many of the leading causes of death in adults: The Adverse Childhood Experiences (ACE) Study. *American Journal of Preventive Medicine*, *14*(4), 245–258.

Finn, J. (2020). *Just practice: A social justice approach to social work* (4th ed.). Oxford University Press.

First Kids 1st. (n.d.). *Funding child welfare services*. Retrieved February 23, 2021, from https://www.issuelab.org/resources/34042/34042.pdf

Gone, J. P. (2012). Indigenous traditional knowledge and substance abuse treatment outcomes: The problem of efficacy evaluation. *American Journal of Drug and Alcohol Abuse*, *38*(5), 493–497.

Hatchers, S. M., Agnew-Brune, C., Anderson, M., Zambrano, L. D., Rose, C. E., Jim, M. A., Baugher, A., Liu, G. S., Patel, S. V., Evans, M. E., Pindyck, T., Dubray, C. L., Rainey, J. J.,

Chen, J., Sadowski, C., Winglee, K., Penman-Aguilar, A., Dixit, A., Claw, E., ... McCollum, J. (2020). COVID-19 among American Indian and Alaska Native persons—23 states, January 31–July 3, 2020. *Morbidity and Mortality Weekly Report, 69*(34), 1166–1169. http://dx.doi.org/10.15585/mmwr.mm6934e1external icon

Mohatt, N., Thompson, A., Thai, N., & Tebes, J. (2014). Historical trauma as public narrative. *Social Science and Medicine, 106*, 128–136.

National Congress of American Indians. (2019). *Healthcare: Reducing disparities in the federal health care budget.* http://www.ncai.org/07_NCAI-FY20-Healthcare.pdf

Pevar, S. (2012). *The rights of Indians and tribes* (4th ed.). Oxford University Press.

Stannard D. (1992) *American holocaust: The conquest of the New World.* Oxford University Press.

Thornton, R. (1987). *American Indian holocaust and survival: A population history since 1492.* University of Oklahoma Press.

Townsend, J., Zapata, E., Rowlands, J., Alberti, P., & Mercado, M. (1999). *Women and power: Fighting patriarchies and poverty.* Zed Books.

Tuhiwai Smith, L. (2012). *Decolonizing methodologies: Research and Indigenous peoples* (2nd ed.). Zed Books Ltd.

Wexler, L. (2014). Looking across three generations of Alaska Natives to explore how culture fosters Indigenous resilience. *Transcultural Psychiatry, 51*(1), 73–92. https://doi.org/10.1177/1363461513497417

# 23

# Indigenous Knowledges, Social Justice, and Disaster Risk Reduction

MARJORIE BALAY-AS, PHD, AND JAY MARLOWE, MSW, PHD

> The effect of mining on our lives is far more than the effect of a hundred typhoons.
> —Kankanaey community leader

---

**Overview**

In this chapter Marjorie Balay-as and Jay Marlowe demonstrate the significance of Indigenous knowledges to inform effective social work practice related to disaster risk reduction. Drawing from community-based research with the Indigenous Kankanaey in the northern Philippines, they examine how the five key concepts of Just Practice relate to Indigenous peoples' everyday lives and the contexts and power structures that surround them. They explore the impacts of development aggression, such as large-scale mining, that are putting the Kankanaey people's survival at risk. The authors show how social workers and other professionals can formulate disaster responses that reflect Indigenous peoples' varied perspectives, concepts, and contexts.

---

## Introduction

Indigenous knowledges and practices have great potential to inform effective disaster preparedness and response. Drawing from a critical ethnography with the Indigenous Kankanaey in the northern Philippines, this chapter uses the Just Practice Framework in the context of work with Indigenous peoples related to disaster risk reduction (DRR). The authors consider how social workers and other professionals can formulate disaster responses that capture Indigenous peoples' varied perspectives and situations, including the ways they conceptualize and respond to hazards and disasters. We examine how the framework's five key concepts relate to Indigenous peoples' everyday lives and the contexts and power structures that surround them. We conclude with a reflection on the (often) small and necessary steps involved when working to attain socially just and meaningful disaster risk reduction (DRR) with Indigenous peoples. We highlight the significance of nonviolent resistance to development aggressions that make Indigenous peoples vulnerable to everyday hazards and disasters.

## Marjorie's Story

I (Marjorie) am an Indigenous Kankanaey woman of the northern Philippines. As Indigenous peoples, we have always lived in harmony with our natural environment. Natural hazards such as typhoons are interwoven with our everyday life. As such, we have developed knowledge systems that have allowed us to live with these natural processes. However, outside influences like those from multinational corporations and their powerful agendas have affected our traditional ways of life. "Development aggression"—unjust development practices forced upon Indigenous people in disregard for human rights (Nadeau, 2005)—along with harsh natural phenomena and other hazards are increasingly affecting our community. Our responses to these hazards are becoming more dependent on technocratic knowledge and approaches than on Indigenous ways of knowing and practice. With the increasing encroachment of development aggression, such as large-scale mining in our lands, the Indigenous Kankanaey people's survival is at risk.

In this chapter, my co-author, Jay, and I present a case study of the Indigenous Kankanaey community of the northern Philippines to highlight how development injustices are affecting our community; how Indigenous people variably conceptualize and respond to hazards and disasters; and how community development social workers can be better prepared to engage with Indigenous communities to attain socially just and meaningful disaster risk reduction (DRR). We contend that binary, either-or thinking, which has been used in framing Indigenous versus Western scientific knowledge, has resulted in a devaluation of Indigenous knowledge and practice (Balay-as et al., 2018). We bring the Just Practice Framework (Finn, 2020) to bear as a tool for critical thinking and practice regarding DRR that recognizes the complex interplay of meaning systems, power relations, histories, and contexts and that opens possibilities for Indigenous peoples to actively participate in and contribute to defining and driving DRR in ways that are more meaningful, relevant, and empowering to them. In addition, we show how the processes of *engagement* and *teaching-learning* were central to the study, just as they are central to practice in Indigenous communities.

## Marjorie's Research

Over the course of 10 months in 2016, I conducted critical ethnographic research (Madison, 2005) with the Kankanaey, a group of Indigenous peoples of Kibungan in the northern Philippines. The three villages involved in the study—Palina, Madaymen, and Lubo—have directly experienced the effects of various stages of large-scale mining, from permit application to exploration, operation, and abandonment. I had previously worked as a community development social worker and community organizer in the region. This was during a period of active struggles by Indigenous people for self-determination and in resistance to development aggression in the form of large-scale mining, logging, dam-building, and commercial construction. Over time I began participating in anti-mining advocacy and became reconnected with rural farmers in far-flung regions of the country whom I had met in my community organizing days. I was gaining a clearer picture of systemic injustice through dialogue and connection in my own Indigenous community and with Indigenous people elsewhere. This led to my interest in learning more about disasters and their relationship to development aggression via graduate studies in New Zealand. I returned to my home region as both "insider," having grown up in the province, and privileged "outsider," having studied abroad in pursuit of a doctoral degree (Balay-as, 2019).

## Bringing the Just Practice Framework to Bear

Through my community research, I sought answers to a few key questions: How do Indigenous perceptions of disasters advance theoretical understandings and practical applications of community development in social work? How do Indigenous peoples perceive and respond to disasters? In what ways are the Indigenous understandings of disasters relevant to community development? How does the practice of community development integrate Indigenous perspectives and capacities in DRR policy formulation and program implementation? The Just Practice framework provided a helpful lens for understanding people's lived experience and considering possibilities for social justice–oriented practice. In the following sections we use the framework to explore issues of DRR in relation to the experiences of Indigenous Kankanaey people.

### MEANING

Meaning refers here to the meanings ascribed to hazards by various actors, such as the different professionals, agencies, and corporations, and the Indigenous peoples themselves. As I entered into this project, I understood that the increasing impacts of natural hazards on Indigenous communities had caught the attention of Western media and fueled their concern with promoting international aid. I was also aware that disasters are interpreted in diverse ways, and increased Western attention may not necessarily result in relevant responses to what people in specific contexts want or need. For some Indigenous peoples, the concept of "disaster" may not translate meaningfully into their Indigenous languages. Such is the case of the Indigenous Kankanaey in the Philippines.

Before I started my fieldwork, I assumed that there would be a collective Kankanaey perspective on disasters. I was wrong. The mere process of trying to understand, define, and translate "disaster" into the local language was almost endless. After listening to the discussions among the people, I started to get confused about my own perspectives about disasters. Community leaders themselves reported that there are not clear translations or definitions of "disaster" in the Kankanaey language. They say that these terms refer more aptly to threats or challenges to daily life in general.

Elders spoke about "natural hazards" rather than "disasters" and their relationship to them as one in harmony with nature. For elders, natural hazards, such as typhoons, have always been part of everyday human experiences. However, younger Kankanaey posed challenges to elders' views and invoked claims of "scientific knowledge" to understand disasters. Members of the younger generation of Kankanaey, such as university students and young professionals, made a clear distinction between what they called "natural disasters" and "man-made disasters." They derived their understandings from school, books, television, and social media that reflect dominant Western perspectives. They also talked about their social contact with people outside of their villages as another factor influencing their perspectives. The younger generation also expressed appreciation for the value of traditional ways of knowing. Likewise, elders believed that these new perspectives could enhance existing ones and even help develop better responses to disasters. However, elders emphasized that whatever perspectives the younger generation may have, these should always go back to the concept of a *collective* existence of thinking and acting well not only for themselves but also for others.

This discussion of meaning reveals the intimate connection of meaning and power. Discourses on disaster are *socially* constructed (Perry, 2007) and require analyses that highlight the inherently colonizing power of language (Fanon, 1967). Outsiders, such as NGOs and community development workers, bring their own meanings to bear. These perspectives are often reflected in institutional responses to disasters. They may reflect donor mandates or specific DRR frameworks that may be at odds with varied local meanings and may lead to very different and culturally dissonant responses. The naming of disasters as such, the technocratic responses, and how these benefit powerful structures and institutions require careful consideration in developing socially just approaches to understanding and action. Further, to understand Indigenous peoples' perspectives, one must consider the multiplicity of voices that emanate from the different ways people experience and respond to disasters. One must also examine the power relations that influence how people can actually make their voices heard and their perspectives recognized in DRR policy and planning.

## CONTEXT

Context highlights how different actors come together and the settings in which they are based that include sociocultural, political, and economic considerations (Marlowe, 2014). For example, it was in the contexts of community gatherings and consultations that I began to learn how people in the three villages variably conceptualized and responded to hazards with their own distinct ways of producing knowledge through a process of "collective voice." This collective voice does not necessarily mean a homogenous perspective. It is about being provided the opportunity to tell their own stories in a context of dialogue that is meaningful to their everyday life.

*At-ato*, or bonfire sessions, are considered sacred contexts where sharing and learning take place. They are Kankanaey spaces where knowledge is constructed and passed down orally to the next generation. Bonfire sessions facilitate the coming together of all members of the community, elders and younger people alike, to tell their stories, listen to others' stories, and learn from one another. Participation in the bonfire sessions is open and voluntary. Everyone gets the chance to share their thoughts, including children and outsiders or visitors, but no one is forced to speak. Most of the time, an elder will sit at the bonfire to offer wisdom on the topics being discussed.

Bonfire sessions were significant contexts for learning about people's struggles with life in general and their specific experiences with and ways of responding to disasters. Their stories often focused on how they have survived their daily struggles with life. Besides "celebrating survival," these were contexts for transferring knowledge and skills to the young who were present. Bonfire sessions may go on for hours, filled with chanting and storytelling. The knowledge and wisdom shared on disasters were often derived from storytelling and riddles and highlighted by the elders' chants. The elders' presence and guidance in this space of dialogue contributed to their ways of protecting their Indigenous communities by making sure that the stories to be told outside of their villages are sufficient and accurate in capturing what disasters mean to them as Indigenous Kankanaey.

Engaging with the Indigenous Kankanaey people's everyday lives also provided a context for understanding the meanings and experiences of disasters and how these related to their current issues and struggles. Kankanaey people raised their issues with land—the oppressive land laws and relationships entangled in these—which to them was the greatest source of vulnerability when facing disasters. Elders and members of the younger generation alike described mining as the greatest hazard or threat to their community. As one community leader described, "The effect of mining on our lives is far more than the effect of a hundred typhoons." An elder in the village of Palina agreed with this and added that they had survived typhoon after typhoon in the past. Mining, on the other hand, put at risk not only their physical survival but their cultural survival as well. Contextual understanding was key to learning how oppressions and injustice were manifest in people's everyday lives.

## POWER

Power infiltrates and mediates the relationships among the different actors and directly affects disaster work with Indigenous peoples. Community leaders in the mining-affected villages described how the government had relocated Indigenous families as a supposed DRR measure. Community leaders argued that forced relocation of villagers served to pave the way for more intrusions by a powerful mining company. Further, relocation coincided with the Arroyo government's intensified campaign to promote large-scale mining as an engine for improving the national economy in the early 2000s. Thus, as a DRR response, relocation was inherently disempowering.

Some Kankanaey elders and villagers shared their experiences about the use of power by mining corporations to inflict physical violence and to use lawsuits in an attempt to halt the growing resistance movement of the Kankanaey people. Their narratives reflected their experiences with the operation and abandonment of open pit mines, which practically rendered an entire village uninhabitable due to effects of heavy siltation of their farms, rivers, and pasture lands and the drying of sources of water. In talking about these effects of mining, people from all three villages strongly agreed that development aggression via mining was the most powerful threat to their villages.

The people who spoke in these community gatherings reported that they were lured by the promises of the mining company for a better life, only to have to live with disempowering consequences. Women in particular poignantly narrated their experiences with the mines. Aside from the siltation of rice fields and contamination of water systems, they reported that people in the community were experiencing new forms of disease and illness. Community leaders say that the effects are intergenerational. Women expressed worry for the health and survival of their children. The community does not have enough water to supply their farms, and this has greatly affected their agricultural yields. In effect, the village chief said, they have lost their farm capital. Many people have consequently incurred debts from middlemen, meaning that they can now barely provide for the education of their children and their family's basic needs.

In recounting these power relations, elders repeatedly spoke about how some educated members of the community use their education and privilege to exercise power over others in advancing their own agendas. Elders warned community members about the use of power from one's education to exploit and oppress others as the greatest form of betrayal of one's own people and community. Kankanaey folktales and parables shared during the bonfire sessions also talk about how greed results in unequal power relations among them. Storytellers often ended their stories with lessons emphasizing how the obsession for power isolates one from Indigenous communal life.

The women who sat in a separate bonfire session with me and who strongly opposed the entry of mining into their villages shared more of these stories of power and violence in the context of their mining struggle. They talked about the number of crimes that are associated with having mining operations in their community. These women noted that alcoholism and substance abuse among the young became increasingly prevalent during the operation of the mines. They observed a dramatic increase in cases of domestic and sexual violence at the height of mining operations. They lamented how there was nothing they could have done at that time as women to address the power of men over them. Their power analyses were embedded in their everyday struggles as Indigenous women. Overall, their voices and experiences reveal the importance of contextual understanding of workings of power such that the power of people and communities can be tapped through organizing and advocacy work.

## HISTORY

History encourages us to consider Indigenous peoples' previous experiences with hazards and how meaning systems and contexts may have changed over time to inform current and future social work practice on DRR. As the elders narrated their histories, they described how their local practices have sustained them over time as a people, despite the challenges they face to their daily life. This includes the challenges brought by natural hazards. These practices are expressed in their everyday relationships with nature and with one another. Through community conversations and participation in everyday life in the villages, I listened to stories about food security, collective production, shared values regarding collective well-being, and the rejection of wealth accumulation as a cultural value. Women described how collective production sustained not only everyday life but also their physical environment. Indigenous peoples' resilience to disasters is based on their collective relationships as a community reproduced over time.

Community leaders described how, historically, there was always something to use from their environment in order to survive. They explained this within the context of nature's capacity to provide for almost everything that humans need. Women recounted how nature was able to provide for the people after every heavy rain or typhoon. They listed a number of edible plants and herbs that come out only after strong typhoons. One woman recalled a childhood experience:

> After a long typhoon, we usually consumed the food that was stored in the house. We do not have refrigerators to keep degradable food because we took these directly from the farms or the mountains. We cannot take more than what we need. Once the typhoon is over, our parents

would set out to check on the farms and animals and to gather food for us. My friends and I would race to the rivers to collect mushrooms that have grown from the logs that were washed into the riverbanks and gather those edible ferns, too.

However, this may no longer be the case. There are no longer wild fruits and edible plants to gather and eat. They have become extinct with the conversion of forest mountains into open pit mines and other forms of Western development.

On the one hand, stories of history are stories of loss. On the other, they are stories of resistance, struggle, and survival. There is a long history of Indigenous peoples' struggles to oppose oppression and exploitation. These stories offer a source of inspiration in resisting power and challenging the status quo. Among these are the oppositions that stopped the construction of the Chico Dam project from 1977 to the early 1980s (Bantayog, 2015). Another form of success and change is the landmark passage of Indigenous People's Rights Act of 1997 that has provided greater voice and representation. Among the Indigenous Kankanaey of Kibungan, their continuing resistance to mining operations (as a form of hazard) and the associated oppressive agendas (as a form of a disaster) resulted in them bringing to Congress and the Senate a proposed law for the exemption of the municipality from large-scale mining and other extractive operations. This proposed law passed in Congress, and while it was not successful in the Senate, the solidarity and support of many that emerged from the advocacy was already a winning moment for them. Social workers have been part of this history of struggle and resistance among Indigenous peoples.

## POSSIBILITY

Possibility asks us to consider the potential for more effective, socially just DRR informed by the past, present, and future. Possibility is intertwined with Indigenous peoples' struggles for survival. Kankanaey community leaders alongside the elders believe that DRR research and continuing dialogues with them can become a venue to facilitate just and meaningful relationships not only among them but also with outsiders. For instance, the elders have emphasized the role of Indigenous spaces of solidarity and dialogue, such as the bonfire, in fostering a continuing understanding of Indigenous perspectives and knowledge on DRR alongside scientific perspectives. According to the elders, the community bonfires used to be exclusive spaces only for insiders, but these are now open to outsiders to promote dialogues for peace and solidarity.

Possibility is further illustrated in the context of Indigenous peoples' nonviolent resistance to development aggression. The elders underscored that while they have Indigenous knowledges and sustaining practices that they have mobilized in response to the oppressions that manifested from mining agendas and activities (as a form of a disaster for them), these were often in tandem with external support from organizations and professionals such as social workers, development workers, and lawyers. The challenge in nurturing this possibility is for social workers to ensure that non-oppressive relationships are the foundation for present and future DRR practices with Indigenous peoples.

Challenging power as a means of creating possibility can be risky for individuals, agencies, and communities. A possibility focus does not mean we do not anticipate or think about risk. Rather, it means that we are not paralyzed by it. A possibility focus is trying to find ways in which we can work with others and identify the small steps to social justice so that meaningful and sustainable change can be realized. It may mean that sometimes big steps are required, but often these big shifts are accompanied by a lot of background work.

## Reflection on Engagement and Teaching-Learning

This case study provided the opportunity to critically reflect on the processes of engagement and teaching-learning that were central to my research. For example, entering my Indigenous community and gaining access to people's lives and stories required a process I call "re-embedding." I discovered parallels between the experiences of this re-embedding process and the performance of chants by elders in the evening bonfires. As I watched and listened to a group of elders chanting, I realized that one could not simply jump in and participate once the chanting had already started. One evening, three elders were chanting about people of the village in one of these *at-ato*. A fourth elder came in and sat quietly on the outskirts of the bonfire and carefully listened to decipher the story being told. Slowly, he stepped into the bonfire and was acknowledged by the one who had been chanting at that time. Then he waited for a specific tempo before adding his voice into the chant. According to the elders, this process allows them to fully understand the story being told so that they can meaningfully contribute to the construction of knowledge that is being communicated in the chants.

Reflecting on this wisdom by the elders, I asked myself when the right tempo was for me to participate in the Indigenous peoples' ongoing conversations about disasters and their lives in general. More questions came to mind: Had I listened carefully enough to be able to meaningfully engage in telling people's stories? How would joining these ongoing Kankanaey chants about disasters as a researcher affect the rhythm of the conversation? I participated in many bonfire sessions and went through these "stepping back and listening" moments or "re-embedding" experiences numerous times. At times, the process filled me with a sense of belonging that I was among my people sharing and celebrating a collective life. In other moments, the bonfire sessions were to welcome me as a researcher, both insider and outsider to the community. These experiences provided food for thought about the significance of respectful, ethical, and culturally driven approaches to *engagement* in social work practice with Indigenous communities.

I also gained insight into the *teaching-learning* process as community leaders and members engaged in conversation regarding the questions I posed about hazards affecting their lives. In one community, for example, the village leader explained to community members why I was there. Community members discussed their struggles for survival in general and how they were able to sustain themselves, their families, and their community. Then they connected these challenges with their experiences with natural hazards. After these discussions within their groups, the participants gathered together and related these stories to their concepts about hazards and disasters. A community leader facilitated the process with the elder quietly observing most of the time. He never intervened in the discussions. He waited until his wisdom was sought to clarify or to deepen the dialogues. This experience reminded once again that we are all teachers and learners and that part of our responsibility as social workers is to honor culturally driven contexts and practices for shared learning.

## Conclusion

The Just Practice framework offers a path for social work practice on DRR with Indigenous peoples to sense and honor social justice along the process. Given this, social workers working for DRR with Indigenous peoples must consider ways that the Just Practice framework can be translated according to how Indigenous people think of and practice social justice in relation to their everyday lives and relationships. A continuing dialogue is necessary in understanding one another. Solidarity often emerges from meaningful conversations. In relation to development aggression, Kankanaey elders explained that in order for dialogues on DRR to be relevant, they have to become expressions of solidarity with their people's struggles.

However, there are times when dialogues may not be enough. From a development aggression agenda, "understanding" may be seen as an expensive and time-consuming commodity when valuable resources are under a community's feet. Thus, Indigenous peoples have taken more "radical" steps for social justice. These include nonviolent resistance and directly challenging the status quo. The continuing struggles for Indigenous peoples in the Philippines have led them to rally and demonstrate peacefully as a form of resistance. This is not a call to arms, but it recognizes that capitalist interests and agendas are powerful forces that will resist change. Social workers need to recognize that the human rights agenda is inseparable from this kind of work (see Ife, 2001).

This chapter illustrates how Indigenous knowledges can facilitate an understanding of hazards and disasters in relation to development aggression. The discussion of a socially just DRR with Indigenous peoples offers insights on how social workers can meaningfully engage with them. While there is still hard work ahead to confront pervasive injustice, this case study illustrates how a social justice–informed lens can help navigate this important terrain in safe and empowering ways.

## QUESTIONS FOR REFLECTION AND DISCUSSION

We encourage readers to reflect on the following questions when considering the challenges and possibilities of socially just DRR practice with Indigenous communities.

1. How do we understand different perceptions about "disasters" when working with Indigenous peoples and other stakeholders?
2. How do Indigenous peoples practice social justice in their everyday relationships and ways of life, and what does this mean for us as social workers?
3. How do Indigenous peoples understand their vulnerabilities to hazards in relation to the context of their lives and struggles against development aggression?
4. What are the sources of power in Indigenous communities, and how do sources and relations of power relate to disaster events?
5. How do Indigenous people narrate their history, and what do their histories tell us about hazards, disasters, and development aggression?
6. What are the possibilities for dialogue among Indigenous peoples, and how might these inform social work practice?

## REFERENCES

Balay-as, M. (2019). *Disasters through an Indigenous lens in the Philippines* [Doctoral dissertation, University of Auckland]. https://researchspace.auckland.ac.nz/handle/2292/45962

Balay-as, M., Marlowe, J., & Gaillard, J. C. (2018). Deconstructing the binary between Indigenous and scientific knowledge in disaster risk reduction: Approaches to high impact weather hazards. *International Journal of Disaster Risk Reduction, 30*(Part A), 18–24. https://www.doi.org/10.1016/j.ijdrr.2018.03.013

Bantayog. (2015). *The Cordillera resistance against Chico Dam and Cellophil.* http://www.bantayog.org/the-cordillera-resistance-against-chico-dam-and-cellophil/

Fanon, F. (1967). *Black skin, White masks.* Grove Press.

Finn, J. (2020). *Just practice: A social justice approach to social work* (4th ed.). Oxford University Press.

Ife, J. (2001). Local and global practice: Relocating social work as a human rights profession in the new global order. *European Journal of Social Work, 4,* 5–15.

Madison, D. (2005). *Critical ethnography: Method, ethics, and performance.* Sage.

Marlowe, J. (2014). A social justice lens to examine refugee populations affected by disasters. *Advances in Social Work and Welfare Education, 16*(2), 46–59.

Nadeau, K. (2005). Christians against globalization in the Philippines. *Urban Anthropology and Studies of Cultural Systems and World Economic Development, 34,* 317–339.

Perry, R. W. (2007). What is a disaster? In H. Rodríguez, E. L. Quarantelli, & R. Dynes (Eds.), *Handbook of disaster research* (pp. 1–15). Springer.

# 24

# Social Work and Social Justice on the U.S.–Mexico Border

*From Critical Consciousness to Collaborative Action*

JANET L. FINN, MSW, PHD

**Contributors:** Kimberly Garner, MSW, Miriam Hertz, PhD, and Shaunagh Mc Goldrick, MSW

> Getting caught for breaking the law is one thing. Inhumane treatment is another. Why do they treat us like animals? Like bacteria?
> —Mexican migrant recently deported from the United States

---

**Overview**

In this chapter Janet Finn uses the five key concepts of Just Practice to reflect on an MSW immersion course focused on social justice on the U.S.–Mexico border. Participants explored the complex meanings of migration and considered the contested history of inclusion and exclusion that has played out along the border. They bore witness to state power in the context of Operation Streamline hearings and to possibility as they engaged with migrants, humanitarian aid workers, and human rights activists on both sides of the border. Finn illustrates the value of the Just Practice concepts and processes to inform critical inquiry and action.

---

## Introduction

For three years (2014–2016) my colleague Scott Nicholson and I (Janet) led a weeklong immersion learning experience in Tucson, Arizona, United States; and Nogales, Sonora, Mexico, in which participants explored the challenges and possibilities for social work and social justice on the U.S.–Mexico border.[1] Through Nicholson's close ties with human rights, community development, humanitarian aid, popular arts, and labor activists and organizations in Tucson and Nogales, we were able to learn firsthand about pressing social justice issues on the border. This chapter offers a reflection on our experiences of bearing witness, accompanying, developing critical consciousness, and making commitments to action. We show how the *Just Practice* concepts of *meaning, power, history, context,* and *possibility* were manifest in our experiences and how they framed our critical reflection on those experiences (Finn, 2020).

## Getting Started

The idea for the course emerged as a result of ongoing conversation and collaboration between Scott and me, both White social workers with a commitment to social justice in the Americas. For over a decade, Scott brought activists from Central and South America to the Missoula community and the University of Montana to raise consciousness about human rights issues. I incorporated these learning opportunities into my social work courses. When Scott began doing human rights work along the U.S.–Mexico border, we decided to develop a social work course that would place participants directly in the geopolitical and cultural context of the border. We launched the course in 2014.

Our student group varied over the years from seven to 10 members with diverse positionalities regarding race, gender, sexuality, and ability. Our collective experience began 2 months prior to travel with pre-trip readings and conversation. Together we probed questions of *meaning, context, power,* and *history*: What does it mean to understand migration as a human right (Ho & Loucky, 2012)? What about the meaning of home and community and the right to stay in one's home community and country (Solnit, 2008)? How can goods and dollars move so freely across borders, but human beings cannot? How can we better understand the contexts of everyday life that drive migration—such as economic and environmental survival, escaping violence, loss of livelihood, reuniting families, and the hope of opportunity? How is it that millions of undocumented people are forced to live "shadowed lives" in order to support their families (International Labor Organization, 2014)? Why has the United States seen a 10-fold increase in deportation of undocumented migrants in the last 25 years? Why has migration across our southern border become constructed as a "threat to national security"?

## History Lessons

In order to grasp the complexities of present-day border politics, we had to learn about the contested history of inclusion and exclusion that has played out since the Treaty of Guadalupe Hidalgo of 1848, through which 55% of Mexican land

---

[1] The chapter is dedicated to Scott Nicholson, who passed away in June 2017.

was taken over by the United States (Cho et al., 2004, p. 82). In the ensuing years, Mexican workers have been recruited to fill U.S. labor needs, and then scapegoated, deported, and denied entry when U.S. economic conditions soured. For example, Mexican immigration was encouraged in the wake of the Chinese Exclusion Act of 1882, which sparked a farm-labor shortage in the Southwest. In 1917, when overall U.S. immigration policy took a hostile turn, an exemption was made for Mexico to encourage migration of Mexican workers (Cho et al., 2004, p. 90). Mexican migration to the United States increased significantly between 1920 and 1930 (Nevins & Mizue, 2008). However, when the Great Depression hit the United States, Mexican workers became viewed as "surplus labor." Between 1929 and 1939, hundreds of thousands of people of Mexican descent were forced to leave the United States (Cho et al., 2004).

In 1942, faced with agricultural labor shortages during World War II, the Bracero program was initiated, bringing more than 5 million temporary workers from Mexico to the United States. Ironically, while the Bracero program was still underway, "Operation Wetback" was launched in 1954 to suppress migration from Mexico to the United States. Operation Wetback targeted emerging Mexican American communities and resulted in the deportation of more than 3 million people (Cho et al., 2004). As these historical patterns suggest, the presence of nearly 34 million persons of Mexican descent and more than 11 million Mexican-born immigrants living in the United States today, with and without official documentation, has deep historical roots (Israel & Batalova, 2018).

Our first trip in 2014 coincided with the 20th anniversary of the passage of the North American Free Trade Agreement (NAFTA). We posed questions about the meaning and power of NAFTA. What have been the consequences of NAFTA's history on the lives and livelihoods of Mexican agricultural and industrial workers? We learned that many Mexican farmers were put out of business as heavily subsidized U.S. corn poured into Mexico in the wake of NAFTA (Ho & Loucky, 2012; Public Citizen, 2014). Mexican farmers earned 70% less for their harvests as U.S. corn imports to Mexico quadrupled (Sierra Club, 2009). Thirty percent of farm jobs in Mexico were lost in the wake of NAFTA, affecting 2.8 million farmers and additional millions of family members (Ho & Loucky, 2012, p. 20; Nagengast, 2009).

In Tucson, our group got a compelling history lesson from attorney and human rights activist Isabel Garcia. As Garcia walked us through a history of U.S. imperialism, she challenged us to consider the meaning and power of our collective ignorance as U.S. citizens regarding immigration policy and the U.S.–Mexico border (Garcia, 2010). She asked us to consider ways in which ignorance is not accidental but *produced* and to recognize the dangers inherent in historical amnesia. Garcia spoke of the ways in which ignorance, fear, and arrogance combine in crafting a sense of exceptionalism that informs U.S. immigration policy.

Garcia drew our attention to the progressive militarization of the U.S.–Mexico border since the 1980s (Garcia, 2010). Over the last 40 years, and accelerating after the passage of NAFTA and the events of 9/11, U.S. border policy has become increasingly repressive as evidenced through the United States building walls, funneling migrants to dangerous and potentially deadly crossing points, and expanding budgets for the U.S. Border Patrol and Immigration and Customs Enforcement (ICE; "America's Deportation Machine," 2014; Cantu, 2018; Ho & Loucky, 2012; Nevins & Mizue, 2008). Arizona, argues Garcia, became a funnel for undocumented migration. As a result, the numbers of deaths in the Arizona desert began to grow and death itself became normalized (Ferguson, Price, & Parks, 2010; Ho & Loucky, 2012). The Southwest desert has earned the nickname "America's killing ground" as thousands of people have died trying to cross it ("America's Deportation Machine," 2014). Humane Borders, a Tucson-based humanitarian aid organization, has documented 3,339 migrant deaths along the Arizona border alone between 1999 and 2018 (Humane Borders, 2018).

## Learning in Context: Tucson

During our time in Tucson, we stayed in the homes of members of the Tucson Human Rights Coalition. As we shared meals and conversation, we listened to family stories of migration and learned about the complexities of citizenship status within families. Our hosts described everyday fears of deportation and family separation. They also described the critical work of the coalition to provide human rights education and advocacy for undocumented residents and their families. We met with worker-leaders of the Southside Worker Center, which supports the collective empowerment of immigrant day laborers to access dignified work and just wages. We shared a meal with members of *Mariposas sin Fronteras* (Butterflies without Borders), a Tucson-based group dedicated to support, accompaniment, and advocacy for LGBTQ+ people held in immigration detention. We learned of the profound vulnerability of queer and trans people in detention and the significance of having advocates on the outside who send letters, make visits, and spark public awareness in order to resist rendering them silenced and invisible.

## Bearing Witness to Power in the Context of Operation Streamline

With our historical consciousness sparked, we turned our attention to a very specific context in which the unequal power relations that characterize the border play out daily. That context is Operation Streamline, an expedited court process that targets unauthorized immigrants apprehended along the border with Mexico (Robertson et al., 2012). At the time of our visits, the Operation Streamline program in Tucson was convicting between 40 and 80 migrants per day with the misdemeanor charge of "illegal entry" or felony charge of "illegal re-entry" (Slack et al., 2013).

Operation Streamline began in 2005 and was implemented in Tucson in 2008 (Robertson et al., 2012). Through this policy, undocumented immigrants who are caught by border patrol attempting to cross from Mexico into the United States are prosecuted in the federal court (National Immigration Forum, 2020). Prior to Operation Streamline, first-time crossers were returned to their home country by border patrol or faced civil charges; only people with prior criminal records faced criminal charges in federal court. Today, individuals caught crossing the border face criminal charges. Those who are convicted via Operation Streamline are funneled directly into the U.S. prison system. They face sentences of 30 to 180 days in federal detention centers, most of which are run on contract by private prison operations (Robertson et al., 2012; Slack et al., 2013). According to No More Deaths, a Tucson-based social justice organization, Operation Streamline has "drastically increased prosecutions, making 'illegal re-entry' the most commonly filed federal charge" (No More Deaths, 2012, p. 1).

Further, Operation Streamline has created a profitable market for the private prison industry. For example, CoreCivic (formerly known as Correctional Corporation of America) and GEO Group are the two largest ICE detention contractors. These two private prison corporations had a combined total revenue of 4.1 billion dollars in 2018, about one-quarter of which came from ICE detention contracts (Noguchi, 2019). More than half of all federal prosecutions are now for immigration-related offenses.

We recount here one of our visits to Operation Streamline on a January afternoon in Tucson. A bailiff assigned us seats in the courtroom, where we witnessed a group of 64 men and one woman, all with wrist, waist, and ankle shackles and wearing shoes with no laces, being led in by federal marshals and seated together on the far side of the court. We learned that each had been given an opportunity to meet briefly with an attorney earlier that day, wherein they were informed of the terms of a possible plea bargain. The primary aspect of the plea agreement is that a felony charge, which carries a sentence of 2 years or more, is dropped in exchange for a plea of guilty to a misdemeanor charge, which carries a sentence of up to 6 months. The defendants, with few options and little understanding of the legal technicalities, generally accept the terms of the agreement and appear in court to receive sentences ranging from time served to 180 days.

A judge called the court to order; marshals brought the defendants before her in groups of five. An interpreter sat in the witness stand, translating the proceedings into Spanish for the defendants. One by one, the charges against each defendant were read and translated, to which the defendants uniformly responded in Spanish "*culpable*"—guilty—and were given their individual sentences. Over the course of 1 hour and 17 minutes, an average of 1 minute and 11 seconds per person, the presiding judge sentenced the defendants to a total of 6,900 days (19 years).

In reflecting upon the meaning and power of the courtroom scene we witnessed, some members of our group likened Operation Streamline to a tragedy, while others described it as a cruel farce, with court personnel as unwitting actors and the defendants bearing profound consequences. Others depicted Operation Streamline as an assembly line approach to (in)justice. A public defender with whom we spoke aptly characterized the process as "McJustice." Each of us was left to critically consider the meaning of guilt. As one member of our group wrote: "'*Culpable*'—guilt—is now a muddy concept for me. Who is guilty, and of what, is a question that doesn't leave my mind."

## Bearing Witness to Possibility: Action and Accompaniment on the Border

Operation Streamline provided us with a disturbing example of the workings of "power over" vulnerable individuals and groups (Townsend et al., 1999). In contrast, our time in the company of human rights, labor, community, and arts activists gave us the opportunity to bear witness to the possibilities of power within, power with others, and power to enact social justice (Townsend et al., 1999). Over the next several days, our groups visited shelters and accompanied both humanitarian aid workers and migrants as they navigated physical, emotional, and legal challenges of life in transit along the border. In Nogales, we visited Grupos Beta, a Mexican government agency that provides aid to migrants, including those who have recently been deported from the United States. We were introduced to the *Comedor* and *Casa Nazaret*, programs of the Kino Border Initiative (KBI). KBI is a faith-based initiative that strives to accompany migrants and communities affected by the consequences of migration. The work of KBI combines direct humanitarian aid, research, public education, and advocacy for migrant rights (Danielson, 2013). The *Comedor* offers meals, basic medical assistance, and human rights education to migrants. Our group served meals, washed dishes, and listened to migrants' stories. *Casa Nazaret* is a shelter for women and children who have been deported. We also visited the San Juan Bosco shelter, which has provided dinner and shelter for thousands of migrants for 40 years. In each setting we witnessed the intimate and elemental power of accompaniment and came to appreciate its central importance to effective advocacy.

In these venues, we had the opportunity to talk with persons seeking shelter and support and to learn about their journeys. We heard accounts of fathers and mothers, recently released from jail and deported, who were determined to cross again in order to reunite with their children. A man in his 30s, recently deported, spoke of knowing no other life but that in the United States, where he had resided since he was a young child. He has a wife, job, and family in the United States. A woman in her 20s had become separated from her husband on the journey north from Oaxaca. They had left their infant daughter in the care of her grandmother and had planned to cross to the United States together in search of work. Her voice filled with desperation as she begged for help in locating her husband. Another man in his 30s, recently deported, told of his plan to find seasonal work in Mexico to get by until he made another attempt at returning to the United States. He lamented that labor wages in Mexico would leave him with little to send to support his family in the United States.

We learned of harrowing trips north from southern Mexico, Guatemala, El Salvador, and Honduras as desperate conditions of poverty and violence forced individuals and families to strike out in the hopes of physical and economic survival in the United States. We heard accounts of the ubiquitous sexual violence against women migrants, with "help" provided in the form of emergency birth control, given the high likelihood of rape along the journey north. We met women recovering from illness at *Casa Nazaret* and heard accounts of babies being delivered in the shelter after mothers, nearly full-term in their pregnancy, were deported from the United States and dropped at the border. These experiences deepened our thinking about the meaning of reproductive justice in the context of migration. We faced challenging questions from a young Mexican woman who asked why we would not use our privilege and our ready access to the United States to help bring her and others across the border. If we truly believed U.S. border policies and practices were unjust, why would we not take direct action in defiance of the law? Her questions haunted us as we reflected on our roles as witnesses.

Our home base while in Nogales was *El Hogar de Esperanza y Paz* (Home of Hope and Peace, HEPAC), a community center that provides a nutritious daily lunch for more than 100 schoolchildren from the most impoverished families in the neighborhood. HEPAC, guided by principles of liberation theology and popular education, offers adult education classes, facilitates community workshops that address issues of trauma and violence, organizes children's camps during school vacation, and operates a women's artisan cooperative. Our time in HEPAC provided a context for learning and critical reflection on our border experiences and opportunities for dialogue with community activists committed to helping people exercise their right to home and community (Solnit, 2008).

While migration is a human right, so is the right to a sustainable life in one's home community and country. We engaged with activists who've worked for decades to build sustainable community opportunities that mitigate against the need for out-migration. For example, we met with a labor activist who developed skills in popular education through workshops at HEPAC and then led the multi-year struggle to create the first independent union in an assembly plant in Nogales.

Our understanding of the meaning of community and the power of the border was expanded during a visit to the *Taller de Arte Público Yonke* (Junkyard Public Art Workshop, or *Taller Yonke*). *Taller Yonke* raises consciousness through public art, with particular attention to the dynamic context of border culture and the meaning and power of the border wall. Border art pieces have featured clouds and human feet transcending and transgressing the border and sensual scenes of humans, animals, and spirits creating a community of peace, in contrast to the militarization of the border.

We returned to the Arizona side of the border to hike one of trails used by migrants. We followed the practice of the Tucson Samaritans, a volunteer group whose mission is to relieve suffering and prevent death in the desert, and left water and food along the trail—acts that are becoming criminalized. The hike allowed time for critical reflection. Our individual and collective privileges, as well as the severe realities of crossing the border as a migrant, came into even sharper focus. The abandoned items we encountered on the trail hinted at the stories of those who had passed through the area and sparked a range of emotions and questions among us.

On one hike our group came across three backpacks that appeared to be very recently abandoned. Nearby were three oranges, a cell phone charger, and a knee brace strewn along the trail. Scott called out to let the owners know we were humanitarians with food and water; his call was met with silence that sparked more questions. What happened to the owners of these belongings? Where are they now? What can we do to ensure migrants are treated with dignity, respect, and compassion?

## From Critical Reflection to Creative Action

Our learning experiences challenged us to recognize our responsibilities as social justice workers. They also served as catalysts for ongoing reflection and action. Upon return to Montana, our groups sought opportunities for ongoing teaching-learning. We shared our experiences with campus and community audiences. We prepared handouts with access to websites and publications for audience members to learn more. We made connections with the Montana Immigrant Justice Alliance (MIJA), a statewide organization dedicated to educating and advocating for immigrant rights, and we hosted films and speakers on immigrant rights. We have encouraged those with whom we speak to express their concerns to their elected representatives, continue their own critical education, and support the work of organizations such as No More Deaths, Samaritans, and Humane Borders. Our efforts have been guided by the concept of "reverse mission" as described by Faye Abrams and colleagues (2005). Having had the privilege to listen and learn from those living the everyday realities of violence and violation along the U.S.–Mexico border, it is our responsibility to use our privilege as a tool for advocacy and action. It is our responsibility to participate in the immigration debate and to add our voices to those demanding humane migration policies that honor the dignity and rights of migrants and their children and families. Finally, it is our responsibility to grapple with our ethical positions both personally and professionally. At what point do we say "enough!" to injustice and join as allies in acts of solidarity and civil disobedience in the pursuit of social justice?

## Postscript, 2021

In January 2020, I (Janet) went on a water drop deep in the Sonoran desert with a group of humanitarian aid volunteers. Our crew included three 20-somethings from the Northwest, a Catholic nun, a retired math teacher, a former army medic, and a couple of snowbirds escaping the cold of northern climes. It was an all-day journey to several sites in the desert to leave water for migrants. This eclectic bunch had followed remarkably different paths to the border. The conversations were rich, and the experience reaffirming of the fierce hope that guides social justice work. We had come together by way of a meeting of the Samaritans, a group of people of conscience dedicated to providing humanitarian aid to travelers in the desert. The Samaritans also provide care and support for two migrant shelters near the border in Mexico and engage in community-building work to raise consciousness about human rights on the border. Unfortunately, Covid-19 has disrupted the work of many cross-border humanitarian aid organizations, leaving migrants facing ever more precarious circumstances (Reidy, 2020). Possibility, however, lies in determined, collective action for policy change. The Biden administration has laid the groundwork for comprehensive immigration reform. By joining in solidarity with consciousness-raising efforts, humanitarian aid work, and policy advocacy initiatives, social justice workers can help bring the promise of justice for migrants to fruition.

## QUESTIONS FOR REFLECTION AND ACTION

1. What do you see as the responsibility of social workers to advocate for both migration as a human right and the right to home and community?
2. What actions are happening in your community or state in support of the rights of migrants? What individual and collective action could you take in support of these efforts?
3. What are key policy changes that need to be made to honor the rights of migrants and non-citizen residents of the United States? What forms of policy advocacy might you engage in to support just immigration policy?
4. Consider Garcia's argument that ignorance of history is not accidental but produced. What does she mean by this? What other examples can you point to that illustrate the ways in which ignorance of history is produced?
5. If you were to write to your political representatives advocating for just immigration reform, what are three main points you would make?

## REFERENCES

Abrams, F., Slosar, J., & Walls, R. (2005). Reverse mission: A model for international social work education and transformative intra-national practice. *International Social Work*, 48(2), 161–176.

America's deportation machine. (2014, February 8). *The Economist*. https://www.economist.com/briefing/2014/02/07/the-great-expulsion

Cantu, F. (2018). *The line becomes a river: Dispatches from the border*. Riverhead Books.

Cho, E., Paz y Puente, F., Louie, M., & Khokha, S. (2004). *Bridges: Building a race and immigration dialogue in a global economy*. National Network for Immigrant and Refugee Rights.

Danielson, M. (2013). Documented failures: The consequences of immigration policy on the U.S.-Mexico border. Kino Border Initiative.

Ferguson, K., Price, N., & Parks, T. (2010). *Crossing with the virgin: Stories from the migrant trail*. University of Arizona Press.

Finn, J. (2020). *Just practice: A social justice approach to social work* (4th ed.). Oxford University Press.

Garcia, I. (2010). U.S. border militarization and immigration policing and deepening the humanitarian crisis in Arizona. *Injustice for all: The rise of the U.S. immigration policing regime* (pp. 23–25). http://nnirr.org/drupal/sites/default/files/injustice_for_all_-_the_rise_of_the_u.s._immigration_policing_regime.pdf

Ho, C., & Loucky, J. (2012). *Humane migration: Establishing legitimacy and rights for displaced people*. Kumarian Press.

Humane Borders. (2018). *1999–2018 recorded migrant deaths and Humane Borders water stations* [Map]. https://humaneborders.org/wp-content/uploads/deathmapcumulative_letter_2018.pdf

International Labor Organization. (2014). *Hazardous work*. ILO. http://www.ilo.org/safework/areasofwork/hazardous-work/lang--en/index.htm

Israel, E., & Batalova, J. (2018). *Mexican immigrants in the United States*. Migration Policy Institute. https://www.migrationpolicy.org/article/mexican-immigrants-united-states-2019

Nagengast, C. (2009). Afterword: Migration, human rights and development. In *International migration and human rights: The global repercussion of U.S. policy*, edited by Samuel Martinez (pp. 253–269). University of California Press.

National Immigration Forum (2020). Fact sheet: Operation Streamline. September 1, 2020. https://immigrationforum.org/wp-content/uploads/2020/09/Streamline-Fact-Sheet-FINAL-1.pdf

Nevins, J., & Mizue, A. (2008). *Dying to live: A story of US immigration in an age of global apartheid*. City Lights Publishing.

No More Deaths (2012, March). Fact sheet: Operation Streamline. https://nomoredeaths.org/wp-content/uploads/2014/10/nmd_fact_sheet_operation_streamline.pdf

Noguchi, Y. (2019). *Under siege and largely secret: Businesses that serve immigration detention*. https://www.npr.org/2019/06/30/736940431/under-siege-and-largely-secret-businesses-that-serve-immigration-detention

Public Citizen. (2014). *NAFTA at 20*. Public Citizen's Global Trade Watch.

Reidy, E. (2020, June 29). Briefing: Coronavirus and the halting of asylum at the U.S.-Mexico border. *The New Humanitarian*. https://www.thenewhumanitarian.org/news/2020/06/29/Mexico-US-coronavirus-mass-expulsions-asylum-halt

Robertson, A., Beaty, R., Atkinson, J., & Libal, B. (2012). Operation Streamline: Costs and consequences. Grassroots Leadership.

Sierra Club. (2009). *NAFTA's impact on Mexico*. http://vault.sierraclub.org/trade/downloads/nafta-and-mexico.pdf

Slack, J., Martinez, D., Whiteford, S., & Peiffer, E. (2013). *In the shadow of the wall: Family separation, immigration enforcement, and security*. Center for Latin American Studies, University of Arizona.

Solnit, R. (2008, November/December). The most radical thing you can do. *Orion*. https://orionmagazine.org/article/the-most-radical-thing-you-can-do/

Townsend, J., Zapata, E., Rowlands, J., Alberti, P., & Mercado, M. (1999). *Women and power: Fighting patriarchies and poverty*. Zed Books.

# Epilogue

JANET L. FINN

As varied as these accounts of social justice work are, they share common ground. Each contributor approaches practice with passion and commitment, a capacity to see or search for connections between immediate personal struggles and broader social forces, and a fierce sense of hope. They are bricoleurs who have taken the Just Practice concepts and processes as raw materials and molded them into critical and creative approaches to justice-oriented practice. Moreover, they approach their work with humility, openness, and loving connection to individuals and communities. They have reclaimed the practice of love that is at the heart of social justice work.

We hope these case studies inspire readers to center social justice in their own practice. We encourage readers to listen deeply to the stories of those they serve, to continually question their own assumptions, to invite others to the table, to seek out possibilities for creative partnerships and practices, to find their own voices as advocates, to speak truth to power, and to take bold and courageous action. It is up to us to fan the fires of hope as we nurture and accompany others in naming and claiming their right to dream.

# Contributors

**Marjorie Balay-as, PhD,** is a registered Indigenous Kankanaey social worker from the Philippines. She has a doctorate in social work from the University of Auckland. She has extensive professional experience in community development and civil society participation with international organizations, the United Nations, and local NGOs in the Philippines.

**Jen Barile, MSW,** is senior officer, advocacy partnerships, with the International Rescue Committee (IRC) Headquarters. Previously, Jen served as resettlement director of IRC–Missoula. Jen has also worked with youth in foster care, survivors of domestic violence, migrant farmworkers, and individuals experiencing homelessness.

**Katie Baumler, MSW,** is a school social worker in New Zealand. Katie began her social work career in the United States as a child protection specialist. She relocated to New Zealand in 2012 and has practiced as a registered social worker in a variety of roles, including food bank coordination, home-based family support, and school social work.

**Robyn Brown-Manning, PhD, MPhil, LMSW,** is a doctoral lecturer at the Silberman School of Social Work at Hunter College of the City University of New York and adjunct assistant professor at Iona College in New Rochelle. She teaches child welfare practice and anti-oppressive service delivery. Her research examines the experiences of African American mothers raising sons and the use of mindfulness and meditation in the classroom.

**Erin Butts, MSW,** works for Great Falls (Montana) Public Schools as the district's student mental health coordinator. She has worked in the areas of integrated school mental health research, practice, and policy since 2010. Erin is committed to the development of trauma-informed, system-wide approaches to social work in schools.

**Sarah Butts, MFA,** is a theater director and educator. She has written and directed several original documentary theater works addressing mental health, stigma, trauma, and loss. She directed *A Heart Without: Real Stories of Homelessness*, which was recognized at the 2012 Institute for Children, Poverty, and Homelessness Conference in New York.

**Kara Byrne, MSW, PhD**, is an assistant research professor in the College of Social Work at the University of Utah. She is currently part of an interdisciplinary research team developing assessment and treatment approaches to address child traumatic stress in children's advocacy centers and primary care provider settings.

**Amy Capolupo, LCSW**, is director of Disability Services for Students at the University of Montana and has worked in that office for the past 15 years. Her expertise is in providing reasonable accommodations to students with disabilities and implementing policies and procedures that incorporate access and universal design.

**Marissa Cirilo, LCSW**, is the coordinator for Harold Washington College's Wellness Center in Chicago. Marissa leads programming that focuses on enhancing partnerships and support services for college students, including the Healthy Food Market, which addresses food insecurity and hunger on campus.

**Vickii Coffey, MSA, PhD**, is an assistant professor of social work at Governors State University in University Park, Illinois. Her teaching focuses on social policy and social justice. Her practice addresses violence against women and experiences of formerly incarcerated persons. Her research addresses mass incarceration, reentry, violence against women, and the intersections of race, class, and gender therein.

**Deanna Cooper, LCSW**, is director of the BSW Program and 2+2 Program and the University of Montana. In addition to her 10 years as clinical director of a model jail-based treatment program, she has worked in rural health care supporting veterans and their families and as a school social worker, establishing prevention programs for children and families impacted by poverty and substance abuse.

**Eric Crabtree-Nelson, LCSW**, has worked over the past decade in child welfare and outpatient counseling and as a college administrator. Eric is also a licensed clinical social worker in private practice. He brings an ability to bridge the micro and macro worlds of social work and to make solutions come alive through innovative thinking and collaboration.

**Sonya Crabtree-Nelson, LCSW, PhD**, is associate professor of social work at DePaul University in Chicago, Illinois. Sonya has 15 years of direct practice experience working in the areas of child welfare and domestic violence. Her current research interests focus on trauma, resilience, ethics, and clinical practice.

**Katherine Deuel, MS, MSW**, has worked as an educator, conservationist, mediator, and organizational consultant. She is the executive director of Home ReSource, a nonprofit community sustainability center in Missoula, Montana, dedicated to social, economic, and environmental justice.

**Laura Dresser, MSW, PhD**, is an assistant clinical professor of social work and associate director of the Center on Wisconsin Strategy (COWS), a national think-and-do tank promoting equity, sustainability, and democracy at the University of Wisconsin–Madison. Laura is a labor economist and expert on low-wage work.

**Sarah Fielding, LCSW**, is a clinical social worker in private practice. For the past 10 years, she has worked in a variety of roles in a community-based youth home setting, primarily with adolescent girls who are survivors of trauma and abuse. She approaches her work through a trauma-informed, relationship-based lens.

**Janet L. Finn, MSW, PhD**, is a professor of social work at the University of Montana. A former child welfare social worker, Finn has a background in both social work and anthropology and has authored and edited numerous books and articles about community, women, childhood, youth, social justice, and transnational issues.

**Charles P. Hoy-Ellis, LCSW, PhD**, is an assistant professor at the University of Utah, College of Social Work. His scholarly focus is on the health and well-being of LGBTQ midlife and older adults. He has more than 15 years' direct practice experience as a clinical social worker with the LGBTQ community and is a collaborator with the Aging with Pride: National Health, Aging, Sexuality, and Gender Study (NHAS).

**Diane Kempson, MSW, PhD**, is an associate professor of social work and MSW program director at the University of Wyoming. She has extensive practice experience in mental health and with underserved populations. Her passion for working with family systems has shaped her appreciation for the complexity and interconnectedness of systems and her practice therein.

**Jesse Littman, MSW**, was a caseworker with the International Rescue Committee (IRC) in Missoula, Montana, from 2016 to 2020 and now serves as immigration legal representative for IRC–Missoula. Littman previously worked in South America with immigrant groups and with detained asylum seekers on the U.S.–Mexico border.

**Jay Marlowe, MSW, PhD**, is an associate professor of social work at the University of Auckland and current Rutherford Discovery Fellow through the Royal Society New Zealand. His research addresses refugee settlement, transnationalism, trauma, disasters, and the way in which refugees can participate as peers in civil society.

**Jen Molloy, MSW, PhD**, is an assistant professor of social work at the University of Montana. Her research explores restorative justice practices in education and juvenile justice. She teaching social work with groups and communities, organizational leadership, and social justice approaches to social work practice.

**Kao Nou L. Moua, MSW, PhD**, has over 15 years of experience working with marginalized young people as an advocate, program coordinator, and researcher. Her other practice areas include organizational change and culturally informed interventions and services. Her research is related to Hmong American youth, oral tradition, and indigenous methodologies.

**Ann P. Rall, MSW, PhD**, is an associate professor of social work at Eastern Michigan University. She has worked as a community organizer for 40 years, confronting issues of poverty, racism, sexism, homophobia, and ableism. She is involved with Michigan Welfare Rights Organization (MWRO) and helped found the Detroit People's Water Board.

**Amie Thurber, MSW, PhD**, is an assistant professor at Portland State University School of Social Work. Thurber is concerned with the spatialization of persistent inequities and the possibilities for building more just communities through innovations in policy, practice, and participatory inquiry that foster place attachments, social ties, and civic action to promote flourishing neighborhoods.

**Willie F. Tolliver, DSW**, is an associate professor and director of Social Justice and Equity Education in the Silberman School of Social Work at Hunter College. His teaching, research, and practice interests include transformative leadership, spirituality and social work, decolonizing social work, and centering race and racism in human behavior and the social environment.

**Ashley Trautman, MSW, JD**, is an assistant professor at the University of Montana School of Social Work and a juvenile justice specialist at the National Native Children's Trauma Center (NNCTC). She provides training and technical assistance on childhood trauma to tribal communities across the country. Her teaching interests include social policy, tribal sovereignty and history, the Indian Child Welfare Act, diversity, and cultural humility.

**Elizabeth Urschel, LCSW, MFA**, is a clinical social worker in private practice. She specializes in grief, loss, and trauma and uses narrative methods to facilitate healing. Urschel has worked in child welfare and mental health systems and with adults experiencing homelessness. She holds an MFA in creative writing, which informs her narrative approach to practice.

**Marilyn Bruguier Zimmerman (Nakota, Dakota, Ojibway, Newe), MSW, PhD**, is senior director of policy and programs at the National Native Children's Trauma Center (NNCTC). She served on the U.S. Presidential (Obama) Commission to Eliminate Child Abuse and Neglect Fatalities and the Advisory Committee of the Attorney General's (Holder) National Task Force on American Indian/Alaska Native (AI/AN) Children Exposed to Violence. She has expertise in trauma-informed systems change serving AI/AN children and families.

# Index

ability
   collective, 63, 232, 262
   corporate law office, social work practice in, 218, 219, 222, 223
   as facilitator, 72
   Indigenous rights, 228
   IRC-Missoula, 111
   positionality and, 75
   possibility and, 191, 202
   social justice activism, 85
   of students to learn in school, 117, 194, 202
   technologies in, 202, 203
   of tenants to litigate actions, 74, 78
   trauma response, 238
Abrams, F., 268
accessibility. *See* disability rights
accessibility checklist, 218, 221–23
accompaniment
   African Americans, 33
   empowerment and, 112–13
   healing and, 32, 53
   Home ReSource, 233–34
   IRC-Missoula, 112–13
   jail-based treatment, 157
   oppression and, 31, 43
   privilege and, 31
action, collective, 187–88, 191–92
action process, 3–4
ACT.UP, 29
adultification, 168
adverse childhood experiences, 130
advocacy
   mental health care access, 209–10, 213–14
   Michigan Welfare Rights Organization, 89
   migrants, U.S. Mexico border, 268
affinity groups, 222, 223
affordable housing. *See also* housing equity/equality
   in Detroit, 83
   in Nashville, 95, 97–99, 101–2
   in Salt Lake City, 74
African Americans
   action/accompaniment, 33

biopsychosocial assessments, 14–20
Black codes, 20, 21
in child welfare system, 20–23, 168
colonization impacts on, 187
Covid-19 impacts on, xiii
engagement, 32–33
incarceration, 162–64, 168
ageism, 33, 34
agency
   action and, 4
   context of practice, 2
   historical perspective and, xi
   in incarceration, 164
   possibility and, 213
   power in, 2
   Pride liberation movement, 28–29
   in therapeutic relationship, 40
   tribal, 242, 243
AI/AN youth. *See* National Native Children's Trauma Center
*ako*, 145
Alexander, M., 187
American Civil Liberties Union (ACLU), 152
American Indian/Alaska Native (AI/AN) children. *See* National Native Children's Trauma Center
American Indian boarding schools, 21, 43, 240
Americans with Disabilities Act of 1990 (ADA), 193–94, 197, 199
anti-oppressive, 23, 190, 258
anxiety/anxiety disorder, 15, 26, 61, 134, 139–41, 157, 170
Arlethia G. Mayes Healthy Market. - food security/insecurity
arts-based activism, 90–91
assessments
   biopsychosocial, 10–20
   Just Practice (*See* Just Practice framework)
assimilation, 239–42, 245, 246
autism spectrum disorder, 48–56

Balay-as, M., 251–52
Barile, J., 105

276

Barlow, M., 87
Beery, Z., 202
biopsychosocial assessments, 10–20
    Just Practice application to, 11–14
    Meaning section, 12, 16–17
    narrative construction, 17
    Power and History section, 13, 20–21
    Power and Possibility section, 13, 21–22
    Similarities in Positionality section, 12, 18–20
Black codes, 20, 21
bonfire sessions *(at-ato)*, 254–58
    collective voice, 254
    context, 254–55
    critical reflection, 258
    development aggression, 251, 252, 259
    history, 256–57
    Indigenous ways of knowing, 251, 253, 254
    meaning, 252–54
    mining, 254–55
    possibility, 257–58
    power, 253–56
    re-embedding process, 258
    resiliency, 257–59
    resistance, 257–59
    teaching-learning, 259
borderline personality disorder, 211
border politics. *See* migrants, U.S. Mexico border
born accessible, 195, 200, 202
boundaries with youth in care, 41–42
Bracero program, 263
Bradley, M., 74
brown, a. m., 188
Bryant, Anita, 29
building materials reuse store. *See* Home ReSource
Butts, E., 128–29, 132
Butts, S., 131–32
Byrne, K., 70

Caban, A., 132
Cahill, C., 74
Canaday, M., 27
case manager/management, 156
case studies
    child abuse/neglect, 16, 48–56
    child sexual abuse, 16, 18
    colonization/oppression, 42–44
    employment, 21–22
    forcible separation, 21
    foster care, 18, 39, 48–56
    gender/gender identity, 30–34
    gender socialization, 32–33
    LGBTQ adults, 30–34
    oppression, 14–23
    overwhelming feelings, coping with, 15
    parent-child connection, 39–44
    redlining, 20
    segregation, 21
    social identity, 18–20
    trauma, 17–18, 20, 48–56
celebration
    field seminar, 188
    field seminars/fieldwork, 188
    home ReSource, 234–35
    IRC-Missoula, 113–14
    language and, 114, 157
    survival and, 254–55
Chang, S., 89
child abuse/neglect, 16, 18, 48–56
child removal, 41, 43, 240–41, 246
child sexual abuse, 16, 18, 48
child welfare system
    African Americans in, 20–23, 168
    Native Americans in, 43, 44, 240, 244, 247
    neglect, signs of, 83
    parental rights loss, 154–55
    silencing of families by, 70
Chinese Exclusion Act of 1882, 263
Cirilo, M., 176, 178–80
cisgenderism, 19, 25, 26, 30–32, 34, 150, 180
Civilian Conservation Corps (CCC), 27
Coffey, V., 162–63
cognitive approaches, 121, 122
collaboration
    corporate law, 219–20
    food security, 175–81
    housing equity, 72, 75–76
    interprofessional, 130, 207, 208, 216–20, 224
    jail-based treatment, 153
    leadership, 16, 31, 47, 63, 91, 217, 222–23, 245
    processes, xii, 3–4, 20, 30, 70–76, 78, 112, 199
    Social Workers in Schools, 143, 146
    verbatim theater, 130–36
collective action, 187–88, 191–92
collective trauma, 20
collective voice, 254
colonization
    African Americans, impacts on, 187
    language and, 253
    Māori people, impacts on, 144
    Native Americans, impacts on, 151–52, 245, 246
    sexual objectification and, 33
    in social work and nonprofits, 190
    trauma and, 43, 240, 242
color line, 96
communication. *See also* dialogue; listening
    autism spectrum disorder, 48, 51, 52
    in biopsychosocial assessments, 19, 22
    CRAFT approach, 157
    criminal justice system, 154
    engagement as, 3, 198
    faculty meetings circles, 121
    homelessness, support of, 62, 67
    parent-child connection, 44
    re-embedding and, 258
    refugee resettlement, 106, 107, 112
    in restorative justice, 123
    restorative questioning, 117–18, 122

278  Index

telecommunications, 194
tenant-landlord policy, 74
within therapeutic relationship, 30, 48, 51, 52
in verbatim theater, 130, 136
community-building circles, 117–18, 121
community deliberation, 63–64, 67
Community Voices for Housing Equality (CVHE), 71. *See also* housing equity/equality
　context, 73
　history, 77
　meaning, 76–77
　participatory action research (PAR), 70–71, 78–79
　possibility, 78
　power, 75–76
　privilege, 75
competencies, 5–7
consciousness raising, 110, 130, 267
context
　corporate law office, social work practice in, 217, 219–20
　cultural humility and, 142, 146
　in decision-making, 217
　dialogue and, 252, 254
　disability rights, 200–201
　disaster risk reduction, 254–55
　food security, 178
　homelessness, 59
　Home ReSource, 230–31
　housing equity, 73–75
　incarceration, 167–68, 170
　IRC-Missoula, 107–9
　jail-based treatment, 151–52
　LGBTQ adults, 26–29
　mental health care access, 210–12
　Michigan Welfare Rights Organization, 83–84
　migrants, U.S. Mexico border, 264
　Nashville Neighborhood Story Project, 95
　National Native Children's Trauma Center, 241
　oppression and, 11–12, 20–21, 36, 254–55
　poverty and, 38, 228
　resistance and, 108
　restorative justice, 118–19, 121
　River House, 38
　Social Workers in Schools, 142–43
　transformation and, 83–84
contraband camps, 96
Converge Action Team (Great Falls), 136
Conyers, J., 89
co-researchers, 70–78, 164
Cornerstone Theater, 131
corporate law office, social work practice in
　ability/disability, 218, 219, 222, 223
　accessibility checklist, 218, 221–23
　collaboration, 219–20
　context, 217, 219–20
　decision-making processes, 222
　diversity, 219, 222–23
　history, 217–19
　inclusiveness, 218–19, 221–23
　meaning, 217, 222

　organizational change, 223–24
　positionality, 217–18, 220
　possibilities, 217, 222
　power, 217, 221
　teaching-learning, 223
Council on Social Work Education, 4
Covid-19, xiii, 91–92, 182–83, 247
Crabtree-Nelson, E., 176, 178, 179
CRAFT approach, 157
criminal justice system. *See also* incarceration; jail-based treatment
　mass incarceration statistics, 168
　psychological biases, 167
　punishment allocation in, 167–68
　race/ethnicity differences, 152–54, 160, 168
　shame, 155, 159, 160
　stigmatization, 155, 169–70
　structural forces, 167
　treatment of women in, 165–67
critical friend, 119–20
critical reflection
　dialogue and, 121, 246, 267
　disability rights, 198
　disaster risk reduction, 258
　food security, 178–79
　healing and, 22
　Home ReSource, 234
　IRC-Missoula, 113
　migrants, U.S. Mexico border, 268
　narrative and, 21, 23
　oppression and, 43
　privilege and, 3, 20, 267–68
　restorative justice, 122–23
culpable, 265, 266
cultural humility
　in clinical practice, 43, 78, 241, 246
　context and, 142, 146
　dialogue and, 111
　importance of, 241–42, 246
　IRC-Missoula, 111
　National Native Children's Trauma Center, 241–43
　teaching-learning and, 243
cultural identity, 141, 142
Culture Clash, 131–32
culture of disbelief, 38
curiosity, 3, 53, 145, 146, 211
CVHE. *See* Community Voices for Housing Equality (CVHE)

data visualization project, 90
Daughters of Bilitis, 28
decision-making
　collaborative, 217
　context in, 217
　ethical, 217
　processes, 66–67, 113, 221–22
　strategies, 60, 186, 218
decolonization. *See* colonization
Deegan, P., 209
deportation, 262–64

depression, 26, 32, 132, 212, 239
DetroitMindsDying.com, 91
Detroit People's Water Board coalition (PWB), 82
Detroit to Flint Water Justice Journey, 88
Detroit Water and Sewerage Department (DWSD), 82
development aggression, 251, 252, 259
*Diagnostic and Statistical Manual of Mental Disorders (DSM)*, 28, 29
dialogue. *See also* communication
    benefits of, 125, 259
    community, 72–73, 76–78
    context and, 252, 254
    critical reflection and, 121, 246, 267
    cultural humility and, 111
    development, 76, 120, 219
    meaning and, 142
    in neighborhood engagement, 67
    organizing, 76
    possibility and, 257
    process, 4, 72–73, 123, 259
    restorative questioning, 117–18, 122
    within therapeutic relationship, 52–53
    verbatim theater, 131
disability rights
    accessibility, 194–95, 198–202
    born accessible, 195, 200, 202
    context, 200–201
    critical reflection, 198
    EITA task force, 195–96, 198, 200
    history, 199–200
    meaning, 198–99
    National Federation of the Blind, 196, 198, 200–202
    positionality, 197–98
    possibilities, 202
    power, 201–2
    teaching-learning, 198
disaster risk reduction
    bonfire sessions *(at-ato)*, 254–58
    collective existence of thinking/acting, 253
    collective production, 256
    context, 254–55
    critical reflection, 258
    development aggression, 251, 252, 259
    history, 256–57
    Indigenous ways of knowing, 251, 253, 254
    Marjorie, 251–52
    meaning, 252–54
    mining, 254–55
    peace, 257
    possibility, 257–58
    power, 253–56
    re-embedding process, 258
    resiliency, 257–59
    resistance, 257–59
    solidarity dialogues, 257
    teaching-learning, 259
discipline in schools, 117–19
discrimination, 26, 96–98, 101, 152

dissociative identity disorder (DID), 211
DRR. *See* disaster risk reduction

East Side Clinic. *See* mental health care access
economic injustice, 131, 150
economic justice, 82
EITA task force, 195–96, 198, 200
embodied approaches, 121
emergency managers, 82, 84
emergency psychiatric assistance, 211–12
*Emergent Strategy* (brown), 188
empowerment
    accompaniment and, 112–13
    engagement and, 251
    fair housing exposition, 78
    of immigrants, 264
    jail-based treatment, 160, 163–64
    meaning and, 232, 233
    possibility and, 171, 217, 222, 231
    power and, 75, 106–8, 209, 212, 255
    of refugees, 106–8
    systems of care, 38–39, 41
    teaching-learning and, 145, 251
    through reflexive process, 32
    water rights, 85
engagement
    as communication, 3, 198
    empowerment and, 251
    field seminar, 187, 188
    field seminars/fieldwork, 187, 188
    homelessness, 60–67
    Home ReSource, 233
    IRC-Missoula, 112
    jail-based treatment, 153–54
    listening and, 120, 253, 258
    Michigan Welfare Rights Organization, 85–86
    oppression and, 246
    poverty and, 41
    restorative justice, 120–21
    Social Workers in Schools, 139–41, 145
    of stakeholders, 60–67
    survival and, 217–18
    verbatim theater, 134, 135
evaluation
    IRC-Missoula, 113
    restorative justice, 123–24

family separation, 264
*Farmington Report* (2005), 152
Federal Transient Program (FTP), 27
field seminar, 184–92
Finn, J., 11, 217, 218, 223, 261, 268–69
Flowtown Revue, 90–91
food security/insecurity
    collaboration, 175–81
    context, 178
    Covid-19 impacts, 182–83
    critical reflection, 178–79
    establishment of, 175–77
    history, 178, 256
    meaning and, 76, 177–78, 181

# Index

positionality, 179–80
possibilities, 178, 182
power, 177–78
privilege, 179–80
program survival, 176
stigmatization, 175, 181
teaching-learning, 178–79
formerly incarcerated persons, 162–64, 169–71
foster care system, 18, 21, 39, 41, 43, 46–48, 54, 155
Frank, L., 186
Freedom of Information Act (FOIA), 87, 90

Galeano, E., 191
Garcia, I., 263–64
gender
    entrapment, 165
    identity, 29, 30, 31, 129–30
    oppression, 36, 167, 228
    socialization, 33
gentrification. *See* neighborhood gentrification
globalization, 73
Goldstein, E., 17
Great Depression, 27, 263
Greater Chicago Food Depository, 175–77, 181
Great Falls Public Schools. *See* verbatim theater
group home. *See* youth in care
group work, 62–63, 99, 151
Grupos Beta, 266
Gupta, A., 38

habitus, 122
Harold Washington College, 175
Hartland Partnership Center, 71, 72, 78
hate crimes, 26, 152
healing
    accompaniment and, 32, 53
    community, 245
    critical reflection and, 22
    evidence-based practices, 242
    family and connection in, 41, 53
    incarceration, 168
    instincts towards, 53
    positionality in, 245
    possibility and, 243
    sweat lodge, 157–60
    systemic barriers to, 119–20
health equity promotion model, 29
Healthy Student Market. *See* food security/insecurity
heterosexism, 2, 25, 26, 29, 31–34
historical trauma. *See under* trauma
history
    bonfire sessions (at-ato), 256–57
    Community Voices for Housing Equality (CVHE), 77
    corporate law office, social work practice in, 217–19
    disability rights, 199–200
    disaster risk reduction, 256–57

food security, 178
homelessness, 59
Home ReSource, 230
housing equity, 77
inclusiveness and, 176
IRC-Missoula, 109–10
jail-based treatment, 151–52
LGBTQ adults, 26–29
    of mental health care access, 207–9
Michigan Welfare Rights Organization, 84
migrants, U.S. Mexico border, 262–64
narrative and, 98, 144, 213
Nashville Neighborhood Story Project, 98, 100
oppression and, 13, 26–27
poverty and, 38, 77, 240
racism and, 38
resistance and, 257
river House, 38
Social Workers in Schools, 144
survival and, 257
HIV/AIDS pandemic, 29
*Hogar de Esperanza y Paz* (Home of Hope and Peace, HEPAC), 267
homelessness
    assessment, 60–61
    community deliberation, 63–64, 67
    context, 59
    history, 59
    meaning, 60–62
    misconceptions of, 64, 65
    power, 60, 62, 65–66
    services, improvement of, 67
    stakeholder engagement, 60–67
    teaching-learning, 61–62
    work groups, 62–63, 65–67
Home ReSource
    accompaniment, 233–34
    action, 233–34
    celebration, 234–35
    context, 230–31
    critical reflection, 234
    engagement, 233
    history, 230
    meaning, 232
    organizational culture, 233
    possibility, 232, 235
    power, 231
    social change, 231–32
    teaching-learning, 233
    triple bottom line business model, 228
    zero waste, 232, 233
homosexuality. *See* LGBTQ adults
housing equity/equality
    collaboration/team building, 72, 75–76
    community dialogues, 72–73
    CVHE, 71–72
    globalization context, 73
    history reframing, 77
    local-level context, 73–75
    meaning, 76–77

participatory action research, 70–71, 78–79
possibility, 78
power, 75–76
privilege, 75
state resettlement policies, 73–74
tenant-landlord policy, 74–75, 77
tenant rights, 71–72
trauma/resilience, 73, 77
Humane Borders, 264, 268
human rights
  disregard of in development aggression, 251, 252, 259
  language of, 107, 109
  migrants, U.S. Mexico border, 262–64, 266, 269
  of refugees, 107
  right to dream, 191
  in social work practice, 259
  to water, 87–89
humility. *See* cultural humility
Hunter, R., 70

Immigration Act of 1882, 109, 110
Immigration and Customs Enforcement (ICE), 264, 265
immigration/immigrants
  deportation, 262–64
  empowerment of, 264
  migrant trail hike, 267–68
  racial/ethnic differences, 109, 111, 142
  refugee resettlement program, 105–8
  undocumented, 262, 264–65
  xenophobia, 109–10
incarceration
  of African Americans, 162–64, 168
  agency in, 164
  context, 167–68, 170
  meaning, 168–69
  possibility, 171
  power, 165–71
  racial/ethnic differences, 152–54, 160
  stigmatization, 155, 169–70
  transcendental phenomenology, 162, 164
inclusiveness
  corporate law, 218–19, 221–23
  food security, 176
  history and, 176
  housing equality, 73–75
Indian Child Welfare Act, 43, 240
Indian Health Service (IHS), 242
Indigenous community. *See* disaster risk reduction; National Native Children's Trauma Center
Indigenous knowledge/ways of knowing, 240, 241, 243, 245, 251, 253, 254
Indigenous People's Rights Act of 1997, 257
Indigenous rights, 42–44, 144, 228, 256.
  *See also* disaster risk reduction; National Native Children's Trauma Center
integrated behavioral health, 207
intergenerational trauma. *See under* trauma

International Gatherings of Social Movements on Water, 90
International Rescue Committee. *See* IRC-Missoula
interprofessional collaboration, 130, 207, 208, 216–20, 224
intersectionality, 19, 29, 34, 197
IRC-Missoula
  accompaniment, 112–13
  celebration, 113–14
  community-based PAR, 113
  consciousness raising, 110
  context, 107–9
  critical reflection, 113
  cultural humility, 111
  empowerment, 108, 112
  engagement, 112
  ESL instruction, 111
  evaluation, 113
  forcible displacements, 109
  history, 109–10
  immigrants as public charges, 109–10
  language as barrier, 107, 108
  meaning, 106–7
  power, 107–8
  refugee resettlement program, 105–8
  teaching-learning, 112
  translation services, 108, 111
IRC–Missoula Refugee Advisory Board, 113

jail-based treatment
  accompaniment, 157
  case manager role, 156
  collaboration, 153
  context, 151–52
  CRAFT approach, 157
  engagement, 153–54
  families, inclusion of, 155
  hate crimes, 152–54, 160
  history, 151–52
  meaning, 151–52
  methamphetamine, 154–55
  peer mentors, 157
  positionality, 152–53
  power, 151–52
  resiliency, 160
  resistance, 160
  shame, 155, 159, 160
  stigmatization, 155
  sweat lodge, 157–60
  systemic racism, 152–54, 160
  teaching-learning, 155–56
  transitional services, 156–57
  trust, 153, 154
  Wellbriety model, 157–58
Jennings, A., 89
Jim Crow laws, 20, 21
Jorgensen, C., 31
Just Practice framework
  applications of, xii–xiv
  to biopsychosocial assessments, 11–14

## 282  Index

concepts, xi–xii, 1–2
disaster risk reduction, 252
to field seminar, 185–88
Home ReSource, 229
IRC-Missoula, 112–14
in Nashville Neighborhood Story Project, 101–2
National Native Children's Trauma Center, 243–44
processes, xi–xii, 3–4, 224

Kankanaey. *See* disaster risk reduction
Kino Border Initiative (KBI), 266

language
  as barrier, 107–10, 253
  celebration and, 114, 157
  colonization and, 253
  as commonality, 186, 187
  of human rights, 107, 109
  of intervention and termination, 224
  meaning and, 76, 142, 224
  possibility and, 111
  power and, 66
  of pride and liberation, 28–29
  sign, 199, 200
  stigmatizing, 181
  supportive in trauma-informed practice, 239
  in therapeutic relationship, 31, 49, 54
  in tribal programs, 240, 242, 245
Lavender Scare, 27–28, 33
Lavitt, M., 212
LGBTQ adults
  ageism, 33–34
  context, 26–29
  health equity promotion model, 29–30
  history, 26–29
  homosexuality, 27
  intersectionality, 33
  medical establishment labeling of, 28–29
  preferred pronouns, 31
  Pride liberation movement, 28–29
  racism, 33
  sexual objectification, 33
  stigmatization of, 26, 31
  Stonewall Riots, 28–29
liberation, 22, 28–29, 267
listening. *See also* communication
  active, 78, 132
  benefits of, 198
  engagement and, 120, 253, 258
  radical, 17
  skill development, 156, 220
  in social work practice, 3, 17, 78, 139
  teaching-learning and, 233
  within therapeutic relationship, 146
Littman, J., 105
Ljunggren, T., 135–36

macro practice, 184–85, 191, 192, 217
Mahaffey, M., 89

Māori model for health, 141, 146
*Mapping the Water Crisis* (WPD), 90
March for Refugees (Utah), 78
*Mariposas sin Fronteras* (Butterflies without Borders), 264
mass incarceration, 163, 168
Mattachine Society, 28
Maurer, M., 202
McCarthy, Joseph/McCarthy era, 27–28
meaning
  corporate law office, social work practice in, 217, 222
  dialogue and, 142
  disability rights, 198–99
  disaster risk reduction, 252–54
  empowerment and, 232, 233
  field seminar, 189
  field seminars/fieldwork, 189
  food security, 177–78
  food security/insecurity and, 76, 181
  Home ReSource, 232
  housing equity, 76–77
  incarceration, 168–69
  IRC-Missoula, 106–7
  jail-based treatment, 151–52
  language and, 76, 142, 224
  mental health care access, 209–10
  Michigan Welfare Rights Organization, 82–83
  narrative and, 82–83, 97–99, 209–10
  Nashville Neighborhood Story Project, 97–98
  restorative justice, 120, 122
  Social Workers in Schools, 142
  transformation and, 97
  verbatim theater, 135, 136
Medicaid, 47, 157, 183, 211
meditation, 135
memory, politics of, 209–10
mental health care access
  advocacy, 209–10, 213–14
  context, 210–12
  East Side Clinic closure, 208–9
  emergency psychiatric assistance, 211–12
  history of, 207–9
  integrated behavioral health, 207
  meaning, 209–10
  narrative, 209, 213
  person-in-environment approach, 210
  politics of memory, 209–10
  possibility, 213–14
  power, 208–9, 212–13
  teaching-learning, 210–11
mentors, 107, 157
Michigan Welfare Rights Organization
  accountability, 87
  advocacy, 89
  arts-based activism, 90–91
  context, 83–84
  Covid-19 impacts, 91–92
  engagement, 85–86
  history, 84

legal action, 89
meaning, 82–83
possibility, 85
poverty, 82–83
power, 84–85
teaching-learning, 86–87
micro practice, 191
micro *vs.* macro practice, 191–92
migrants, U.S. Mexico border
　action/advocacy, 268
　civil/criminal charges, 264–65
　consciousness raising, 267
　context, 264
　critical reflection, 268
　HEPAC, 267
　history, 262–64
　ICE detention contracts, 265
　Operation Streamline, 264–66
　plea agreements, 265
　possibility, 266–68
　power, 264–66
　reproductive justice, 267
　reverse mission, 268
　teaching-learning, 266–68
mining effects on land/lives, 254–55
minority stressors, 26, 29
Montana Immigrant Justice Alliance (MIJA), 268
motivational interviewing (MI), 155–56, 160
MWRO. *See* Michigan Welfare Rights Organization

narrative
　collective history loss, 98
　construction of, 11, 16, 17
　critical reflection and, 21, 23
　history and, 98, 144, 213
　of incarcerated women, 166
　individualizing/victimizing, 91
　meaning and, 82–83, 97–99, 209–10
　positionality and, 18, 212
　power and, 212, 255
　sharing, 14
　shifting, 88
　stigmatizing, 66
　therapy, 47
Nashville Neighborhood Story Project
　affordable housing crisis, 95, 97–99
　color line significance, 96
　context, 95
　contraband camps, 96
　discrimination, 96–98, 101
　gentrification-as-revitalization, 97
　history, 94–95
　meaning, 97–98
　narratives, 97–98
　place-history, 98, 100
　power, 98–99
　racialization, 96
　resident displacement, 95–97, 100

　social ties, 98, 100
　stigmatization, 96–98, 101
　tenant organizing, 99
National Federation of the Blind (NFB), 196, 198, 200–202
National Native Children's Trauma Center
　assimilation, 239–42, 245, 246
　boarding schools, 21, 43, 240
　child removal, 240–41, 246
　context, 241
　Covid-19 impacts, 247
　cultural humility, 241–42
　evidence-based practices, 242, 245
　historical trauma defined, 240
　identity, 240, 245, 246
　Indigenous ways of knowing, 240, 241, 243, 245
　meaning-making, 241–42
　positionality, 244–46
　possibility, 243
　power, 242
　privilege, 246
　technology, 247–48
　trauma-informed approaches, 242–46
　tribal sovereignty, 242, 243
　trust responsibility, 246–47
National Nurses Union, 90
Native American Religious Freedom Act (1978), 159
Navajo, 151–53, 157–60. *See also* criminal justice system
neighborhood gentrification. *See also* Michigan Welfare Rights Organization; Nashville Neighborhood Story Project
　as-revitalization, 97
　context, 94–95
　redlining, 20
　water shutoffs, 81–87
neoliberal, 38
Netroots Nation, 90
New Deal, 27
New Zealand, 138, 142, 144, 146, 252. *See also* Social Workers in Schools
Nicholson S., 261
NNCTC. *See* National Native Children's Trauma Center
Nogales, 261–62, 266, 267. *See also* migrants, U.S. Mexico border
No More Deaths, 265, 268
North American Free Trade Agreement (NAFTA), 263

Office for Civil Rights (OCR), 193
Operation Streamline, 264–66
Operation Wetback, 263
oppression
　accompaniment and, 31, 43
　anti-oppressive, 23, 190, 258
　assessments and, 11, 14
　challenging, 34, 192, 257

context and, 11–12, 20–21, 36, 254–55
critical reflection and, 43
dynamics of, 3
engagement and, 246
gender, 36, 167, 228
heterosexist, 25
history and, 13, 26–27
by police, 28
possibility and, 29–30, 257–58
power and, 21, 190, 209, 255–56
in social work practice, 192, 212
systemic, 14, 19, 136, 150, 152–53
teaching-learning and, 33
within therapeutic relationship, 26
organizational change, 123, 223–24, 258
organizational culture, 233

parent-child connection, 44
Paris Gibson Education Center, 130
participatory action research (PAR), 70–71, 78–79.
  See also housing equity/equality
participatory planning, 188
peer mentors, 157
People's Water Board (Detroit), 83–91
performance process in verbatim theater, 135
person-in-environment approach, 210
Philippines. See bonfire sessions (at-ato)
politics of memory, 209–10
Poor People's Campaign: A National Call for Moral Revival, 90
possibility
  ability and, 191, 202
  agency and, 213
  bonfire sessions (at-ato), 257–58
  Community Voices for Housing Equality (CVHE), 78
  dialogue and, 257
  disaster risk reduction, 257–58
  empowerment and, 171, 217, 222, 231
  field seminar, 190–91
  healing and, 243
  Home ReSource, 232, 235
  housing equity, 78
  incarceration, 171
  language and, 111
  mental health care access, 213–14
  Michigan Welfare Rights Organization, 85
  migrants, U.S. Mexico border, 266–68
  National Native Children's Trauma Center, 243
  oppression and, 29–30, 257–58
  poverty and, 243
  Social Workers in Schools, 144–46
  survival and, 257
  sustainability and, 191
  verbatim theater, 135–36
Poverello Center. See homelessness
poverty
  advocacy, 89–90
  context and, 38, 228
  engagement and, 41

gentrification, 95
health disparities in, xii
history and, 38, 77, 240
homelessness, 66
housing equality, 70, 77
learning impacts, 117
migration motivations, 267
positionality and, 19
possibility and, 243
in punishment allocation, 167–68
statistics, 129
water rights, 81–83, 89–91
power
  in agency, 2
  concept, 2
  corporate law office, social work practice in, 217, 221
  disability rights, 201–2
  disaster risk reduction, 253–56
  dynamics, 23, 75, 179, 201, 212, 239
  empowerment and, 75, 106–8, 209, 212, 255
  field seminar, 189–90
  field seminars/fieldwork, 189–90
  food security, 177–78
  homelessness, 60, 62, 65–66
  Home ReSource, 231
  housing equity, 75–76
  incarceration, 165–71
  IRC-Missoula, 107–8
  jail-based treatment, 151–52
  language and, 66
  mental health care access, 208–9, 212–13
  Michigan Welfare Rights Organization, 84–85
  migration, 264–66
  narrative and, 212, 255
  Nashville Neighborhood Story Project, 98–99
  National Native Children's Trauma Center, 242
  oppression and, 21, 190, 209, 255–56
  power over, 2, 13, 23, 39, 66, 108, 123, 165–67, 169, 171, 186, 189–90, 231, 242, 255, 266
  power to act, 2, 13, 212, 231
  power within, 2, 13, 164, 212, 223, 242, 266
  power with others, 2, 266
  privilege and, 75, 212, 242, 255–56, 267–68
  resistance and, 2, 84
  restorative justice, 118, 120, 122–23
  Social Workers in Schools, 143
  verbatim theater, 135, 136
praxis, 19, 22
preferred pronouns, 31
presence, 51, 73, 166, 167, 208, 254, 263
Pride liberation movement, 28–29
prison ministry program, 171
privilege
  accompaniment and, 31
  assessment framing, 14, 19
  critical reflection and, 3, 20, 267–68
  differences in perception of, 181
  male, 179, 228
  positionality and, 152, 179, 228, 246, 252

power and, 75, 212, 242, 255–56, 267–68
systems of, 34
White, 3, 43, 228
problematizing, 3, 188, 189
professional development, 144, 218–20, 222, 223, 233
professional distance, 42
psychiatric disorder, 28, 29
public charge, 109–10

Quijada Cerecer, D. A., 74

racial/ethnic differences, 109, 111, 142
racialization, 96
racial justice, 59, 187
racism
  advocacy, 82
  Black codes, 20, 21
  challenges posed by, xii
  context of practice, 2, 43, 153
  dialogue, 134, 187
  history and, 38
  in immigrant resettlement policy, 74
  institutional, 144
  internalized, 33
  intersectionalities, 129–30
  in school discipline policy, 117, 129
  slavery, 20, 21
  structural, 19, 34
  systemic, 19, 41, 43, 44, 90, 152, 228
  teaching-learning and, 33
  White, 160
radical listening, 17
rapport, 139, 144–45, 154. *See also* trust
recovery, 155, 157–58
redlining, 20
re-embedding process, 258
re-entry, post-incarceration, 169–71
reflection. *See* critical reflection
reflective approaches in restorative justice, 121
reflexive praxis, 19, 22
reflexivity, 1, 19, 22, 26, 32, 118, 233, 246
Refugee Act of 1980, 106–7
refugee advisory board, 106, 111, 113
refugee communities, 70, 76, 105, 113
refugee resettlement program, 105–8.
  *See also* IRC-Missoula
Rehabilitation Act section 504, 197
rehearsals, 128, 134–35
Reisbig, D., 131
relational orientation, 122
resiliency
  bonfire sessions *(at-ato)*, 257–59
  disaster risk reduction, 257–59
  housing equity, 73, 77
  jail-based treatment, 160
resistance
  action and, 3–4
  context and, 108
  to development aggression, 251, 252, 255–59

heritage of, 84
history and, 257
in housing equality, 67
nonviolent, 251, 255, 259
power and, 2, 84
Pride liberation movement, 28–29
sweat lodge, 157–60
teaching-learning and, 121–22
as theme in theater, 128
in therapeutic relationship, 42, 43, 130
to treatment, 154–57
of youth, 38
restorative conferencing, 117, 118
restorative justice
  cognitive approaches, 121–22
  community-building circles, 117–18, 121
  concepts of, 117–18
  context, 118–19, 121
  critical friend role, 119–20
  critical reflection, 122–23
  discipline in schools, 117–19
  embodied approaches, 121
  engagement, 120–21
  evaluation, 123–24
  implementation of, 119–20, 123
  meaning, 120, 122
  positionality, 119–20
  power, 118, 120, 122–23
  racial/ethnic disparities, 117, 118, 124
  reflective approaches, 121
  relational orientation, 122–23
  restorative questioning, 117–18, 122
  teaching-learning, 121–22
restorative questioning, 117–18, 122
reverse mission, 268
revitalization, 97
River House. *See* youth in care

Samaritans, 269
San Juan Bosco shelter, 266
"Save the Children" campaign, 29
school projects. *See* restorative justice
school social work. *See* Social Workers in Schools
secondary settings, 217, 221, 224
segregation, 21, 101
self-determination, 252
sex as biology, 31
sexual abuse
  of children, 16, 18, 48
  of women in criminal justice system, 166
sexual and gender minorities. *See* LGBTQ adults
sexual objectification, 33
shame in criminal justice system, 155, 159, 160
slavery, 20, 21
Smith, A. D., 132
social change, 231–32
social identity, 11, 18–20, 26, 217
Social Workers in Schools
  collaboration, 143, 146
  context, 142–43

cultural identity, 141, 142
engagement, 139–41, 145
history, 144
Māori model for health, 141, 146
meaning, 142
possibility, 144–46
power, 143
responsibility/loyalty, 140
teaching-learning, 140, 142–43, 145–45
trust, 140–41, 144–45
Social Workers Registration Board (New Zealand), 144
sodomy, 27
sovereignty, 228, 242, 243
special rapporteurs, 88
stakeholder engagement, 60–67
stigmatization
criminal justice system, 155, 169–70
food security, 175, 181
incarceration, 155, 169–70
jail-based treatment, 155
of LGBTQ adults, 26, 31
Nashville Neighborhood Story Project, 96–98, 101
Stonewall riots, 28–29
street demonstrations, 89–90
structural forces in criminal justice system, 167
structural violence, 70, 152, 167
student activism. *See* verbatim theater
substance-use treatment. *See* jail-based treatment
suicidality, xii, 26, 130, 239
survival
celebration and, 254–55
within children, 130
crime, 167
disaster risk reduction (*See* disaster risk reduction)
economic, 262, 267
engagement and, 217–18
food security program, 176
history and, 257
migration and, 262
possibility and, 257
teaching-learning and, 259
water rights, 85
of youth/families, 136
sustainability
awareness of, 231
community, 267
economic, 227, 262
organizational change, 123, 258
possibility and, 191
principles of, 227
tenant organizing, 99
tribal programs, 246
sweat lodge, 157–60
systemic oppression, 14, 19, 136, 150, 152–53
systemic racism, 19, 41, 43, 44, 90, 152, 228
systems of care, 38–39, 41

*taha hinengaro* (mental health), 141
*taha tinana* (physical health), 141
*taha wairua* (spiritual health), 141
*taha whānau* (family health), 141
*Taller Yonke*, 267
teaching-learning
bonfire sessions *(at-ato)*, 259
corporate law office, social work practice in, 223
cultural humility and, 243
disability rights, 198
disaster risk reduction, 259
empowerment and, 145, 251
field seminar, 186–88
food security, 178–79
homelessness, 61–62
Home ReSource, 233
IRC-Missoula, 112
jail-based treatment, 155–56
listening and, 233
mental health care access, 210–11
Michigan Welfare Rights Organization, 86–87
migrants, U.S. Mexico border, 266–68
oppression and, 33
racism and, 33
resistance and, 121–22
restorative justice, 121–22
Social Workers in Schools, 140, 142–43, 145–45
survival and, 259
verbatim theater, 135
team, building, 208
technology, 202–3, 247–48
Tectonic Theatre Company, 132
tenant-landlord policy, 74–75, 77
tenant organizing, 99
tenant rights, 71–72
*te whare tapa whā* model, 141, 146
therapeutic group home. *See* youth in care
therapeutic relationship
agency in, 40
artist identity, 54–55
attachment, 54
communication within, 30, 48, 51, 52
connection/communication, 50–54
dialogue within, 52–53
eye contact, 50
healing instincts, 53
language in, 31, 49, 54
oppression within, 26
origami creations role, 53–54
power, 49
resistance in, 42, 43, 130
talking/realization, 52–53
trust, 54, 55
training and technical assistance (T/TA), 239, 243–44, 247
transcendental phenomenology, 162, 164. *See also* incarceration

transformation
  context and, 83–84
  meaning and, 97
  neighborhood gentrification, 94–95
  professional development as, 222
  religious faith as, 163–64, 168–69
  restorative justice as, 117–19, 124–25
  social justice work in, 78–79, 213
  of social work practice, xi–xiii, 1, 23, 153, 211
  of students, 13–15
  technology in, 231
  theater as, 130, 136
transgenderism. *See* LGBTQ adults
transitional services, 156–57
trauma
  adverse childhood experiences, 130
  collective, 20
  colonization and, 43, 240, 242
  historical, 77, 152, 187, 228, 240–45
  housing equity, 73, 77
  intergenerational, 239, 241
  youth in care, 38–39
trauma-informed approaches, 242–46
trauma-informed practice, 239
Treaty of Guadalupe Hidalgo of 1848, 262–63
tribal court, 239
tribal sovereignty, 242, 243
triple bottom line business model. *See* Home ReSource
triple threat, 165
Trump administration, 109, 110
trust
  jail-based treatment, 153, 154
  National Native Children's Trauma Center, 246–47
  rapport, 139, 144–45, 154
  Social Workers in Schools, 140–41, 144–45
  therapeutic relationship, 54, 55
  trust responsibility, 246–47

unattached persons, 27
undocumented immigration, 262, 264–65
University Neighborhood Partners, 70, 71
U.S. Commission on Civil Rights, 152

verbatim theater
  adverse childhood experiences, 130
  collaboration, 130–36
  consciousness raising, 130
  *Converge: E Pluribus Unum*, 127–28
  directing process, 134–35
  engagement, 134, 135
  interviews/screenwriting, 132–33
  meaning, 135, 136
  possibility, 135–36
  power, 135, 136
  racism, 134
  rehearsal/performance process, 135
  responsibility, 134–35
  teaching-learning, 135
  youth influence/creative process, 134
voice, collective, 254

water affordability, 83
Water Affordability, Transparency, Equity, and Reliability Act (WATER) Act of 2017, 89
Water Affordability Program (Detroit), 89
water as a human right. *See* Michigan Welfare Rights Organization
water drop trip, 268–69
Water Justice Journey (Detroit to Flint), 88
"Water Power," 90
water services restoration, 91–92
water/sewerage rates, 83
water shutoffs, 81–87
Watson, J., 89
Wellbriety model, 157–58
We the People of Detroit (WPD), 90
*whanau* (family) perspective, 141
White supremacy, 34, 187
Will See, 90
women in criminal justice system, 165–67
World War II, 27

xenophobia, 109–10

youth in care
  betrayal by authority, 41
  case studies, 39–44
  context/history, 38
  detachment/removal policies, 41, 43
  emotional meltdown, 42
  family trauma/adversity, 38–39
  identity, 42
  meaning/power, 40–41
  parent-child connection, 39–44
  professional distance/boundaries, 41–42
Youth Resource Center (Great Falls), 136

"Zero by Fifty: Missoula's Pathway to Zero Waste" plan, 229, 233
zero waste, 232, 233
Zero Waste Ambassadors Program (ZWAP!), 229
Zettel, A., 176

www.ingramcontent.com/pod-product-compliance
Ingram Content Group UK Ltd.
Pitfield, Milton Keynes, MK11 3LW, UK
UKHW021317180426
11947UKWH00015B/1283